"Birthed in the fires of real world missional controversy, this book crackles with the urgency of the gospel. Drawing from the deep well of Barth's *Church Dogmatics*, Jeff McSwain offers a refreshing vision of Christian life freed to live wholly *in* this world by seeking the true life *hidden* in Christ."

—**Brian Brock**
University of Aberdeen

"There's a remarkable single-mindedness about Jeff McSwain, a theological determination that yields insights impossible to ignore. Here he presses us to read Barth's doctrine of sanctification through Luther's *simul iustus et peccator*, and in the process uncovers a wealth of connections and resonances with immense practical consequences for the life of the church. Provocative and game-changing, Barth—and the Gospel!—will never sound quite the same again."

—**Jeremy Begbie**
Duke University

"McSwain argues persuasively that the *simul* . . . is a powerful key to Barth's theology as a whole. Breaking new ground, yet firmly committed to all the key truths championed by Barth, McSwain's theological insightfulness is evident on every page. An impressively comprehensive knowledge of Barth's *Dogmatics* is also on display, along with a truly Barthian passion for the truth and the importance of the gospel . . . McSwain's thesis is both fascinating and challenging. It will richly reward careful engagement."

—**Douglas Campbell**
Duke University

"In an original contribution, McSwain succeeds in demonstrating how Barth's version of the Lutheran *'simul iustus et peccator'* is radicalized by its extension to the incarnate Son and thereby to the race as a whole, transferring the pattern of Chalcedonian Christology (the so-called 'two natures' doctrine) into the field of anthropology. The result is a significant recasting of our ways of thinking about numerous core doctrines, including creation, atonement and incarnation as well as redemption and fall."

—**Trevor Hart**
author of *Regarding Karl Barth*

"I have literally been waiting for years for this book—a book that explores in depth what the sanctification of Jesus Christ means for the sanctification of humanity. In this excellent, accessible, and innovative work, Jeff McSwain carefully examines how Karl Barth reappropriates the classic doctrine *simul iustus et peccator* while also creatively imagining ways Barth's understanding could enliven the life and ministry of the church today. This is a beautiful contribution to the growing theological literature on sanctification and discipleship."

—**Kristen Johnson**
Western Theological Seminary

"McSwain casts his net wide, but discerningly, fastidiously mirroring Barth's understanding of tradition and the Bible. *Simul Sanctification*: Jesus Christ incarnate is at once the Righteous One of God, and the One who assumes sinful human flesh. From Gregory to the Chalcedonian anthropology he finally makes sense, and adds to the *corpus*, of Barthian studies, and progress on Barth's theological actualism: of a singular Jewish man of humble origins who re-presents in every human being."

—**P. H. Brazier**
author of *Barth and Dostoevsky* (Pickwick, 2016)

Simul Sanctification

Princeton Theological Monograph Series
K. C. Hanson, Charles M. Collier, D. Christopher Spinks, and Robin A. Parry, Series Editors

Recent volumes in the series:

Koo Dong Yun
*The Holy Spirit and Ch'i (Qi):
A Chiological Approach to Pneumatology*

Stanley S. MacLean
*Resurrection, Apocalypse, and the Kingdom of Christ:
The Eschatology of Thomas F. Torrance*

Brian Neil Peterson
*Ezekiel in Context: Ezekiel's Message Understood in Its Historical
Setting of Covenant Curses and Ancient Near
Eastern Mythological Motifs*

Amy E. Richter
Enoch and the Gospel of Matthew

Maeve Louise Heaney
Music as Theology: What Music Says about the Word

Eric M. Vail
Creation and Chaos Talk: Charting a Way Forward

David L. Reinhart
*Prayer as Memory: Toward the Comparative Study of Prayer
as Apocalyptic Language and Thought*

Peter D. Neumann
Pentecostal Experience: An Ecumenical Encounter

Ashish J. Naidu
*Transformed in Christ:
Christology and the Christian Life in John Chrysostom*

Simul Sanctification
Barth's Hidden Vision for Human Transformation

Jeff McSwain

Foreword by Alan Torrance

PICKWICK *Publications* • Eugene, Oregon

SIMUL SANCTIFICATION
Barth's Hidden Vision for Human Transformation

Princeton Theological Monograph Series 232

Copyright © 2018 Jeff McSwain. All rights reserved. Except for brief quotations in critical publications or reviews, no part of this book may be reproduced in any manner without prior written permission from the publisher. Write: Permissions, Wipf and Stock Publishers, 199 W. 8th Ave., Suite 3, Eugene, OR 97401.

Pickwick Publications
An Imprint of Wipf and Stock Publishers
199 W. 8th Ave., Suite 3
Eugene, OR 97401

www.wipfandstock.com

PAPERBACK ISBN: 978-1-5326-4107-7
HARDCOVER ISBN: 978-1-5326-4108-4
EBOOK ISBN: 978-1-5326-4109-1

Cataloging-in-Publication data:

Names: McSwain, Jeff, author. | Torrance, Alan J., forward.

Title: Simul sanctification : Barth's hidden vision for human transformation | Jeff McSwain ; forward by Alan Torrance.

Description: Eugene, OR: Pickwick Publications, 2018. | Princeton Theological Monograph Series 232. | Includes bibliographical references.

Identifiers: ISBN: 978-1-5326-4107-7 (paperback). | ISBN: 978-1-5326-4108-4 (hardcover). | ISBN: 978-1-5326-4109-1 (epub).

Subjects: LCSH: Barth, Karl, 1886–1968—Criticism and interpretation. | Sanctification.

Classification: BX4827 .B3 M379 2018 (print). | BX4827 (epub).

Manufactured in the U.S.A.   08/09/18

Unless otherwise noted, all Scripture quotations are taken from the New Revised Standard Version Bible, copyright © 1989 National Council of the Churches of Christ in the United States of America. Used by permission. All rights reserved.

Scripture quotations marked (NIV) are taken from the Holy Bible, New International Version®, NIV®. Copyright © 1973, 1978, 1984, 2011 by Biblica, Inc.™ Used by permission of Zondervan. All rights reserved worldwide. www.zondervan.com The "NIV" and "New International Version" are trademarks registered in the United States Patent and Trademark Office by Biblica, Inc.™

To my beloved Susan,
who championed me to, and through, this transformational project

The "old" and "new" worlds are indirectly identical, the new already present in the old in that its reconciliation in Jesus Christ has already taken place. What is still to come is its manifestation (i.e. "apocalyptic" eschatology!)

—Karl Barth

Contents

Foreword by Alan Torrance | ix
Preface | xi
Acknowledgments | xvii

    Introduction: Humility and Confidence | 1
1. *Simul* Sanctification: "no easier way" | 26
2. Can We Speak of a Chalcedonian *Anthropology*? | 46
3. Chalcedonian Change and the Spirit of Righteousness | 60
4. No *Partim-Partim* in Participation! | 75
5. Hercules at the Crossroads | 98
6. Freedom to *Be* Transformed | 120
7. The *Simul* as a Matter of Life and Death | 137
8. A *New* Perspective on the Cross | 159
9. When Is the *Simul*? | 179
10. The Darkness Shall not Overcome It | 197
11. The Humanity from Heaven and the Humanity of Earth | 212
12. A Kinship of Being: How Far Can We Go? | 228
13. Taking Scripture with *Totus* Seriousness | 244
14. Seeing through the *Simul* | 260

    Conclusion: Consummation | 281

    Final Reflections | 291

Bibliography | 309

Foreword

When Gregory Nazianzen affirmed that "the unassumed is the unhealed" he saw himself as reminding the church of the account of salvation that characterizes and, indeed, underwrites the witness of the New Testament. That the eternal Son took what was ours that we might have what is his was not merely a central theme in Patristic thought. It lay at the heart of John Calvin's account of the *mirifica commutatio* (the wonderful exchange manifest in the incarnate Son) and it would become a central affirmation in the soteriologies of Karl Barth, Hans Urs von Balthazar, and T. F. Torrance as also the many contemporary theologians influenced by them.

The fundamental question that this raises concerns what precisely the eternal Son has assumed. Was it the perfect form of our humanity that is assumed—that is, without all that negates our humanity, namely, sin? Or is it (as Barth and others suggest) our dysfunctional, alienated humanity that he assumes and which is thereby restored and redeemed in him? Is this to present us with a choice—might it be possible to affirm both? That is, might there be a christological basis to "the *simul*" that lies at the heart of redemption? This question becomes particularly pertinent if, with McSwain, we affirm that what Christ assumed was more than a merely generic or universal humanity but the particular humanity that characterizes each of us as individuals—that is, if each of us can be said to find "our particular humanity" assumed, redeemed, and created anew in him.

With rare theological insight and rigor, the author drills down to the core of Barth's christological basis for sanctification. As McSwain demonstrates, the implications from this starting point are vast. It is clear that he is pushing boundaries out of a passionate concern to grapple with the salvific relevance not merely of the message of Jesus Christ, or the work of Jesus Christ, but of the very *person* of the incarnate Son. Although it will prove controversial, this is a deep-thinking and courageous monograph that both demands and inspires serious, theological engagement.

Alan Torrance

Preface

In December, 2007 Reality Ministries Inc. was birthed from a cauldron of theological adversity. We have continually been premised on the conviction that the gospel of Jesus Christ is the gospel for all or not the gospel at all, and that God's grace is not contingent on a person's capacity to respond. Unfortunately this latter statement has been taken to mean that free human response is not important to the gospel! There is much more that could be said on this score.[1] However, after five exciting years committed to our burgeoning new ministry, "founder's fatigue" began creeping in and my wife Susan encouraged me to revisit the PhD idea. The return to St. Andrews in September 2013 was a great refreshment—an intensity of a different sort!

My original PhD proposal centered on the theme of theological anthropology, and projected conversation partners included Karl Barth and Gregory of Nazianzus (fourth century). I am continually drawn to Gregory because of his insistence that Jesus Christ incarnate is at once the Righteous One of God and the One who assumes sinful human flesh (without sinning).[2] I had ruminated for years about the duality of the Chalcedonian

---

1. Just months before this book was published, Mark Galli's *Karl Barth: An Introduction for Evangelicals* hit the shelves. Interestingly Galli uses my saga with Young Life as "Exhibit A" in illustrating how Barth's theology can be threatening to the so-called Evangelical way of evangelism. In 2007 I had been invited upon request to present to Young Life leadership my position paper on evangelism, which I titled "Jesus is the Gospel" (non-published, copyright 2007). This essay immediately preceded my termination for "theological differences." Typical Evangelical suspicions (antinomianism, "soft on sin," universalism) negatively postured my dialogue with Young Life from shortly after my return from masters work in Scotland in 2002. My contentment to engage with Young Life leadership on the level of purely objective inclusion and real belonging in Christ—more expansive in scope than Dortian Calvinism and more real (less hypothetical) than Arminian doctrine—did not alleviate enough of the perceived threat to prevent my demise.

2. See Gregory's letter to Cledonius (101): "The unassumed is the unhealed; but what is united to God is saved. If only half Adam fell, then what Christ assumes and

formula of 451 (Christ as one person, two natures—divine and human) and what it had to say about Christology *and* anthropology (one *human*, two "natures"—true and false).³ While Gregory and Cyril of Alexandria's⁴ position has not been the prevalent view of recent centuries, I knew Barth held to a similar scriptural belief about Christ's assumption of fallen flesh. To me, probing the theological history of the assumption was important enough—we all need to know that it is actually God who embraces us at our worst, not an intermediary. However, I was also keen to press forward to better apprehend how Barth could hold to Christ's human assumption of *sarx* with all its ignominious connotations while maintaining at the same time an understanding of the incarnate Christ (not only the resurrected and ascended Christ) as the true human.

Since the time of my theological metamorphosis in January of 2000 (shared in *Movements of Grace*)⁵ my immersion in the *Church Dogmatics* has provided great inspiration in my Christian journey. Already aware of

---

saves may be half also; but if the whole of his nature fell, it must be united to the whole nature of him who was begotten, and so be saved as a whole." See also Oration 20.13, where Gregory teaches concerning Christ: "He who is rich is a beggar—for he goes begging in my flesh, that I might become rich in his godhead." The flesh of which Gregory speaks is diametrically opposed to Spirit. It is not humanity *per se* which is oppositional to God, but sinful humanity. Christ assumed sinful humanity to cleanse, sanctify, and restore it in himself, raising us with him and returning us to the original Adam. Therefore, exhorts Gregory, humans should bring "gifts for your king, for your God, for the one who became a corpse" (20.13–14,16–17). See also Oration 30.5–6: "In the character and form of a Servant, he condescends to His fellow servants, and assumes a form which is not his own, bearing all me and mine in himself, that in himself He may consume the bad, as fire does wax, or as the sun does the mist of the earth, and that I may partake of what is his by being conjoined to him."

3. Note quote marks. It will be clear throughout the book that humanity at base has one *true* nature, not two.

4. Cyril of Alexandria died in 444, but his strong theological influence leading into the Council of Chalcedon obviously echoed Gregory's teachings on the assumption: "what has not been taken up has not been saved"; *In Ioannis Evangelium*, MPG LXXIV, 89 CD; as cited by Dorries, *Edward Irving's Incarnational Christology*, 207. The extended quote is even more clearly derived from Gregory, "The Word of God united himself with the whole nature of men, that he might save the whole man. For what has not been taken up has not been saved." In line with Athanasius and Gregory, Dorries notes that on Cyril's view, humanity's holistic cleansing included body *and* soul, so that in Christ's solidarity with sinful humanity, and without interruption to his divinity, Christ offered "his soul in redemptive exchange for the soul of all." It appears impossible to fully ascertain whether the Chalcedonian Council concluded that Christ's human nature comprised either our sinful flesh or pristine (pre-fall) flesh, in spite of the wide circulation of Cyril's writings.

5. https://wipfandstock.com/movements-of-grace.html/.

Barth's penchant for employing the Chalcedonian pattern in areas other than Christology, it was clear to me that only an anthropological argument firmly rooted *in* Christology could prevent my proposal from being easily dismissed as a cheap imitation or copy of the Chalcedonian pattern pasted *onto* anthropology. A cute parallelism would not do. The challenge was to articulate Barth's biblical belief that, because of the inter-connection of his Christology and anthropology, the one human being Jesus Christ is simultaneously true human and false human. Additionally, I must explore the degree to which Christ's humanity informs the true and false composition of every human being, by virtue of our concrete derivation from the Second Adam. Further still, even if I could prove that Barth understands the humanity of Christ and therefore all humans in this way (as a one person-two selves duality), what effect might this have on the growth and day to day life of the Christian disciple?

To my pleasant surprise, the PhD seminar that fall of 2013 was led by John Webster and the text was *CD* IV/2. At some point during that semester I remember the joy I felt when, half-asleep in my Scotland bedroom, the idea presented itself which I can only conclude was an answered prayer. It was the emergence of a thesis topic from our recent reading (paragraph 66) on Karl Barth's doctrine of sanctification, specifically his radical recalibration of Martin Luther's *simul iustus et peccator*, "simultaneously righteous and sinner" (or the *simul* for short). In subsequent talks with Alan Torrance (once again my supervisor), and doctoral studies friends such as Jonathan Lett, Joseph Sherrard, Travis Stevick, Forrest Buckner, and Tim Baylor, I become more and more convinced that Barth's *simul* is the ideal framework from which to present his understanding not only of human duality but also of human transformation. In Barth's *simul* there converges the depth of *peccator* depravity assumed by Christ (à la Gregory) and the *iustus* vindication of the ongoing and dynamic "vicarious humanity of Christ" as later elaborated upon by Barth's pupil, T. F. Torrance. Instead of allocating valuable space to other major theological voices, I settled on a project that would be a singularly thematic, full-on engagement with Barth, looking at the *simul* as a scarlet thread, especially throughout *Church Dogmatics*, around which to weave Barth's doctrine of sanctification most coherently.

It is my hope that decades of experience in grass roots ministry and non-profit social justice work will continually enhance my ability to work alongside others mutually interested in the interface of Barth's theological vision and contemporary culture, even while keeping the cultural discussion supremely theological. In his powerful book, *The Christian Imagination: Theology and the Origins of Race*, theologian Willie Jennings aptly decried the "current practice of teaching systematic theology (and all its varieties—dogmatic, pastoral, and so forth—and all its historical epochs) and then of teaching missions (historically conceived) or intercultural studies or both as separate realities."[6] This concern was echoed at the 2017 Ecclesiology and Ethnography Conference in Durham, England, where I was graciously invited to give a systematic theology paper. My friend Pete Ward, the director of the conference, spoke about his dislike of the term "practical theology." I agree with Pete; "practical theology" too easily puts the cart before the horse. Conversely, if we pursue the knowledge of God through the revelation of God's self in the muck and mire of incarnate existence, we will invariably be doing theology in a way that begs for sound practical expression.

One Barth scholar, after reading my original dissertation, heartily commended my work before adding the phrase, "and of course provocative." Admittedly, with the "provocative" part comes a certain amount of fear and trembling. Someone audacious enough to make, in my knowledge, what are unprecedented theological moves in Barth studies might be either a poor or a great scholar. I hope I'm not the former, and I don't pretend to be the latter. If this book is meant to be a stimulating contribution to Barth scholarship, it will admittedly not be because I have demonstrated clinical command over Barth's original language, although I have drawn support from *Kirchliche Dogmatik* at a few key points. I have taken it upon myself in this book to demonstrate, with apologies in advance to some fine Barthian scholars, that Barth's theological actualism (see Introduction) has been vastly underestimated. Similar to the hidden mystery of true human anthropology itself, I believe the meaning of Barth's actualism has been in a sense hidden; this hiddenness could be due to the fact that it is not explicitly articulated in his work itself, or perhaps due to the interpretive lens through which one reads Barth. Like his magisterial Alps, Barth's *Church Dogmatics* is undeniably impressive, even in terms of volume alone. Excerpted quotes, like snapshots of the scenery, will always garner some interest. However, there are heavily forested areas which, in working our way up the slope, preclude us from accessing just how compelling his theology is for everyday living. Apart from being dropped at the summit, which in this analogy is the full-blown actualism of his sanctification theology, one will not see the exhilarating trails which can only be slalomed from above.

In the face of the vicious and systematic inhumanity of the early and mid twentieth century, it would not surprise us to see any theologian of that era react with a transcendent escapism (if not atheism or agnosticism). Barth's theology does not apologize about transcendence. However, instead

---

6. Jennings, *The Christian Imagination*, 115.

of escapism he confronts us with a radical transcendence-orientation simultaneously rooted in the revelation of a crucified God. Am I right to maintain what I am calling Barth's Christo-anthropological actualism as simultaneous to the facts of what is often a Hobbesian human existence: "solitary, poor, nasty, brutish, and short"? By beginning at the summit of Barth's eschatological realism, am I anticipating Barth's direction for his proposed Volume V, or merely imaginating?

There may have been others in other languages, or even in English (I have not exhaustively read the secondary material) who have presented Barth's actualism like this. Nevertheless, in parading my view out for the world I fear, in my worst moments, like the king with no clothes, being exposed amidst charges of redeploying Barth's view as a Platonic, dualistic one. Against this fear, I continually draw comfort from Barth's unrelenting reliance on a real incarnation, which makes dualism unthinkable. I am emboldened by remembering the Apostle's preaching of a gospel which could only be foolishness to the Greeks, even while employing Platonic themes (trading dualism for duality, e.g., 2 Cor 3–5).[7] And I am impassioned about Barth's approach being a viable and life-giving way forward to engage with an increasingly secular and pluralistic world.

I do not bemoan a post-Christian culture. To the degree that such a transition evicts us from what has been called Christian nationalism, it is actually quite a refreshing idea. When Christian forms are exalted "to be served," they threaten to obscure the God who came "to serve" (Matt 20:28). In view of the pervading political and religious polarization taking place in our country, the solution to any "us vs. them" mentality is not a sloppy theological inclusiveness, or what David Tracy might label a "lazy pluralism." Instead, the way of the cross provides a uniquely exclusive inclusivity. As the Savior of the World Jesus Christ is the most inclusive person ("and I, when I am lifted up, will draw all people to myself," John 12:32) and also the most exclusive person ("I am the way, the truth and the life, no one comes to the Father except by me," John 14:6). And yet it is not facts about Jesus Christ that we want the world to know, even his exclusive inclusivity; rather, we desire others to know *him* ("this is eternal life, that they might know you, the only true God, and Jesus Christ whom you have sent," John 17:3). This knowing is much more than an intellectual knowing; it is a holistic, intimate,

---

7. Against all intimations that Christianity owes its thinking to Plato, here is where we can enjoy flipping the Harnakian derivative, noting that Plato was apprehending a reality which preceded him, even if he picked up the suitcase by the wrong handle. See the C. S. Lewis chapter "The Grand Miracle," in *Miracles*, for a wonderful reflection on reality, revelation and how other religious and mythological expressions relate to the prior reality of Jesus Christ.

knowing, a knowing often lost on the wise men and scholars of this age. The gospel is about knowing the heart of a God who loves us before we could ever love him, and who demonstrates that he loves us even more than he loves himself (1 John 3:16). Henri Nouwen once remarked, "To know the heart of Jesus and to love him are the same thing."[8] My fundamental desire is for this book, within the language of academic discourse, to be in the vein of Nouwen's comment.

This project marks an end and a new beginning. It represents the final sweep of my formal theological studies (PhD 2015) and the ongoing expressions of what I have gleaned from Barth as he has relentlessly pushed me back to the Word. Perhaps the outworkings of Barth's *simul* sanctification have their most practical import for the church and world in the years ahead, but regardless, the beneficial effect Barth's teaching has had on my own life and family is immeasurable. In this vein I want to give primary thanks to God, Father, Son, and Holy Spirit: to whatever degree this project reflects your kingdom, thank you for giving me strength to swim upstream against conventional wisdom. To the degree I have misrepresented you, thank you for your forgiveness and the continued opportunity to grow from grace to grace.

Mom and Dad, you have walked every step with me in love, interest, and prayerful support. Emily, Caroline, Malissa, and David, what a joy to live with you and to share Christ's abundance together through thick and thin. And to my wife Susan, to whom this book is dedicated, I can never express how grateful I am to be your husband, to be loved by you, and to learn from you and grow with you.

All Saints' Day 2017

---

8. Nouwen, *In the Name of Jesus*, 41.

Acknowledgments

I AM THANKFUL TO MY MENTOR AND FRIEND ALAN TORRANCE, WHO TOOK me on for MLitt work in 2001 and over the course of an eleven year interval continually nudged me towards the terminal degree.

I am thankful to Jeremy Begbie, who also encouraged me towards publication of this book and who has provided such wonderful affirmation for our work here in Durham.

I am thankful for my longest running friends in the local Barth reading group, Douglas Campbell and Alan Koeneke, and all the others who have joined the fun along the way.

I am thankful for those who read preliminary copies of this book in various forms and who provided constructive feedback: Kristen Johnson, Dustin Lampe, Jonathan Lett, Eddie Lowe, Emily McSwain, Sangwon Yang, Anthony Mullins, Mako Nagasawa, Ethan Taylor, Nikki Raye Rice, David Sittser, and Greg Little.

I am thankful to my personal editor and friend, Todd Speidell, who provided helpful critique and expertise to this book. Additionally, the staff at Pickwick were a joy to work with: thanks especially to editor in chief K. C. Hanson, Matt Wimer, Jeremy Funk, Daniel Lanning, Ian Creeger, Shannon Carter, and Sallie Vandagrift.

The woodcut of Jesus in the Garden is graciously contributed by local artist Janice Little. It is one of a series of Janice's "stations of the cross" woodcuts at our North St. Neighborhood chapel, where all types of people gather for morning and evening prayer.

Jesus in the Garden by Janice Little.

Introduction
Humility and Confidence

"believers . . . will meet unbelievers sincerely, in the humility of a full and honest solidarity with them; but also confidently, having regard to the, in the long run, irresistible power of the matter they represent."[1]

One Little Word

APPROXIMATELY 500 YEARS AGO, OCTOBER 31, 1517, TRADITION HAS IT that Martin Luther hammered his "95 Theses" to the door of the Wittenberg Church. Centuries later, Luther became an ongoing conversation partner for another hugely influential German-speaking theologian, Karl Barth. It is easy to imagine Luther's words to "A Mighty Fortress is Our God" ringing in Barth's ears as he penned the Barmen Declaration against Hitler's co-opting of the German Church. Perhaps "one little word shall fell him" consciously or subconsciously sparked Barth's resounding conviction: "Jesus Christ, as attested to us in Holy Scripture, is the one Word of God whom we must hear and whom we must trust and obey in life and in death."[2] What is beyond conjecture, however, is the way our Swiss Dogmatician latches on to and enlarges Luther's controversial notion which describes Christians as *simul iustus et peccator* (simultaneously righteous and sinner). Barth re-appropriates

---

1. *CD* II/1, 96.
2. The first line of The Barmen Declaration (1934) is quoted as the heading for §69. The ensuing pages of *CD* IV/3.1 are replete with references to both Luther's hymn and to Barmen, sometimes in what appears to be an intentional proximity. See 274: "As the Word of God spoken in Jesus Christ is not against man but for him, so man for his part, as the one he really is, cannot be radically against the Word spoken to him but only for it. The battle continues, but it bears this aspect. Again it is the case that one little word can fell His adversary."

Luther's *simul* as his pivot point for all matters of human sanctification (and which for Barth includes conversion). In fact, George Hunsinger has stated that the *simul* for Barth "constitutes the framework for sense and nonsense for soteriology as a whole."[3] The *iustus* dimension represents truth and life; the *peccator*, untruth and death.

Christians often think of sanctification as having to do with Christians being conformed to Christ. But what does the humanity of Jesus Christ himself and Jesus' own sanctification—"for their sakes I sanctify myself" (John 17:19)—have to do with ours? How can Barth speak of sanctification without implementing the typical construct of progressive, or zero-sum, sanctification?[4] How could the *simul*, in what sounds like a static paradox, have anything to do with real Christian growth and transformation? In addressing these questions I will seek to establish that it is Barth's vibrant Christo-centric definition of humanity which remains dimensionally rooted against human sin, shame and satanic activity. Barth's moves here provide an expansive context for the Holy Spirit's role in all matters of sanctification. Barth's radical appropriation of Luther's *simul* provides an apt lens through which the christological and Trinitarian purposes of creation may emerge. To this end, I will propose 1) sanctification is to be retrospectively grasped with Barth by looking through reconciliation to creation (through Christ's reconciling work "the secret of creation is perceptible"[5]), and 2) equally important for sanctification is that it subsequently be envisioned *from* creation without reference to reconciliation at all, i.e., from creation alone, as part and parcel of *iustus* humanity created in Christ.

Theological anthropology cannot very well be *anthropology* if it does not apply to every human being. Even if we accept the *simul*'s usefulness for Christians, what do we make of a wider appropriation of the *simul* in light of Barth's emphasis on Christ as the Second Adam? Should Barth's rephrasing of the *simul*, "I was and still am the old man . . . I am and will be the new man,"[6] extend to humanity in general? Barth's application of the

---

3. Hunsinger, "A Tale of Two Simultaneities," 326. According to Arnold Come, *An Introduction to Barth's Dogmatics for Preachers*, it is the view of French theologian Henri Bouillard that "*simul iustus et peccator* is the most persistent theme in Barth's theology, and that everything else is build around it" (158).

4. To be clear, by zero-sum sanctification I mean a sliding scale built upon a 0–100 percent ratio whereby more righteousness means less sinfulness and vice versa.

5. *CD* III/1, 36.

6. *CD* IV/1, 544. The "saying" in quotes is my succinct paraphrase of Barth. Barth's actual quote in *CD*: "I was and still am the former man . . . I am already and will be the latter man." Regrettably, because of Barth's reliance on old man-new man-one man language in articulating the *simul*, I have maintained the use of "man" and masculine

simul may help us to better understand why we often see so much good in unbelievers and so much evil in believers. Yet, if sin persists in the life of the Christian, what can it really mean for us to be a "new creation" and that "the old has gone" (2 Cor 5:17)?[7] How does the fact that Christians believe they are not only risen but also ascended with Christ, and seated with him in the heavenly realms (Eph 2:6), square with the practical challenges to faith that confront them in this fallen world every day?

Theological questions invariably emerge after senseless tragedies like that on December 14, 2012 in Newtown, Connecticut. On that day a man entered an elementary school and gunned down twenty children and six teachers. In her article "Where was God at Newtown?"[8] Diana Butler Bass (a self-proclaimed theist) concludes that one could not say God was at Newtown unless one were to determine God to be either ruthless or powerless; the Voltarian riddle here does its work. However, the author also concludes that God was not really absent, only apparently absent (i.e., hidden). She thereby expresses the overall conclusion that the best one can say about God in the situation of Sandy Hook Elementary is to adhere to a version of the *Deus absconditus*: in her words, "God is in all places and nowhere." The author's way of expressing the apparent absence of God is essentially to posit a God who is mostly withdrawn and inaccessible when the world feels darkest. Does God just sit idly by, wringing God's hands when darkness mounts an offensive?

On Barth's view, the omnipresence of God can never mean God's omni-absence—and any hidden "god" who is *not really* absent is certainly not *really* present. Instead, for Barth the God who is hidden *is* the God who is revealed to be present in Jesus Christ. Barth could not take more seriously the biblical teaching that Jesus Christ is the fullness of deity in bodily form (Col 2:9). While true that Jesus Christ is often hidden, just as true is that Jesus Christ is never absent; for Barth, Jesus Christ is just as present in his hiddenness as he is in his revealedness.[9] It follows that while Barth can in

---

language in quoted material but use inclusive language in my own prose. Additionally, I have chosen to preserve UK spelling when it occurs in quoted material.

7. When it comes to exegeting the lives of Christians from a purely sequence-driven version of sanctification, we must continue to ask: Why do Christians continue to prove themselves in the present to be all the things supposedly past? How are Christians so easily mistaken for those liars, cheats, adulterers, and blasphemers who "will not enter the kingdom of Heaven?" (1 Cor 6:9–10).

8. Diane Butler Bass, "Where Was God in Newtown?"

9. See *CD* II/1, 473–483, for Barth's discussion on presence and absence—e.g., "God is not less present here or there" (473); "Omnipresence cannot mean God's omni-absence" (472); "But there is no non-presence of God in His creation" (476).

one sense affirm Luther's *Deus absconditus*, he is chagrined over Luther's failure to resist rigorously the cleavage that so easily occurs between the God hidden and the God revealed. Barth's point is that, if the *Deus revelatus* only partially, or not fully and accurately, reveals the *Deus absconditus*, then when it comes to figuring out what God is actually like, we are left to pure speculation.

For Barth, when God becomes a human being he lives not only as a singular Jewish man of humble origins, but he also represents in himself every human being—the whole spectrum of the human race. Jesus Christ is the true and original human being beloved by God, and at the same time the representative human sinner—and therefore "the greatest of all sinners"[10]—being "forsaken" by God. In his person, Christ defines the goodness of humanity, and he also delimits the evil and brokenness of humanity. The implications are somewhat startling: every single human being exists in the human being of Jesus Christ, eternal Son of God. In terms of Barth's beloved Colossians, we could describe the *simul iustus et peccator* as the simultaneous, twofold, "Christ is your life" (see 3:4) and "Christ is your death" (see 3:3). In Barth's view, then, righteousness is not primarily a forensic term[11] to be fitted into a legal scheme of atonement but signifies true life from above, life derived solely from the life of God. Righteousness and life cannot be separated in Barth's view any more than sin and death.

How does this—Christ's life for us even amidst tragedy and death—translate to the murders at Sandy Hook Elementary? Where was God at Newtown? Jesus Christ either defines or delimits the being and action of every person involved, most particularly the victims. God's presence in this world, states Barth, is "the presence of the crucified."[12] On this side of the veil, Barth encourages us to hope in the one who perfectly understands and loves us, who suffers with us and who is, even when hidden, the farthest from being absent—he is the Victor, but he is in Barth's words "the Victor of Gethsemane and Golgotha."[13] In the confusing simultaneity of righteousness

---

10. *CD* IV/1, 281. We will discuss what Barth does and does not mean by "forsaken" beginning in chapter 7.

11. As we shall see, especially in chapter 7, Barth is not opposed to all implementation of forensic themes in regards to justification or even adoption (although for adoption "filial" or "covenantal" would be preferable to "legal"). When it comes to the atonement, I think of "forensic" as shorthand for the overall structure housing penal substitution; we could say punishment and satisfaction are two peas in the forensic pod. The "forensic, legal language of justification," states Mark Dever, "make clear the reality of our guilt and the required penalty" ("Nothing But the Blood").

12. *CD* IV/3.1, 395.

13. *CD* IV/3.1, 390 (emphasis added). In her important book, *Sex, Race, and God*,

and sinfulness or their *teloi*, life and death, Barth's *simul* provides a gospel framework communicating an ever-present God revealed in Jesus Christ, a God who in the end does not rescue us from death but in it and *through* it to the other side.

Barth said of Mozart that the composer heard the harmonious and discordant notes together but both within an envelopment of light.[14] So too the *simul*. The *simul* would not be helpful if Barth's adaptation of "total depravity" were not framed in the highest possible doctrine of creation and the unremitting goodness of humanity properly understood. The *simul* would not be a productive instrument for sanctification if the end of Christ's human narrative was not redemptive for lives tragically cut short or if the verdict were ever in doubt. Indeed, for those witnessing the crucifixion event on that darkest of days, the verdict *was* in doubt; that is the day, on Barth's view, the great God almighty humbled himself to be most small. By doing so, in his death and burial he swallowed all the darkness that opposed him, so that we might testify with Barth by Easter light: "However small and weak it might be, light will always be the power that banishes darkness; and however great and mighty it may be, darkness will always be the impotence that yields before light."[15]

Susan Brooks Thistlethwaite conveys the autobiographical account of one of her students who had been raped while disposing of trash at a trash dump in a deserted back alley. Writes Thistlethwaite: "As she lay there on the heap of trash, injured and bleeding and wondering whether she was about to be killed, she had a vision of Jesus as a crucified woman who said to her from the cross, 'You don't have to be ashamed, I know what you are suffering'"(93). Obviously to hold that Jesus of Nazareth was God does not mean that God is a man, nor does it mean that Jesus as God cannot equally represent or identify with different genders. Thistlethwaite remarks of her own metamorphosis regarding how the power of Christ's death supernaturally translates to women: "When I first saw Edwina Sandys's sculpture 'Christa' in the Cathedral of St. John the Divine in New York City, I was unsettled and disliked it intensely. The figure is of an unclothed woman crowned with thorns, arms outstretched in the form of a crucifix but without a cross behind it. I said to my companion, 'Women are routinely crucified in contemporary society. This will tend to legitimate violence against them.' Yet since then, because of the healing these statues seem to evoke in women who have survived sexual and domestic violence, I have revised my view. 'Christa' is not experienced by many women as legitimating violence against them but as identifying with their pain and freeing them from the guilt that somehow . . . they deserved what they got"(93).

14. *CD* III/3, 298; Barth describes Mozart as hearing music in very *simul* terms: "Mozart saw this light no more than we do, but he heard the whole world of creation enveloped by this light. Hence it was fundamentally in order that he should not hear a middle or neutral note, but the positive far more strongly than the negative. He heard the negative only in and with the positive. Yet in their inequality he heard them both together."

15. *CD* III/1, 123.

Barth asserts that it is Christ's passion that *most* profoundly reveals God's true divinity, "the divine form hidden under the form of a servant." He did not endorse theories that suggest Christ "surrendered, or even curtailed" his deity in going to the cross. For Barth, a better explanation from Philippians 2 is simply that Jesus did not "treat His equality with God as His one exclusive possibility . . . It was not an inalienable necessity for Him to be only like God and only distinct from the creature." Barth continues, "His freedom is seen in the fact that He is able to do something different. He can so empty Himself that, without detracting from his form as God, He can take the form of a servant, concealing His form of life as God, and going about in the likeness of man."[16] Even when God fully "stoops" down to us, says Barth, he remains fully on high. By becoming one with the creature (i.e., with humanity), the Creator reveals his strength through his weakness, his power through his smallness.[17]

> *The Prince of Darkness grim,*
> *we tremble not for him;*
> *His rage we can endure,*
> *for lo his doom is sure,*
> *one little word shall fell him.*[18]

This book, focused on Barth's *simul iustus et peccator*, is not about theodicy per se, although hopefully the connection is apparent. If the asymmetrical themes of righteousness and sin, light and darkness, cannot be maintained along with that of life over death, then not only does Paul's conviction to preach "Jesus Christ and him crucified" have no relation to the *simul*, but it is also a conviction with no bearing at all on our lives in this fallen world. Conversely, we will suggest that it is only the *simul*'s intimate connection to "Jesus Christ and him crucified" that makes the duality of the *simul* good news for sanctification and conversion.

The Simul's Scaffolding

As suggested in the preface, what follows is not meant to be a study on Barth as much as an engagement with Barth. It is a project constituted in large

---

16. *CD* II/1, 516.

17. *CD* II/1, 527. For God becoming one with humanity, see *CD* II/2, 163: "In Him is light and no darkness at all. But when God of His own will raised up man to be a covenant-member with Himself, when from all eternity He elected to be one with man in Jesus Christ, He did it with a being which was not merely affected by evil but actually mastered by it."

18. Excerpt from the hymn, "A Mighty Fortress is Our God."

measure by an interactive reading with the primary text of *Church Dogmatics*.[19] The reader will note that I have taken the liberty of using *iustus* and *peccator* as modifiers (i.e., *peccator* humanity instead of *peccatum* humanity) in order to provide an implicit connection back to the historic dictum itself: *simul iustus et peccator*. My suggested reading of Barth's theological anthropology (i.e., that which recognizes Jesus Christ as not only God and human but also as true and false human) is likely to stretch our understanding of the freedom of God past the "Thomist limitation."[20] Barth continually asks for our traditional conception of immutability to be checked at the door.[21] The hope is that what emerges will be a provisional corollary of the original

---

19. I am operating in the perspective of Barth scholars such as John Webster, who believe Barth's approach in the *Church Dogmatics* years (1932–67) is relatively consistent throughout and not requiring special treatment in view of year of production. See John Webster, "Introducing Barth," 13.

20. *CD* II/1, 537. In his discussion starting on page 534, Barth takes Aquinas to task for presumptuously exalting the Aristotelian principle of non-contradiction as "an absolutised system" determining what God can and cannot do. Instead of ascribing to ourselves "creaturely reliability" in positing such principles, we should look to God as the only reliable source for what is possible. "We shall always seek and find the limit of what is possible in Him, not in what is created . . . The limit of the possible is not, therefore, self-contradiction, but contradiction of God" (536).

21. See Barth's discussion on immutability, *CD* II/1, 494–496. Barth is suspicious of the term immutable. He thinks of it as an inhibitive concept in light of God's freedom to reveal himself in various forms; immutable does not mean immobile. Barth therefore can cleverly promote "the immutability of the freedom of God," which keeps the doctrine of God from being imprisoned in petrifying theological constructs, providing constancy (the term he prefers to immutable), but also elasticity. "There is such a thing as the holy mutability of God," insists Barth, "He is above all ages. But above them . . . as the One who—as Master and in His own way—partakes in their alteration, so that there is something corresponding to that alteration in His own essence. His constancy consists in the fact that he is always the same in every change. The opposite of his constancy, that which is ruled out by it, is not His holy mutability, but the unholy mutability of men" (496). Our study will explore the extent that, for Barth, Jesus Christ represents the holy mutability of God *and* the unholy mutability of humanity—the righteous constancy and "the wicked inconstancy" (496) of humanity in his one person. Barth believes the death and resurrection of Jesus Christ and the Savior's willingness to submit to the threshing of the Cross reveals the negative aspects of fallen humanity and the re-emergence of true humanity, but again, it also reveals the "divine form hidden under the form of the servant," the true identity of God: "God is 'immutably' the One whose reality is seen in His condescension in Jesus Christ, in His self-offering and self-concealment, in His self-emptying and self-humiliation. He is not a God who is what He is in a majesty behind this condescension, behind the cross on Golgotha. On the contrary, the cross on Golgotha is itself the divine majesty, and all the 'exaltation' necessary on account of His deity" (517).

formulation—a "Chalcedonian *anthropology*"[22]—for the church, providing encouragement for disciples through sharing with Christ the Spirit-filled life of transformation to which we shall refer as *"simul* sanctification."

In presenting Barth's reformulated *simul* as the backbone of his theology of sanctification, Barth asks us to consider each person as a singular person, and yet as two persons, two totally opposite persons in one person. This single-subject duality, then, comprises two determinations—the *iustus* (true) self and *peccator* (false) self. A series of questions might naturally follow here: Could we say "one subject, two subjectivities"? But is it possible to hold to two subjectivities without two subjects? And if one of the "subjects" is merely parenthetical, what legitimate theological or practical use could it have? As with other dimensional concepts, language fails to adequately capture what Barth is after. Like describing the One and the Three of the Trinity or in regards to the Hypostatic Union, we can only consider the fullness of one dimension when we "think away" the other. As difficult as this may be, Barth does not see any more responsible way to understand Scripture, and therefore he appears convinced that if we grasp the scripturally derived interpretive key to the *simul* (Jesus Christ and him crucified), it will be to our advantage in reading Scripture and in opening ourselves to the transforming work of the Spirit in our lives.

In spite of the Christian's "freedom as the new man in Jesus and in the Holy Spirit," writes Barth, the Christian is in "bondage as the old man . . . in the flesh." The two, oppositional determinations of the believer are both total. "Total freedom" and "total bondage," Barth insists, "clash in one and the same man."[23] Sanctification therefore involves the believers' ability to recognize within themselves a "quarrel" between "two total men who cannot be united but are necessarily in extreme contradiction."[24] Paul's words reflect the Christian's struggle: "So then, with my mind I am a slave to the law of God [connoting total freedom], but with my flesh I am a slave to the

---

22. I call this "Chalcedonian anthropology" because of its portrayal of humanity as revealed in Jesus Christ, and because it follows the Chalcedonian pattern of dual aspects (in this case *iustus* and *peccator* humanity) in a single subject. It will continually be made clear that "Chalcedonian anthropology" is an imperfect corollary to the original—by its nature it is a provisional term which loses its function when the contradiction inherent to the *simul* is removed as revealed in the death and resurrection of Christ, and ultimately manifest on the Day of Redemption.

23. *CD* IV/2, 496–97. Between these two determinations, instists Barth, there can be no cooperation: "For how can there be co-operation between total freedom and total bondage? How can the Spirit give assistance to the flesh, or the flesh to the Spirit?"(497).

24. *CD* IV/2, 570, 571. In his *simul* existence, "Paul's old self" and "Paul's new self" have nothing in common except for one thing, "Paul."

law of sin [connoting total bondage]" (7:25).²⁵ In spite of Jesus' admonition in Matthew 6:24, asserts Barth, Paul confesses to having two masters—this is "the plight" he shares with all human beings.²⁶

In this book I will use at different times both the word "dimension" and "determination" to describe the two aspects of Barth's *simul*: *iustus* and *peccator*. "Determination," preferred by Barth, better carries the dynamic and oppositional movements of the two aspects of the one person "at serious odds with himself."²⁷ The word "dimension," I think, better carries the simultaneity of the situation.

Introducing the Christo-anthropological

For my first book I coined the phrase "dynamic Christo-realism"²⁸ to describe how I see Barth and those he influenced, Dietrich Bonhoeffer and the Torrances (T. F. and J. B.), understanding who Jesus Christ is as the one in whom all things exist and hold together (Col 1:17). Within God's one great recapitulating act Christ re-gathers all things in heaven and on earth to himself (Eph 1:10). In the vanguard of this soteriological inversion, Paul tells us, we find the pinnacle of God's creation, the human being. In other words, it is not the human being who shares the redemption of "all things,"

---

25. Importantly, the thinking about the true and false dimensions of human existence, represented here in 7:25 by oppositional slaveries, cannot be allowed to devolve into a spatial dichotomies like mind-body or inner-outer. Paul does use these images in Romans 7, but in the context of the section Barth adheres to Paul's overall meaning of two, whole, mutually exclusive determinations, *totus iustus* and *totus peccator*. "Inner" will retain great importance for our study in its non-spatial meaning, being useful in conjunction with the "hidden" dimension of humanity. In other words, for Barth the inner man (7:22), dimensionally not spatially understood, is true humanity.

26. *CD* IV/1, 589.

27. *CD* IV/2, 570.

28. What I call Christo-realism is very different from the concept Christian Realism as promoted by Reinhold Niebuhr. Again, on Barth's view, sin is absurd and irrational since there is no root for it in reality, so that it is categorically impossible; yet the fact remains, it exists. That is why Barth calls all sin, and its defacing, distorting negation, "the impossible possibility." Conversely, Niebuhr's "Christian realism" begins with the fallen "reality" and calls grace "the impossible possibility." In other words, Niebuhr adopts the human perspective as reality because it is more practical and reflective of our experience, a position commonly assumed by people in the world today as is evidenced by the common adjectives "harsh" and "brutal" as modifiers for reality. When Barth occasionally implements the word "reality" (see *CD* I/2, 305) to describe the darkness, he is not reversing field to agree with Niebuhr but only communicating that our experience in this world is indeed harsh and brutal, more so and especially in contrast to the "real reality" of Jesus Christ (see *CD* IV/2, 227).

but quite the opposite: "the creation itself will be set free from its bondage to decay and will obtain the freedom of the glory of the children of God" (Rom 8:21). Grace is thus comprehended by the human being Jesus Christ, the one representing God to humanity and humanity to God, and in turn all creation exists within this covenant relationship. Instead of Christo-realism, then, which is a broader term, in this book I am implementing the more precise term "Christo-anthropological" to describe the true and pure relationship, the dynamic covenantal union, between God and all human beings *en Christo*. I want to emphasize here that the *iustus* dimension (or determination) of humanity that I am employing from Barth's *simul iustus et peccator* is representative of the Christo-anthropological being-in-act of every human; righteousness is not a forensic label ("a title tacked on"[29]) or even an indicative *state* of human being. *Iustus* humanity means every human's union and communion with Christ and ongoing participation in him.

A quick search will produce numerous results concerning what has been called Barth's theological actualism. Much of the discussion is related to Jesus Christ as uniquely revealing God's being-in-act, which includes the governing of God-talk by the incarnation and helpfully tilts us away from static categories that seem to limit God's activity (as in our review of immutability, above). Because of the inner-connection of Christology and anthropology, Barth's actualism implicitly includes human being-in-act as derived from and contained within Christ's being-and-act. My reading of Barth's actualism, however, seeks to move the discussion beyond its usual limits. If Paul Nimmo, for instance, describes Barth's actualism as "the context of all ethical action and of the human person,"[30] I would like to further propose that the being-in-act of Jesus Christ is not only the context of these ethical actions but also the specific content, i.e., that the being and act of the true human Jesus Christ *is* literally the being-in-act of every human in the fullness of the Holy Spirit.[31] This means that the actuality of all human

---

29. *CD* I/1, 94.

30. Nimmo, *Being in Action*, 2.

31. Nimmo does not deny that Barth's "actualist ontology" has specific content, the "fundamental and particular" content is the being-in-act of Jesus Christ as the elected human and the electing God (8). With this we fully concur. However, when it comes to the depth of the content—the nature of derivative human participation within the being-and-act of Jesus Christ—the angle of my divergence from Nimmo's path is acute. While I will not take up Nimmo again, his parsing of passive from active participation in the quotation that follows is consistent with other interpreters who lend a shallowness to Barth's actualism compared to our Christo-anthropological consideration: "On the one hand, there is that participation in Jesus Christ which is true of all individuals in light of the divine election and the history of Jesus Christ." This is Nimmo's "passive mode" of participation. "On the other hand . . . there is that participation in Jesus

obedience, on every level, always precedes the possibility of human obedience. All pneumatological and epistemological aspects are intrinsic to what is already actual for every human in Christ. Correspondingly, for humans in Christ, there is never a higher magnitude of divine command than there is of our true and actual human response to that command. An incommensurate human response could only result in what Barth calls an "ethical vacuum" incumbent on us to fill, a potential for us to attain, a spiritual tank to be topped off. Instead of leaving us naked or even partially exposed before God's expectations, Barth provides a glorious picture of every human *en Christo*, and therefore clothed in the Law.[32] More precisely, Barth might admonish us, it is a law deeper than "the law and the prophets"—the Law of the Spirit of Life.[33] Against all notions of an "ethical vacuum," Barth's Christo-anthropological actualism provides a life in the Holy Spirit "full of realistic content" on the one hand (when it comes to *iustus* humanity) and accountability on the other (when it comes to *peccator* humanity).

As will be clear in chapter 3 and chapter 4, it is the Christo-anthropological dimension of human life—every human being's actual, active, and ongoing participation in Christ and in and by the Spirit—which forms Barth's baseline definition of human identity as I understand it.[34] For that reason Christo-anthropological (connoting *iustus* humanity) should not be

---

Christ which represents the active correspondence of the ethical agent to her original determination, that is, her response *in act* to the passive participation that is already real in Jesus Christ" (173). I will argue beginning in chapter 4 that such a parsing of Barth's concept of participation dictates a misreading of Barth's *de jure*—*de facto* language and reintroduces the very theological pitfalls Barth seeks to avoid.

32. *CD* II/2, 563. Barth's fondness for submarining Luther's juxtaposition between law and gospel has perhaps switched over in this case to playing off of Calvin (who spoke of Jesus Christ being clothed in his gospel) as a way of showing the deep unity of gospel and law, properly understood (see chapter 5).

33. I capitalize the Law of the Spirit of Life (see Rom 8:2) in recognition of the subjectivity of God in which all real human subjectivity is located, e.g., the Law of Christ.

34. On my view, it is problematic to affirm Barth's premise that Jesus Christ is humanity, to subsequently talk about his non-static being-in-act, to recognize that there is no ontological difference between humans, and then to pull up short on granting humans the fullest actual participation within those assertions. Such a compromise invariably leads to internal interpretive conflict, where as readers of *CD* we are likely to introduce Barth as inconsistent in places where it is our own inconsistency which is the problem! Apart from our dimensional compass of Barth's *simul*, could Barth be anything but incoherent when he makes statements such as, "Even regenerate man continually has to recognise himself as unregenerate man" (*CD* II/1, 144)? If, in our immanent-mindedness we are prone to dismiss out of hand Barth's transcendent view of humanity because we perceive hints of Docetism, Platonism, or even Gnosticism, then we are sadly left to grasp at what is within our reach.

confused with my other term "anthro-dimensional." Anthro-dimensional refers to all the positive *and* negative dimensions of humanity. Put differently, the Christo-anthropological does not include the dimension of *peccator* humanity because it does not originally or ultimately belong; however, because parasitic *peccator* humanity is never without the Christo-anthropological (*iustus* humanity), human transformation (for the one person) is possible at all times, from within or without the *simul* (see Rom 8:11).

My PhD thesis was originally entitled "*Simul Sanctification*": Karl Barth's Reappropriation of Luther's Dictum "simul iustus et peccator." For the revamped book I have changed the subtitle to *Karl Barth's Hidden Vision for Human Transformation*. The deletion of the dictum should not be taken as de-emphasizing the *simul*. I believe more than ever that the *simul*, with its *iustus* determination replete with Barth's (non-Lutheran) actualism, provides an organizational construct for the most faithful approach to human sanctification. Our sanctification is powered in a sense from the Christo-anthropological dimension, the dimension which adequately defines humanity beyond the *peccator* dimension and to our deepest unity with Christ. However, I would not want to give the impression that a "dimension"—even a righteous dimension—is the key to human holiness! Sanctification is unequivocally driven by Jesus Christ the Son of the Father, in the power of the Holy Spirit.[35]

Hidden Vision

At this point I would like to make three general comments about the subtitle. As has already been inferred, Barth's vision for sanctification is a *hidden vision*. The hiddenness of Barth's vision is reflected in the dimensional nature of the *simul* itself. In the midst of our *simul* (contradictory) existence the true Christo-anthropological character of humanity might not only feel hidden but downright elusive! As a way of encouraging the saints, my intent is that this book will contribute depth to the powerful and hopeful biblical concept of hiddenness.[36] On this side of the veil, what we are given to know

---

35. I say this as a preemptive strike against all notions that the "Christo-anthropological dimension" or the "simul" actually *do* anything as acting subjects, even if they are occasionally presented as subjects in my prose!

36. Against all Gnostic notions of a secret knowledge, God's revelation of himself in Jesus Christ for the sake of every human being is the most public knowledge possible. This is what Barth calls "the open secret": the good news that Paul declares has already "been proclaimed to every living creature under heaven" (Col 1:23; see Col 1:25–28; 2:2–3)! See also Eph 3:8–9: "Although I am the very least of all the saints, this grace was given to me to bring to the Gentiles the news of the boundless riches of

about God and humanity will always be hidden to a degree. Thankfully "hidden" does not mean hopelessly "blocked." In the transcendent and immanent light of Christ, we know "in part"—we *do* see as God reveals and by his Spirit grants us epistemic access—even if for now "we see through a mirror dimly." We look forward with great anticipation to the day when the distortion recedes, the partial gives way to perfect and full revelation, the *peccator* dimension of humanity dissolves away from the Christo-anthropological, and we "know fully, even as we are fully known."[37]

Vital to Barth's hidden vision is his discussion of humanity in its "pure form" and "impure form" (his terms). Especially pertinent in this connection is Barth's section in the middle of *CD* IV/3 between the first and second components of his four-part excursus on Job. It is in our consideration of this excursus, a critical juncture of our study (chapter 8), where Barth provides strongest support for our hypothesis of a delicately nuanced christological *simul* from which every human being's *simul* is derived. Because of the relatively intricate theological moves necessary to support the above contention, some preemptive articulation may be helpful. First, I believe Barth's articulation of the relationship between the pure and impure "forms" of humanity is a clarifying and deliberate tactic against any suspicions that his account is platonic. Commandeering the word "form" for his own purposes (and away from platonic concepts of *methexis*, or human participation *within* a higher form) the pure form of humanity *is* participation. This real participation in union with Christ is just as real on earth as in heaven.[38] Headed-off therefore is an imagined straight (dualistic) correlation in Barth's meaning between A) the *peccator* determination of humanity and the "impure form" of humanity on one hand, and B) the *iustus* determination and "pure form" of humanity on the other. Barth's "pure form" of humanity *is* essentially the *iustus* determination, but the "impure form" of humanity is *not* simply equated with the *peccator* determination. Instead, Barth's "impure form" of humanity describes the one "overall" human (or humanity) in *simul* contradiction.[39] The "impure form" of humanity comprises both the *iustus* and

---

Christ, and to make everyone see what is the plan of the mystery hidden for ages in God who created all things." See also 1 Cor 2:7.

37. The quoted phrases are from 1 Cor 13:9–12.

38. Ironically, it is less thoroughly actualistic views of Barth's actualism (unlike the Christo-anthropological actualism we are espousing) which paint him more platonically; these views typically insert hypotheticals which in some way distance human participants from the human Jesus Christ in a manner Barth's eschatological realism does not countenance.

39. Again, because we are so accustomed to zero-sum constructs we will be prone to mistake Barth's concept of the "impure form" as a *partim-partim* instead of a

peccator dimensions, i.e., the two total (*totus*), asymmetrical determinations (two "subjectivities") of humanity as they exist in the single subject.[40]

Secondly, an understanding of the accompanying *totus peccator* can wait for further discussion, but suffice here to emphasize that no amount of sinfulness can affect, in Barth's view, the being and presence of the pure form (the dynamic *iustus* determination) of humanity. As two mutually exclusive determinations in one space, the *peccator* determination can never mix with the *iustus* determination, nor can it displace it. It can, however, hide it. The *peccator* determination can only be an obscuring, evil, and incomprehensible distortion which conceals the real, unadulterated presence of one's true and pure humanity. What we have, then, are two total oppositional dimensions that by non-theological observation are refracted by their opposite. Without the eyes of faith, the one person in view is defined as less than whole or complete (something less than totally *iustus* or totally *peccator*). The result? We inevitably surmise the two "totals" as equal to an incomplete! For Barth, this is the enigma of the "impure form."

Third, when it comes to theological anthropology, it is the accompanying narrative of Job in Barth's discussion of pure and impure forms which grabs our attention. This is because Barth makes a good number of allusions to Job as a kind of Christ figure. Both Job and Jesus, asserts Barth, have a pure, hidden form of their humanity, in spite of their sufferings and struggles of faith. As we shall see, there is a place in Barth's discussion where he paints Job directly in *simul* terms, recognizing the impure, overlapped form of his humanity. While Barth does not directly describe an "impure form" of Jesus' humanity (instead he describes the corrupt humanity Christ assumes as an "alien" form), his unmistakable association of Job with Jesus perhaps provides a clue for us as to what Barth could be posing as a carefully qualified christological *simul iustus et peccator*. If so, this could only corroborate

---

totus-totus. "Impure form" to us may sound like a mixture of *iustus* and *peccator* which essentially corrupts the integrity of each (as in pure water being contaminated), but there is no such mixture at play! There is only our experience and perception of two total, unalloyed, dimensions *as* a mixture.

40. In conjunction with the above note, saying this still another way may help to reinforce the non-diminishing quality of the *iustus* dimension, even when theologically housed in the "impure form" of humanity: Barth understands the "impure form" of humanity as totally pure (because the pure *iustus* dimension is never diminished) but not *merely* totally pure (because of the additional "overlap" of the totally corrupt *peccator* dimension). While *iustus* humanity can, in Christ, exist on its own, *peccator* humanity is by nature parasitic and cannot exist on its own, not even as an "impure form" of humanity. Still, in its mirrored (pseudo-holistic) and evil parasitic essence it attains symmetrical stature with *iustus* humanity, not to be proven asymmetrical apart from death and resurrection.

our thesis that Barth is presenting a second Chalcedonian duality within the first—a presentation not only of a true God and true human in one person, but also discerning within the original duality two functioning determinations within the one humanity, a simultaneously true and a false humanity (e.g., Christ as not only the pure form of humanity but also simultaneously the impure form of humanity, having assumed corrupt flesh). A christological *simul* could only be a temporal duality, although we must consider with Barth to what degree a *peccator* determination for Jesus, combined with his divinity, can avoid running corruption straight back into the depths of God's eternal being. Barth does not say, for instance, that Jesus sinned, but in a way perhaps not posed since Gregory, Barth makes us consider afresh what it would mean if he had.

Fourth, Barth continually asks us to walk by faith, resisting the temptation to consider others from a human point of view (2 Cor 5:7, 16). His "pure form" and "impure form" provides language for humanity which always directs us back to the one human subject (i.e., the pure form *of Job* or the impure form *of Job*). In the end, as revealed in the passion of Christ, the *iustus* dimension of humanity and the pure form of humanity prove to be synonymous. After the final judgment, in the unconflicted Kingdom, there is no *peccator* humanity and therefore no impure form of humanity. Even when Barth gives the old, false self a subject status, it is always as such a bracketed subject status (deadly as it is). Unlike the *iustus* predicate with its true *iustus* subject, *peccator* humanity never stands on its own. A fully independent *peccator* humanity (as in a straight dualism) could only substantiate a Lutheran idea of original sin, occluding the truth of original belonging. It should be clear that the same potential misunderstanding does not arise with Barth's concept of impure humanity, as the *iustus* dimension is always and already there, and can only be defaced.

In sum, because the pure form of humanity is just as concrete and real here as it is there in "the heavenly realm," any insinuation of a Platonic metaphysical dualism impressed on Barth's duality is categorically untenable. While heaven (including the pure, *iustus* form of humanity) may constitute the hidden *backside* of this life, it is not the "static background"[41] of human experience. A dimensional view postures the true "Pat" being seated with Christ in the heavenly realms simultaneous to the true Pat being seated at the coffee shop; conversely, a dichotomous, non-dimensional, view could only put Pat's true self in heaven, and Pat's false self (or something less than Pat's true self) on earth at the coffee shop. In Barth's view, then, humans have eternal life even in the midst of *simul* contradiction because humans

---

41. *CD* III/3, 468.

really exist, in different ways, in both spheres. "The 'old' and 'new' worlds are indirectly identical," notes Barth, "the new already present in the old." Elsewhere he adds, "Eternal life is not another, second life beyond our present one, but the reverse side of *this* life, as God sees it, which is hidden from us here and now. It is this life in relationship to what God has done in Jesus Christ for the whole world and thus also for us."[42]

Human Transformation

With all the talk about dimensions, we must not lose sight that this book is about *human* transformation. Again, Barth's emphasis on Christology includes not only the never-diminished truth of Jesus Christ as God, and not only the abiding incarnational truth of Jesus of Nazareth, but also the inherent anthropological connection of Jesus Christ—the Second Adam—*as humanity*. While recognizing anthropology as "a consequence and analogy of Christology,"[43] it is just as important to acknowledge that in Barth's view, who we are as humans in the humanity of Christ, and who we are in the Spirit, are not two different things. Humans in Christ are humans in the Spirit. It follows that our individual spiritual bodies are never extrinsic to our humanity; they are not floating above our human bodies, which are wracked by sin on this side of the veil. Barth understands our spiritual human bodies to be always present in their fullness even if they are hidden, interrelated as heaven is to earth. As we will see in chapter 11, Barth takes fully seriously the biblical statement that we are "hidden with Christ in God" (Col 3:1): "The saying in Col 3:1 may well be regarded as the normative biblical definition of heaven . . . where we ourselves are secretly present. Where is this heaven? The answer is that it is where Christ is."[44]

In this book I will seek to rebut the conventional adage that if humans are too heavenly-minded they are no earthly good. Such a belief could only be premised on the faulty notion that the ascended Christ is in heaven but not on earth. Barth is adamant that apart from Christ there is no humanity, but because humanity exists in Christ and the Spirit, and because by the

---

42. Busch, *Karl Barth*, 488.

43. *CD* III/3, 500. Due to the work of Willie Jennings, *Christian Imagination*, and J. Kameron Carter, *Race*, I am more aware than ever of the potential that an emphasis on Jesus Christ as the Second Adam may de-emphasize the Jewishness of the humanity of God, Jesus of Nazareth. That is not my intent. In "Final Reflections" (after the Conclusion) I wrestle with the possibility that my theological anthropology may open the door to supersessionist notions which are implicitly racist.

44. *CD* III/3, 438. In this connection, Barth does not hesitate to assert that Christ himself *is* the hidden kingdom of God: *CD* II/1, 606.

Spirit Christ exists just as much here as he does there, the fullest integrity is given to human life on earth.⁴⁵ Our spiritual bodies in Christ, then, are fundamentally a material dimension of our earthly existence, not only our heavenly existence. In the revelation of Jesus Christ we discover with Barth that the new humanity is the true humanity; again it is this understanding of humanity, along with the dimensional nuancing described above, which allows theologically for a fullness of our true humanity to be present without resorting to a zero-sum construct. On Barth's dimensional view, we could say our true selves are "here" and "there" in a manner the zero-sum game does not afford.⁴⁶

Transcendence and immanence are often perceived as mutually exclusive or spatially cordoned off from one another. On one hand, Christians are not unaccustomed to biblical phraseology which notes that they are seated with Christ in the heavenly realms (Eph 2:4–6). On the other hand, they rarely think of this transcendent occurrence happening simultaneously to their being seated at a table in a downtown coffee shop! Most Christians, especially in the West, probably have not dwelled on the dimensional thinking necessary to affirm such a duality (one person "seated" in two places—heaven and the coffee shop), and most certainly have not thought of the possibility that the life of every human being may be structured in a similar way.⁴⁷ Further, many have not given due consideration to the unenviable theological alternatives to such a universal claim.⁴⁸ I believe taking Barth seriously

---

45. It is from this location in the transcendent and immanent Christ that all human activism on behalf of other oppressed humans springs. A Christ who is seated in heaven, Barth, insists, "brings us fully into the historical context of the divine activity . . . If Christ is seated at the right hand of God, this does not mean that He has a mere place of honour as a spectator, and that He is now indolent" (*CD* III/3, 438–39).

46. As will be developed throughout our study, this perspective protects us from implementing spatial metaphors as if our true humanity after the fall (or even the "image") consists of relics, residue, or a "core"; at the same time it encourages us to grasp the dimensional (non-spatial) meaning of words like "inner" and "heart" when they are employed in Scripture.

47. But what exactly is the nature of the relationship of being seated here and being seated there? Is Starbucks in heaven too? As much as they might wish (Starbucks that is, not the heavenly beings) there is no grounds for such a claim (apologies!). In all seriousness, however, such a conception could only be Platonic, as if starting with a particular and predicating a universal. In chapter 13 we will discuss how to go around the circle of analogy in the theologically correct direction.

48. Ephesians 2:4–6 reads: "But God, who is rich in mercy, out of the great love with which he loved us even when we were dead through our trespasses, made us alive together with Christ—by grace you have been saved—and raised us up with him and seated us with him in the heavenly places in Christ Jesus." Alternatives in reading Ephesians could include the Dortian (Five Point) Calvinist position, that only some

involves learning to recognize his Eastern mind: thinking dimensionally, refusing to walk by sight, braving the world of the counter-intuitive. Eastern theologians may (please pardon the over simplifications) decry a lack of transcendent, dimensional paradigms by Western sequential thinkers. Conversely Eastern thinkers may be pigeon-holed as esoteric or mystical, or at least polemicized by Westerners as emphasizing Christ's resurrection over the cross. My presentation of Barth postures him differently—he is first and foremost a theologian of the cross, but with a dimensional mind. Barth understands the cross to be the supreme incarnational and historical testimony of the redemptive love of God. In one very important aspect, however, thanks to a constructive (not contrastive) relationship between transcendent and immanent concepts, Barth does not see the cross and resurrection as purely sequential. It is apparent that on Barth's view, unless one perceives "newness of life" (Rom 6:4) as being an active indicative truth of humanity in Christ—a creaturely dimension simultaneous to the cross—one will not be able to entertain or appreciate what sounds like an oxymoron: the "quickening power" not of Christ's resurrection, but of Christ's death.[49] Here Barth stands with Athanasius, whose portrayal of the renewing of the image by the superior Image was meant to communicate exactly that, a renewing, and not a re-doing.[50] In the theology of new creation, Christ's work cannot mean

---

people—the elect minority—are eternally seated in the heavenlies. While this position is logically primary in their view, Dortian Evangelicals will grant this seat to believers retroactively, which functionally puts them closer to the Arminian position. For most Arminians, persons who become Christians are then granted a seat with Christ even though there is often some theological maneuvering *after* conversion towards a more Reformed understanding of election. In contrast to both Dortian Calvinism and Arminianism, however, it is both the *universal scope* and *finished work* of Jesus Christ in the Spirit which is so important to Barth's doctrine of judgment and his avoidance of abject universalism, as we shall see.

49. *CD* III/1, 280. This quickening power of the Spirit might be crudely portrayed as follows: picture a boat sailing upstream, in full sail (the fullness of the wind is never questioned), and then an immediate reversal of the current, as in the throwing of a lever, so that the fullness of wind and current are in perfect unison. In the previous iteration, the boat against the current is still empowered by the wind, as is proven in its course upstream, but the power with fullness of wind *and* current, and no resistance, can only be imagined.

50. See Athanasius, *On the Incarnation*, (13); "With humanity being dehumanized, and clouded by demonic deceit which hid the knowledge of the true God," says Athanasius, God could only act in keeping with his character, "to renew his image in humanity . . . by the coming of the very Image of God, our Lord Jesus Christ . . . Therefore the Word of God came in person, so that, being the image of the Father, he would be able to recreate humanity afresh in that image." Athanasius continues by stating that this re-creation was effected by the doing away of death and corruption

re-doing any more than Christ's incarnate death necessitates re-incarnation. In the annulment of the *simul*, the crucified God does not create a new reality, but instead reveals a different kind of immutability—the "eternally new" reality of God himself.[51] It will become increasingly clear, especially in chapter 8, that Barth's dimensional account of the *simul* challenges the common conception that Eastern-minded theologians axiomatically privilege the resurrection over the cross.[52]

Human *Transformation*

Finally regarding the subtitle, the third word to highlight is the word *transformation* as it regards human sanctification. As with transcendence and immanence, "transformation" is typically understood contrastively. Transformation is couched in terms of an increase of the good or a decrease of the bad. The more ground I can gain for good against bad, therefore, the more transformation I will have. As common as it is for Christians to think this way in matters of sanctification, if we play this faulty equation out to its *telos*, we would have to explain why bad things are needed in heaven in order for transformation to occur! Scripture tells us plainly that transformation indeed does occur, not only in the midst of decay—and even when decay is apparently winning ground in this life—but also when there is no more decay (2 Cor 4:16–18; see 3:17–18). It follows that perhaps a better way to think of transformation in heaven, and in general, is to imagine transformation occurring before and without need of a "Fall" of humankind. Once we recognize this created economy in Christ (revealed in redemption), we will begin to understand Barth's concept of non-contrastive transformation.[53] Instead of being couched in a contrast, this transformation is in the Spirit of

---

by the death of the one who assumes them in his human body, Jesus Christ, thereby renewing humanity according to the Image of God. The source of the above inclusive language quotation is christianhistoryinstitute.org.

51. CD II/1, 500.

52. It will hopefully also become clear that Barth's more Western emphasis on "penal satisfaction" (due in part to his refusal to dismiss judgment passages in the Old and New Testaments as they converge with the cross) fits into a more Eastern or dimensional understanding of "satisfaction" unanticipated by typically Western systematicians.

53. Non-contrastive transformation occurs in spite of the *totus* aspects of the *simul* (i.e., transformation can and does occur in spite of humans being already *totus iustus* and in spite of human being already *totus peccator*). As we shall see in our first chapters, although Christians may experience an increase in righteousness or a decrease in sinfulness, Barth's *simul* logic holds that Christians need not capitulate to zero-sum categories to explain such experiences.

Righteousness who brings transformation because *of who the Spirit inherently is*, and because of who we are as Spirit-breathed human beings.[54] By asking "When is the *simul*?" (chapter 9), and by following Barth's guidance that reconciliation was not *ex nihilo*, as was creation, we will begin with revelatory permission to "peek" behind the fall to consider the pure form of humanity. In fact, if the Job excursus provides Barth's most intimate look at a christological *simul*—Christ in solidarity with humanity amidst the "tangled skein" of our existence—then I will likewise propose (chapter 12) that Barth's discussion of the angels provides a discreet, if oblique, glimpse of untangled *iustus* humans fully alive as participants in the Trinitarian communion.

Even with such a fullness given to humans, it is the emphatic humanizing of this true Spirit-filled human nature which carries an intrinsic guarantee against all suspicions of mechanical universalism. If, as we conjecture here, Paul and John understand "in Christ" and "eternal life," respectively, to be indications of righteously dynamic human life as created and redeemed, then it should be expressly obvious that to go against this free, true life of the Spirit is to court self-destruction. As with the cross and resurrection, when Christ returns we will all be with him (Col 3:4), appearing on the Day when the Judge calls every person to account (2 Cor 5:10). In the clear light of Jesus Christ and him crucified, we will be exposed in the revelation truth that our old selves were crucified with him (Rom 6:6). The deliverance we have always been meant to understand, the definitive un-insinuation of the false self from the true self, will be clearly laid out before us. For every human present on that Day, all undeniably *simul (totus) iustus et (totus) peccator*, repentance and belief will never be so important.

Instead of imagining the work of the Spirit as an extension *to* Christ's perfect work, Barth urges us to understand the Spirit's work as an aspect *of* the Son, Spirit, and Father's completed and perfect work. On Barth's view, and *contra* the old adage, practice (even Spirit aided) does *not* make perfect, but participation by the Spirit in the perfection of Christ's humanity, given to us, is truly transformational, especially when practiced in community (Heb 10:24–25). To know Christ, then, is literally and actually to know *our very own* transformation, individually and corporately.[55] This is

---

54. As will be discussed beginning in chapter 3, if we grant a Spirit-filling to all humans as created beings, the fall becomes even more impossible to fathom. Because of its irrational and absurd nature, Barth believes the fall can never be explained, only described.

55. See *CD* III/4, 74; in the "great" revelation of Jesus Christ, states Barth, we find the "little revelation" of our own being in act: the "revelation of the fact that we know Him and therefore ourselves."

because knowledge is deeper than mere noetic cognizance and therefore unavoidably issues forth as Christian ethics in a holistic way that ethics based on imitation can never attain. It will hopefully be clear throughout this book that Barth's theological anthropology allows him a reciprocal freedom of expression such that what is true for the individual is true for the corporate and vice versa. This perspective—anchored at bottom by the fact that there is no ontological difference between human beings—has the effect of blunting potential criticism that Barth is too individualistic in his discussion of the Christian life. Consistently from Volume I to Volume IV Barth emphasizes that God is "for me" precisely *because* he is for us, or that *because* he is for us, he is also "for me."[56] In light of this realist premise, to the extent the church understands that it also exists and operates within the "for us" (*pro nobis*) of God's universal reconciling economy, it is empowered; to the extent the church attempts to create its own insular "for us" (vs. "them") it is diminished.

It should not be surprising that some will confuse what I have said about Barth's "Eastern mind" with the "new age" mentality.[57] This age-old philosophy charges us to look deep within, or to meditate profoundly enough to "get in touch" with our center, the core of our being. If not already, by the end of this book it should be patently clear that even with all his talk of the "old man" and the "new man" (or "old self" and "new self"), Barth incessantly warns us against all delusions of the *self-discovery* of a true self. As universal as "Christ in you, the hope of glory" (Col 1:27) may be, the hope of glory is never unattached from Jesus Christ. "Know thyself!," in other words, is no way to thy true self. Instead, reminds Barth, only in discovering Jesus Christ can one find one's true self in him while experiencing, in the Spirit, real transformation.

Mapping the Journey

By interrogating what Barth calls a "kinship of being" between Jesus Christ and humanity, it will be important to steer clear of theological conflation at every level; distinction will be vigorously maintained between God and humanity, humanity and Jesus Christ, and God and sin or death. I mentioned above that the term "anthro-dimensional" includes all the positive and negative dimensions of humanity. For instance, the Christo-anthropological,

---

56. See *CD* I/2, 697; *CD* IV/1, 212, 688.

57. For the reason of this potential confusion, "Hebraic" may be preferable to "Eastern," but I have chosen "Eastern" to make clearer the contrast (i.e., *contra* "Western" or "the Latin West").

plus the added contradiction of the *peccator* dimension, is humanity in its provisional form, i.e., under the *simul*. Even out from under the *simul*, however, there is another sort of anthro-dimensionality which must be maintained.[58] The remaining bi-dimensionality of humanity in Christ ensures that the *iustus* humanity of Jesus, although perfectly like ours, is also different from ours. Jesus Christ is humanity, Barth insists, but humanity is not Jesus Christ. Unlike ours, Jesus Christ's humanity is always by nature the humanity *of God*.[59] There can be no conflation, no flipping of the derivative, no reversal of the phrase "God is humanity" as one might vainly conjecture by means of a misconstrued *analogia entis*.[60] Even while unimaginatively intimate, human adoption into the relations of God via union with Christ is always undeserved and by grace alone. Even if fundamentally in the fully transcendent realm there is no opposition between God and the pure form of humanity, there was a time when humanity "was not."

Chapter 1 of our study seeks to outline Barth's radical appropriation of Luther's *simul* for sanctification and conversion, most especially his disciplined maintenance of the severe *totus* aspect of the phrase and, reasoned christologically, his implicit universal application of the *simul* to every human being. Chapter 2 contends that Barth, by means of scriptural and revelatory witness, expresses a more nuanced understanding of Christ's

---

58. If the term anthro-dimensional is, in the first sense a provisional term (because it includes the *peccator* determination), we must admit that in the second sense "anthro-dimensional"—because of the remaining bi-dimensionality even without the *peccator*—is also a temporal term distinguishing uncreated from created. This theologically protects against humanity, even the creaturely Christo-anthropological, being necessary to the Son of God.

59. Even when it comes to an incarnation into *iustus* humanity (non-corrupt human flesh), God's condescension is always involved. As clear from the Phil 2 hymn, God condescends not only to suffer and die, but even more fundamentally to become human in the first place.

60. I consider Keith L Johnson's book, *Karl Barth and the Analogia Entis*, an even-handed treatment of Barth and the *analogia entis* controversy: Barth was concerned that an "analogy of being" between God and humanity, based on both being described as the image of God (see 2 Cor 4:4; 1 Cor 11:7), would encourage reading back into God starting with humanity, i.e., humans starting with their own being and existence. Even if revelation is used to explain this, the explanation can still find its false start in creation. Notes Johnson: "Humans are not 'capable' of entering into relationship with God because they are in the image of God, therefore, but rather, they enter into this relationship *only* because 'the One who is the image of God' exists *for* them by entering into time as a human being" (217; Johnson's internal quotes are from *CD* III/2, 225). To the extent the *analogia entis* conversation failed to hold to the centrality of Jesus Christ as the reference point for God, humanity, and image, Barth was unforgiving, at one point describing the concept as the "anti-Christ."

humanity than is ostensibly provided in the Chalcedonian definition. What emerges is a second duality revealed within Christ's one human person—the duality of a true, *iustus* humanity and a corrupt, *peccator* humanity.

It will be imperative in chapter 3 to elucidate the comprehensive nature of Barth's actualism, especially in the realm of humanity's dynamic and free *iustitia* in the Spirit. Chapter 4 attempts to clarify our view of Barth's Christo-anthropological actualism, especially pertaining to the concept of participation, by comparing and contrasting it with other views. The actual extent of Barth's so called non-libertarian human freedom in Christ and the Spirit will be questioned in chapter 5; we will consider Barth's position as a subversion of the typical monergist-synergist spectrum. In order to appreciate the benefits regarding Barth's Spirit-charged epistemological program for sanctification, chapter 6 continues to consider Barth's resistance to being framed within a Cartesian paradigm. In chapter 7, central to assessing the menace of the *peccator* determination will be an examination of Barth's theology of the cross. I will argue that Barth employs a single-subject latitude in order to maintain the severe and mutually exclusive determinations of the old human and new human inside of the one human Jesus Christ. This human *simul* duality, in contrast to the fundamental divine-human duality of Chalcedon, is proven by resurrection revelation to be ultimately provisional in nature, but chapter 8 will further investigate the relation of the pure (*iustus*) and impure (*simul*) forms of humanity through the nexus of the suffering of Job and the passion of Christ. In chapter 9, I surmise Barth's position regarding the annulment of the *simul* as well as its beginning, taking a harder look at the themes of creation and fall. Considering Barth's doctrine of creation, chapter 10 submits that Barth's *simul* is reflective of the original antithesis between God and nothingness, under which Christ first placed himself so that we would know both his solidarity in the darkness and his victory over it. Any analysis of Barth's *simul* would be incomplete without a discussion of its relation to time and eternity. Accordingly, chapter 11 presents Barth's Christ-defined matrix of *iustus* and *peccator* humanity as emblematic of human birth but expressly not of human creation; this is predicated on Barth's interpretation of the two creation sagas centered in Genesis 1 and 2 and the distinction between pre-temporal, supra-temporal, and post-temporal eternity. Chapter 12 will re-engage with Barth the question of the relationship between concepts of *theosis* and our created and redeemed *iustus* humanity. Most particularly, I seek to prove that Barth's section on angels at the end of volume III/3 is a clue to his conviction about the heavenly and earthly determination of humans as most truly humanized.

If the first twelve chapters form the kernel of my systematic argument (the original PhD) as to what I believe Barth is saying, then the remaining chapters are less clinical. Still engaging with Barth, I have given myself a bit more interpretive freedom to implement his theology. Chapter 13 revisits Barth's understanding of biblical texts from a realist perspective. I argue that Johannine passages regarding human love and obedience are rooted in Barth's Christo-anthropological actualism and Trinitarian reality as I understand it, as are scriptural teachings on prayer and the shema. Chapter 14 presents the summative thesis that short of the *eschaton*, humans continue to dwell in the overlap of the *simul*'s two mutually exclusive determinations, but by "looking through" Barth's *simul* to recognize true, created, and redeemed humanity in Christ, believers are equipped in the Holy Spirit to interpret their lives, resist evil, and to engage the world around them most hopefully. From my reading of Barth I make the assertion that his theology of the *simul* implies a simultaneous three heaven cosmology.[61] I conclude in the last chapter, "Consummation," the importance of *simul* sanctification for robust Christian discipleship. Not to be put off until later, the inherent judgment of the *simul*—"whosoever is not with me is against me"—reveals the same Holy Spirit of the second heaven to be operative in the first heaven (our current earthly existence). Consummation, in one sense, comes after the conclusion; it is the term Barth uses for the final *revelation* of the reconciliation of the world as finished in Christ. On Barth's view, consummation is redemption unveiled—a redemption that includes humanity finally freed completely, not only actually but also existentially from the imprisonment of the *simul*. The time between now and the consummation is a time when the completion and fullness of Christ's work comes to bear by the Holy Spirit in transformative ways. In this vein, after the Conclusion I will offer some "Final Reflections" which explore how "*simul* sanctification" can be constructively embodied in the life and ministry of the church.

In sum, while I hope that this book can be an entry point for beginners with Barth, for veteran readers I am offering what I perceive to be a fresh reading by making six main interrelated theological moves: 1) the introduction of a double-duality construct; that is, a second duality (true human, false human, one human) within the original Chalcedonian duality (one person, divine and human natures), and from this a proposed christological *simul iustus et peccator* from which our anthropological *simul* derives, 2) Barth's *iustus* determination of the *simul* is filled out with all the pneumatological and epistemological content of Barth's Christo-anthropological actualism,

---

61. As we will see, my first heaven, second heaven, and third heaven constructions are, I believe, complementary to Barth's pre-, supra- and post-temporal eternities but certainly not equivalent (the first heaven, for example, is most related to Barth's supra-temporal eternity). Similar to the three eternities, however, the three heavens are not to be separated, only distinguished.

meaning that every person is freely and joyfully participating in Christ in a fullness of the Holy Spirit, 3) far from being Docetic, this counter-intuitive understanding provides us with a literally *new* theology of the cross that gives fullest force to the suffering, sinfulness, and evil of our lives and world, the parenthetical un-reality that hurts so badly precisely because it does not fundamentally or ultimately belong,[62] 4) while Barth's *iustus* determination for humanity cannot be diminished at all by the mutually exclusive and deadly determination of our *peccator* humanity, it follows that for Barth our true created humanity, again derived from Christ's humanity, transcends not only our death but also our birth (or conception), 5) as true humans in Christ with material spiritual bodies (never a soul without a body), we are also simultaneously and inseparably false humans; it is from within *simul* contradiction that we must repent and believe, recognizing by the Spirit our freedom and deliverance from the flesh in the death of Jesus Christ ("for we know that our old self was crucified with him that the body of sin might be destroyed, and we might be no longer be enslaved to sin," Romans 6:6), and finally, 6) what I call the "second heaven" functions as a linchpin to Barth's sanctification theology, protecting it against so-called triumphalism; this otherworldly "eternal dimension" (*einem jenseitigen Zusammenhang*) brings the critical clarity of judgment to bear at the frontier of Barth's supra-temporal and post-temporal realms of eternity. As human beings of the first heaven we live under the contemporaneous judgment of the second heaven. Under this judgment of grace we have constant opportunity by the "sword of the Spirit" to recognize ourselves in both the crucified and risen Jesus Christ and to share a Doubting Thomas moment with all due humility and confidence: "My Lord and my God" (John 20:28).

---

62. By a "new" theology of the cross I do not mean never before advanced, but instead a theology of the cross that emphasizes the *new* as always in the same space as the old, and highlighting the contrast of the latter.

Simul Sanctification: "no easier way"

"Luther's 'simul (totus) iustus, simul (totus) peccator,' has thus to be applied strictly to sanctification and therefore conversion if we are to see deeply what is denoted by these terms . . . the same man, in the 'simul' of to-day, is both the old man of yesterday and the new man of to-morrow"[1]

MARTIN LUTHER'S PHRASE SIMUL IUSTUS ET PECCATOR, DESCRIBING THE Christian to be simultaneously righteous and sinful, has undoubtedly been controversial since Luther introduced it at Wittenberg in his Romans lectures of 1515–16.[2] For many "the *simul*" is considered a useless paradox. Those already uneasy with what they consider to be Luther's antinomian tendencies spy in his enigmatic phrase worrisome sponsorship for both false comfort and sinning "boldly." Surely it is not surprising when the Christian sins, but shall we go so far as to classify the saint as a sinner?

Historically, even those impacted by Luther's teachings on justification have struggled to embrace the Reformer's insistence on the *simul* and its static categories in light of Scripture's admonitions to "be transformed." John Wesley, for example, famously converted at Aldersgate while listening to a reading of Luther's commentary on Galatians, later voiced great distrust in Luther's view of sanctification.[3] Wesley, always wary of antinomianism, preferred a gradualist model of Christian progress meant to eventually

---

1. *CD* IV/2, 572.

2. Mann, *Simul iustus et peccator*, 1.

3. See Walls, "John Wesley's Critique of Martin Luther," 31; Wesley is cited from late in his career: "Who has wrote more ably than Martin Luther on justification by faith alone? And who was more ignorant of the doctrine of sanctification, or more confused in his conceptions of it?"

translate into perfection or "full sanctification." Opposite of full sanctification is the potential for Christians to lose salvation altogether (for those not progressing), making for a rather tenuous concept of justification, or at least an uneasy and fragile assurance of justification for believers. The more objective emphasis of Luther and the more subjective emphasis of Wesley are indicative of the two poles between which Protestants have continually sought to understand how their justification relates to their sanctification and vice-versa. Is the supposed healthy tension between the objective and subjective poles really possible to attain? Is it possible to speak of sanctification and true genuine human subjectivity without devolving into a subjectivism where any real objective meaning is at risk?

Barth's Reappropriation

Karl Barth's emergence from nineteenth-century German Liberalism includes an expansive christocentric view of sanctification that holds together justification and sanctification and their objective and subjective aspects in unprecedented ways. Not without irony, it is actually Barth's radical adaptation of Luther's *simul* in matters of sanctification and conversion that causes him to eschew both Luther's monergist conception of justification and the Reformer's juxtaposition of Law and Gospel.[4] Throughout our study I will contend that Barth's version of Luther's *simul* includes helpful antidotes where gradualist (Wesleyan) thinking may be prone to overreact to Luther's static categories.

The first question this raises is, "To what extent and in what form did Karl Barth reappropriate Luther's *simul*?" For Luther, it must be remembered, the discussion about the *simul* and sanctification only begins when Christian believers are assured of their justification and thereby declared *iustus*. On Barth's view, however, sanctification (like justification) is related less to the beginning of a believer's faith experience and more directly to the person of Jesus Christ and all to whom *he* is related! Because of *who* Jesus Christ is, Barth's scope for sanctification (and justification) is universal and actual. Sanctification is not contingent on a person's expression of faith. As the Second Adam, Jesus Christ is the primary human being who includes and sanctifies all humans in his own humanity; all persons are positively incorporated into his saving work. The actual sanctification of every human being in Christ is so comprehensive that Barth views even our participation "as objective before it ever becomes active."[5] George Hunsinger elaborates,

---

4. These themes will be discussed in chapter 5.
5. Hunsinger, "A Tale of Two Simultaneities," 330.

Barth's doctrine of universal objective participation breaks with almost the entire Latin theological tradition, including perhaps especially the ever dominant Augustinian tradition. One has to go all the way back to early Greek fathers like Athanasius to find relatively comparable associations of the phrase *in Christ* with the word *all*. Barth boldly allots certain New Testament passages like I Corinthians 15, II Corinthians 5, Romans 5 and Romans 11, where similar universalistic associations occur, a weight of significance they have not enjoyed for centuries.[6]

Hunsinger goes on to say, "It should not be surprising if for many conscientious believers Barth's position, at least initially, should seem implausible or counter-intuitive or fraught with unfortunate consequences."[7] Indeed, full sanctification by grace, extended to all, is a departure from Luther and one of the most difficult aspects of the doctrine for a Lutheran *or* Wesleyan to assimilate![8] The fact that Barth adamantly holds to this view of justification and sanctification is evidence of his certainty that any *iustitia* gifted to humanity originates ontologically in the depths of the Giver himself, in his history, and not in the individual conversion experience.[9]

On Barth's view, the full sanctification of Jesus Christ accomplished in his birth, life, death, resurrection, and ascension interpenetrates the full justification accomplished in the judgment of the cross, together making them simultaneous aspects "of the one redemptive act of God in Jesus Christ."[10]

---

6. Hunsinger, "A Tale of Two Simultaneities," 327–28.

7. Hunsinger, "A Tale of Two Simultaneities," 328.

8. Spross, "Doctrine of Sanctification," 72. Spross is a Wesleyan who cites Barth's universal scope and his exhaustively objective theology of sanctification as major drawbacks: "[Barth] would be extremely uncomfortable with the heavy emphasis on the subjective appropriation of sanctification common in most Wesleyan circles. His monergistic view of sanctification would seem quite alien to the synergistic approach of the Wesleyans." Barth would also be uncomfortable with his theology being described as purely monergistic; his personalist ontology arguably preserves and even enhances human subjectivity while relocating it, as we shall see beginning in chapter 3.

9. In this book we regard anthropological ontology (nature of being) as meaning the being-in-act of the humanity of the Son of God, which by nature is a dynamic and relational understanding of being rooted in Trinitarian Persons and which, by grace, personally implicates all human beings created and redeemed in Christ. This ontological reality cannot be added-to or subtracted-from by positive or negative existential expressions. Obviously, even though there is no ontological epistemological or pneumatological distinction between believers and unbelievers, there is existential variance.

10. Spross, "Doctrine of Sanctification," 64. The phrase in quotes is directly from Barth, *CD* IV/2, 507.

While not to be confused with our *simul iustus et peccator*, this "other *simul*" of justification and sanctification is obviously correlated to the former and provides the christological foundation for extending the *simul iustus et peccator* to all of humanity. *Iustitia* and *peccatum* are plainly central features to this one act of redemption, this sanctifying and justifying story, whereby: "For Christ also suffered for sins [*pro peccatus*] once for all, the righteous for the unrighteous [*est iustus pro iniustus*], in order to bring you to God" (1 Pet 3:18).[11] In chapter 3 we will consider more deeply how the *simul* applies to Jesus Christ himself, the first-century Jew from Nazareth. For now it suffices to recognize that it is Barth's doctrine of simultaneous justification and sanctification—premised on his interconnection of Christology and anthropology—which by implication allows us to apply Barth's *simul iustus et peccator* as a universal framework.[12]

One aspect of the *simul* that Barth carries over from Luther is an insistence on the *totus* element of the concept: *simul* (*totus*) *iustus et simul* (*totus*) *peccator*.[13] When it comes to *totus peccator*, Barth and Luther do not disagree on scope: humanity is *totally* sinful. For both theologians, the concept *totus peccator* intends to engender humility in believers, a continually abject dependence on God's grace. Following Luther, Barth believed gradualist, zero-sum sanctification theories can only delude believers into imagining 1) they are able to leave their sinfulness behind, or 2) they are earning favor by their obedient performances—favor that as *iustus* humans they have already been given—hence obscuring righteousness with self-righteousness. Lutheran scholar Gabriel Fackre advances the importance of "Lutheran sobriety." We should "heed the Lutheran admonition to be wary of the organic metaphor in describing the Christian life, a process of growth in which the sanctified life moves naturally to fuller and fuller realization, or so stressing the possibilities of life in Christ that its impossibilities are discounted.

---

11. Regarding Barth's commentary of this verse, see *CD* II/1, 398; *CD* IV/1, 257–58: 1 Pet 3:18 signifies for Barth, as we shall see, not a forensic swap of one for the other—a straight up exchange of unrighteousness for righteousness—but instead involves the Righteous One standing (all the time righteous) at the same time fully in the human condition of the flesh, "the nature of man as he comes from the fall." All Scripture references are from the New Revised Standard Version (NRSV) unless otherwise noted.

12. Importantly, Barth would not approve of a universal application of the popular replacement "simultaneously saints and sinners," seeing as he does the biblical distinction between the church (the communion of saints) and the world.

13. The reader should note that our use of the phrase *simul iustus et peccator* always assumes the *totus* component.

Rather, the Christian life struggles against sin at every step of advance, its power increasing commensurate with that advance."[14]

In spite of Fackre's admonitions, Lutherans have traditionally looked to versions of the *simul* that provide at least some sense of growth and change. It is symptomatic amongst Christians, not only Wesleyans, to chart progress—attempting to quantify more holiness or less unholiness—in the realm of sanctification. If Lutherans, even including Luther himself, do not consistently hold to a *simul* and *totus* through and through, it would be understandable.[15] Conversely, Barth sternly resists any mode of Christian discipleship susceptible to the flimsiness of subjective analysis (i.e., psychologism).[16] Barth's appropriation of Luther's *simul* is therefore unapologetically disciplined in a manner that might cause even Luther to cringe. If Michael Root[17] is right, and the outer person and inner person nuances of Luther's thought were developed to "de-paradox" his own *simul* (thereby

---

14. Fackre, "Affirmations and Admonitions," 23, 24.

15. Fackre, "Affirmations and Admonitions," 23. Fackre reproduces the Lutheran segment of the Joint Declaration on the Doctrine of Justification signed by the Lutheran World Federation and the Roman Catholic Church (1999). It is obvious that a desire for rapprochement has caused Lutherans to take a less severe line on the *simul*. Of Luther's own compromise, see Root's interpretation below.

16. See Anderson, "The Problem of Psychologism," 352: Anderson makes the helpful point that Barth is not out to extinguish the subjective aspects of sanctification, or to deny the importance of "psychological phenomena." In turn, "The 'more or less' of conversion experience does not nullify the objective ground of the '*totus-totus*,' but bears relative witness to it."

17. Root, "Continuing the Conversation," 56–57. Root, another Lutheran, points out that an oversimplification of Luther's *simul* is the cause of the static paradox charge. Root asserts instead that Luther's letter *Against Latomus* "should be a touchstone . . . of a Lutheran understanding of the *simul*" and that *Against Latomus* is indicative of Luther's teaching on the *simul* throughout his career beginning as early as 1515–16. Essentially, Root believes what has been most often overlooked is Luther's distinction between "grace" and "gift," which are particularly applied in justification to the outward and inward aspects of a person respectively. While "grace" grants God's favor, and in Luther's words "an outward good," "gift" relates to the internal process of transformation against "the corruption of nature" (again Luther's words). The internal is the realm of the Spirit, the indwelling Christ, and faith. Notes Root: "While externally, in relation to God's judgment, the justified person is wholly justified, internally, the self is still divided between the new self, constituted by faith and the indwelling Christ, and the old self, still resisting. These two realities are not related statically or equally; even internally the justified is not equally just and a sinner. While sin earlier ruled the self, it is now ruled by the new self"(57). Root's assertion, if correct, relaxes considerably what has been historically been perceived as a loaded tension in the *totus* version of Luther's *simul*, but it also widens the split between justification (outer) and sanctification (inner), further marginalizing the latter in Luther.

providing for a semblance of gradualism), Barth will have none of it. Relaxing the contradiction in the *simul* is not the way to dynamism for Barth. Barth's version is most severe, a "black and white" *simul* which involves a whole (*contra* the inner-outer nuance) *peccatum* and a whole *iustitia* in the one human being, i.e., two whole and two total, mutually exclusive dimensions, or what Barth calls "determinations."

Hans Küng has noted the whole, total, and actual nature of Barth's assertion of human righteousness in Christ. "Justification is not merely an external pasted-on 'as-if.' Man is not only called just. He *is* just. He is a new man—not just outwardly but *inwardly*, not just partly but *totally*, not just negatively but *positively*. That is an indisputable presupposition." Küng affirms the righteous, just, side of Barth's *simul*. In the same breath, however, the Catholic theologian questions whether Barth's *simul* overstates sin in the believer, pondering "whether or not there is sense in calling a man who is fully justified inwardly a sinner."[18] Indeed, even those who appreciate Barth's controversial universal application of humanity's righteousness in Christ can be troubled that "Barth finds it perfectly natural to continue to speak of the Christian as a sinner in the present tense."[19] Confounded by his "dialectical" descriptions of the sinful righteous and the saintly sinner, Barth's version of the *simul* seems like a theological regression to many, untenable because of its apparent intractability, its lack of a "growth" provision for sanctification.[20] Even if Barth values the "Lutheran sobriety" and incessant dependence on the grace of God that his *simul* provides, surely he has more in mind?

Incoherent or Keystone?

In his incisive article "An Analysis of *Simul Iustus et Peccator*," Thor Hall would have us take a step back for some logical perspective before dismissing Barth's *simul* as incoherent or unuseful. The potential reward is too great for such a rash decision, Hall asserts, because throwing the phrase out of our Christian vocabulary "represents a rather superficial approach to the

18. Küng, *Justification*, 236.

19. Spross, "Doctrine of Sanctification," 71.

20. Sonderegger, "Sanctification as Impartation in the Theology of Karl Barth," 310. Not even considering for the moment the scandalous implications of Barth's *simul* in its universal application, Sondregger marks Barth's approach on sanctification as a "radical departure . . . from his Reformed household," noting that the Belgic, Westminster, and Heidelberg professions all contain some sort of gradualism in the sanctification process, i.e., a "more and more" and a "less and less" in regards to Christians' righteousness and sinfulness respectively.

problems of Christian thought and doctrinal formulations. With such an attitude to traditional theological concepts one could never be sure whether the reason for the rejection is that the authors of these formulations did not know what they were speaking about, or whether it is we, their successors, who do not grasp the deeper motifs within their thought."[21]

With Hall's cajoling admonition in hand, it behooves us to grapple with the reasons as to why Barth arguably reappropriated Luther's *simul* in a fashion which allows us to apply its determinations in a manner even more exhaustive and wide-ranging than the original. While Barth turns to the *simul iustus et peccator* in every volume of *Church Dogmatics*, we should not be surprised at Barth's intentionality to highlight the *simul iustus et peccator* especially in the sections on justification ("The Justification of Man," *CD* IV/1, §61) and sanctification ("The Sanctification of Man," *CD* IV/2, §66). We have already noted the correlation between Barth's *simul* and the "other *simul*," that of justification and sanctification. Interestingly, and hinting at our Christo-anthropological conclusion, Barth frames the "twofold" simultaneity between justification and sanctification directly in relation to the words of the Chalcedonian definition: "From the christological *without confusion* and *without change* of Chalcedon we can deduce at once that the same is true of justification and sanctification. As the two moments in the one act of reconciliation accomplished in Jesus Christ"[22] and two pages later, "If we have also to accept the *without separation* and *without division* of Chalcedonian Christology, justification and sanctification must be distinguished, but they cannot be divided or separated."[23] Justification and sanctification, Barth concludes, "both take place simultaneously and together, just as the living Jesus Christ, in whom they both take place and are effective, is simultaneously and together true God and true man, the Humiliated and the Exalted."[24] The point of this is clear: Barth does not want us to stray far from the fact that his theology, whether talking about God or humanity, justification or sanctification, humiliation (pertaining to assumed sinfulness) or exaltation (pertaining to righteousness), is always rooted in God's revelation of himself in Jesus Christ.

So what does Barth want to communicate about the importance of the *simul* for our day-to-day lives? Why is it critical? Barth himself provides an

21. Hall, "An Analysis of *Simul Iustus et Peccator*," 182.
22. *CD* IV/2, 503. The italicized words are translated from Barth's original Greek.
23. *CD* IV/2, 505. The italicized words are translated from Barth's original Greek.
24. *CD* IV/2, 507. Barth obviously enjoys invoking the Chalcedonian formula throughout the *Dogmatics*, applying it directly, as here and above, or alluding to it in order to provide the unitary or "twofold answer" (509) for apparently dualistic situations.

explanation in the middle of his section specifically addressing sanctification (§66):

> Luther's *simul (totus) iustus, simul (totus) peccator*, has thus to be applied strictly to sanctification and therefore conversion if we are to see deeply what is denoted by these terms, and to understand them with necessary seriousness. It is certainly hard to grasp that the same man stands under two total determinations which are not merely opposed but mutually exclusive; that the same man, in the *simul* of to-day, is both the old man of yesterday and the new man of to-morrow.
>
> But there is *no easier way* of seeing and understanding the matter. Static and quantitative terms may seem to help, but they are not adequate to describe the true situation. They involve a separation into constituent elements. It is true that the situation seems to cry out for this separation. It seems to be much more illuminating if, instead of saying that the whole man is still the old and yet already the new, in complete and utter antithesis, we say that he is still partially the old and partially the new. But if we put it this way, we mistake the matter.[25]

In light of Barth's own comments above, it would not be a stretch to suggest that the *simul*, described here in the middle of §66, is the keystone for Barth's whole argument on sanctification "and therefore conversion" because for Barth what is true of sanctification is also true for conversion. Both rely on continual *metanoia*, not a *metanoia* that is purely noetic (as in the Greek world) however, but a *radical change of mind* which cannot help but produce a radical change in behavior (i.e., Christian ethics performed in an attitude of love). The result of this combination—"the performance of very concrete acts in practical alteration of a prior human attitude"[26]—is what Barth calls the "life-movement," or *Lebensbewegung*,[27] of the disciple

---

25. *CD* IV/2, 572. Section break is not original to *CD*. Emphasis in second section is added to connect with chapter title.

26. *CD* IV/2, 564–65. Barth warns against segmenting the mind and body, which could only return us to an intellectual emphasis. First, tying together Hos 6 and Rom 12, Barth notes that sacrificial acts apart from love mean nothing; they do not evidence conversion. Secondly, while *metanoia* (Rom 12:2) invariably includes embodiment, just as true is that this reschematization of our minds (Rom 12:2) takes place within "the overall movement" of Rom 12:1, the presentation of our "whole persons" (Barth's understanding of "bodies") as living sacrifices to God.

27. Barth, *Die kirkliche Dogmatik* (hereafter *KD*); *KD* IV/2, 641. Barth uses this uniquely descriptive German word in paragraph 66 on Sanctification almost as much as in the rest of *KD* combined.

who lives in conversion. It is "the life-movement from the old to the new man"[28] in "correspondence to the life-giving movement of his Lord . . . and the mystery of the life-giving Spirit."[29]

As Barth counsels us in the indented quotation above, however, sanctification can only be stymied by forgetting the *simul*, the twofold determination, revealed in the truth of Jesus Christ. It is plain that the sanctifying "life-movement" from the "old man" to the "new man" should not be understood to mean we are one or the other, but always both. As Barth warns, "static" or "quantitative" terms can only do harm because they compromise the "necessary seriousness" the gospel gives to both our righteousness and sinfulness. In fact, Barth is so concerned to communicate this point that he paints the twofold determination of every human being into even bolder relief as a "quarrel" between "two total men . . . who cannot be united but are necessarily in extreme contradiction."[30]

Remembering Hall's advice to press in to the apparent paradox, at this point our only consolation may be from Barth's comment that the *simul* is "certainly hard to grasp"! In submission to Barth's progression, we must first trust Barth's directive to take both sides of the *simul* with "necessary seriousness." To begin with, the righteousness given to us by Christ is not a legal fiction; it is not for Barth some kind of declared forensic justice that shields humans but never really touches them. While Luther (as per Finnish research[31]) had better days emphasizing the impartation that takes place in our union with Christ, it was the outward-inward nuancing of Luther driven by his imputation model that Barth is out to avoid here. Notes Hans Küng, "It must be formally stated that Karl Barth clearly teaches the *interior justifying* of man. Not that he has denied the forensic justification of the Reformers but that he has revised and deepened it, taking it seriously in its divine character . . . for Barth what is juridically pronounced is ontologically

---

28. *CD* IV/2, 567.

29. *CD* IV/2, 529.

30. *CD* IV/2, 570, 571.

31. See Braaten and Jenson, eds., *Union with Christ*. I have endeavored not to present Luther as advocating a simplistic forensic model, i.e., the granting of a passive or static legal righteousness to those justified, even though that is the way he is often perceived. I found Jordan Cooper's pithy volume *The Righteousness of One* to be a helpful summary of Finnish research as juxtaposed to traditional scholastic views of Luther. Cooper draws out the active righteousness embedded in the ontology of Luther encouraging believers towards their participation in union with the person of Christ. Clearly, to adopt a more ontological reading of Luther would position him in closer proximity to Barth, even if his understanding of participation does not approach Barth's Christo-anthropological actualism.

made just."³² Citing the real ontological relationship between the Son of Man and humanity, Barth continually points all credit for the sanctification and conversion of human beings back to their Head; "It is in His conversion that we are engaged."³³ As Barth asserts pejoratively, "in virtue of our being in Him and with Him, in virtue of the fact that by His Holy Spirit He has clothed us with that which properly He alone is and has; in virtue of the fact that He allows us to have a share in that which belongs to Him. What more do we want?"³⁴

As alluded above, "clothing us" could be used, and often is, to express merely a legal, forensic covering over the justified sinner, yet for Barth the metaphor is his way of maintaining the Creator-creature distinction; he insists that the sharing which takes place between the two is always "from above to below" and never the other way around. The human righteousness given and received in grace is therefore always derivative. However, as Daniel Migliore adds, derivation does not equate to "ontological deprivation";³⁵ it really *is* the righteousness of Christ given to humans. Much more than courtroom rhetoric of a declared justification, the ontological renewal of humanity in Christ is so thoroughgoing for Barth that it includes all the ethical and agential dimensions of human subjectivity, as Migliore relates:

> Barth's doctrine of sanctification cannot be abstracted from the comprehensive theological ontology in which it is embedded. It presupposes a realistic understanding of God to be God for humanity; it presupposes a realistic trinitarian understanding of God as the God who lives in eternal self-giving love, who freely enters into fellowship with humanity in Jesus Christ, and who freely gathers, builds up, and commissions a new community of men and women in Jesus Christ by the power of the Holy Spirit; it presupposes a realistic understanding of the union of the eternal Word of God and human nature in Jesus Christ in which all humanity is included. "There is no one," Barth contends, "who does not participate in Him."³⁶

Migliore here reflects on what I have already described (Introduction) as Barth's Christo-anthropological actualism. Even when mentioned

---

32. Küng, *Justification*, 69.

33. *CD* IV/2, 583.

34. *CD* IV/2, 583. I credit Daniel Migliore with renewing my attention to this remark by Barth.

35. Migliore, "Participatio Christi," 289.

36. Migliore, "Participatio Christi," 289–90. Migliore's internal Barth quote is from *CD* IV/2, 271.

throughout our study without its christological prefix, it is necessary to impress upon the reader that "actualism" as it pertains to humans is always derived. In view of Barth's *simul*, we will therefore define Barth's actualism as the radical concept that real human subjectivity and all levels of *iustus* human participation are contained comprehensively in the person of Jesus Christ. Barth's actualism includes the following tenets: 1) Every human being is wrapped up in the being-in-action of God the Son, the Son of Man, in the fullness of the Holy Spirit, and in the love of the Father. 2) To be incorporated into this union with Christ by grace means true agential freedom, whereby any extraneous human subjectivity to the dynamic human righteousness we already have in Christ can only be unrighteousness. As we shall see in chapter 4, misunderstandings regarding Barth's actualism arise when the above tenets are ignored. In sum, we can say with Barth that because "all *he* [Jesus Christ] is and does applies to us," we are actually participating with him as "part of Christ's own self" before we are conscious of it.[37] It will become increasingly clear for sanctification that, on Barth's view, actuality always precedes possibility.

Past Dualism to Duality

We earlier mentioned Barth's shared conviction with Luther about humanity as *totus peccator*, but considering Barth's even more basic understanding of a universal *totus iustus* humanity and the comprehensive nature of his Christo-anthropological actualism, can Barth really take sin seriously enough? Anyone presupposing Barth to be "light on sin" need look no further than his remarkable excursus on Friedrich Nietzsche where Barth commandeers Nietzsche's dark view of human barbarity into his indictment against humanity as (*totus*) *peccator*.[38] Indeed, Barth's graphic descriptions of the seriousness of sin can be decidedly Lutheran, but Barth's eventual purposes are considerably non-Lutheran.[39] The convincing work of Jesus Christ in the atonement is what allows Barth to address sin and its heinous consequences most seriously; it is the extent of what Jesus Christ has assumed, suffered and accomplished in dealing with human sin which exposes sin's dreadful seriousness. A person is "measured," says Barth, "by

---

37. Barth, *Learning Jesus Christ Through the Heidelberg Catechism*, 128. This book is a compilation of Barth's lectures given primarily at University of Bonn in 1947, hereafter noted as *Heidelberg*.

38. *CD* III/2, 231–42.

39. Unlike Luther, Barth does not unleash his *totus peccator* indictment (in face of God's perfect law) as a crushing blow to prepare us for the gospel (see chapter 5).

what God has done for him."⁴⁰ Total grace exposes total need, not the other way around, this the repentant person can freely acknowledge. Conversely, by attempting to "arrest" this judgment of grace—the abject dependance exposed by the depths the Savior has plumbed—persons only confirm that they are unrighteous transgressors.⁴¹ The unrepentant person, notes Barth, "will always be distinguished by the fact that he still has a great deal to say in his own favour."⁴²

Because Barth firmly believes it is the love of God epitomized by Jesus Christ on the cross that unmasks our sinfulness, he believes the same tack should be taken in proclaiming the gospel, for to see our sinfulness outside of the grace which has outpaced it could only be destructive. Notes Allen Jorgenson, "[W]hile the Lutheran perspective is teleologically ordered to Christology, Barth's approach is archeologically ordered. Christ is clearly the beginning point for Barth's harmatology."⁴³ We can safely say that Barth begins and ends *Church Dogmatics* with this archeological or "retrospective" viewpoint, but the question remains as to why Barth, a theologian known for beginning with the end in mind, would cling in his doctrine of sanctification to a description of the *simul peccator* which is *so* far from being light on sin that it returns us to the the idea of a true *simul* paradox: "It is not merely that man lacks something which he ought to be or to have or to be capable of in relation to God. He lacks everything. It is not merely that he is in a dangerous and damaged state, but in his being toward God he is completely finished and impotent. He is not only a sick man but a dead one."⁴⁴ Barth does not hesitate to describe depraved and degenerate humanity in its "inhumanity, perversion and corruption."⁴⁵ Known for his systematic rigor, at times it appears Barth is stepping backwards into a Lutheran mindset which he has long since conceptually surpassed. Notes Spross: "Barth took the sinfulness of sin so seriously that he incorporated [into the three full volumes on reconciliation] a paragraph in each volume detailing specifically the multiple and nefarious aspects of sin that threaten

---

40. *CD* III/2, 605.

41. *CD* IV/2, 742.

42. *CD* II/2, 769.

43. Jorgenson, "Karl Barth's Christological Treatment of Sin," 448. Jorgenson contrasts Barth's approach with the Lutheran Confessions which he quotes: "the knowledge of sin is necessary. For the magnitude of the grace of Christ cannot be understood . . . unless our diseases be recognized."

44. *CD* I/2, 257.

45. *CD* III/2, 27. Cf. "distorting" (26); "degeneracy" (28); "depravity" (29).

to undermine and destroy the reality of the reconciliation that has been provided for mankind in the atoning work of Jesus Christ."[46]

"Threaten" indeed! With every assurance on the *iustus* side of the matter, we still find it difficult to avoid looking over our shoulder to the *peccator* side, where the old man appears quite formidable. "I was and still am the former man: man as a wrongdoer": this is the Christian's proper testimony, insists Barth.[47] Barth's statement brings us back to Küng's concern about overstating sin in the believer. How does keeping the old man in the present tense help us in matters of sanctification? It is daunting to think of sanctification as a tug-of-war of sorts between two "total" forces, and while apparently this is being presented by Barth, a tug-of-war or two kingdoms motif is exactly the picture of sanctification Barth is out to repudiate.[48] Admittedly the word picture of the "quarrel" between "two total men" (the old and new man) can sound dualistic, but Barth artfully and consistently implements the mutually exclusive determinations within the overriding framework of a duality; he refuses to allow for the twofold determination to devolve into some kind of endless dialectic between two equal forces or states. For all the apparent equality expressed in the *simul*, the *iustus* dimension and the *peccator* dimension are *not equal in the same sense*.[49] As we have already insinuated, the key to breaking the apparent logjam of *simul* (*totus*) *iustus et* (*totus*) *peccator* is recognizing the asymmetry at play. This interpretive key can be summarized in three basic statements: 1. both aspects as *totus* are 100 percent, but the *100 percent totus iustus* is deeper than the *totus peccator*; 2. the two aspects are simultaneous with each other, but *iustus* has a future and *peccator* does not; 3. the two dimensions are dynamic, but *iustus* is moving in the direction of life and freedom, while *peccator* is moving in the direction of death and bondage.

With these basics in mind, we still have to acknowledge the considerable conceptual difficulty involved in shifting paradigms from dualism

---

46. Spross, "Doctrine of Sanctification," 69.

47. *CD* IV/1, 544; cited in introduction.

48. This is another place where Barth distances himself from Luther. Barth calls Luther's two kingdoms theology an "unfortunate doctrine" because it sets up a static antithesis between light and darkness (*CD* IV/3.1, 151). See *CD* IV/3.2, 712: "In Him there is not the clash of two kingdoms, but the one Kingdom of God in reality." Within his un-Lutheran operating framework, Barth does allow himself in *CD* III/3 to speak of "two kingdoms" in a very carefully qualified sense. The anti-ontology of evil is a destructive dynamic (523–24) under the "alien lordship" of Satan (526). The "kingdom of falsehood" (527) is a "mimicry" of reality (528). It can only exist as a "negative reflection" (530).

49. *CD* II/1, 627.

(two determinations existing in two spaces) to duality (two determinations existing in one space), and that is why the simultaneous dimension of the formula bears further elaboration. We remember Barth's words, "the same man, in the *simul* of to-day, is both the old man of yesterday and the new man of to-morrow." To put it another way, the whole person, the one human being, is wholly the old self and wholly the new self at the same time. It is exactly here that Barth wants to talk about sanctification and conversion as "transition" and "movement"; but Barth appears to want us to talk about transition without mention of sequence. How do we do this? What can be the meaning of "old" and "new" if these terms are simultaneous?

In grasping Barth's *simul*, it may prove beneficial to break the sequential and simultaneous aspects of one of Barth's statements into two separate comments before bringing them back into relationship. First, (A) "We are totally evil when we enter his judgment, and totally cleansed when we leave it."[50] This statement is simple, and it is sequential. But we know by now that on Barth's view this bare sequential understanding is not adequate, so to the above we attach Barth's subsequent, complementary comment: (B) "In the one sentence of God we are both *semper peccatores* and *semper iusti*."[51] The *semper* ("always") gives the character of the present tense. These two dimensions "stand opposed, not in dialectical equilibrium, but with a preponderance of the second over the first"[52] The word "preponderance" signifies that there is a weightiness to the truth of humanity "totally cleansed"—dictated by the salvation history of Jesus Christ (sequence)—which the other dimension ("totally evil") of the *simul* does not carry, even in its own present, *totus*, existence.

Barth summarizes accordingly, "Luther's *simul iustus et peccator* cannot and should not . . . be taken to mean that the totality with which we are righteous and sinners involves an equal and equally serious determination of our existence."[53] The *simul* is not a "see-saw" between two determinations

---

50. *CD* II/2, 757.

51. *CD* II/2, 757.

52. *CD* II/2, 757.

53. *CD* II/1, 627. Cf. IV/1, 573 for an apparently contrary example of Barth describing the directions of the twofold determination as "equally actual and equally serious." In context we see that Barth's "equally" is not meant to return us to a frozen paradox but only to show just how fine the layers are that Barth is parsing. In other words, Barth *does* want us to take one of the "equally serious" determinations more seriously than the other! "That man is against God is important and must be taken seriously. But what is far more important and must be taken far more seriously is that in Jesus Christ God is for man. And it is only in the light of the second fact that the importance and the seriousness of the first can be seen" (*CD* II/2, 154).

of equal validity.⁵⁴ Barth wants to download the sequential (Christ's death and resurrection for us) into the *simul*, the former being the interpretive key of the latter. We could use Barth's succinct rephrasing of the *simul* to enhance our clarity regarding what can be a strange and difficult paradigm: "I was and still am the old man . . . I am and will be the new man." Here we see the past and future aspects contextualizing and interpreting the present; the "I am" for both phrases signifies the individual's simultaneous and present existence *in the overlap* of past and future, old and new. Again, on Barth's view, *iustus* and *peccator* are both in the present tense, but not in the same sense.

The two spheres—the past (*peccator*) and the future (*iustus*)—directly and emphatically relate to the salvation history of Jesus Christ and what has happened to us in him: in humility the Son of God assumes and comprehends a depersonalizing movement towards nothingness; all the while as Son of Man he reveals in his exaltation the free, Spirit-personalizing movement towards eternal life. When it comes to the sequence, it may help us to think of Jesus Christ first, and then us in him. When it comes to the simultaneity, it may help to think of us first in our present experience, and then Jesus Christ and him in us. Comprehending all aspects of this—either the historical salvation sequence or the present *simul*—is Jesus Christ, our Contemporary, and the Holy Spirit who brings the sequence to bear in our *simul* situation.⁵⁵

The *Simul* versus Psychologism

Thus far we have endeavored to communicate Barth's emphasis to take both the *iustus* and the *peccator* sides of the *simul* necessarily seriously. Extra care is required when discussing the *peccator* dimension because, out of context, the present tense and *totus* aspects of the *peccator* description have potential

---

54. CD II/1, 627. Barth here describes the "right and validity" (preponderance) of the *simul* to be established by the "non-contemporaneity . . . the overcoming and dissolution of the past by the future" (sequence) imported into the "contemporaneity" (simultaneous). To put it another way, the "non-contemporaneity" provides the "preponderance" within the "contemporaneity."

55. See CD III/2, 467. Importantly, Barth does not leave Christ behind (in the historical salvation narrative) in favor of a contemporary operation of the Spirit. As he relates here, his *simul* theology does not "rest merely on a retrospective vision" of Christ's work. In other words, instead of Christ being historical and the Spirit being contemporary, each Person's work is co-extensive with the other, maintaining the *homoousion*. I have been encouraged in my understanding of the sequential functioning inside the *simul* by Hunsinger's "Tale of Two Simultaneities."

Simul *Sanctification*: "no easier way"

for being confusing (*total* usually communicates ascendency) and even debilitating (fostering hopelessness) for Christians. However, as reflected earlier, even though Barth recognizes his approach is counter-intuitive, he sees "no easier way" of appraising the sanctification situation; indeed it would be a massive error to give up either the *totus peccator* or the *totus iustus*, and thereby capitulate to a zero-sum approach that "*seems* to be much more illuminating."[56] But why are the stakes so high for maintaining the *simul*? Why is Barth's claim that his *simul* is the only proper framework for sanctification valid and unique compared to other viewpoints?

As described above, Barth, even more consistently than Luther, refuses to minimize the extent of human sinfulness and the *totus peccator*, and he warns against jettisoning the *simul* for fear of its severity.[57] Other programs of sanctification invariably marginalize the gravity of sin in relation to the righteousness of a believer by either 1) an emphasis on the wrong kind of sequential (the Christian instead of the christological sequence) without regard for the simultaneous or 2) loosening the severity of the *totus* aspect of the *simul*. As for the first alternative, a misappropriation of "the old is gone" (2 Cor 5:17) could lead to a blind emphasis on the *iustus* determination, promoting an over-realized eschatology and an artificial denial of the present destructiveness of sin.[58] In this paradigm (a misunderstanding of "the old is gone" as first and foremost regarding Christian conversion) Christians may even fear the loss of salvation when things go badly; they may feel the need to "get saved" again. What if Christians think they have sin sequestered, only to have it break out with a vengeance? Barth speaks of the man who is sure he has drowned "the old Adam," yet he continually discovers that the old guy is a very good swimmer![59] To continue the metaphor, persons in this anxious state—where the sequence dictating the Christian's analysis is the Christian's own before-and-after narrative—can only grasp at the driftwood floating in their own choppy existential waters. Conversely, fortified with the sequence founded on the salvation history of Jesus Christ, Christians need not be surprised or thrown into an existential crisis by the simultaneous challenge of sin and evil.[60]

56. *CD* IV/2, 572. Emphasis added.

57. *CD* IV/2, 572.

58. See *CD* II/2, 328–29: Barth remarks of believers that "even in their new state they cannot feasibly forget the very real and continuing memory of that state of utter godlessness and merited rejection which even in faith continues in the weakness and perversity of their life and conduct."

59. *CD* III/2, 631.

60. See *CD* IV/2, 516: instead of believers attempting to sequester sin via their own existential sequencing, Barth emphasizes the better sequence of Christ's work erecting

The second alternative to the *simul* is not unrelated to the first. Perhaps confounded by the inadequacy of the Christian sequence (i.e., the simplistic replacing of the *totus peccator* with the *totus iustus* in the mistaken interpretation of "the old is gone, the new has come") the Christian resorts to softening the christological sequence (i.e., the old is "kind of gone," or will be gone someday). In other words, because there is no acknowledgment of the definitive christologicial sequence, where all died and rose in Christ, Christians have forfeited the *simul*'s *totus-totus* framework for sanctification with what Barth calls a *partim-partim*.[61] It is the *partim-partim* approach that forms the basis for what was earlier described as the problem of psychologism. If wary of the over-realization caused by focusing only on the *totus iustus* status, the *partim-partim*—giving neither *iustus* nor *peccator* a *totus* status—serves to under-realize both the *iustus* and *peccator* dimensions, leaving humanity to languish in a no-man's land that is the very worst of both worlds. Echoing Barth, in the *partim* understanding there is no real "already arrived" for the "new man" or for the old. In other words, there is not an established future for the "new man" (he has not *already* risen with Christ), and there is not an established end to the "old man" (he has not *already* died with Christ); there is no "already" but only a "not yet" for both. Christians then find themselves in the unenviable position of quantifying their progress and judging their own performance, as if searching their spiritual experiences for an ever-elusive tipping point.[62]

How does Barth's program avoid this psychological analysis? It is clear on Barth's view that the cognitive meter with which humans seek to quantify sin is itself corrupted by sin, and therefore tilted to underestimate sin's seriousness. Barth does not have to marginalize sin negatively because the resurrection does it positively. In other words, he is able to "maximize" the seriousness of sin because he knows there is a limit to sin, or even better because he knows that Jesus Christ in his death and resurrection has

---

a wall against "the raging flood of human vice," relegating all sin to believers' past (theologically speaking, again not first and foremost the past as in a period before the believer's own existential decision of faith). With the proper sequence in mind, Barth urges recollection "of what has taken place in Jesus Christ, and in Him for them and to them." At the same time, he couches "backsliding" as the forgetful futility of reaching back for, and attempting to bring forward, what Christ has decisively made past.

61. *CD* IV/2, 572.

62. I thank my friend David Sittser for the apt metaphor of the "tipping point." *Contra* this arbitrary approach is Barth's realist interpretation: 2 Cor 5:17 "must surely be taken to mean that this man is a new creature already" (*CD* IV/1, 321); the "old is gone" equates for Barth that to sin "has no future" (*CD* IV/1, 256). In sum, "new creation" is "too strong to be taken only as figurative" or as an expression describing "the changed feelings and self-understanding of Christians" (*CD* IV/1, 749).

"boundaried" or delimited sin. Without such an asymmetry anchored objectively and ontologically in the judgment of Jesus Christ crucified and resurrected, the Christian can only attain, in Barth's words, "a psychological myth which has no real substance."[63]

Here Barth elaborates with another metaphor: "What we see in our own life are all kinds of attempts and fragments, all kinds of half-lights which may equally well be those of sunset or sunrise, which vouch less for our sanctification than . . . against the factuality of our sanctification."[64] It is of critical import to Barth that we confront these arbitrary judgments with the *simul*, recognizing the two *totus* determinations at play in the one person who

> is always this man [the old man] totally and altogether, from top to toe, just as in the same present of the divine pardon he is always that other man [the new man] totally and altogether, from top to toe, the man who goes forward to the goal of his righteousness, who has indeed already arrived, who is alive there as a righteous man. Neither in the one case nor in the other are we dealing with a quantum, rising here and dropping there like a fluid in two communicating tubes, but in both cases we are dealing with a single and a total human existence.[65]

The *simul*, then, uniquely provides foundational support against the changing tides of gradualism by providing knowledge that eternal security is not founded on human mitigation of sin. That is why Barth promotes humanity's death, *in Christ's*, as one of the greatest gifts of grace. Only a definitive full stop for the old man, and then a fresh start for the new man, can provide the best antidote to human psychological fragility and the ill-conceived attempts to marginalize sin and death in a way only death and resurrection can.[66] This is the christological meaning of the old is gone; to the extent

---

63. *CD* IV/2, 572.

64. *CD* II/2, 775. Barth's colorful flair is at its best in describing our psychological games of self-assessment. These pitiable Christians are "only involved in a feat of juggling in which they may achieve a sensational but very dangerous interchange of supreme rapture and the most profound disillusionment"(*CD* II/2, 776).

65. *CD* IV/1, 576. Küng also draws attention to Barth's quantum metaphor (Küng, *Justification*, 64).

66. See *CD* II/2, 774–776. By the Holy Spirit in revelation we are given to see ourselves in Christ's story and thusly to see ourselves accurately. But Barth is extremely wary of collapsing the Spirit into the human spirit, or using the Spirit as an alibi for humans making judgments based on their own knowledge concerning sin and sanctification: "human judgment passed by ourselves on ourselves" (776), says Barth, is "the worst of hallucinations"(775). "When and where are we such believers of ourselves

Christians believe that their old selves have been crucified with Christ, they may rest in this victory as those who have their death behind them.[67]

Barth is obviously convinced that the *simul* fosters a more transparent and genuine Christian life. Again, when the old self emerges, Christians unequipped with the *simul* become psychologically concerned; they may be tempted to hide their sin because they do not want to be thought of as frauds or hypocrites. It is at times like this that persons need to be assured of a safe place where the *total* weight of their sinful selves can land without fear of breaking their relationship with God. Within this assurance, for instance, a white American may find the freedom to confess, "I am a racist," even if his or her life does not overtly reflect it. Not that Christians should publically "own" every sin imaginable because they are *totus peccator*, but on Barth's view this sanguine approach invariably liberates believers to healthy confession when appropriate. An honest acceptance of one's determination as *totus peccator* will be transformative because it is antithetical to the "tissue of lies" which constantly prompts us to absolve ourselves.[68] On the one hand, Barth would furiously resist (in our example) a broad brush view of racial prejudice that threatens to blur the line between victims and perpetrators or weaken the seriousness of a specific offense. On the other hand, it would be strongly preferable to confess "I am prejudiced" because of one's inextricable solidarity with fallen humanity, than to judge oneself as innocent of prejudice because of a self-psychological assessment. The latter for Barth is insidious indeed.[69]

But for Barth, even more damning than judging oneself as innocent is the mistake of judging oneself as partly guilty, that is, calling oneself a "sinner" but refusing to accept the indictment of *totus peccator*. On Barth's view, such a rationalization belies false humility, "a particularly evil form of self-justification," and the "crassest pride" whereby "seduced by Satan" humans falsely lay claim to themselves, as if they were in a position to quantify the extent of their sinfulness.[70] It is only in light of the judgment of God and our execution and rebirth in Jesus Christ that we can accept the gravity

---

that we can believe on the basis of our own witness? . . . [These persons] are ascribing credibility and the force of witness to a supposed 'pneumatic actuality' in the sphere of experience . . . building their houses on the sand . . . they will know nothing of the death of the old man and the life of the new" (775–76).

67. *CD* III/2, 621.

68. *CD* IV/1, 407.

69. *CD* II/2, 742: "Of all the things God hates, the most hateful is that we should not admit ourselves to be the transgressors that we are, but should try to excuse and justify ourselves as what we are."

70. *CD* II/2, 754–55.

of our weaknesses in their fullest declension, having room to acknowledge *past and presently* that we are *totus peccator* because we know we are *presently and future totus iustus*.[71]

In refusing the *partim-partim* approach to sanctification, Barth has attempted to excise all deadly forms of psychologism. Barth knows all too well the insatiable human appetite to create rites of passage which are then used in the attempt to measure and validate human salvation and sanctification, as if God does part and we do part (synergism). In spite of his disdain for the Western *ordo salutis*, Barth is sure that replacing it with another set of psycho-spiritual markers could only feed the wrong thing in the Christian.[72] As in his famous resistance to all forms of natural theology, not the smallest point of contact is to be allowed that could enable human beings, in and of themselves, to apprehend God or to obey God. In Katherine Sonderegger's words, "*simul justus et peccator* . . . wards off any synergy: we do not pull our share of the load because we do not pull any of it."[73]

---

71. Unless people know that they have been given a new life as revealed in the death and resurrection of Christ, they will cling to the old and dress it up as best they can. The self-justifying tendencies are too strong, and people will argue along the line of degree, like a blind man talking about colors, says Barth (*CD* II/2, 747–49). "The secret of grace ['the divine judgment'] must first have been seen if we are to demand of anybody that he forgo his self-justification" (748). "In defiance of every computation, unless God's own judgment gives it force, we will continually excuse and vindicate ourselves" (749).

72. We are thankful to Anderson ("Problem of Psychologism," 339) for pointing us to Barth's rejection of the "psychological pragmatics" (*CD* IV/2, 502) of the *ordo* and in soteriology in general.

73. Sondregger, "Sanctification as Impartation," 313.

2

Can We Speak of a Chalcedonian *Anthropology?*

"For the open secret of what has happened in Jesus Christ is that in Him the transcendent God who yet loves, elects and liberates the world, and lowly man who is yet loved, elected and liberated by Him, are indeed distinct and yet are not separated or two, but one."[1]

OUR INVESTIGATION HAS SHOWN THAT EVEN IF BARTH'S PENCHANT IS NOT to use the *simul* to describe unbelievers directly, it is patently apparent that by describing Christians as *peccator* and non-Christians as *iustus*, he has placed all humans within the *simul*'s operating framework. We will discuss later in the book how and why Barth intentionally seeks to erase the line between believer and unbeliever until it no longer gets in the way of a proper delineation between the two. Those outside the church are, insists Barth, "no different from those inside—within the community. The saints are not, as it were, artless children unfortunately led astray by wicked rascals. They themselves are wicked rascals."[2] Barth challenges our theological categories for what can and cannot fit in the same "space"—"saints" and "wicked" for instance. In the same way, we may seek to theologically quarantine God from wickedness, but by dictating what God can and cannot do we may potentially hinder our ability to best grasp the demonstration of his love.

Having considered the advantages of the *simul* which Barth promotes in practical matters of sanctification, we have still not explored the original source, beyond Luther, from whence Barth derives his theology of the *simul*. How does Barth attempt to anchor his theology in a reality that, while

---

1. *CD* IV/3.2, 712.
2. *CD* IV/2, 666.

Can We Speak of a Chalcedonian Anthropology? 47

helping us to interpret our existence, is not by any means "existential?"[3]—i.e., a theology that does not start with experience to interpret reality? First, Barth is a biblical theologian who is quick to criticize any "theology" not grounded in Holy Scripture.[4] Second, and more importantly, Barth's reference point for every aspect of the *simul iustus et peccator* is the Living Word, God's most direct and reliable revelation of himself, Jesus Christ.[5] In this short but pivotal chapter we will, after considering Barth's scriptural basis for *simul* anthropology, inquire as to what degree his scriptural *simul* anthropology is predicated on a scriptural *simul* Christology.

The *Simul* and Scripture

In Scripture Barth finds Paul's testimony in Romans 7 to be one example of undeniable substantiation for the doctrine of *simul iustus et peccator*. Barth follows a long tradition of interpreters, notably Augustine, Luther, and Calvin, in promoting the belief that Paul is writing of himself in Romans 7 and thereby describing the experience of a mature believer.[6] Paul's autobiographical reference to the present-tense power of sin in his own life provides articulation for a real ongoing struggle in any Christian's life.[7] According to Barth's exegesis of Romans 7, Paul testifies to being both a sanctified human of the Spirit and a "wretched man" of the flesh. The Christian must admit with Paul "nothing good dwells within me, that is, in my flesh" (Rom 7:18). Barth continues, "He is useless, absolutely useless, as far as concerns

---

3. Throughout *Church Dogmatics*, Barth targets Bultmann and Schleiermacher in his critique of existentialism, or what Barth decries as an anthropocentric perspective: "subjectivity from below" (see chapter 3 of our study).

4. See *CD* I/2, 822: "What has to be said is that dogmatics has no freedom to be an autonomous branch of Church theology in independence of the witness of Scripture. It cannot give its own witness from its own sources . . . It may or may not be directly concerned in exegesis. It may or may not make actual textual references. But necessarily it takes the form of its thought from its submission to the biblical *Deus dixit*."

5. See *CD* I/2, 452: Barth asserts we cannot have knowledge of our simultaneous "true being" and our "being as sinners" except as we view them in Jesus Christ.

6. *CD* IV/3.1, 210: Barth writes, "At the very height of his apostolic career Paul can and must write in the present tense and in personal terms a passage like Ro. 7.7–25, in which the contradiction in his existence is plainly to be seen in all its menace." Barth here speaks of the importance of interpreting Romans 7 within the context of Romans 5–8 as a whole, where the preponderance and asymmetry is clearly seen.

7. 1 Timothy 1:15, which we assume with Barth is Pauline (*CD* II/2, 430), would be the other most glaring example, "Christ Jesus came into the world to save sinners—of whom I am the foremost." See *CD* I/1: here Barth emphasizes Romans 7 is not a "glance back to the past but an assertion about the present . . . especially of the Christian."

the good. He is stupid, inhuman, dissipated and discontented. He chooses, but he never chooses the right, only the wrong." In spite of the Christian's "freedom as the new man in Jesus and in the Holy Spirit," states Barth, the Christian is in "bondage as the old man . . . in the flesh." These are two total, oppositional determinations in the one person. "Total freedom" and "total bondage," Barth claims, "clash in one and the same man."[8] In other words, the Christian of Romans 7 is *simul (totus) iustus et (totus) peccator*.

The simultaneity of the whole old self and the whole new self can be difficult to unravel in Romans at times, largely because of the use of the first person "I" or "me," which the reader or hearer could take as referring to either determination of the *simul*. Sometimes Paul, recognizing this potential confusion, feels the need to qualify his language so that we know which determination he is speaking of: "I know that nothing good lives in me, *that is, in my flesh*" (7:18; italics added). Instead of resorting to other ingenious methods of explaining Romans 7, we could say with Barth that Paul's first person language, as confusing as it might be from one perspective, actually provides us with crystal clear substantiation for the *simul*. Indeed, it seems apparent to Barth that Paul is speaking of individual Christians who could go either way at any time, bearing fruit to God, or for death (6:4, 5). It is difficult to dismiss Paul's first-person conclusion to chapter 7 and his self-description of two slaveries, one person: "with my mind I am a slave to the law of God, but with my flesh I am a slave to the law of sin" (7:25b).[9]

---

8. CD IV/2, 496–97. Between these two determinations there can be no cooperation. "For how can there be co-operation between total freedom and total bondage? How can the Spirit give assistance to the flesh, or the flesh to the Spirit?"

9. Obviously "the mind" here described is not the sinful mind of *peccator* humanity (Rom 8:6–8) but instead is indicative of the *iustus* determination of humanity. It is apparent that Barth does not adopt Luther's bifurcation of inner (e.g., mind) and outer (e.g., body) but instead has a holistic understanding of the flesh. Humanity at bottom has only one true human nature, but Barth's use of "sinful nature" is important to communicate the total depravity of the flesh, which protects against falsely restricting the flesh to spatial parameters such as outer or body (vs. inner and mind). See *CD* IV/1, 165: "'Flesh' is the concrete form of human nature and the being of man in his world under the sign and fall of Adam—the being of man as corrupted and therefore destroyed, as unreconciled with God and therefore lost." As mentioned in the introduction and made plain in chapter 8, on Barth's view the "pure form" of humanity is ever-present but hidden. It follows that for Barth the "inmost self" which delights in the law of God (Rom 7:22) is true humanity, what we have called *iustus* humanity. The inner *anthropon* (e.g., Eph 3:16), the "new man," the true or *iustus* self, the created and redeemed self—all are in contradistinction to the old man, the false, *peccator* self and the fallen *anthropon* (e.g., Col 3:9); see *CD* IV/4, 7. Not by looking within, but only by knowing Jesus Christ can one discover one's true self. Fittingly, in the name of "their Liberator" and the "law of the Spirit of Life" (Rom 8:2), human beings are free to live

The implications of Barth's argument from Romans are clear. The Christian never stops being a slave to sin; one does not graduate out of the *totus peccator* aspect of one's earthly life.[10] But Barth calls Christians "disturbed sinners" because, like Paul in Romans 7, they know the asymmetrical context.[11] In other words, in this world believers give the *peccator* determination its full, deadly, due (Rom 6:23a), but they have confidence from the Holy Spirit that the coexistence of false and true humanity have nothing to do with an equilibrium. Again it is the gospel sequence provided in the death and resurrection of Jesus Christ—the work of Christ that includes every human—which dictates the critical asymmetry in the midst of the simultaneous. It is believers who always view themselves with Paul in what Barth calls "the question" *and* "the answer" of Romans 7:24–25a: "Wretched man that I am! Who will rescue me from this body of death? Thanks be to God through Jesus Christ our Lord!" This tension-breaking "turning" at the end of the chapter is for Barth the most "forceful presentation of justification as transition" in all of Scripture.[12] It is an epistemological transition that reaches back to connect with the sequential key of interpretation, which has already been declared in the first verses of the chapter. Indeed, Barth calls section 7:1–6, easily overshadowed by the graphic language that follows, the "controlling statement" of the chapter. The metaphor of the first husband's death and the woman's remarriage to the second husband (1–6) functions as a sequential prelude of Christ-centered assurance, a foundation of *iustus* security; from this standpoint Paul then, and only then, endeavors to articulate the depths of his current and past slavery to sin.[13] It is apparent that Paul

---

in the truth (*CD* III/2, 304–5).

10. See *CD* II/1, 120: "the statements of Rom 7 and 8 form a unity which is not to be severed either biographically or factually."

11. *CD* IV/2, 524.

12. *CD* IV/1, 591.

13. *CD* IV/3, 210: because of its critical function in the chapter, Barth warns against isolating 7:1–6. It guarantees that, while "the antithesis is not yet removed . . . Paul can still regard the history as one of triumph." In regards to triumph, Barth's theology has been criticized as an impersonal "triumph of grace." Barth believes Paul was aware of the same criticism, and that is why (see *CD* IV/1, 582), Paul forgoes the more logically linear alternative of "going straight on from" 7:6 to 8:1, he instead circles back around to make sure that his hearers understand his awareness of their ongoing plight in the flesh. Instead of diminishing the counterintuitive claim that we are "dead to sin," Paul heightens the counterintuitive nature of his argument. In Barth's view, Paul recognizes the purely sequential interpretation of Christian life would ring hollow as too idealistic or not "genuine." "Sin shall not be your master," therefore, is spoken in light of the fact that for many Christians, much of the time, it feels like just the opposite—like sin is the master. To say that the first husband of Rom 7:2–3 has not died would be to lose the

is intent not only on communicating the seriousness of the ongoing conflict (in the midst of humans' created and recreated glory, the fact that it is even a contest reveals the incomprehensible depths of human depravity), but also that Paul purposely employs the *simul* (his own primal version) to protect against the over-realized eschatology that he faced in his churches since the beginning of his apostleship.[14]

Daniel Spross questions, "How can Barth put together opposites like sinners/saints, and refer at the same time to the same person? How does the spirit relate to the flesh in the same person? How can one man be at one and the same time the old man and the new?"[15] Undoubtedly Barth would ask in return (in regards to putting these opposites together), "How does the Bible do it?" As with Romans 7, Barth continually shows us his sources in Holy Scripture. But finally and primarily, Barth would ask, "How does God do it? Do we see in Holy Scripture God's revelation of Godself as the Word who became flesh (John 1:14), a singular man Jesus Christ who like us is (in Spross's words) "at the same time the old man and the new?" Barth's view of Christ's incarnational assumption of corrupt flesh—his real solidarity with human "transgressors"—would appear to suggest a christological *simul* (*totus*) *iustus et* (*totus*) *peccator*. Perhaps the central reason Barth spoke so confidently of the *simul's* application to humanity is that it first describes the humanity of God.

---

sequence; it would be an illegitimate claim as in an adulterous union while still married. But, notes Barth, "with bitter words Paul explains that when he looks at himself and takes stock of himself he finds that the first man is very much alive, that his being in the flesh which (in v5 according to the whole tenor of chapter 6) he has put into the past is still in the present" (*CD* IV/1, 583). Barth's *simul* thereby protects theologically against Docetic and Gnostic elements, as Barth concludes elsewhere in speaking of Romans, "It is clear that what we have here is a history of triumph, but also that it is a genuine history" (*CD* IV/3, 211). In sum, to lose the sequence is to lose the victory and to languish without hope, while to leave the simultaneous behind is to forfeit authentic history for the "imagined freedom" of an over-realized perspective—"to pretend to be elsewhere than on the fatal middle stretch between creation and consummation" (*CD* III/2, 304).

14 See the Thessalonian "couch potato" mentality and Paul's consternation about idleness (e.g., 2 Thess 6). If this lackadaisical attitude follows closely on the heels of the Apostle's teaching, the fact that we are not even tempted towards this kind of over-realism may be an indictment in and of itself.

15. Spross, "Doctrine of Sanctification," 69.

A Christological *Simul?*

Jesus Christ as *simul iustus et peccator*? It is a fair challenge to dispute whether Barth spoke of Christ himself as a living summary of the *simul*. To our knowledge Barth never associates the literal phrase *simul iustus et peccator* directly with Jesus Christ or with the time-honored Chalcedonian definition (AD 451). Barth's affinity for describing unitary things in a twofold manner is well known,[16] however, so it should not surprise us that he applies Chalcedon language to anthropology as well. His allusions to Chalcedon concerning the twofold determination of the new and old man (essentially the *simul iustus et peccator*) are unmistakable. But how far does Barth go to actually wed Chalcedonian *Christology* and his *simul* anthropology? Obviously, Chalcedonian language applied to anthropology and obliquely to the *simul* is not the same as putting forth Chalcedonian Christology as the necessary source and foundation of *simul* anthropology.

Before proceeding, it is pertinent to consider some theological presuppositions which may perhaps inhibit a consideration of intimate relationship between Chalcedonian Christology and a *simul* anthropology: 1) Chalcedon is concerned with "Christology," which carries a heavy connotation of divinity, so that a certain lip service is then paid to Jesus' humanity, mostly to facilitate his atoning death; 2) our humanity is thought to be fundamentally broken and sinful, and Jesus' humanity as authentic but pure, and thereby somewhat disconnected from ours; or, 3) in a combination of

---

16. We have already noted Barth invoking the Chalcedonian formula regarding the "other *simul*," justification and sanctification. Five additional examples of Chalcedonian language are enumerated as follows: 1) regarding Jesus' unique ability to keep the great commandment, truly loving God and truly loving neighbor, "Thus the structure of the humanity of Jesus Himself is revealed in this twofold command. It repeats the unity of His divinity and humanity as this is achieved without admixture or change, and yet also without separation or limitation" (*CD* III/2, 217); 2) regarding the objective (divine act) and subjective (human participation) aspects of the atonement, ". . . we cannot separate but we must not confuse the two" (*CD* IV/1, 643); 3) Barth's comment on the Creator and creature living together, "without the transformation of the one into the other, the admixture of the one with the other, or separation or division between them" (*CD* IV/3.1, 40); 4) concerning Israel itself and its prophetic voice, "there is a general acceptance of their co-existence and co-inherence, of their basic unity, though without any confusion or mixture of the two elements" (*CD* IV/3.1, 63); 5) regarding the relationship of the Christian community with the world, the community can be faithful to Christ "only in exact and honest and sober correspondence to His coming in the flesh." Barth concludes that in the community's "visibility and invisibility, its likeness and distinction in world-occurrence, are the twofold determination of its one and total being, just as Jesus Christ, in whose discipleship it exists in this twofold determination of its one existence, is with the same totality both true man and true God, and as such the one Jesus Christ" (*CD* IV/3.2, 734).

the above emphases, Jesus is God and humanity is wretched, but through the wonderful exchange Jesus is made sin and humans are made God. In this last example, whereby humanity is divinized, humanity is overtaken by divinity in such a way as to relegate humanity to accidental or at least incidental status. The common denominator of these views is that, if Jesus' humanity is maintained at all, it certainly does not have anything in common with sinful humanity. Indeed, it must be questioned whether views two and three should ultimately be considered anthropological—they do not portray true humanity but instead corrupt humanity (view 2) and vacated humanity (view 3).

Resisting different tendencies to sunder Christology and anthropology, Barth admonishes us to keep the two in closest proximity. Notes Barth, "in theological anthropology what man is, is decided by the primary text, i.e., by the humanity of the man Jesus."[17] Barth's criterion for considering humanity is always the humanity of God: "For—this was our starting point—He, Jesus Christ is the holy God and sanctified man in one."[18] He is not simply *Mensch* ("humanity"), asserts Barth importantly, but *geheiligte Mensch*, "sanctified humanity."[19] As stated in the paragraph immediately above, a christological view of anthropology begins with true and good humanity before false and parasitic humanity can be considered. It follows that Jesus Christ, himself sanctified humanity, is also a man *being* sanctified, or, to say the same thing differently, as a man *being* sanctified, Jesus Christ is already sanctified humanity.[20] Either way, in his humiliation-in-exaltation and exaltation-in-humiliation, Jesus Christ assumes and therefore reveals the story of humanity *simul iustus et peccator*. It seems apparent that Barth finds in this revelation not merely the ground for speaking of the *simul* in Chalcedonian terms—the two determinations of humanity appropriated into the "two in the one" and "one of the two" Chalcedon framework—but also the basis for incorporating the *simul* as an internal, albeit hidden, axiom of Chalcedonian Christology itself (i.e., the provisional axiom we have named Chalcedonian anthropology).

It is our assertion that what Barth is implying is a double-duality *within* the traditional Chalcedonian formulation, a duality within the humanity of

---

17. *CD* III/2, 226.
18. *CD* II/2, 778.
19. *KD* II/2, 871.
20. The purposeful repetitive nature of this remark is meant to show the dialectical economy of Jesus' sanctification and its consistency with the derived dialectical economy of human sanctification in general, as per Barth's comment highlighted in the last chapter that persons can only go towards the goal of their sanctification because they have already arrived (*CD* IV/1, 576).

Can We Speak of a Chalcedonian Anthropology? 53

Jesus Christ. Barth consistently describes both the dualities—the christological and the anthropological—as "twofold":

> The work of the divine sentence . . . is that man is placed on this way . . . he becomes the man of this history—the history of Jesus Christ. He becomes the man who in every present has both this past and this future; the one as past and the other as future; the one set aside behind him, the other as a promise before him; irreversible in the same sequence as the death and resurrection of Jesus Christ—but in the sequence not merely the one and the other but both at once . . . not intermingled in any present (as though at bottom they were not two-fold) but both distinct in every present; not separated in any present, but—in that sequence, as moments in that history—indissolubly bound together in every present . . . In every present he is still the man he was, the man of sin, the man of pride, and as such a fallen man. He is not this man to remain such, but to be so no longer, to become another man. But he still is this man . . . the man of this history, caught up in this transition.[21]

The preceding excerpt, located in paragraph 61 on justification, is similar to the by now familiar passage we quoted earlier from the beginning of paragraph 66 on sanctification. Both passages use the phrasing *terminus a quo* and *terminus ad quem* in describing the transition in the simultaneous present of the old and new man. Again from paragraph 66:

> the same man stands under two total determinations which are not merely opposed but mutually exclusive; that the same man, in the *simul* of to-day, is both the old man of yesterday and the new man of to-morrow, the captive of yesterday and the free man of to-morrow.[22]

In an opposite manner to the first excerpt from paragraph 61, the *simul* is clearly spelled out here, while the Chalcedonian association is less obvious. And again, in both paragraphs the warning is against separating, mixing, changing or dividing the two determinations in "the same man," first the man Jesus Christ, secondly and derivatively, all human beings.

If not a direct description of Jesus Christ as *simul iustus et peccator*, Barth's discussion of election—his assessment of the election/rejection of humanity in the Elected/Rejected One—betrays the closest of associations

---

21. *CD* IV/1, 573.

22. *CD* IV/2, 572. Other Chalcedonian allusions related anthropologically to the old and new man, and therefore to the *simul*, can be found in *CD* IV/1, 407, 494, 544; *CD* IV/2, 399–400; IV/3.1, 379–80, 396).

to a christological *simul*. Echoes of Chalcedon are again obvious. Barth asks rhetorically, "How can [a man] be *simul peccator et iustus*?" He is discussing how it is possible that the same man can be "rejected and elected . . . both put to death and alive."[23] His answer, of course, is that it can happen because it has happened in the person of Jesus Christ. Jesus Christ is where "the elect and rejected face each other in one and the same person."[24] "It is strictly and narrowly only in the humanity of the one Jesus Christ that we can see who and what an elect person is," notes Barth. "But, again, it is strictly and narrowly only in the portrait of the one Jesus Christ that we may perceive who and what a rejected man is."[25]

Chalcedonian Anthropology

If commentators have missed Barth's christological association with *simul* anthropology, it is possible that they have been blinded by two mitigating concerns. One concern could be called an over-emphasis and the other an under-emphasis, and these two concerns are not unrelated to the typical presuppositions related to Christology and anthropology articulated above.

The first concern has to do with an overemphasis on the separateness between God and humanity in general. This over-emphasis protects God from encroachment not only from sinful humanity but also from righteous humanity. The result theologically is that *iustus* humanity is granted something less than the true, full and actual *iustitia* of Christ. Barth is always keen to keep God and humanity from being theologically conflated. His wariness and downright distaste of deification or divinization (also known as *theosis*) is plain to see.[26] Having made note of Barth's resistant posture, however, it is worth adding that for Barth, Jesus Christ signifies the deepest, most intimate union possible between humanity and God. Barth, for instance, is able to cite 2 Peter 1:4, about participating in the divine nature, with approval; it means the "exaltation of human essence to fellowship with the divine nature."[27] This is a glorious reality indeed, even if something less than the

---

23. *CD* IV/1, 516–17.

24. *CD* II/2, 350.

25. *CD* II/2, 351, 352. While massively pertinent, I have chosen not to provide a detailed analysis of Barth's theology of election in this book, as I have addressed it with some depth elsewhere. See my *Movements of Grace* (2010).

26. See Barth's argument against divinization or *theosis* in *CD* IV/2, 78–117: "God humbles Himself to man, even to the final and most radical depth of becoming man, not to deify man, but to exalt him to perfect fellowship with Himself" (117). We will resume a discussion of *theosis* in chapter 12.

27. *CD* IV/2, 103. It is interesting to note that Barth's only other citation of this

patristic mantra is usually thought to signify, i.e., the Athanasian "He, indeed, assumed humanity that we might become God."[28] Barth was certainly aware of the many shades of deification in Christendom. What might have troubled him even more than an encroachment on God by humanity was the version of deification that entailed a gradual progression of human beings towards perfection in this life or beyond (*a la* John Wesley), a definite offense to Lutheran sobriety and the *simul*. Again, however, we note that Barth is not against the idea of "full sanctification" properly understood; the ontological *totus iustus* is quite the audacious claim! We suggest, then, that the concern about encroachment is overweighted because of a lack of understanding Barth's anthro-dimensional approach, which, in spite of an incarnational unity, always maintains proper distinctions between Christ and true humanity, and between true and false humanity. Maintaining these theological lines will be paramount throughout our study. As will hopefully be made clear, Barth wants to be as concerned about conflation as incarnate God proves to be—that is, not very concerned but enough. We do not detect in Barth anything like humanity becoming God, but what we do see is something scandalously close.[29]

The second concern against applying the *simul* christologically builds on the first. Not only is conflation between God and *iustus* humanity a theological concern, but an embrace of *peccator* humanity by God might be perceived to pose an even greater threat to the very Godhead itself.[30] An overemphasis to protect the separateness between God and humanity in general certainly breeds an under-emphasis on the implications of "the Word was made flesh"; this may cause theologians to pull up short when assessing the *peccator* dimension in Christology. As mentioned in the Preface, we will continue to observe Barth's insistence that the incarnation of God involves the actual assumption of sinful flesh (*sarx*), the Son of God being born into original sin and a holistic human depravity of body, mind, and

---

verse relates to the Virgin Mary as the most obvious participant in the divine nature! (I/2, 195). The phrase "the divine nature" is translated from Barth's original Greek.

28. Athanasius, *De Incarnatione*, 54:3.

29. Barth's theological discipline prevents him from promoting a "straight oneness" between each of us humans and God, but it *is* a mediated oneness, since we are of Christ, and Christ is of God (1 Cor 3:23). See *CD* I/2, 215: "In Jesus Christ our human nature and kind were adopted and assumed into unity of being with the Son of God."

30. Christ's assumption of merely a pre-fall, pristine humanity would obviously be favorable for theologians who desire to protect God from impurity, or who at least feel an untainted, pristine humanity is necessary to properly present Christ as the unblemished sacrificial lamb. Additionally, there may be a concern that Jesus' assumption of a sinful nature means the inevitability of Christ sinning.

soul.³¹ It is understandable that the mind-blowing condescension of God in becoming a human being might overshadow the *type* of human nature Christ assumed in the incarnation. Barth himself describes Jesus Christ as "the true man," the person who gets it right when every other person gets it wrong.³² This is indisputable. But can we probe the time-honored Chalcedonian formula for something more than the simple christological description of a single duality of God and man in one person, not to be confused, changed, separated, or divided?

With Barth there is perhaps more to Chalcedon than meets the eye. Barth affirms the original duality of Chalcedon at face value, that of the union and distinction of God and humanity in the one man Jesus Christ. But Barth's insistence that the incarnation includes God assuming sinful flesh is in blatant contradiction with Barth's other commitment to Jesus Christ being the true human. These two together could only mean that true humanity was and is sinful flesh, which is obviously not Barth's intent. Or, it could be taken that Jesus is true humanity and false humanity at different times, (i.e., alternatively). Instead, it becomes apparent that Barth is introducing another duality inside the original duality; the fact that Barth is presenting the human being Jesus Christ existing simultaneously in contradiction as "the righteous One"³³ and "the one great sinner"³⁴ is precisely the point. To be clear, the original Chalcedonian duality between God and human in Christ is what Barth calls "a twofold *differentiation*."³⁵ But there is also a second duality at play, that of true and false humanity, in the one human being Jesus of Nazareth. Barth describes this, as we have already noted, as "a twofold *determination*." Differentiation (*Differenzierung*) assuages our above concern about the conflation of God and humanity, while determination (*Bestimmung*) assuages our concern about conflation of true and false

---

31. E.g., *CD* III/2, 335–336; notes Barth, "The New Testament knows nothing of a part of the person of Jesus which does not take part in this event. Even His soul…does not live outside of this event but in the middle of it" (336). References to Christ's assumption of fallen flesh are scattered throughout *CD*.

32. *CD* IV/2, 27: Jesus Christ in his humanity is "not only completely like us, but completely unlike us" at the same time.

33. *CD* IV/1, 95. Barth ascribes the term "the righteous One" alternatively to God (*CD* II/1, 413), the human Jesus ("the righteous One"), and to the human being in Jesus ("the righteous one"), the latter two notably on the same page (*CD* IV/1, 95).

34. *CD* IV/1, 239. We as great sinners, even Judas (*CD* III/4, 409), exist in "the one great sinner."

35. *CD* IV/2, 70: "it is apparent that the mutual participation of the divine and human essence as it takes place in and by Him does so in a twofold differentiation."

humanity—*iustus* and *peccator*, even while Jesus Christ remains the point of reference for all aspects of both dualities.

In positing the second duality (true humanity and false humanity) as a corollary, we must never sever it from the original Chalcedonian duality (Christ's divinity and humanity). In this vein two things must be emphasized. First, if there are three components of the original Chalcedonian formula—"One," God, and "man"—what we are introducing is not a fourth component but a nuance of the third, i.e., a duality regarding "man." Second, once we introduce Christ's assumption of sinful flesh, our staunch adherence to spatial categories could cause us to displace his *iustus* flesh (his true humanity), which Barth will not allow.[36] In other words, even if both aspects of the second duality do not sustain ultimately (namely the *peccator* aspect), the intimate, never-ending connection between true humanity and God mediated by Jesus Christ remains.

The second duality inside of the Chalcedonian duality is easily overlooked, possibly because it was not necessarily what the framers themselves had in mind! At the same time, we do not hesitate to call it Chalcedonian because it is certainly consistent with the spirit of the original, albeit entailing a different look at the God side[37] and a deeper look at the "man" side of the classic christological articulation. Again we summarize this second duality. First, Jesus Christ is "not only a true man, but *the* true man."[38]

> The true man who lived and lives here as the man of God and therefore in direct unity with God as the God of man, did not and does not live for himself, but as the "first-born of all creation" (Col 1:15), as the last Adam who in order is the first (1 Cor 15:45), he lived and lives for all men in the place of all. All people, therefore, are elected, justified, sanctified and called in him.[39]

---

36. *CD* III/2, 336. As we shall see in the next chapter, instead of its purely sequential meaning, Barth uses "displace" as a dimensional term, i.e., a displacement of the old flesh for the new flesh based on revelatory disclosure, and not synonymous with "replacement."

37. By "a different look at the God side" we mean Barth's unique doctrine of God's freedom and immutability that reveals God in Jesus Christ to be all that we are in our sin and death while still remaining himself. Still, Barth's protective dogmatic instincts refuse all conflation of God and humanity and any idea that sin is necessary to the Godhead.

38. *CD* IV/2, 27.

39. Barth, *The Christian Life*, 125.

Secondly, this same true man, "the righteous One," was at the same time made sin[40] so that we might become the righteousness of God, "choosing to suffer the wrath of God in His own body and the fire of [God's] love in His own soul."[41] The proposed correlation is simply this: the twofold differentiation of Chalcedon is Jesus Christ, one person divine and human, and the twofold determination of Jesus Christ is true humanity and false humanity in one person. But *peccator* humanity as a *determination* for Jesus Christ? Indeed, as alluded to above in reference to the one person Jesus Christ being the elected and rejected of God, Barth declares that the eternal election and rejection of humanity has its basis in the "twofold determination of Christ Himself."[42] When the Creator became a creature, states Barth, he made his own the creature's "greatness and wretchedness;" God made himself "the Subject of this twofold determination."[43] It would therefore appear to suggest that for Barth, Jesus Christ, Son of God, is *simul (totus) iustus et (totus) peccator* for the sake of the humanity he came to save. The Son of Man enters our plight as our contemporary even as we share his history, the history that assures the Christian mired in contradiction of the day when he or she will stand with Christ without contradiction.

In a seminal statement from *The Humanity of God*, Barth draws together many of the elements of our above discussion, including Christ's divinity and true humanity, while alluding to Christ's false humanity, and all within the Chalcedonian motif:

> In Jesus Christ there is no isolation of man from God or of God from man. Rather, in Him we encounter the history, the dialogue, in which God and man meet together and are together, the reality of the covenant *mutually* contracted, preserved and fulfilled by them. Jesus Christ is in His one Person, as true *God*, *man's* loyal partner, and as true *man*, *God's*. He is the Lord humbled for communion with man and likewise the Servant exalted to communion with God. He is the Word spoken from the loftiest, most luminous transcendence and likewise the Word

---

40. 2 Corinthians 5:21; while it is often assumed that Paul means Christ was made sin at the cross, Paul does not say so directly.

41. *CD* IV/1, 95. As previously noted, after Barth calls Jesus "the righteous One," he similarly describes new humanity in Christ, "The being of the new man reconciled with God in Jesus Christ is one in which man has a future only as the righteous one that he is before God in Jesus Christ." See 2 Corinthians 5:21, Hebrews 10:38, James 5:6.

42. *CD* II/2, 199. See also *CD* II/2, 260: Barth remarks that Christ's community "must correspond to the twofold determination of its Head."

43. *CD* III/1, 377.

heard in the deepest darkest immanence. He is both, without their being confused but also without their being divided.[44]

The remainder of our study will probe the implications of a Chalcedonian anthropology for sanctification. If Barth is correct, one thing is already obvious: the centuries-old debate arguing whether God assumed a pre-fall, pristine humanity or post-fall, corrupted *sarx* is a moot point. He assumed both. In the midst of re-creation certainty and deathly confusion, the new and old human warred to the end in the One human; in his identification and solidarity with every human, Jesus' own "quarrel with himself" was over when the false was put away and he rose triumphantly in the truth and newness of life, having sanctified himself for humanity's sake (John 17:19). The end result is that, while humans do not become God, they become truly human in a way that allows them to participate in God's very nature in the most intimate communion imaginable. Indeed, if humans are already "hidden with Christ in God" (Col 3:3), might even Barth admit that this is "*theosis*" appropriately understood?

---

44. Barth, *Humanity of God*, 46–47 (italics original).

3

Chalcedonian Change and the Spirit of Righteousness

"We have now to focus all our attention on Jesus Christ as the true and new man in virtue of this exaltation, the second Adam, in whom there has taken place, and is actualised, the sanctification of all men."[1]

THUS FAR WE HAVE PROMOTED THE *SIMUL IUSTUS ET PECCATOR* AS BARTH'S keystone to sanctification, but we have refrained from exploring the *simul*'s interconnection to epistemology. It was our desire to first establish Barth's christological content for the *simul*, especially regarding the revealed sequence and asymmetry that makes the *simul* framework helpful for the Christian disciple; after all, it is not the *simul* that changes us! As we have discovered, Barth's anthropology is derived not from human experiences of God or even first and foremost from Holy Scripture but fundamentally from the human being Jesus Christ revealed in Holy Scripture, the living Word who was made sin that we might become the righteousness of God (2 Cor 5:21). Because Jesus Christ's singular life most accurately reveals to us the *peccatum* totality of false humanity's condition, while simultaneously representing the *iustitia* totality of true human being, we may call Barth's anthropology a "Chalcedonian anthropology," a twofold determination of human nature inside the overarching twofold differentiation of the traditional Chalcedonian formula. Now that we have cleared the ground from all potentially inhibiting factors, including the Western *ordo salutis*, psychologistic tendencies, quantifiable zero-sum games, progressive and gradualist

---

1. *CD* IV/2, 155.

sanctification markers, etc., what more can we say about Barth's actualism and the question of just how change occurs in the Christian?

Towards the end of *Church Dogmatics*, Barth describes the sanctified life as anchored in the person of Jesus Christ: "To live a holy life is to be raised and driven with increasing definiteness from the centre of this revealed truth, and therefore to live in conversion with growing sincerity, depth and precision." Barth scholars will be quick to point out that this particular citation, where Barth uses progressive language regarding sanctification, represents an unusual theme in *Church Dogmatics*.[2] In fact, George Hunsinger uses the word "striking" to describe Barth's lack of attention to Christian development and growth in the realm of sanctification. Barth is certainly not against spiritual transformation, but when it comes to describing *how* change happens, Barth leaves "a large logical space . . . that remains to be more adequately filled."[3] How aware was Barth of this "large logical space"? Should Barth have done more in his theology to better develop the epistemological side of sanctification? If so, how would he proceed without re-cluttering the ground he has already cleared through his implementation of the *simul iustus et peccator*?

"For Their Sakes I Sanctify Myself"

When launching forward into the realm of the motivated Christian disciple, we must take pains to refocus the sanctification question. Instead of asking what change looks like for Christians, we begin with Barth by asking what change looks like in the life of Jesus Christ. Does Jesus, "the sanctifying God and sanctified man in One,"[4] truly provide an ongoing and governing context implicating our lives as *simul iustus et peccator* within the realm of Jesus' own sanctification? Indeed, Barth will continually assert that all aspects of human subjectivity regarding sanctification, conversion, growth,

---

2. Even the above quotation (*CD* IV/2, 566) could be described as less than satisfactory for those desiring a more typical gradualist understanding of sanctification. Still, it says more than Hans Urs von Balthasar was willing to acknowledge, namely that Barth "rejected all talk of growth or progress in the Christian life" (this as stated by Hunsinger), "Tale of Two Simultaneities," 316.

3. Hunsinger, "Tale of Two Simultaneities," 337. The *CD* quote, cited by Hunsinger, is from *CD* IV/2, 566. See McCormack, "Afterword," 372–75, where McCormack jousts with Hunsinger as to whether Barth should have or could have said more about progress or change in light of the existing restraints of Barth's theological program.

4. *CD* II/2, 539.

and change correspond to the objective reality (i.e., to the reality of Jesus Christ and his unique vicarious humanity).[5]

Considering more deeply Jesus Christ sanctifying himself for our sakes (John 17:19)[6] turns our attention to his whole, entire life filled with struggle and obedience. As the author of the Book of Hebrews relates, Jesus Christ learned obedience through his sufferings (Heb 5:8). When thinking about Jesus' growth in Scripture, is it necessary to assume that he, while in the flesh and plight of the *false* human being, was lacking in completeness as the *true* human being? Did Jesus' becoming "the greatest of all sinners,"[7] sacrificing himself "to shed our own wicked blood in his own precious blood,"[8] entail a siphoning off of any of his intrinsic Godness and righteousness that subsequently needed to be refilled, as in a zero-sum model?[9]

As alluded to earlier, Barth's twofold *determination* (*Bestimmung*) in one human being is consistent with and included in the Chalcedonian mystery of God and human in one person, what Barth calls a twofold *differentiation* (*Differenzierung*). It is our proposed *simul iustus et peccator* of Jesus Christ, and expressly the simultaneous aspect of the *simul*, which points us to the "one person" aspect of our humanity. When we say Jesus "learned obedience from what he suffered" (Heb 5:8), we cannot say his true humanity learned it (because it did not need to), nor can or should we say his false humanity learned it (it was incapable of doing so); instead we simply "lean into" the mystery and say that *Jesus* learned it. In the same way, Barth remarks, we do not say our false self has a toothache or our righteous self, but simply "I have a toothache."[10] As with everything regarding our

---

5. See *CD* II/2, 652. The exhaustive nature of the vicarious humanity of Christ, later developed by the Torrances, is outlined here.

6. See *CD* III/2, 213. Regarding John 17:19, "For their sakes I sanctify myself, so that they also may be sanctified in truth": Barth cites extensive biblical support to demonstrate the universality of Jesus' remark, here made to his disciples: "What Jesus is 'for us' or 'for you' in the narrower circle of the disciples and the community He is obviously, through the ministry of this narrower circle, 'for all' or 'for the world' in the wider or widest circle." This universality in Barth will be a constant theme of the present chapter.

7. *CD* IV/1, 280.

8. *CD* IV/1, 280.

9. *Pace* theories of *kenosis* which entail Christ losing divinity or aspects of it in order to become a servant. See *CD* IV/1, 203: God "becomes what He had not previously been. He takes into unity with his Divine being a quite different, a creaturely and indeed a sinful being. To do this he empties Himself, He humbles Himself... He does not need to deny, let alone abandon and leave behind or even diminish His Godhead to do this."

10. *CD* III/2, 394.

humanity, the one person aspect of our lives is derived from Jesus Christ; and just as Jesus Christ is elected and rejected humanity in one person, each of us in our singular person is simultaneously elected and rejected.[11] We are to interpret our own rejection and election inside of that of Jesus Christ:

> In Jesus Christ God has known and loved and chosen and drawn eternally to Himself this very man, in his shameful and wretched isolation, implicated in the sinful fall of Adam and enslaved to Adam's nature . . . wantonly rushing into the arms of divine rejection, and therefore suffering it, the very one whose rejection is borne and annulled by Jesus Christ . . . This, then, is the message which the elect community (as the circumference of the elect man, Jesus of Nazareth) has to approach every man—the promise, that he, too, is an elect man.[12]

In *Church Dogmatics* III/2 Barth elaborates on the importance of Jesus taking on "flesh" while acknowledging the nuances of the word. It is clear to Barth that Jesus became a man in both understandings of the flesh, that flesh of simply the "human mode of being" (true humanity) but also that flesh with "evil connotations" (false humanity, or inhumanity) as the word *sarx* often denotes.[13] Barth describes Jesus' sanctifying struggle against the impurity and deceit of the *sarx* he assumed: "through the whole course of his life He is engaged in that passion and action in the flesh."[14] In the Gospels we most clearly observe in the Garden the two determinations of Jesus' human existence battling until the end, when finally the "weak flesh" succumbs to the "willing spirit" by the power of the Spirit.[15] In his Passion, Jesus transforms the flesh, rendering obedient that which was disobedient; it was a "conquest and renewal of the flesh, its slaying and displacement in the old form and its quickening and coming to life in the new."[16] Again, while perhaps more acute during the Passion, Barth's view is that Jesus' "rectification of human nature" is a lifelong process, "from birth to death, and it is revealed to be such in His resurrection from the dead."[17]

In spite of the historical sequence of these real human events in Jesus' life, however, Barth also asks us to see the simultaneous and proleptic

11. *CD* II/2, 347.
12. *CD* II/2, 317–18.
13. *CD* III/2, 335.
14. *CD* III/2, 337.
15. *CD* III/2, 338.
16. *CD* III/2, 336. Barth calls this elsewhere the "conquest of original sin that took place in Jesus Christ" (*CD* I/2, 355).
17. *CD* I/2, 355.

aspect of Jesus's earthly existence in a way that both includes and transcends sequence. Like justification and sanctification, exaltation and humiliation, Jesus's birth and resurrection interpenetrate one another. "Of the incarnation of the Word of God," remarks Barth, "we may truly say both that in the conception of Jesus by the Holy Spirit and His birth of the Virgin Mary it [the recreation of the cosmos] was a completed and perfect fact, yet also that it was continually worked out in His whole existence and is not therefore exhausted in any sense in the special event of Christmas with which it began."[18]

How seriously can we take Barth regarding this *already-but-not-yet* picture of Jesus' earthly life? Barth refuses, even for Jesus' human life, to endorse a zero-sum process for change, and we are not used to confronting the sanctification question on these terms. It is the same question as to whether real change occurs for us inside of a realism that is already so thoroughly actual. Here Barth tips his hand, for he posits that Jesus is already the resurrected human before he is incarnate "sinner." In fact, Barth says, "The resurrection of Jesus adds nothing new to what happened from the beginning."[19] Can we grasp Barth's meaning here? Are we to understand Jesus Christ as the unchanging Righteous One not *because* of the resurrection but because of *who he is*, i.e., who he is eternally—as the resurrection and the life (John 11:25)—in spite of all of the changes in his temporal and deathly pilgrimage as Jesus of Nazareth?[20] If Barth is right, and the legitimacy of human transformation can be maintained in the context of the already perfect *iustus* of Jesus Christ and every human being, then exciting theological ramifications are ahead. For instance, because the resurrection is a "disclosure and revelation"[21] of what is already true, we begin to see how Jesus' (and thereby every human being's) sanctification connects back to the reality of uncontradicted creation, which points us to the eventual culmination of our

---

18. *CD* III/2, 337.

19. *CD* III/2, 337.

20. See *CD* III/2, 336–37: in Christ, comments Barth, disobedient flesh becomes obedient flesh; irrational flesh becomes rational flesh, the "transformation of the fleshly nature is achieved." In spite of what at first glance are purely sequential phrases, Barth wants us to understand "quickening and coming to life" of the flesh—where "the flesh is slain in its old form and is quickened and comes to life its new"—as revelatory, where displacement has to do with the unveiling of another dimension. Throughout Jesus' life, both dimensions of the flesh are fully present, asserts Barth according to the New Testament. There is never a *partim-partim* between the old and new, a not-yet without an already; the air of resurrection "filled and penetrated the life, words and acts of Jesus, even before his resurrection," states Barth, "from the earliest beginnings the quickening and coming to life of the flesh were in full train."

21. *CD* III/2, 337.

Chalcedonian Change and the Spirit of Righteousness 65

study. In the meantime, it has become more and more apparent that Barth's *simul iustus et peccator* for humanity is based on the simultaneous, total, and mutually exclusive determinations of Jesus' own life in the flesh.

It is apparent that Jesus' words, "For their sakes I sanctify myself," do not mean in Barth's view that Jesus merely sets himself apart as the "already" *iustus* humanity; nor does the phrase mean merely Christ's assumption of a *peccator* humanity that is "not yet" sanctified, i.e., entailing Christ's gradual purification of our sinful humanity over time merely by virtue of his God-nature. The implication of the latter could only be that the incarnation involved an accumulation of rectifying acts which accomplished human righteousness, as in a zero-sum model. Note that in this view Jesus' *iustus* humanity is incomplete if not inconsequential, with the agency for good being a divine force (God, or perhaps Spirit) acting upon Jesus' *peccator* humanity to eventually bring it into *iustus* compliance. Instead of these views, we are surely better off biblically embracing the fact that the Son of God assumes humanity in full *simul* contradiction, under two total determinations, *totus iustus* and *totus peccator*.

For Barth, to "work out your own salvation with fear and trembling" (Phil 2:12) is not a gradualistic enterprise towards perfection for the Christian any more than it was for the human Jesus. Instead, it is a continual revelation of believers' union with Jesus' *iustus* humanity in perfect dependence on the Spirit, an again-and-again participation in the one who turned "right" where the *peccator* flesh beckoned him "wrong." In the same way that we can assert with Chalcedonian confidence that Jesus' divinity did not overwhelm his humanity, we can also assert with Barth that the "fear and trembling" which accompanies the working out of one's salvation "retains its full validity."[22] In other words, it is precisely because it is God's working—stamped with the content of "the living Lord Jesus Christ"[23]—that it can genuinely be every human's working. *Simul* sanctification, then, involves holding on to both the *iustus* and *peccator* aspects of humanity without compromise. Less than Christ-defined views of "sequential" sanctification, for example the misappropriation of 2 Cor 5:17 ("the old is gone, the new has come") mentioned in chapter 1, promote existential 'before and after' conceptions as if shorn from their Christo-anthropological (our death and resurrection in Christ's) moorings. Alternatively, Barth's theologically

---

22. *CD* II/2, 188: The full quotation from Barth reads, "'Work out your own salvation with fear and trembling' retains its full validity, just because the willing and working is God's doing."

23. *CD* IV/3.2, 654. See also: Barth, *Christ and Adam*, 105; "In His life and destiny He represents and anticipates their life and their destiny so that they, without ceasing to be distinct individuals . . . must work out the destiny that overtook them in Him."

disciplined view of sanctification 1) maintains a temporal *iustus-peccator* simultaneity for Christ (and thereby the Christian), and 2) interprets the temporal *iustus-peccator* simultaneity (for Christ and the Christian) to be asymmetrical as revealed by Christ's death and resurrection.[24] Together these components preserve an understanding of growth and change in Christ's life (and thereby the Christian's) within the right economy—that of the Holy Spirit. He is the "Spirit of life," the Spirit who is "life because of righteousness" (Rom 8:2; 8:10).

Venit Spiritus Sancti!

Our study of *iustus* and *peccator* humanity has thus far been largely christological, but the pneumatological aspects of epistemology and sanctification merit our attention as well. What can be said of Barth's view of the sanctifying Spirit's presence in our lives in the midst of our *simul* struggle and transition? Returning to Romans 7, we note Barth's reference to v. 24 where Paul writes, "O wretched man that I am!" This is not, says Barth, an unusual sentiment for a Christian; on the contrary, this cry occurs in a man who at the very same time is gifted with a fullness of the Spirit as testified in Romans 8. We remember Barth's adage that we are measured by what God has done for us. His atoning work exposes our complete lack in and of ourselves ("nothing good dwells within me, that is, in my flesh") while also revealing the complete sufficiency and capacity gifted to us by grace in Christ. Just as there is nothing lacking in the finished work of Jesus Christ, there is no inadequacy of the Spirit given to humans. "We cannot possibly think less of [the Spirit's] work," says Barth, "than we do of that of Jesus Christ Himself."[25] To hold out the Spirit as a second blessing or additional work of grace is to divorce Spirit from Son, as if the Holy Spirit's role is to finish a work Christ has not finished; at that point our anthropocentric penchant for synergizing is suddenly foisted upon the Holy Spirit himself![26]

---

24. It should be constantly recognized that these *simul* situations shared by Christ and the Christian are not only temporal, they are provisional because the *simul* itself is provisional. Additionally, while a Christian interpretation of 2 Cor 5:17 is here in view, the words "the human" could be substituted for "the Christian," especially in light of Barth's conviction to hold together sanctification and conversion as operating within the same economy of the Spirit.

25. *CD* IV/3.1, 358.

26. *CD* I/2, 208. On Barth's view, any degree to which the work of Christ is not coextensive to the work of the Spirit discloses an implicit violation of the *homoousion*. See *CD* I/1, 458: to be "a child of God and to receive the Holy Spirit is one and the same thing."

Chalcedonian Change and the Spirit of Righteousness 67

Conversely, states Barth: "The promise of the Spirit . . . is the power of the resurrection of Jesus Christ . . . In it all things are already given to us and to the world. From the standpoint of the Holy Spirit and His promise, of His presence and action, of the Giver and the gift, there can be nothing lacking here and now to those to whom it is addressed and given."[27] Barth, then, does not segregate the Spirit according to Christian and non-Christian. The Spirit is given to all people without reserve (Acts 2:17).[28] Here two words of clarification are in order. Firstly, Barth does not mean that possession of the Holy Spirit is something that every human being owns as a default accessory or as an internal or eternal right. "Possession of the Spirit is not a human state," says Barth, "Only Jesus has the Spirit lastingly and totally."[29] Secondly, human beings cannot exist without being indwelt by the Spirit. There are indeed intermittent movements of the Spirit amongst humans, visiting us as gifts of "transitory and partial bestowals." However, one must not mistake these movements as concerning a lack of the Spirit's abiding presence in every person.[30] For Barth, the critical distinction is that the presence of the Spirit is always by grace, always because of God's act, always because human beings exist in the humanity of Jesus, who shares his fullness of the Spirit with his brothers and sisters.

Barth constantly turns the tables on those who would want to make the Holy Spirit an exclusifying extra. We noted Barth's exegesis of Acts 2 where, following the Apostle Peter, he declares the Pentecostal blessing to be for the totality of humanity. Barth makes the case that the event of Joel's prophecy being fulfilled at Pentecost is not the exception to the rule but the "central history" of humanity with the same universal scope as the work of Christ. "From God's standpoint, and therefore with final seriousness, we have to do with the totality when we are dealing with the unity between the man Jesus and other men, and therefore with the being and operation of the Holy Spirit."[31] The Holy Spirit should never be taken for granted, but neither is He a "magical third" to be added to or to fulfill Christ's union with every human being; He is an intimate aspect of the gift of union and communion

---

27. *CD* IV/3.1, 359.

28. See *CD* IV/2, 334. Barth is fond of Acts 2:17 and cites it often.

29. *CD* III/2, 334.

30. *CD* III/2, 359. See III/2, 363: "Since we have the Spirit and may therefore live, God is indeed 'in us' according to the Bible. But according to the Bible, the Spirit is always a divine work in man, a divine gift to him."

31. *CD* IV/2, 334.

with Christ established by God with every human being, as veiled as this communion may be.³²

Elaboration is in order regarding what I will continually describe as a main corollary of Barth's actualism: "the exception proves the rule."³³ When human beings in Christ witness something apparently exceptional by means of the Holy Spirit (for instance a great or small act where someone puts others' interests above one's own), the so-called exception actually signifies, or is a window into, the universal reality of Christ that is manifested in the particular human experience. Barth justifies his exception-as-the-rule application out of his conviction as to a) *what reality is* as indicated by Scripture³⁴ and b) what it means for us to experience that reality in profound and miraculous ways. The exception-as-the-rule application is inherently related to Barth's realist conviction that actuality precedes possibility—the actuality of our participation in Christ precedes the possibility of our doing so (participating). Humans can never create reality or add to it, but they can experience it in the Spirit; they can believe and participate in Christ on this existential level *precisely because* of the concrete (mostly hidden) reality in which they fundamentally exist.³⁵ Whether it be the individual (the "spiritual person" of 1 Cor 2:15) or the "Spirit-filled" church, either can function as the microcosm of the whole, a "phenomenal" exception which proves the rule of *iustus* humanity in Christ.³⁶ The subset of persons ("the excep-

---

32. *CD* IV/2, 343.

33. *CD* IV/2, 286. This citation is one of myriad examples where Barth turns to this key principle, said in different ways, throughout *Church Dogmatics*.

34. Biblical themes which pertain to Christo-anthropological reality might include the Kingdom of God (Synoptics), the kingdom of the Son the Father loves (Col 1:13), eternal life (Johannine), and, in general, what it means to be in Christ, Christ being himself reality (Pauline). See *CD* II/1, 606, regarding the Kingdom as Christ's Person: "For He Himself is the kingdom of God which is destined to come but still hidden, and the being of the kingdom is simply His own being."

35. This approach to revealed scriptural truth obviously wards off a humanistic Christian relativism, which offers us a "gospel" that is not real or true for me *until* I experience it or believe it. While Barth's actualism comprehends all things positive in all *iustus* human relationships with God, this should not cloud the fact that Jesus Christ also comprehends, in his incarnate work, all that is essentially un-real and un-eternal, including all aspects of *peccator* humanity, taken to the cross. This will be discussed in depth in chapter 7.

36. By phenomenal I mean something known or perceived by the spiritual senses, not an isolated punctillier spectacle or necessarily a massively astonishing event. It may be helpful to contrast the "exceptions" of spiritual persons with Paul's language describing unspiritual persons in 1 Cor 3:3: they are "behaving according to human inclinations" (NRSV); "acting like ordinary people of the world" (ERV); "acting like mere humans" (NKJV); "acting like people of the world" (NCV); "influenced by your

tion") who are experiencing reality in transformative ways at any given time (for instance, the community at Pentecost) are experiencing the reality of Christ, by the Spirit, in a temporal, representative fashion that witnesses to a cosmic, inclusive truth. That is why "the objective order of all things," insists Barth, should be "understood in accordance with the existence of the believer."[37]

Barth's "exception-proves-the-rule" premise would appear to suggest that, for Barth, even the fullness of the Spirit is itself a universal truth to be experienced by specific people in specific ways.[38] Barth elaborates on the *simul*'s relation to the Spirit in paragraph 66 ("The Sanctification of Man"), where Christians are urged to resist their old "totality" in the flesh and to walk in correspondence with their *totus iustus* determination, or with whom "they already are in their totality, their being in the Spirit." The new being of believers in the Spirit, then, is established long before their temporal choice to become Christians; instead it is a "choice which has already been made, a decision which has been resolved and executed concerning them."[39]

The same tack is taken in Barth's short treatise *Christ and Adam*, his iconic exegesis of Romans 5. Here Barth describes the blessings that are appreciated by believers in Romans 5:1–11, including "peace with God" and "the love of God poured into our hearts by the Holy Spirit, whom he has given us," and then Barth coyly remarks, "If we read that first part of the chapter by itself, we might easily come to the conclusion" that Paul believes Christ's humanity is only determinative for Christians.[40] However, according to Barth, the internal logic of Romans 5 clearly demonstrates that the specific Christian experience of these blessings is evidence of the actual universal blessing, not an addition to it or improvement on it.[41] The fact that peace with God, the Spirit, and faith are not explicitly mentioned in Romans 5:12–21 only reinforces Barth's view that these components are im-

---

corrupt nature and living by human standards" (NOG); "behaving like unregenerate people" (NET); "of the flesh and behaving only in a human way" (ESV). Importantly, because each person is *simul iustus et peccator*, one may prove oneself to be a spiritual or unspiritual person in any given moment.

37. *CD* III/2, 157.

38. Because for Barth the actualities of grace always precede the existential possibilities, it follows that one cannot be "full of the Spirit" unless one is full of the Spirit!

39. *CD* IV/2, 574.

40. Barth, *Christ and Adam*, 109.

41. See *CD* IV/2, 285–86, where Barth expounds on the two key principles he implements in his interpretation of Romans 5, namely that the actual always precedes the existential, and the twin corollary, that in the actualizing event of sanctification which visits certain individuals in time and space, "the exception proves the rule."

plicitly and *already included* in the true, righteous, and dynamic humanity of the true and *iustus* One, the Second Adam.[42] To put it another way, every blessing for everybody is included in Christ's righteousness expounded in Romans 5:12–21; therefore "Our standing as believers is as vv. 1–11 have described it, *because* our standing as men is as vv. 12–21 describe it."[43] Continues Barth, "So it is Christ that reveals the true nature of man . . . Vv. 12–21 are revolutionary in their insistence that what is true of Christians must also be true of all men."[44] "What is said in vv. 1–11 is not just 'religious' truth that only applies to the specially talented, specially qualified, or specially guided men; it is truth for all men, whether they know it or not . . . The assurance of Christians, as it is described in vv. 1–11, has as its basis the fact that the Christian sphere is not limited to the 'religious' sphere. What is *Christian* is secretly but fundamentally identical with what is *universally human*."[45]

Barth has been accused of conflating the Second and Third Persons of the Trinity,[46] but one thing he can never be accused of is conflating the Holy Spirit with humanity or with the human spirit (*a la* Hegel). Over and over again it must be stressed that Barth will grant the Spirit's intimate presence with all human beings on this non-conflationary criteria alone.[47] In the

---

42. Barth, *Christ and Adam*, 109. We are not accustomed to defining *iustus*, or true, humanity in light of the thoroughness of Christ's real and actual subjectivity for us. As strange as it may sound, Jesus Christ has already made humanity's peace with God; he has received the outpouring of the Spirit for us, filling our hearts with God's love; he has had and continues to have *our* faith in God *for us*. This is certainly not a theme reserved for *Christ and Adam*: See CD IV/1, 630: Christ "became the new and righteous man . . . for us and for all men . . . There is not one whose peace with God has not been made and does not continue in Him. There is not one of whom it is demanded that he should make and maintain this peace for himself, or who is permitted to act as though he is the author of it." See also CD IV/2, 288: Jesus Christ represents us "even in our cognition." Epistemology, like pneumatology, cannot be separated from Christology and the gift of true, complete humanity we have been given in Christ.

43. Barth, *Christ and Adam*, 110–11. Italics added.

44. Barth, *Christ and Adam*, 112.

45. Barth, *Christ and Adam*, 111. Italics original.

46. If Barth is guilty of this charge of conflation, so is the Apostle Paul (e.g., Rom 8:9). More positively, Barth's emphasis to maintain the closest possible relationship between Christ and the Spirit is precisely to guard against the pitfall of writing theology "from the perspective of the Holy Spirit's work in us" (phrase in quotes from Anderson, "Problem of Psychologism," 345; cited in chapter 1), preferring instead to anchor God's renewal of humanity in the most concrete historical fashion.

47. Barth's healthy fear of wrongly allocating the Holy Spirit to humanity may explain his reticence to being more direct in presenting the Spirit's fullness as part of the indicative *iustus* determination for every human being.

excerpt below, for instance, while it would be a mistake to imagine "Messianic" as meaning only for Jesus, or only for those who come to faith in Jesus, even worse would be to grant the Spirit to all humans as an inherent "anthropological" possession (thereby engendering a "Messiah complex" contrary to grace). On the contrary, for Barth "Messianic" simply means as revealed uniquely in the Person of Jesus Christ, by grace, for all: "That this Spirit rests on man, is laid on Him and remains over him, that man is full of the Spirit and his being and doing are consequently spiritual, and he himself is spirit because created by the Spirit—these biblical statements are not anthropological but exclusively Messianic. That man in general lives, he owes of course to the Holy Ghost. Hence it can also be said of man in general that the Holy Spirit is given to him, that he receives Him, that he lives by and from the Spirit, that he has the Spirit."[48]

Barth refuses to codify or commodify the work of the Holy Spirit. It is his way of ensuring that we do not commandeer the Holy Spirit into our psychologistic games; the Holy Spirit does not dwell in us in contradistinction to elsewhere or to the exclusion of others. We might say to be "full of the Spirit" for Barth, then, functions as biblical idiom for our operating in the truth of the Spirit's fullness given to humanity.[49] Again, this is a fullness *given*; it is not inherent in humanity. To be "full of the Spirit" is a biblical phrase essentially wedded to Christology and for us purely derivative and relative in nature (after all, who could claim, aside from the Messiah, to have an unadulterated fullness of the Spirit?). We certainly do experience this "fullness" at certain specific times over against others, but this can only be a qualitative or comparative difference. Always careful in the way he uses "progress," Barth describes the transformational dynamic as a revelatory one, or one that progresses "from its present to its future fulness" (i.e., from fullness to fullness). As Barth notes, Paul's words "ever-increasing glory" (2 Cor 3:18) keep any talk of degree and growth as part of an indescribable, non-quantitative economy beyond all zero-sum calculations.[50] Indeed, on Barth's view, believers may anticipate continuing to grow in fullness even

---

48. *CD* III/2, 334.

49. See *CD* III/2, 358: here Barth makes at least an oblique reference in support of our contention in light of Eph 5:18 ("be full of the Spirit"): "By 'Spirit' must always be understood the divine operation of grace in its full scope."

50. *CD* IV/3.1, 359: As for progressing "'from glory to glory,'" Barth states, "Even this is the work of the Lord who is the Spirit, so that it can throw no shadow on the perfection of His work." A comment from Ambrose is appropriate here, even if we are uncertain as to whether he partakes in Barth's view of the exception proving the rule: "For one who is drunk with wine totters and reels, but one who is intoxicated with the Spirit is rooted in Christ" (cited by Hall, *Worshipping with the Church Fathers*, 68).

after the sinful contradiction has been fully removed! Relates Barth: "Even as eternal grace, freed from the whole enshrouding veil of our temporality and corruption, grace will still be the grace of God and not our nature. To that extent, even in the eternal redemption, we shall not be at the goal, and the blessedness of our perfect knowing of God will consist in a being on the way, so that it too will have to be described as *theologia viatorum*."[51]

Even Faith

Having potentially inspired us with his vision for perpetual change even after the consummation, when does our personal transformation *begin*? When it comes to change, what is the import of our individual faith? "The essence of faith is to accept as right what God does... That is why it can and must be said of faith that in and by it we are righteous before God."[52] But wait, whose faith here is in view? Is it ours? If it is ours, insists Barth, it is only ours to the degree our faith is already included in that of Jesus Christ, "the One elected from eternity to be the Head and Saviour of all men, who in time responded to God's faithfulness with human faithfulness as the Representative of all men." Through Christ's birth, suffering, death and resurrection "the change . . . took place for all. In it the turning of all from unfaithfulness to faithfulness took place. In this history of His the Christian life became an event as the life of all."[53]

We will continue to observe that words and phrases typically used by Christians to describe existential change, for instance believing, becoming, quickening, awakening, regenerating, being born again, filling with the Spirit, renewing our hearts, and as we shall discuss, even "participating"—these are all for Barth primarily ontological terms. While Barth does not mean that we should not use these terms (he obviously uses them himself),

---

51. *CD* II/1, 209. Barth can at once say we are already at the goal, having been given fullness, and yet not yet at the goal, acknowledging the Spirit economy of fullness to fullness.

52. *CD* II/2, 583. See *CD* II/1, 159–60: "we have to do the one thing that is needful. We have to believe; not to believe in ourselves, but in Jesus Christ. In Him, along with our enmity against God's grace, our flight from faith too is limited, ended and destroyed. In Him faith finds itself again. In Him the believing man, beyond and despite the darkness which is in himself, finds himself in the light, ready for God."

53. *CD* IV/4, 13. Such comments raise the question as to whether Barth really discerns any difference at all between Christians and unbelievers. We will discuss this important topic in upcoming pages. For now, we can recognize that Barth does see a difference, but it is secondary to our common humanity, a universally shared ontology of human beings in Christ.

he does mean we do not have biblical permission to implement them backwards or to make the secondary meaning the primary meaning. Barth has strong words for this misguided attempt:

> The fact that the change in which man becomes a Christian has its ground and commencement in the history of Jesus Christ characterizes it as a divine happening, in distinction from all the other natural or supernatural changes which are notable enough in their own way. Any description of the Christian life which might seek to assign to it any other basis can only be the description of a tree hewn off from its root. Whatever may become of it, one can never again ascribe its own life to it. It can have its own life only in unity with the root. Similarly, man's own life as the Christian life is possible and actual only in unity with its origin in Jesus Christ.[54]

Before proceeding, we emphasize again that Barth is by no means out to denigrate spiritual experiences of Jesus Christ and his reality. Undoubtedly, the existential faith-event involves the whole person psychologically,[55] emotionally, and spiritually; the event experienced by the person may even have visceral effects. To deny these liberating experiences, says Barth, is to take our "appreciation of the objective superiority too far," creating a wooden Christianity without living Christians! Particularly pertinent to our study is Barth's warning that "even the trinitarian god of Nicene dogma, or the Christ of the Chalcedonian definition, if seen and proclaimed in exclusive objectivity and with no regard for this accompanying phenomenon, necessarily becomes an idol like all others."[56]

We may find it refreshing to hear from Barth that even subjectivity can be overly objectified. He calls this problem "subjectivism from above" when "all anthropology and soteriology are thus swallowed up in Christology."[57] While aware of threats on both fronts, Barth here is out to avoid the overly objective scheme of epistemology while not over-correcting to the opposite scheme of Schleiermacher and Bultmann, where resides "the no less fatal

---

54. *CD* IV/4, 17.

55. Clifford Anderson aptly summarizes that Barth's "anti-psychologistic doctrine of sanctification admits psychological phenomena" even though "subjective experiences of conversion cannot themselves bear any objective weight" ("The Problem of Psychologism in Barth," 351). Just as importantly, asserts Anderson, "if theologians start by describing psychological experiences they will never reach the objective reality of conversion" (345). This point comports exactly to Barth's critique of Neo-Protestantism.

56. *CD* IV/3.2, 655–56.

57. *CD* IV/4, 19.

mystical, liberal or existential picture of Christians without Christ."[58] For Barth, the latter could only be "subjectivism from below," for in this event, "Christology is now swallowed up by a self-sufficient anthropology and soteriology. It need hardly be said that the New Testament witnesses, even when they appeal most strongly to man himself, even in their most urgent calls for repentance, decision, faith, patience and love, never think or speak thus."[59]

It is apparent that Barth views the two poles of subjectivism from above (dehumanizing monergism) and subjectivision from below (humanistic synergism) to be theologically insufficient. What then is his solution? Barth relentlessly contends that the most genuine human subjectivity and meaningful spiritual experiences issue forth out of "true Christocentricity."[60] When Jesus Christ "takes the place" of a person, insists Barth, it is the opposite of oppressive–it is liberating.[61] And again, whose place does Christ take? All person's places, declares Barth, whether they know it or not, this because of a universal commitment made by the true Light who enlightens every person: "It is a pledge to all: What I was and did, I was for you and did for you," and, "It is a promise for all: What I was and did for you, what you already have and are in Me, shall and will, in the same divine power as that in which I was raised from the dead, be manifested and brought to light as the reality of your poor life, as your eternal life." This pledge and promise means, Barth concludes, "Jesus Christ is not just available in some way" for every person, as from a distance; instead, "He is present for, with, and in" every person. Barth's "true Christocentricity," then, can function as a synonym for what we have called Barth's Spirit-charged[62] actualism, his equivalent of Paul's humanising statement "Christ, who is your life" (Col 3:4). In *simul* terms, this is *iustus* humanity.

---

58. *CD* IV/3.2, 656.

59. *CD* IV/4, 20.

60. *CD* IV/4, 19.

61. *CD* IV/4, 21. We will unpack just how Barth is able to hold to true human freedom *within* a christocentric model in chapter 5 and chapter 6.

62. See *CD* IV/4, 29: Barth again confirms that while liberation is a work of the Spirit, it is "not a different work, a second work alongside, behind or after the work of the reconciling covenant action of the one God accomplished in the history of Jesus Christ and manifested in His resurrection."

No *Partim-Partim* in Participation!

"Subjective revelation can consist only in the fact that objective revelation, the one truth which cannot be added to or bypassed, comes to man and is recognised and acknowledged by man. And that is the work of the Holy Spirit. About that work there is nothing specific that we can say. We can speak about it only by sheer repetition, that is, by repeating what is told us objectively, that 'God was in Christ reconciling the world unto himself.' The work of the Holy Spirit is that our blind eyes are opened and that thankfully and in thankful self-surrender we recognise and acknowledge that it is so: Amen."[1]

WE HAVE SPOKEN OF BARTH'S UNAPOLOGETIC INSISTENCE THAT THE *TOTUS iustus* determination of our lives includes the fullness of the Holy Spirit given to humanity in Christ's perfect sanctifying work, even in matters of personal faith and conversion. How then do we square this with Barth's descriptions of the Spirit's epistemic role in differentiating Christians from unbelievers? Most notably, what do we say about Barth's use of *de jure, de facto* language as a manner of explaining human appropriation or of persons "coming to

---

1. *CD* I/2, 239. We return here to the "rare" quote on sanctification indicated in chapter 1, "To live a holy life is to be raised and driven with increasing definiteness from the centre of this revealed truth, and therefore to live in conversion with growing sincerity, depth and precision." By a reliance on "the who" of sanctification—"the centre of this revealed truth"—we are now able to interpret this statement with all of its revelatory objective force. Barth incessantly asks us to recalibrate all understanding of subjective growth from within his dynamic Christo-anthropological paradigm. Jesus Christ, as Barth states elsewhere, "is the source of an objective growth: in him God's confirmation of us grows stronger, the power of his grace increases in my life" (*Heidelberg*, 108).

faith"? Indeed, Barth maintains throughout *Church Dogmatics* that all people are sanctified by what Christ has done for their sakes; likewise, he insists based on the revelation of Jesus Christ that there is no difference ontologically between persons.[2] All are *totus iustus* in the Righteous One. However, Barth also maintains throughout *Church Dogmatics* that Christians belong to God in "a special way" and that they are marked off, having attained to a "real subjectivity" through being awakened to the truth of Jesus Christ by the Holy Spirit.[3]

"Special" Anthropology

Let us turn now to several theologians who display varying grasps of Barth's concept of sanctification—what we might rightly describe as actualization within Actualization (the anthropological uniquely maintained within the Christo-anthropological).[4] Calvinist scholar Anthony Hoekema, author of *Karl Barth's Doctrine of Sanctification*, is one who expresses consternation over Barth's approach to the objective and subjective aspects of sanctification.[5] Citing Barth's *de jure, de facto* language regarding sanctification, Hoekema contends Barth is saying everyone is sanctified objectively, and yet not everyone is sanctified subjectively.[6] To Hoekema this is tantamount to an internal contradiction casting serious doubt on Barth's program of sanctification, not to mention his whole doctrine of God! Here, says Hoekema, Barth "is in real trouble as far as his conception of the Trinity is concerned." Continues Hoekema: "God the Father, [Barth] has said, has sanctified all men in Christ; Jesus has been sanctified by the Father for all men. But the Holy Spirit is only given to some, so as to enable them to grasp

---

2. *CD* III/4, 651–652.

3. See *CD* IV/1, 148; *CD* IV/3.1, 281; *CD* II/2, 322.

4. We capitalize Actualization here to denote Barth's "supreme actuality" (*CD* IV/4, 17), which in this case he is using to describe how the existential activity of human baptism is a powerful sign of the "supreme actuality" of universal human baptism as it has occured in the death of Christ: "it taking place now and here inasmuch as it took place then and there."

5. Hoekema, *Karl Barth's Doctrine of Sanctification*.

6. Hoekema, *Doctrine of Sanctification*, 11. In this connection Hoekema cites *CD* IV/2 (511): "The sanctification of man, his conversion to God, is, like his justification, a transformation, a new determination, which has taken place *de jure* for the world and therefore for all men. *De facto*, however, it is not known by all men, just as justification has not *de facto* been grasped and acknowledged and known and confessed by all men, but only by those who are awakened to faith." Note that in no way does Barth say here what Hoekema accuses him of, namely that "objectively all men are sanctified, whereas subjectively not all men are sanctified" (Hoekema, 10).

their sanctification and make it effective. Why? Is God at odds with Himself? Do the Father and Son desire one thing, and the Holy Spirit another? Do the Scriptures ever give us the impression that there are elect people to whom the Holy Spirit is not given?"[7]

If Hoekema has indeed "caught" Barth, exposing him with these rhetorical questions, we cannot begrudge Hoekema's accompanying statement that "Barth's contention that all men are objectively sanctified is meaningless." But from our last chapter—outlining Barth's view of human subjectivity as existing *within* divine-human objectivity—we recognize immediately that Hoekema is operating on a series of mistaken assumptions. While Barth would agree with Hoekema that Scripture never posits that there are elect people from whom the Spirit is withheld, Barth would also insist with Hoekema that the Trinity is not to be divided, nor the Son and Spirit placed "at odds." That Hoekema gets Barth wrong is clearly attributable to his simplistic equation of Barth's *de jure* and *de facto* sanctification to objective and subjective sanctification, respectively. A person sanctified *in principle* but not *in fact* is simply not sanctified—to this Barth would heartily concur!

That Barth apparently does not fathom how he could fall prey to such obvious errors shows that he is operating in a wholly different paradigm from Hoekema. For Barth, the fact that all are elect, and all are given the Spirit, provides the unique ontological context for real human subjectivity, taking seriously both our being in-act and our act in-being. Our true human "subject-self" is none other than Jesus Christ, the one who substitutes for, and represents, every human being to God.[8] What Barth describes as "the place" or location of true human subjectivity—the place from which all Christian expression of faith, prayer, confession, etc., derive—is a Person.[9] As Barth states later in the same volume, "His name, and therefore He

7. Hoekema, *Doctrine of Sanctification*, 22.

8. CD IV/1, 755: "What do I acknowledge and recognize and confess as this subject? . . . The first thing is that Jesus Christ is, in fact, just for me, that I myself am just the subject for whom He is. That is the point. That is the newness of being, the new creation, the new birth of the Christian."

9. CD IV/2, 658–59: To the extent that any human beings live the Christian life, they owe it to the being of Christ. He is "the air which they breathe, the ground on which they stand and walk. As we are told in John 15:4f, they have no being or life apart from Him, just as the branches are nothing apart from the vine . . . 'Without me ye can do nothing.' But they need not try to do anything without Him. He *is* the vine, and they *are* the branches" (italics original). While the Holy Spirit is not himself described as the vine in John 15, this environment of real subjectivity is a Trinitarian one because of how God has breathed into us at creation and chosen to reveal himself to us in Jesus Christ, the true human who fully and perfectly relies on the Spirit in his life of

Himself, is the place where salvation took place for all men . . . His name is a field of force."[10] To elaborate, the force field Barth describes is the dynamic matrix of grace where Jesus Christ by the power of the Spirit lives to the Father and fulfills the covenant for us in response to God ("I will be true to you, you shall be true to me"). This is the covenant which, as Barth emphasizes, includes and transcends the history of Israel and is actually part of the fabric of creation itself.[11] Astoundingly, it is not only a covenant which Christ fulfills from humanity's side, but one which Christ fulfills from *both* sides: "For—this was our starting-point—He, Jesus Christ is the holy God and sanctified man in one. In His person God orders and man obeys . . . In His person God's gracious Yes to man, which is the meaning and content of his command, coincides with man's grateful Yes to God; the command of God with the obedience of man."[12]

Barth obviously subverts the typical objective—subjective faith paradigm by making Jesus Christ as mediator both the object and subject of faith. This is precisely why substituting *de jure* for the objective component and *de facto* for the subjective aspect of sanctification is to shortchange the mediating role of Jesus Christ for all things human, thereby jeopardizing what Barth presents as the objectivity of true human subjectivity.[13] It appears lost on Hoekema that Barth's actualization is working on two levels,

---

filial obedience, the same Spirit in whom we are given to rely in union with Christ and apart from whom the ascended Christ would not be present to us.

10. *CD* IV/4, 94.

11. *CD* IV/1, 38–39. Hoekema comments on this covenantal language of Barth's without understanding Barth's full intent.

12. *CD* II/2, 778. We say our personal yes to God in union with the one who has already said and is saying our most personal yes to God for us. Grace is a Yes to a Yes! For other examples in *CD*: II/2, 188; IV/1, 570, 646; IV/2, 180, 241, 271; IV/3.1, 47, 379, 381; IV/4, 66. In Barth's *Humanity of God*, 47, there is a very similar description to the above quotation. It is noteworthy that Barth includes all human aspects in Christ's vicarious representation, including the epistemological and, as with the above, not only obedience but also gratitude: "in this oneness Jesus Christ is the Mediator, the Reconciler, between God and man. Thus He comes forward to *man* on behalf of *God* calling for and awakening faith, love and hope, and to *God* on behalf of *man*, representing man, making satisfaction and interceding. Thus He attests and guarantees to man God's free *grace* and at the same time attests and guarantees to God man's free *gratitude* . . . Thus He is in His Person the covenant in its fulness, the Kingdom of Heaven which is at hand, in which God speaks and man hears, God gives and man receives, God commands and man obeys" (italics original). See also McSwain, *Movements of Grace*, for an exposition of this theme of the double movement of grace.

13. If *de jure* is "in principle" and *de facto* is "in practice," or "in actual fact," the unavoidable hypothetical element introduced by the former term can be problematic for understanding Barth's actualism.

and that when Barth says one's sanctification is subjectively actualized by the Spirit, it patently does not mean that this one's sanctification is not "already-actual" in the Spirit. Hoekema's confusion is again due to misinterpreting the nuances of Barth's universal *simul* application. In other words, he does not understand all matters of human subjectivity, including epistemology and pneumatology, be be included in the determination of *iustus* humanity. The result is Hoekema's misconstrued summary of Barth: "the Holy Spirit is only given to some, so as to enable them to grasp their salvation and make it effective."[14] Hoekema surmises that Barth has simply relocated Hoekema's prized double predestination schema into the Third Article, where the Spirit selects some people to the exclusion of others. Surely Barth is not so ignorant as to trade one form of determinism (Dortian Calvinism which he abhors), for another, pneumatological version! At this point let us turn to the specific passage in *Church Dogmatics* which Hoekema believes provides an undeniable foundation for his disparagements:

> It is the Holy Spirit, the being and work of the Holy Spirit in this special form, that is still lacking in the world at large. That God did not owe His Son, and in that Son Himself, to the world, is revealed by the fact that He gives his Spirit to whom He will. The hand of God the Reconciler is over all men. Jesus Christ was born and died and rose again for all. The work of the atonement, the conversion of man to God, was done for all . . . To that extent, objectively, all are justified, sanctified and called. But the hand of God has not touched all in such a way that they can see and hear, perceive and accept and receive all that God is for all and therefore for them . . . But the hand of God has touched and seized Christians in this way—which means the presence and activity of the Holy Spirit.[15]

Exactly to what extent is Barth making the blatant internal contradiction Hoekema supposes? While Barth's comment "still lacking in the world at large" seems to dispute our contention of a fullness of the Spirit for all, we immediately note that Barth is talking of the Holy Spirit in this "special form." What is this special form, and what does it mean when he speaks elsewhere of Christians belonging to Christ in a "special way?" Barth can at one time speak of the baptism of the Holy Spirit visiting certain individuals

---

14. Hoekema, *Doctrine of Sanctification*, 22. One has to wonder if Hoekema here has projected the Calvinist distinction of effectual and ineffectual calling onto Barth's epistemology. That a subset of humanity has awakened to faith by the Holy Spirit expressly does not mean some human beings do not have the Spirit.

15. Hoekema, *Doctrine of Sanctification*, 21, quoting from *CD* IV/1, 148.

in this second, existential, or special form, and the sanctifying baptism of all individuals in the first, primary, or ontological form. These two aspects are the "two forms of the one factor." For Barth, the fact that these forms are actually "identical" to one another does not diminish the distinctiveness or significance of the second form. It only means the second form, while a manifestation of the real, does not in any way add to the first, even while actualizing it.[16] So in the ultimate and actual and ontological sense, there is no lack of the Spirit, but in the second form, the existential realm, the work of the Spirit is still lacking full manifestation. We see this existential lack every day in our lives and in people around us. The fullness of the Spirit is hidden. As always, Barth does not want to collapse the Holy Spirit into the human spirit, so he remarks about God not "owing" the Spirit to anyone; "He gives His Spirit to whom he will."[17]

It is important to notice what Barth does and does not say in this passage about specific manifestations of the Spirit. He says the hand of God is over all persons; this statement is directly related to the objective aspect of reconciliation, including justification, sanctification (including all aspects of human subjectivity) and calling. Then he talks about the hand "touching" all persons, albeit in two different "ways." These "ways," however, can be seen as more descriptive of the participatory responses of persons than they are prescriptive of God's touching some to the exclusion of others. When we observe those who are "seized" and become Christians, we give credit where credit is due; as Barth relates, it is only by "the presence and activity "of the Holy Spirit that this can happen. However, Hoekema's logical misstep is to assert that Barth means it is by the hand of God when it *does* happen and it is also by the hand of God when it *does not* happen. In his nuanced view of God's sovereignty, Barth will not go there; he will not make God party to the falsehood of unbelief, nor will he try to explain evil or what he considers to be un-reality. Importantly for Barth, no one is *not* included in the good work of the Spirit in the sanctifying, converting, subjective dimension of grace, and the fact that some come to faith while others do not simply cannot be explained.

Hoekema fails to realize Barth's realist premise that God's choosing of humanity includes every human being choosing God, and that Barth's use of *de facto* has absolutely nothing to do with humans or with God (the Spirit) taking an additional step to make human subjective response "effective."

---

16. *CD* IV/4, 29–30.

17. We could only speculate as to whether this phrase provides a trigger for Hoekema to a hyper-Calvinist rendition of Romans 9, thereby inhibiting him from seeing Barth's meaning.

As we have seen, the *simul iustus et peccator* is the antidote to all of these humanistic and synergistic intermediating tendencies. A great advantage of the *simul* is that it leaves our epistemological questions in the right places. The non-gradualist gap left between the stark, mutually exclusive determinations of the *simul* (the gap that every pundit wants to fill in or bridge) is actually our friend, because it opens us to the Holy Spirit to do His work—His miraculous, unexplainable work: "Just as our spirit cannot produce the Word of God, so too it cannot receive it . . . A sheer miracle must happen to [a person] . . . if his life shall be a true Christian life, which is a life within the hearing of God's word. This miracle is the office of the Holy Spirit."[18]

The *simul* has guided us to "practice" the habit of seeing with Chalcedonian eyes how two things are happening in one space. From this perspective it should be increasingly clear what Barth means by his phrases that the Holy Spirit makes persons Christians or that Christians do belong to Christ in "a special way." We misinterpret Barth by putting the "special" accent on our experience if by this we mean some people are special to the exclusion of others. Again, we continually strive to root our language about humanity in the *simul* and in the original Person of the *simul*, Jesus Christ. "Special" for Barth is rooted in the *iustus* determination of Jesus Christ and in all humanity *iustus* in him. It is therefore a Christo-anthropological term, first and foremost, not an existential one. We are not used to thinking of Jesus Christ as the original Adam, before the fallen Adam of Romans 5. Barth is clear about this: "Here the new point is that the *special* anthropology of Jesus Christ—the one man for all men, all men in the one man—constitutes the secret of "Adam" also, and so is the *norm* of *all* anthropology."[19] It is apparent that, on Barth's view, "special" is actually the norm.

But again, if "special" is the norm for Barth, how can "special" have any helpful, discriminatory meaning at all? It must be emphasized that Barth is not trying to create a flat experiential landscape when it comes to Christian encounters with the Spirit; Barth likens concrete manifestations of the reality of the Spirit to rising "mountain peaks out of the plain of God's general presence."[20] Barth is not asking us to "dumb down" the "special presence" of God as the Spirit moves in particular circumstances, but only that we take a higher view of the "general presence" of God. Notes Barth, "It is only the One who is present in the special manner and place who is also the God present in the world as a whole,"[21] and continuing a few pages later, "We

---

18. Barth, *Holy Spirit and the Christian Life*, 10–11.
19. Barth, *Christ and Adam*, 36; italics original.
20. *CD* II/1, 477.
21. *CD* II/1, 478. See II/1, 484: "It is the one unique and simple presence, the

therefore cannot speak of the relativity of the special presence of God without speaking of the reality of the special presence of God."²² It is obvious that for Barth the relationship of the "general presence" to the "special presence" of God is not remotely similar to the Calvinist contrast between "common grace" and "special grace" (or "effectual grace").

The *Simul* and *de jure–de facto*

After extricating Barth from Hoekema's "would-be" prison of contradiction, we might do well, without coming to the same conclusions as Hoekema, to question Barth's distinction between the *de jure* and *de facto* aspects of sanctification. Is it possible that Barth unwisely reintroduces anthropocentric space that he does not want to reintroduce when it comes to this distinction? Did he feel he was being overly objective and too severe with his *simul*, deciding to accommodate more typical perspectives on human subjectivity? One critic has proffered that, after Barth's sections on "The Christological Basis for Sanctification" and "The Objectivity and Actuality of Sanctification" (both CD IV/2, paragraph 66), in which he provides great examples of the thoroughness of grace, Barth falls off: "even one as deeply concerned from first to last with the theocentrism and Christocentrism as is Barth must acknowledge the subjective appropriation that makes this reconciliation a personal reality."²³ Does Barth make this kind of intentional allowance? Does he make an unintentional one?

---

proper presence of God as the one and simple God in His creation, in which both His special presence in all its diversity and also His general presence with its dynamic identity possess their beginning and their end."

22. *CD* II/1, 483.

23. Spross, "Doctrine of Sanctification," 66. By the time of *CD* IV/3, Barth certainly does not show himself impervious to criticism that he has supposedly conflated the Spirit with Christ or, as contrasted against Bultmann, minimalized existential Spirit-experiences. For example, there are instances in *CD* IV/3.1 See 350–57, where Barth focuses, almost to the extreme, on the promise of the Holy Spirit and particularly the Spirit's special movement in the existential events of our "temporal" or "historical sphere." This relates especially to one's becoming a Christian, or to being "spiritual" as opposed to "unspiritual." At these times, where Barth's language about pneumatology and epistemology threatens to ignore everything that came before, his language must be kept well inside the consistent framework of Barth's theological actualism to be coherently grasped. Readers of Barth, seizing what we might call "existentialist friendly sections" like this in *CD*, might unfortunately operate without our principles for Barth's actualism, i.e., that epistemological actuality always precedes epistemological possibility and that Holy Spirit experiences and actions are not exceptions to the rule but rather exceptions which *prove* the rule. We will discuss such an example in the section below. In reference to the section noted here (from *CD* IV/3.1), it is

We have defined Barth's actualism as the theological concept that real human subjectivity and all levels of human participation (for all persons) are contained comprehensively in the person of Jesus Christ, in the freedom and power of the Holy Spirit. I have mentioned what we can now formalize as twin corollaries to Barth's Christo-anthropological actualism that must always be kept before us: 1) actuality precedes possibility on every level, and 2) the exception proves the rule. Together these corollaries comprise the Christo-anthropo-logic that, because "there is no one who is not participating in Him,"[24] when humans *do* participate in actions of sanctification and conversion, it is because, in Christ, they are already doing so. Additionally, even though phenomenal Holy Spirit experiences cannot be quantifiably captured, to the extent that we can apprehend these manifestations, we can define them not as exceptions *to* the rule, but as exceptions *which prove* the rule of our *iustus* humanity in Christ. These manifestations—actions that

---

readily apparent that unbelievers can live as if what is "already actualised" (280) is "non-actual" (354). Indeed, acting "as if" Christ is not there can fuel the perception of a separation of the non-believer and Christ or the Spirit (354). But while there is, in a sense, a perceived lack of the Spirit, or a factual lack of Christian activity, Barth refuses to "simply" say that the unbeliever lacks these things, for in the dimensions of reality not yet perceived, this person is indeed already the "recipient, bearer and possessor" of the promise of Christ and the Spirit (355). The fact that one "lacks" is Barth's way of saying that one is not yet at the place of experiencing *no lack*, i.e, the fulness one already has in Christ (Col 2:10) remains in *simul* contradiction. That is why, in *simul* terms, Barth chasens believers in this world to also always consider themselves unbelievers. Acting "as if" or looking "as if" they are outside the faith cannot undo the actual reality, even if the Spirit's work is apparently "wasted on them" (540). One need only to read the first pages of the very same *CD* part-volume IV/3 to see Barth re-establish this actualist frame by denigrating all Bultmannesque efforts to assign value to subjective revelatory experiences without due credit to the foundation of actual objective, subjective, and therefore universal reconciliation. See *CD* IV/3, 10: "when it is a matter of the Christian community and the life of the individual Christian, we shall have to speak of the work of the Holy Spirit in which the event of reconciliation is concretely active and perceptible in this character of self-declaration . . . But, as already indicated, it does not have this character only when it is active and perceptible in this work . . . this work of the Holy Spirit creates new facts only to the extent that the revelatory character of reconciliation is confirmed in it." Of this basis of reconciliation Barth continues, "This objectivity of even [reconciliation's] revelatory character must be emphasized so expressly because misunderstanding can so easily creep in, as if the problem of the knowledge, understanding and explanation of reconciliation . . . were really a problem of the theory of human knowledge and its spheres and limitations, its capacities and competencies, its possible or impossible approximation to this object. Only too easily the reference to the enlightening work of the Holy Spirit can be understood as the final and then, like a *Deus ex machina*, the very doubtful word of such a theory of knowledge."

24. *CD* IV/2, 271.

bear witness to reality—may be less obvious than we would like, even in the community of faith. Barth therefore recognizes that humanity's ongoing participation in Christ is as hidden as it is counterintuitive.

As we have already seen, Barth's actualism is easily misunderstood; for all Christ has done for every human in the Spirit, hypothetical factors can still be mistakenly inserted which dictate that sanctification is not actual or personal until a final step takes place. By its very nature, the verb form of actual, "to actualize," gives the impression of a move from incomplete to complete, as if something is not actual until it is actualized; it is not difficult to see how *de jure-de facto* language fit into such a context could be misleading. In his book *Participation in Christ: An Entry into Karl Barth's Church Dogmatics*, Adam Neder expands Barth's *de jure-de facto* motif into a reference point from which to articulate Barth's entire program of sanctification; unfortunately his analysis betrays an inconsistent grasp of Barth's principles of true human subjectivity.[25] It is only in acts of faith and obedience, according to Neder, that the "objectively true becomes subjectively true." On Neder's view, the Holy Spirit makes present the objective and future truth in this occasion of faithful human response. The objective truth, then, is a promise that is future, apparently for all people, but there is not a present subjective truth—an ongoing *iustus* determination in Christ—for all people.[26] Neder's overall reading unavoidably shifts the locus of participation to obedient acts as a way of actualizing sanctification *as if it is not already personally actualized* for every individual person.

God's being is in his act, and his act is in his being.[27] Purely derivatively, and by grace alone, Barth's anthropological ontology in Christ is likewise

---

25. Neder, *Participation in Christ*. Neder begins by helpfully reminding us that, for Barth, Christ's presence in human beings is not an inherent anthropological quality, but only by grace. His initial portrayal of Barth's *simul*—the *totus peccator* aspect communicating our utter dependence of God's grace for the purposes of obedience—is also sound (12). When it comes to the *iustus* aspect, I appreciate Neder's appraisal that Barth resists static substantial categories, which can be described apart from God's being-in-act: there can be no "essence" without "actualization" (97n.). Neder rightly maintains that Barth's theology is not occasionalist, citing Barth's comment (103) that "the command of God secretly fills every moment of our lives" (*CD* II/2, 612). However, because he does not define the command so as to include fullest human subjectivity (Christo-anthropological actualism), Neder, not unlike other interpreters, fails to consistently provide a robust assessment of Barth's actualization and therefore of *iustus* humanity.

26. Neder, *Participation in Christ*, 55–56.

27. *CD* IV/3.2, 534. See *CD* III/2, 347; Barth claims Acts 17:28 is "the missionary message of Paul." See *CD* II/1, 475; also *CD* IV/2, 53, where Barth takes pains to distinguish Paul's appropriation of a Greek playwright from Pantheism.

construed. Act and being are never separated for any reason. Has Neder seized upon one aspect of Barth's articulation (i.e., the idea of living *to* sanctification instead of *from* it), creating for himself an imbalanced viewpoint in favor of being-in-act over act-in-being? If so, what evidences Neder's move in this perilous direction? Fundamentally it is his interpretation that, for Barth, union with Christ and the indwelling of the Spirit do not apply to everyone universally. When the summons is heard, asserts Neder, humans "embrace it by joining themselves to Christ." Neder's misreading of *CD* 4/3.2 (paragraph 71.3) portrays a view that only in our active response, in our becoming Christians, does Christ enter us and unite himself to us.[28]

Neder wants to promote Barth's program of sanctification and participation as "thoroughly actualistic."[29] He correctly points out that there are times in *Church Dogmatics* when, in Neder's words, "union with Christ" functions as "a synonym" for "*de facto* participation in Christ."[30] Yet, granting his comment about *de facto* participation in Christ, how might Neder describe *de jure* participation with Christ? In Neder's mind, is Barth proposing a different ontology for non-*de facto* participants? Are they not also united to Christ? If righteous union with Christ and ongoing participation in him is not actual, ontological and universal, can we escape the conclusion that for Neder the *de jure–de facto* distinction has morphed into something different from Barth's intention (i.e., a dualism)? As with other theologians, perhaps a desire not to promote Barth as an outright universalist has

---

28. Neder, *Participation in Christ*, 79–80. See 85. Apparently oblivious to Barth's rules of Christo-anthropological actualism as we have described them, Neder's analysis is symptomatic of readers of Barth who have underestimated Barth's actualism and have set off on a misguided trajectory. In keeping with the corollary of actuality before possibility, Barth in the referenced section of *CD* is adamant about that fact that one cannot be united with Christ unless one *is* united with Christ; the experience of being united with Christ is therefore a fresh expression of an established truth. For humans to "enter in to their union" (*CD* 4/3.2, 540) with Christ is for them to live into what is real. This union has not only been established by Jesus Christ as God, "the Subject who initiates and acts decisively in this union" (541) but it is also established by Jesus Christ as the human Subject, "the only legitimate partner of the covenant"(544) with God. Thus, states Barth, to believe is for a person "to do the natural thing proper to him as the man he is in Christ and therefore in truth," and therefore, Barth continues, the "decision or leap of his faith, obedience and confession consists in the fact that he takes himself seriously as the man he is and recognises himself to be in Jesus Christ instead of immediately forgetting his true self" (544). This person "unites himself with Christ," Barth concludes, "because in truth he is not outside Him but within Him" (545).

29. Neder, *Participation in Christ*, 78, 80.

30. Neder, *Participation in Christ*, 78. "Union with Christ *happens* in revelation," Neder asserts correctly (xiv), but it happens in revelation because it pre-exists revelation. It happens because it is and has been happening.

induced Neder to promote a Barth who is less "thoroughly actualistic" than Neder himself avows?[31]

Neder's interpretation of Barth's actualism appears uncomfortably close to Schleiermacher's concept of "actualisation" whereby, critiques Barth, "the encounter of man with God . . . is to be understood as the actualisation of a generally demonstrable religious capacity of man."[32] On Barth's view, Schleiermacher's approach evinces the virus of Neo-Protestantism, the introduction of an anthropocentric subjectivity, or a "possibility to actuality" framework.[33] Conversely, it bears repeating that Barth describes the *iustus* person as "the man who goes forward to the goal of his righteousness, who has indeed already arrived, who is alive there as a righteous man."[34] While not to the degree of Schleiermacher, Neder's depth of actualism (or lack of depth) prompts a slew of questions. If people do not believe, or obey the summons, are they still obedient in Christ? If people do not respond to the summons, are they still united to Christ and indwelt by the Spirit? What about people who do not hear the good news: are they *de facto* sanctified? What about those with cognitive impairments: are they less sanctified than those who actively acknowledge Christ's decision on their behalf as the reality of their lives?

As with Hoekema, Neder interprets Barth's *de jure-de facto* terminology in such a way as to aid and abet the extraction of the existential events of our sanctification from the objective truth of our sanctification in Christ, as if to give them their own ground.[35] For Neder, Barth's "grace" is appar-

---

31. E.g., Greggs, *Barth, Origen and Universal Salvation*. Like Neder, Greggs unfortunately tends to a limited, under-realized, view of Barth's actualism. See Greggs's discussion delineating passive (universal) and active (Christian) participation (33), and his embracing of Barth's *de jure-de facto* language for the same purpose (135).

32. *CD* I/1, 193.

33. See *CD* I/2, 238–52 for a penetrating discussion of the relationship of subjective and objective revelation. Barth contends that the danger of Neo-Protestantism is rooted in its abandonment of "the insight that the Holy Spirit is none other than the Spirit of Jesus Christ" (250).

34. *CD* IV/1, 576. When it comes to sanctification, in Barth's view persons are home before they start: "still on the way, and yet already at the goal" (*Heidelberg*, 93). See *CD* IV/1, 591, where Barth comments similarly about a believer's justification: "The completion of his justification has precedence over its commencement."

35. Another contributing factor to Neder's underestimation of the thoroughness of Barth's subjectivism could be Neder's emphasis on Barth's words "guarantee" and "promise"—this cannot help but accent Barth's actualism to the future and away from the present; it then becomes all too easy for actualism to morph into potentiality or possibility, thereby vacating all objective content. Küng's elucidation is helpful at this point: "The promise is pledged now, here, today, in the midst of this present time. It

ently only as good as being joined to Christ, which everyone is not; it is in this sense that his version of participation "misses us." Perhaps unwittingly, Neder has replaced Barth's model of participation and real, hidden, human holiness with a hypothetical holiness waiting to be realized. We continue to hold that for Barth what is true for Christ in the event of Christ's human subjectivity is also true, objectively by grace, for all individual persons in all aspects of their genuine subjectivity. In Barth's words, every person is "already immitted into this event."[36] Unless we enfold subjective participation as part and parcel of objective sanctification, the idea being that we are all personally included and already participating in Christ, then how can there be real objective truth? And, if there is no objective truth, how could there be such a thing as "participation" (which by its very nature is always *in* the truth). Fundamentally, if Neder is right about Barth, Hoekema is right about Barth, and there is no inbetween: "Barth's contention that all men are objectively sanctified is meaningless."[37]

Let us be plain about this: *de jure* participation for Barth only makes sense when *de facto* participation is established in advance. *De facto* functions as logically primary to *de jure*.[38] Neder's mistake is to posit that Barth's use of *de jure-de facto* introduces a before-after sequence from non-union to union. This ignores the previously established, actual union with Christ for all people revealed in the legitimate sequence of the salvation history of Jesus Christ.[39] We have outlined how Barth imports the legitimate sequence (i.e., that of the Christ event, into Luther's *simul*) but the illegitimate sequence of Neder's does not comport with Barth's *simul* at all. By introducing the wrong kind of before-after, the simultaneous and universal aspects of the *totus peccator* and *totus iustus* determinations are compromised. As with Luther, Neder's persons do not have a thoroughgoing *iustus* determination

---

is entirely certain, direct and real. Man even now possesses the totality" (Küng, *Justification*, 65). If, conversely, Neder firmly held to "guarantee" and "promise," without the full Christo-anthropological actualism we are promoting, he would be left with universalism or limited atonement.

36. *CD* II/1, 31.

37. Hoekema, *Doctrine of Sanctification*, 21. Cited above.

38. To redeploy Nimmo's terminology (Introduction), "active participation" is logically prior to "passive participation."

39. See *CD* IV/2, 300: Union with Christ, asserts Barth, is every person's "sure foundation"; it is a fact not contingent on "our recognition and response." See *CD* IV/2, 300. This principle need not contradict Neder's contention that in other places Barth speaks of union with Christ as synonymous with *de facto* participation, this as long as *de facto* participation is described as a Spirit-led manifestation of actuality and as not a further stage of actualization (or especially as a transition from non-union to union). It is precisely on this point that Neder is unclear.

until they are Christians.[40] Therefore, to the extent Neder categorizes persons as receiving union (and therefore *iustitia*) as judged by their existential actions, he is bound to underestimate sin. Without the protection of the *simul*, the seriousness of sin can only fade into the background because it is contained in the "before" of an illegitimate *de jure-de facto* existential sequence. To put it another way, because acts of obedience reveal union with Christ, Neder's non-*simul* sequencing forces him to make definitive judgments about the goodness of isolated actions: "where obedience takes place, it is exclusively obedience." He is critical of Barth for failing to follow suit.[41]

Neder's inadequate perspective on Barth's actualism fails to consider that Barth *does* acknowledge that there is purely good action in human behavior, only that it is invariably obscured by the overlap of the *peccator* determination. In our day to day *simul iustus et peccator* experience, then, taken as a whole, our participatory activity is purely good to the extent that it is. Only in reality, *sans peccator*, is it pure, pure and simple. This is an appropriate time to introduce what I call a third corollary (along with the twin corollaries of *actuality before possibility* and *the exception proves the rule*) of Barth's Christo-anthropological actualism: the *to-the-extent* deduction. This third corollary protects us from the trap of another form of psychologism (chapter 1), a moralistic temptation to capture any action as simply and purely good. Because precise quantification is never possible, one lives in correlation to the reality of Christ only "to the extent" that one does, and always in the miraculous power of the Spirit.

The simultaneous presence of the *totus iustus* and the *totus peccator* determinations ensures that there will always be a "to the extent" aspect in play for every human action in this world. To misunderstand this is to misunderstand Barth's *simul*. Therefore, it appears obvious that Neder disagrees with Barth because Barth's *simul* disagrees with Neder's rendition of *de jure-de facto*! By insisting that, when a person becomes a Christian, the Christian moves from *de jure* to *de facto* "status" and over to the other side of the ontological ledger, or by insisting that by his acts of obedience the Christian leaves the *peccator* behind and enters a *iustus* dimension different

---

40. Neder is correct when he advances: "it is clear that for Barth, as for Luther before him, the *simul* doctrine denotes an eschatology"(85). However, Neder (along with Luther) has not only underestimated the scope of *iustus* humanity, Neder has also underestimated the *present-tense* comprehensive concreteness of Barth's eschatological realism. On Barth's view, as soon as Christ has done and is doing something *for us*, it is never *without us*. Again, when it comes to *iustus* humanity, the future means now.

41. Neder, *Participation in Christ*, 85–86. Neder's view betrays an un-nuanced or un-dimensional view of human behavior resulting from the lack of a universal *totus-totus simul* construct.

from others who are not united to Christ and indwelt by the Spirit, Neder has painted himself into a holiness corner.

In a way more nuanced than Hoekema, who rawly equates Barth's *de jure* with objective sanctification and *de facto* with subjective sanctification, Neder presents a Barth who ostensibly keeps the subjective aspects of participation within the objective, but who ultimately draws a line between actual (*de jure*) and actualized (*de facto*) participation in Christ. In the end, Neder's reading simply offers a more sophisticated version of splitting subjective from objective; in light of Barth's Christo-anthropological actualism, we might say Neder is splitting "subjective from Subjective." Where does this leave us? Based on the potential for theological confusion, can we at least pose the question to Barth regarding the wisdom of using *de jure-de facto* at all? Is Barth to take some of the blame for leading Neder and Hoekema down their wayward paths? Before issuing a verdict on that score, let us turn to one more theologian who has quite a different view on Barth's epistemology.

Actual Subjectivity

In *Regarding Karl Barth*, Trevor Hart offers us a reading and explanation of Barth's epistemology that does not allow human subjectivity to escape the freedom found uniquely in the objective truth of Jesus Christ. Firstly, notes Hart, Barth takes Acts 17:28 fully seriously; human *being* exists in the *being* of God, the being of God revealed to us in the Son who is *homoousios* (one being) with the Father. Jesus Christ is himself the Creator who takes on flesh and becomes a human being like us. "We exist, we have our being, only in relation to him; a relationship which we cannot deny without deceiving ourselves, and out of which we cannot opt without ultimate consequences." Hart continues, "Now what we are and who we are are matters no longer determined simply by our relationship with God as such, but precisely by our relationship to this man, *Deus incarnates*."[42] Hart discusses theological variants on how "actuality" is understood, but he reminds us that actuality for Barth is based first and foremost on *who Jesus Christ actually is*. It is in the history of Jesus Christ "that the divine intention for humankind has been actualized (not just anticipated)."[43] Secondly, the actual truth and historical

---

42. Hart, *Regarding Karl Barth*, 59.

43. Hart, *Regarding Karl Barth*, 58. Note that for Hart, *contra* Neder's reading, Barth's actualism is not weighted towards the future. Again, because of Jesus Christ there is no human being who is not actualized human being. But there is such a thing as actualization within Actualization, actualizing within Actualizing; this is what we

reality of Jesus Christ gives us the freedom "to discover ourselves 'in him.'"[44] What Barth says below about justification equally pertains to sanctification:

> We have found it at the place where it is reality and truth, the reality and truth which applies to us and comprehends us, our own reality and truth . . . It is all true and actual in Him and therefore in us. It cannot, therefore, be known to be valid and effective in us first, but in Him first, and because in Him in us. We are in Him and comprehended in Him, but we are still not He Himself. Therefore it is all true and actual in this Other first and not in us.[45]

While exhaustingly reminding us (above) that human agency is derived from Christ's true history, Barth presents us with the other part of his counterintuitive "riddle": that Christ's history is no less "our true history, in an incomparably more direct and intimate way than anything which might present itself as our history in our own subjective experience."[46]

Hart points out that human faith is never "an activity in which something virtual is actualized" but always a participation in "something which is already real and already has our name stamped upon it."[47] We are now beginning to see just how different Hart's approach is from Neder's. We earlier suggested that Neder's use of the *de jure-de facto* distinction unavoidably lands him in a self-justifying position of which neither the Apostle Paul nor Barth would approve. In contrast, Hart notes, "Having excluded justification by works . . . [Barth] did not intend now to bring in at the eleventh hour an alternative 'work' in the performance of which we achieve the self-justification which has hitherto eluded us." Hart continues, "Faith, insofar as it can be referred to as a work at all (i.e., as something we *do*) has no intrinsic self-justifying value whatever, but is simply that human action which God accepts as the realization and appropriation of his own justifying work."[48]

---

call participation, rightly understood. In other words, all elements of human subjectivity remain vibrantly within Christo-anthropological Subjectivity.

44. Hart, *Regarding Karl Barth*, 58.

45. CD IV/1, 549; cited by Hart, 58n. As we have seen for Barth, justification and sanctification are simultaneous concepts which interpenetrate one another. Later Hart affirms regarding sanctification, "But notice at once *it* too is achieved first and foremost in the history of the man Jesus Christ" (71).

46. CD IV/1, 547; cited by Hart, 61.

47. Hart, *Regarding Karl Barth*, 67.

48. Hart, *Regarding Karl Barth*, 65. Again, Hart's offering is focused on justification, but whether it is self-justifying or self-sanctifying, the principles remain the same in Barth.

For Barth, as Hart accurately relates, "faith has the character of acknowledgement;" the problem is that this acknowledgment cannot "issue naturally from our capacities."[49] Not surprisingly, Hart notes the emphasis on human incapacity to be crucial for Barth, and this is where Hart affirms the importance of the *simul*. In concurrence with our study, Hart notes several critical aspects of the *simul*'s two mutually exclusive and total determinations. First, "there is not a process taking place in us which at any given stage could be adjudged more or less complete."[50] In other words, there are no zero-sum games or fluid tubes of "more and more" dictating in turn a "less and less." Second, these are not forensic determinations; all humans really are righteous,[51] and all humans really are sinful. Third, *totus iustus* and *totus peccator* are not static states, but dynamic ontological movements in opposite directions (towards life and death, respectively). But because believers know the history of Jesus Christ, they are given to know the future, in their present. As Christians we can know ourselves to be people in transition, who, because of our implication in the history of Jesus Christ, can live by "the relationship of our prior existence (*totus peccator*) to our future hope (*totus iustus*) . . . a history in which our present is determined by the assurance of things hoped for and the conviction of things not seen just as surely as it is by our continuing sinfulness."[52] And last, the distortion caused by the overlap of the *simul* prevents us from seeing ourselves as the *totus iustus* or the *totus peccator* in exclusion from the other. We must rely on the disclosure of our true humanity and false humanity revealed in Christ and in his life, death, and resurrection history to see the seriousness of each determination; this is true especially because in our experience "the *totus peccator* seems to overwhelm the *totus iustus*."[53] Hart, with Barth, calls sin in its utter perversity nothing less than an "ontological condition,"[54] albeit at bottom a false one.

So if we go back once again to completely clear the ground of self-justifying tendencies (to the degree we are able!), how exactly does Hart attempt to describe the epistemological transition from unbeliever to

49. Hart, *Regarding Karl Barth*, 65.

50. Hart, *Regarding Karl Barth*, 54.

51. See CD IV/1, 636; cited by Hart, 58. "It is not just a mere figure of speech to say that in faith man finds that the history of Jesus Christ is his history . . . that he can regard himself as justified in His righteousness because it is his own righteousness."

52. Hart, *Regarding Karl Barth*, 55.

53. Hart, *Regarding Karl Barth*, 55. See also Hart, 60.

54. Hart, *Regarding Karl Barth*, 52: "Sin is an ontological condition and not merely an external forensic relation." What Barth understands to be the counterfeit, albeit deadly, anti-ontology of "nothingness" will be discussed in chapter 7.

Christian without resorting to unsound *de jure-de facto* tactics? While with Barth Hart is wary of speaking of progress wrongly understood, he recalls Barth's words of Christian life as a "pilgrimage" in Christ, "from an ever new past through an ever new present to an ever new future."[55] By encountering Christ crucified and risen—recognizing the "Whence of the *totus peccator* and the Whither of the *totus iustus*"—one recognizes one's life in Christ's and is "caught up" in the Whither.[56] As Hart relates:

> In discovering this truth about ourselves, in finding ourselves in Jesus Christ, we are thrown into a crisis and launched into a "way"—the way of hope and of living in accordance with the object of our faith. [We are] caught up in a transition, called to live life as those in relation to whom the supreme reality . . . is shown to be that which has taken place in Jesus Christ. [This] "story" which we discover to be our own . . . projects us into the crisis of eschatological transition, living out the Kingdom of God in the midst of the world, living by faith in that reality which lies beyond our experience, but which stands over against us as our reality nonetheless.[57]

This life of participation, devoid of "progress" to be measured or quantified, is full of exciting transformation and Spirit dynamism: "thrown," "launched," "caught up," "discovering," "projected," etc. With words like these, who needs "progress"? But what again triggers this *metanoia*? It simply happens under proclamation of the gospel.[58] It happens, states Barth, by the "self-demonstration of the justified man" to faith.[59] This self-demonstration, Hart reminds us, is sourced uniquely in the "self-revelation of Jesus Christ to the sinner." Jesus Christ is the one "in whom our justification [and sanctification] is a completed reality prior to and apart from our

---

55. CD IV/1, 602; cited by Hart, 55. The importance of the word "new" for Barth will become more obvious as our study progresses.

56. Hart, *Regarding Karl Barth*, 63. See CD IV/1, 558, 573; cited in Hart.

57. Hart, *Regarding Karl Barth*, 62.

58. CD III/1, 349; here Barth speaks of human recognition and response as an "echo" inside of the larger self-communication of God. This is not an echo that takes place over the human's head, but neither "does it rest on any of his inherent faculties, nor is any of these faculties capable of this recognition. It merely takes place." Technically speaking, when it comes to repentance, one cannot "change one's mind" any more than one can decide to believe—it happens in the Spirit and under the Word. We should therefore beware the dangers of posturing repentance as something that we do.

59. CD III/1, 349. See CD IV/1, 629; 636: the human's "faith is a real apprehension of his real being in Christ."

acknowledgement of it."⁶⁰ It follows that "self-demonstration" occurs when this foundational reality of Christ "impinges on our existence."⁶¹

Barth articulates this self-demonstration in various ways through his *Church Dogmatics*. For instance, regarding God's self-disclosure to the human person, Barth states, "God vouches to him—the ontological order demonstrates itself in the noetic." In other words, "the knower" finds oneself included in the content of God's own existence, "distinct from God but allied to Him."⁶² So again, is sanctification and conversion for Barth simply about noetic assent? In relation to God's revelation and its accompanying validation to those who "know," Barth could not be more clear: "Its truth has come home to them . . . This event, this confirmation, in contrast to mere cognizance, we call knowledge. Cognizance becomes knowledge," Barth continues, when the person "becomes a responsible witness to its content."⁶³ Barth will have nothing of a noetic Christianity that is devoid of embodying the gospel.⁶⁴

If Hart captures well this life of dynamic discipleship under the aegis of the justified and sanctified human Jesus Christ, we again ask, is Barth wise to implement the *de jure-de facto* explanation for epistemology? An audacious question. As we have seen, our utmost intimacy with Christ is one thing (it is hidden even from us); our experience of this intimacy is another (we experience it to the extent that we do). This appears to be what Barth is trying to communicate with *de jure* and *de facto*. In other words, the couplet functions as an epistemological description which serves Barth's Christo-anthropological actualism (where *de facto* is logically primary); it regards the revelatory status of the situation. Any time Barth speaks of subjective, *de facto* sanctification in terms of a group of people, less than identical with the world (i.e., not universal in scope), he is speaking purely of the existential

---

60. Hart, *Regarding Karl Barth*, 66. Bracketed material added with permission of author.

61. Hart, *Regarding Karl Barth*, 64. This less muscular description of awakening to sanctification (i.e., it "reaching" us instead of us reaching for it) only makes Neder's hypothetical-laden approach to participation feel heavier.

62. *CD* III/1, 349.

63. *CD* I/1, 188.

64. See *CD* I/2, 792–93: "We are only repeating what we have often said before when we state again that *only the doer of the Word is its real hearer*, for it is the Word of the living God addressed to the living man absorbed in the work and action of his life . . . It is not as if man first exists and then acts. He exists in that he acts." See also *CD* IV/2, 538: "Faith is not obedience, but as obedience is not obedience without faith, *faith is not faith without obedience*. They belong together, as do thunder and lightning in a thunderstorm."

realm where concrete reality in its universality and particularity is revealed, where existential and actual converge, and where Christians on this side of the veil "pass from one small and provisional response, from one small and provisional perception and love, to another."[65]

But do we need *de jure-de facto* to get the point across that humans may become who they already are in Christ or are we just as well off without this Barthian phraseology? We suggest that when understood with Hart in the spirit of Barth's intent as outlined above, it is a legitimate way of understanding sanctification and conversion, especially in relation to describing the existential manifestation of their reality. However, because of its potential to be co-opted by "decisionist" evangelicals, cluttering ground Barth has already cleared in regards to gradualist and synergist subtleties, we are right to question it. Perhaps it is Hart's taking of Barth's *simul* with sober seriousness that keeps him from employing Barth's *de jure-de facto*, the latter being a theological formulation that Hart knows can be misconstrued as "light on sin." Regardless, Hart manages to communicate Barth's intent regarding epistemology just fine without the *de jure-de facto* distinction. One the one side, Hart has helped to establish Barth's conviction that all aspects of *iustus* human subjectivity are firmly ensconced in their proper christological and pneumatological (and therefore epistemological) location, the humanity of God. On the other side, away from anthropocentric concerns, it remains to be elaborated just how Barth's theology of sanctification and conversion avoids the accusation of being, in Philip Rosato's words, an "intra-divine act" over the heads of human beings.[66] How helpful is the *simul iustus et peccator* when it comes to real human freedom and personal transformation? Is it true, as Rosato charges, that Barth "robs man" of "his proper freedom" by refusing him "a genuine role in either accepting or rejecting God's gracious activity on his behalf?"[67] This will be the focus of the upcoming chapters.

Experiencing Fullness

As has hopefully been made plain, it is Barth's uniquely rigorous endorsement of Luther's *simul iustus et peccator* that prevents him from accommodating any semblance of a gradualistic "more-and-more" motif for sanctification, as in Wesleyan perfectionism.[68] In light of Barth's actualism,

---

65. *CD* IV/2, 286.
66. Rosato, *The Spirit as Lord*, 167.
67. Rosato, *The Spirit as Lord*, 142.
68 Hunsinger, "Tale of Two Simultaneities," 337–38. Again, it is to be mentioned that Luther does not remain as disciplined as Barth in maintaining the *simul* against

quantitative versions of "more" lose their meaning; how can one improve on *totus iustus*? At the same time, we have opined that Barth's view is transformative within the *iustus* direction simply because of *who* the Holy Spirit *is* as revealed and determined by the life sequence of Jesus Christ through death and on to unadulterated resurrection glory. As the gospel of Jesus Christ is proclaimed, there is a sense in the hearer of deep calling to deep (Ps 42:7), an experience of the Spirit that Barth describes using another Psalm, "in your light we see light" (Ps 36:9).[69] For those who have epiphanies, or for Christians who have moments of "more," these occasions of a superabundance of grace are certainly *experienced* as temporal "lessenings" of the *peccator* contradiction. Barth would not deny this, even if he might counter that being filled with the Spirit does not require a commensurate "lessening." Indeed, with Luther, Barth would have us remain soberly mindful that any kind of "less-and-less" contradiction cannot be counted on by Christians. The hope which transforms, however, does not rely on a contrast in order to be effective, now or later; it is anchored on the day when the veil is removed and all notions of "less-and-less" contradiction evaporate into a glorious "no contradiction." In the meantime, the *simul* protects and mitigates against any efforts to wedge-in a semi-Pelagian human slice of credit that Barth's own *de jure-de facto* distinction may unwittingly introduce. The *totus* determinations of the *simul* serve Barth to reject any *partim-partim* in participation! In Christ, as *totus iustus*, we are all righteous participants—obedient believers who love God; as *totus peccator* we are wicked, disobedient, unbelievers who hate God.[70] Our decision of faith, our love for God, must irrupt from within this *iustus/peccator* overlap.

Again it is the *iustus* determination of grace being unleashed in the alteration of our lives by Jesus Christ crucified and risen that empowers "Christians" to proceed.[71] By now we know with Barth that this happens

---

gradualism. Instead of "more-and-more," Hunsinger describes Barth's understanding of sanctification as "again-and-again." Alternatively still, Daniel Migliore offers a "better and better," quoting Barth: "Actual progress will show itself concretely just in this: that we understand better and better that we are all absolutely dependent on grace" (Migliore, *Commanding Grace*, 300).

69. It is only in God the Spirit that a person can turn to God or pray to God, insists Barth; "We can comprehend God in ourselves only as we comprehend ourselves in *God*, just as we can, of course, comprehend ourselves in God only as we comprehend *God* in ourselves" (*CD* I/1, 465). Italics original.

70. See *CD* II/2, 317: Barth describes humanity's hatred of God.

71. "Christian" is a provisional term. While Barth does give "Christian" some ontological "play," it appears obvious that Barth means what Christians are meant to be about (i.e., not concerning the label but the content). To put too much emphasis on the word "Christian," as in the well-known phrase of Karl Rahner, "anonymous Christian,"

uniquely by the Holy Spirit, and, while there cannot be any diminishment of the Spirit's fullness, and no lack in his gift to every human, there *can* be experienced an increase. For Barth, this is what glory is all about.[72] But again, every human? It has been the intent of this chapter to demonstrate Barth's conviction that the *totus iustus* indicates an ongoing sharing of every person in the life of Christ, including his fullness of the Holy Spirit. Concerns about universalism will be addressed soon enough, but suffice it to say that Barth's avoidance of universalism as a system is not in any way related to compromising the actual and ongoing *totus iustus* reality of every human being by grace alone. Indeed, it is the universalist scope of scriptural testimony which drives Barth's Christo-anthropological realism. From this basis we have assessed some accompanying governing principles of Barth's program for sanctification, namely the notion of change occurring within completeness (as witnessed first in Christ himself), the synchronized work of Christ and the Spirit, and the three corollaries to Barth's actualism: the actuality-before-possibility motif, the idea that phenomenal, "special," exceptions prove the rule, and the to-the-extent deduction. These give Barth a potent articulation for the sanctification of all people in Christ in which

---

is not helpful, and can only give an artificial encouragement towards universalism.

72. CD II/1, 209; as noted earlier, even after the removal of the veil and after the Church is no longer encompassed by error, believers are still "on the way" to greater realizations of God's glory; they never attain full comprehension. See CD IV/1, 327–28: Barth speaks of God's glory being unbounded even now, regardless of being less manifest because of the overlap of the ages. We could assert that glory is not boundaried anymore than "being filled" relates to the proverbial "brim." Surely the Holy Spirit delights in his superabundance in synchronization with Christ's perfect work. But can we say that the Spirit adds his "personal more," his "surplus," not only revealing and particularizing Christ's finished work but also exceeding it? That is the view of Rogers, "The Eclipse of the Spirit in Barth," 188. Rogers argues that Barth can do more by taking a cue from Athanasius to give distinct freedom and creativity to the Holy Spirit in his theology of reconciliation, as rooted in the Spirit's self-giving in Trinitarian life. Also see Rosato, *The Spirit as Lord: The Pneumatology of Karl Barth*. Rosato is another who speaks of an eclipse of the Spirit in Barth; the Spirit is dominated, marginalized and relegated to "a purely noetic function" (161) by Barth's Christology; this eclipse of the Spirit is also an eclipse of man, whose nature and spirit are erased and dominated by the Holy Spirit. "For Barth, the Spirit does not surpass the work of Jesus Christ but is fully bound to its primacy and unfailingly committed to its noetic apprehension. . . . The Spirit and man do not have the privilege of developing or furthering the work of Christ in any ontic sense" (161). Rosato appears to desire a notion of libertarian freedom that fundamentally and unsurprisingly chafes against Barth's personalizing ontology: "in the end the human person possesses no real freedom or proper identity of his own."; Barth's "pneumatomonism" refuses to endow man "with a free spirit of his own" (142, 143); "a soteriologico-pneumatological history which is being worked out with man's cooperation is lacking in the *Church Dogmatics*" (168).

Christians, specially, can believe (1 Tim 4:10) and therefore unavoidably embody.

We have come full circle from the charge laid before us by George Hunsinger at the beginning of chapter 3, namely, to investigate more deeply the "how" of sanctification in light of the "large logical space" left by Barth's *simul* and its two mutually exclusive determinations. For those still stymied by the *simul*, left with unsatisfactory answers about the epistemological aspects of sanctification and conversion, we can only wonder if the wrong questions are being asked.[73] The gap is not a separation between humans and Christ, a human incompleteness or lack of wholeness or even holiness; it does not not make room for the wrong kid of human becoming (as in one becoming something one at present is *not*); and it certainly is not a place where the Holy Spirit must step in to finish something that Christ has not finished. The gap or space of which we are painfully aware is simply the mutual exclusivity of the *iustus* and *peccator* dimensions which simultaneously interweave our lives. We have sought to establish that these stark mutually exclusive determinations of the *simul* do us great service and that any efforts to "fill in" the logical gap can only do more harm than good. As surely Barth would acknowledge, even the most magnificent words in the most carefully nuanced fashion cannot get us over Hunsinger's ditch. In light of Barth's program for *simul* sanctification, Christians are summoned to proclaim the gospel of the one and only Son of God, Jesus Christ—who is also for us *iustus* and *peccator* humanity warring in one person—and by a miracle of the Spirit let "the teleology of the dispute" speak for itself.[74]

---

73. For instance, instead of how this can happen, perhaps the better question is who?—who makes it happen; in whom does our sanctification occur? In answer, we can say that Jesus does it all, even our believing; this includes even our believing in the fact that Jesus Christ does our believing, and our believing in our believing of that fact, and our believing in our believing in our believing of that fact, etc. . . . *ad infinitum*! We can never "get outside" of Christ's representative agency for us, as if making an assessment as a bystander. Thankfully, knowledge of the *ad infinitum* nature of grace is not required for real change to take place! I said something similar to this in McSwain, "Sheep or Persons?"

74. *CD* IV/2, 577.

5

Hercules at the Crossroads

"It is true that man's God-given freedom is choice, decision and act. But it is genuine choice; it is genuine decision and act in the right direction. It would be a strange freedom that would leave Man neutral, able equally to choose, decide, and act rightly or wrongly! What kind of power would that be! Man becomes free and is free by choosing, deciding, and determining himself in accordance with the freedom of God."[1]

WHEN IT COMES TO HUMANS AND JESUS CHRIST, BARTH HAS MADE AN EXtravagant claim: "There is no one," asserts Barth, "who is not participating in Him."[2] Without questioning the idea that free choosing is part and parcel of the true human experience, Barth is clearly reformulating the categories for what freedom and choosing really are for the *iustus* human as designed by God. We have described Barth's actualism as the freed human faith and obedience of every person as located in the Spirit and, on the most concrete level, participating in the ongoing humanity of Jesus Christ. In Christ, *iustus* humanity has been given a fullness (Col 2:10) that cannot be added to or subtracted from; everyone is irresistibly implicated. Such a counter-intuitive concept may be at first difficult to differentiate from theological monergism, which for matters of sanctification brings with it undesirable by-products such as antinomianism, false comfort, and universalism. With the help of the *simul*, we will consider in this chapter how Barth interrogates predominant strains of monergism and synergism in early Protestantism, questioning the extent to which Barth can, while categorically rejecting synergism,

---

1. Barth, *Humanity of God*, 76–77.
2. *CD* IV/2, 271.

avoid the typical alternative of monergism. Barth's reading of Deuteronomy 30 with its commands, as it connects with creation and the new covenant, demonstrates his refusal to trade dehumanizing constructs of agency and obedience for humanistic ones. Instead, Barth relentlessly points us to the hidden "Person in the imperative."

Barth's Hercules allusion is a favorite. He turns to it throughout *Church Dogmatics* because it provides the perfect foil to his own notion of human freedom and choosing. Hercules, as related by Xenophon, agonizes at the crossroads of decision between the beautiful maidens Virtue and Vice.[3] Hercules eventually chooses to follow the heroic path of the angelic Virtue, spurning the enticing Vice. Because Hercules epitomizes for Barth the inappropriate muscularity of humans determining their own destiny, his emphatic "No Hercules at the crossroads" functions to clear the ground of all non-christological starting points, whether they be soteriological, pneumatological, or epistemological.

The Erasmian Legacy[4]

Barth largely attributes the synergist expressions of early Protestantism to the teachings of a reform-minded Catholic, the vastly influential Desiderius Erasmus.[5] In his 1524 treatise *Freedom of the Will*, Erasmus taught that, in spite of the challenges presented by the fall, human beings are capable of choosing good; at the same time, they are free to choose evil. It is clear that Erasmus views such an understanding of free will to be fully compatible with the grace of God.[6] God initiates, taught Erasmus, and humans cooperate: "as we show a boy an apple and he runs for it . . . so God knocks at our soul with His grace and we willingly embrace it."[7] Erasmus's line of thought—that a person cannot respond to God independently, but in cooperation with God a person can respond—would prove to be largely congruent with that of Arminius in the next century and eventually with the teaching of John Wesley.[8]

---

3. Grafton, Most, and Settis, *Classical Tradition*, 997. Barth's use of Hercules is not mentioned by the authors.

4. Subtitle borrowed from Dodds, *Exploiting Erasmus: The Erasmian Legacy and Religious Change in Early Modern England*.

5. CD II/2, 67–68; Barth links the sixteenth-century Erasmus with the seventeenth-century Arminians; the latter were "the last exponents of an understanding of the Reformation which Erasmus had once represented against Luther."

6. Erasmus, *Freedom of the Will*, 47.

7. Erasmus, *Freedom of the Will*, 80.

8. John Wesley was an unabashed follower of Arminius. Arminius's ties to Erasmus are not as clear, but all evidence points to Arminius's respect for and reliance on

Luther responded vociferously to Erasmus in his polemic *On the Bondage of the Will* (1525). It should not surprise us that the Father of the *simul* contended that God alone has free will and Erasmus's attempts to give humanity a capacity it did not have must be rejected. The unbelieving human is purely *peccator*, corrupt through and through, and fully dependent on the free, sovereign mercy of God. Human response to God, involving justification by faith, is solely a matter of the divine decision. For Luther, any kind of cooperation with God is out of the question: "God foreknows and wills all things, not contingently, but necessarily and immutably."[9] Luther arguably never demurred from his monergist views expressed in *Bondage of the Will*, and therefore has more in common with Calvin regarding double predestination than modern Lutherans would perhaps care to admit.[10]

Erasmus. See Dodds, who acknowledges that while the Dutch Remonstrants (Arminians) were more *against* predestination than they were *for* free-will, it cannot be denied that there was "a high degree of similarity" between their teaching and that of Erasmus (331, 330, n. 170, n. 169). As the Remonstrants' teaching landed in England, relates Dodds, the Erasmian legacy there provided fertile soil: "Erasmian texts published and translated in England . . . contained free will theology that was so similar to the rhetoric espoused by English Arminianism that it would be highly problematic to assume English Arminianism developed almost overnight as an offshoot of Dutch theology" (197). Most English Arminians did not know the debt they owed to Erasmus, continues Dodds, but they shared the fate of their unacknowledged forefather in being demonized as Pelagians by wrathful monergists like Daniel Featley, *Pelagius Redivivus or Pelagius Raked out of the Ashes by Arminius and his Schollers*, 1626 (198).

9. Luther, *Bondage of the Will*, 83.

10. For an interesting comparison, see Block, "Why Lutheran Predestination Isn't Calvinist Predestination," and Mattson, "Double or Nothing: Martin Luther's Doctrine of Predestination," Mattson draws heavily from Luther's *Bondage of the Will*, which, as Mattson demonstrates, carries forward the double-predestinarian view Luther prescribed in his previous *Commentary on Romans* (see Mattson, 10). Block's view is more reflective of later "Philipist" Lutheranism as influenced by Philip Melanchthon; the *praevea fide*, or "foreseen faith," view of election won out over Luther's strict monergism at Concord (1577). Ironically, Erasmus's teaching was most assuredly assimilated by Melanchthon before it was embraced by Arminius. Because of his perceived influence on Melanchthon, Barth calls Erasmus one of the fathers of Neo-protestant liberalism (I/2, 668); he is not the only one to note Erasmus's association with Melancthon. Dodds cites sixteenth-century English texts claiming that Melanchthon "got his Pelagianism from Erasmus" (112). Erasmus, followed by Melanchthon, were the two most influential religious authors in sixteenth-century England (305). As Barth describes it, *contra* the Calvinist *decretum absolutum*, the post-Luther *Formulas of Concord* should in one sense be commended for beginning with God's love and Christ's work for the whole world. But by emphasizing the idea of foreknowledge and the idea that God elects *those whom he foresees* will choose God, Barth insists that the Philippists could only affirm God's purposes of election secondarily, compromising the integrity of God's freedom and calling the whole meaning of election into question

Barth is quick to claim that by lapsing from Luther's strict monergism, later Lutherans (notably the Philippists who followed Philip Melancthon) ironically found themselves in the same synergistic waters as those swimming in the legacy of Erasmus.[11] This was a rationalization Luther's *simul*, with its *peccatum* bankruptcy, was meant to prevent.

Lutherans, however, were not the only Protestants to resist the *decretum absolutum*, and they were not the only ones to resort to synergism in doing so. If, in Barth's view, the Lutherans wanted to hold on to election by dressing it up a different way (implementing the concept of *praeveas fide* or "foreseen faith"), the Dutch Reformed Remonstrant movement inspired by Jacob Arminius essentially jettisoned all remnants of hyper-Calvinist (monergist) election, putting forth instead the idea of *fundamentum electionis*. This concept promoted Christ as the basis, or platform of election, upon which human beings were free to go in either direction. Thus, on Barth's view, the Arminians certainly recognized God's foreknowledge of people's

---

(*CD* II/2, 74). In other words, asserts Barth, the Lutheran solution was one in which creatures' "free" decisions were allowed "virtually to precede the decision of the divine will, and thus to limit and determine the divine will itself." The well-meaning Lutheran doctrine of Concord therefore threatened, in Barth's words, to "become the entrance-gate for a new Pelagianism" (75). Additionally, on Barth's view it carried with it the same epistemological problems of the more strictly monergist double-decree. In other words, if not everyone is elect, how is one to know for sure if he or she is in the fold? If believers turned to the movement of the Spirit in their lives as validation of the divine decision and to upbraid their assurance of being elect, how could they not avoid a new monergism of the Spirit? (74) By introducing a back-door or retroactive view of election, while at the same time portending to be a legitimate God-purposed version, Barth sensed this Philippist model of election to be remarkably dangerous (70). See also *CD* II/1, 569 and following: Barth critiques the same problems with Molinism, or "middle knowledge," which continues to be recycled by those seeking the best of both poles (see Perszk, ed., *Molinism*). Melanchthon's theology, notes Barth, was an open door for Lutheranism's formal embrace of *scientia media*: "Man's freedom is not governed by the divine knowledge . . . It forms a factor over against it which God knows, but cannot, or will not, or at any rate does not control" (577). See Tanner (*God and Creation in Christian Theology*, 141–52), for another rather scathing indictment of Molinism. Similar to Barth's sensitivity to Erasmian intrusions, Tanner has a keen eye for what she calls "Pelagian structures of discourse" in theology. Tanner enumerates helpful ground-rules for maintaining sound discussion between the poles of God's transcendent sovereign will and at the same time the fullness of human integrity and "creatured efficacy." Like Barth, Tanner is desirous to promote a "non-contrastive" agential relationship between God and God's creatures. While affirming this aspect of Barth's thought, Tanner is not at all clear in her relatively non-christological account of agency that she is satisfied with Barth's claim of human agency being enhanced, liberated and distinctly humanized exclusively within the mediation of Christ.

11. *CD* II/2, 73.

decisions of faith, but not for the purpose of integrating it into an overall explanation for God's sovereign election. The result was, according to Barth, that their promoting of Christ as the *fundamentum electionis* entailed "no divine decision at all." In reaction to the absolute decree, Arminians in the spirit of Erasmus "did not contend for the dignity of Jesus Christ, but for the dignity of man standing over against Jesus Christ in an autonomous freedom of decision."[12] While the prevenient grace of Arminius and the later John Wesley (both used the term) assured that no one can make a decision of faith apart from the grace which is actively "sufficient" for the salvation of all people, it elevated the human into a Erasmian sphere of bi-lateral freedom.[13]

In his sermon "The Image of God," Wesley outlined what he perceived to be the scene in the Genesis garden: "Man was made with an entire indifference, either to keep or change his first estate: it was left to himself what he would do; his own choice was to determine him in all things. The balance did not incline to one side or the other unless by his own deed. His Creator would not . . . weigh down either scale. So that, in this sense, he was the sole lord and sovereign judge of his own actions."[14] While Wesley perceived the first humans as endowed with the liberty to proceed in either direction from a neutral starting point, he also recognized that the fall "locked up" humanity's spiritual senses and that Adam consequently found himself "in the same condition as if [he] had them not."[15] In Wesley's view it is the Holy Spirit who restores the spiritual senses; importantly, this is the universal restoration described as prevenient grace, a restoration of spiritual faculties to all human beings everywhere, at all times *after Christ's coming*, enabling them to find themselves back at the fork between free choices.[16] A person

12. CD II/2, 68.

13. See Arminius, "The grace sufficient for salvation is conferred on the Elect, and on the Non-elect; that, if they will, they may believe or not believe, may be saved or not be saved" (cited in Peterson and Williams, *Why I Am Not An Arminian*, 110); and "Free will is unable to begin or to perfect any true and spiritual good, without grace . . . This grace [*praevenit*] goes before, accompanies, and follows—it excites, assists, operates that we will, and co-operates lest we will in vain" (cited in Summers, *Systematic Theology: A Complete Body of Wesleyan Arminian Divinity*, 79–80). See John Wesley, "Salvation begins with what is usually termed preventing (and very properly) preventing grace, including the first wish to please God" and "First. God worketh in you; therefore you can work: Otherwise it would be impossible" (both from Sermon 85, "On Working Out Our Own Salvation," III.3, public domain).

14. Wesley, Sermon 141, "The Image of God," cited in Vickers, "Wesley's Theological Emphases," 195.

15. Wesley, cited in Vickers, "Wesley's Theological Emphases," 200.

16. Vickers, "Wesley's Theological Emphases," 200–201.

cannot make a decision of faith apart from the Holy Spirit's assistance. It stands to follow that, because prevenient grace can be resisted, it does not lead to universalism; at the same time, because prevenient grace is universal, it does not reflect a limited atonement. Thus Wesley's prevenient grace attempts to navigate between both forms of theological monergism.

In sum, on Barth's view, while Lutherans and Arminians were right to dispose of the Calvinist double decree and its "Absolutism," they did not have a good solution to put in its place; once distancing themselves from Calvinist dehumanizations, they were left by default with "man's electing of God."[17] Likewise, Calvinists were rightfully repulsed by what they considered semi-Pelagian aspects of synergism, but their monergist solution was woefully inadequate in upholding the God-given integrity of true human freedom. Again, these historical positions (which are continually recycled) are meant to provide contra-distinctive context for elucidating Barth's desire to present a biblically sound way to theologically maintain God's sovereign initiative in election, the unlimited love of God, and the effective (not just sufficient) work of Christ for the whole world—while also maintaining the true freedom of every person in it. In continuing our discussion on election and freedom, we will address two main questions: 1) If we eliminate (as we think is wise) Calvinist double-predestination as an option,[18] and only consider the other Protestant theologies which can seriously maintain the indiscriminate love of God for all humanity, to what extent can Barth himself avoid monergism in his efforts to biblically describe the relationship between a free God and a free humanity? And 2) if, for fear of universalism, we reject Barth's view of freedom and choose one of the Erasmian views reflective of God holding the apple for us to reach out and grasp, how will we be sure we are not picking our own poison?[19]

---

17. *CD* II/2, 76.

18. Defiance of the dualistic (for Barth non-christological) Dortian decree is a place where Wesley and Barth could not agree more. Wesley once said of the Dortian decree that it "destroys all [God's] attributes at once. It overturns his justice, mercy and truth. Yea, it represents the most Holy God as worse than the devil . . . No Scripture can mean that God is not love, or that his mercy is not over all of His works" Cited in Maddox, *Responsible Grace*, 39.

19. *CD* II/2, 594; "The free will of man has nothing to do with permission, freedom and joy. It is in his free will that he is tricked and tricks himself out of all of this, reducing himself to that servile state and service, however free and happy he thinks himself to be."

No Hercules in the Garden

It is apparent that Barth spies in the Arminian approach to "grace" a coin with two dangerous sides: one essentially allows for a rationally free resisting of this grace, and the other essentially provides a rationally free enablement for humans to cooperate with God. The result is a bidirectional freedom very different from Barth's free *iustus* determination for elected humanity. The real point for Barth is that human obedience and sanctification have nothing to do with the human capacity to cooperate with God or with a "free agency" which suggests humans are as free to decide for God as they are to decide against God. Barth cites the instructions given by God about the tree of the knowledge of good and evil as an indication that even in the Garden Adam (including Eve) did not have "the equal choice of obedience or disobedience." Setting Adam up as "a Hercules at the crossroads" could only call God's character into question, says Barth, virtually making God the tempter. Instead, continues Barth, "What is implied by the tree of knowledge of good and evil, and underlined by the prohibition, is simply that the given possibility of obedience is not the possibility of one choice as opposed to another, but of a free decision."[20] What, then, is "a free decision"? Barth elaborates on human choice in the Garden:

> It is true that some play is given to man, that freedom is ascribed to him. But his freedom is not, of course, a freedom of choice between obedience and disobedience. This is denied him by the fact that God . . . has made him good [and] has therefore ordained and equipped him only for what is good, and who, as his Creator, has cut him off from evil, i.e., from what He Himself as Creator negated and rejected. No play is given him on the edge of the abyss. He is not allotted a place midway between obedience and disobedience.[21]

In sum, while God did not give Adam the freedom to disobey, God did create Adam in God's own image with the freedom to obey. Along with God's prerogative to establish human freedom in a uni-directional fashion, Barth can maintain that this human freedom of decision is not in the least mechanical. Obedience "is not physically necessary," Barth insists, nor is "disobedience physically impossible."[22] But after emphasizing that disobedience is impossible in God's free economy, is Barth now saying it is possible? Additionally, how can Barth say there is no deviation in freedom without

20. *CD* III/1, 264–65.
21. *CD* III/1, 263–64.
22. *CD* III/1, 264.

employing a contrived or mechanical schema? Obviously this fine line cannot be walked without the *simul*. For humans in *simul* contradiction, it is glaringly evident in our lives and world that disobedience is physically possible. For *iustus* humanity, however, obedience is "not physically necessary" because "compulsion" with its negative connotations simply does not exist in the uncontradicted dimension of humanity—the sphere without the *simul*.[23] Coercion does not exist where humans are irresistibly free. It follows that the way God set things up, there has never been a neutral place for humanity to stand, not even for the real *imago Dei*, the Son of Man. The grace of God, Barth elaborates, reveals in Jesus Christ

> the human image with which Adam was created to correspond and could no longer do so when he sinned . . . This human image is at the same time God's own image. The man Jesus, who fulfils the commandment of God, does not give the answer, but by God's grace He is the answer to the ethical question put by God's grace. The sanctification of man, the fact that he is claimed by God, the fulfillment of his predetermination in his self-determination to obedience, the judgment of God on man and His command to him in its actual concrete fulfillment—they all take place here in Jesus Christ. The good is done here—really the good as understood critically—beyond all that merely pretends to be called good. But it is not done because, like Hercules at the cross-roads, this man chooses between good and evil and is good on the basis of His choice to be good.[24]

If for Barth there is no Hercules at the crossroads before the fall, there is certainly not one after. Like Luther, Karl Barth was wary of all forms of perfectionism and any ideas of progressive growth in holiness that would feed the wrong thing in us in regards to human agency. To this end he endeavored to sweep away all crumbs of the Erasmian legacy: "Is there a worse threat to freedom itself than the establishment of man as his own lord and lawgiver? Who can exercise a worse tyranny over us than the god in our own breast? . . . If you wish to see a man enslaved, you have only to free him in the manner in which Erasmus . . . once wished to see him free."[25]

For Barth, the way to oppose Erasmus's view of freedom is not to mitigate humanity's bankruptcy and helplessness (i.e., to lessen the *peccator* side of the *simul iustus et peccator*). Indeed, Barth grieved the tendency amongst

---

23. An example of *iustus* compulsion, apart from negative connotations, would be 2 Cor 5:14 (NIV), "Christ's love compels us."

24. *CD* II/2, 516.

25. *CD* I/2, 667–68.

Neo-protestants to make way for "freedom" by downplaying the Christian's slavery to sin, "the wretchedness of man, and his incapacity to know God and to do good."[26] Unfortunately, the consequence of lapsing from this severe understanding of the *peccator* dimension of humanity was reflected in later Lutheranism and in Protestantism in general, even through the exalted Reformation mantra of *justification by faith*. While standing with Luther regarding the incapacity of *peccator* humanity, Barth rejects Luther's monergist conception of justification by faith to the extent that it entails passive (purely *peccator*) humans being objectified, or acted upon by God. At the same time Barth rejects all wrongheaded Erasmian notions of justification by faith—a perceived justification by "*my* faith" which only returns one to self-justification at the crossroads of faith. Here Lutherans, Wesleyans, and yes, even Calvinists[27] find themselves standing again with Hercules. Faith is not, asserts Barth,

> the way which—another Hercules at the crossroads—man can equally well choose and enter, which he can choose and enter by the same capacity by which he might go any other way. Even in the action of faith he is the sinful man who as such is not in a position to justify himself, who with every attempt to justify himself can only become more deeply entangled in his sin . . . for there is as little justification of man "by"—that is to say, by means of—the faith produced by him, by his treading the way of faith, by his achievement of the emotions and thoughts and acts of faith, by his whole consciousness of faith and life of faith, as there is a justification "by" any other works. Faith is not at all the supreme and true and finally successful form of self-justification.[28]

---

26. *CD* I/2, 666.

27. Calvinists, for all their monergism, must approach evangelism like Concordian Lutherans (i.e., Philippists who promote "foreseen faith"). They do not know who the elect are until human decisions are made, therefore in evangelical proclamation they often resort to assuming all of their audience are not elect. This practical Arminianism ("preach like Wesley, but believe like Calvin") in Calvinists' evangelizing is at bottom disingenuous, because it starts its hearers off in hell and as children of the devil, giving them the consolation of heaven only after repentant decisions are made. At that point converts can be assuaged that they are elect and, contrary to what was preached, have actually been adopted and beloved children of God from all eternity. Speaking autobiographically, this approach produces great dis-ease amongst Calvinists, but they are not equipped with the biblical alternative to what we might call this "Calvinist conundrum." Uneasy in evangelistic enterprises, Calvinists may gravitate to the established church where they can reverse the assumption.

28. *CD* IV/1, 616–17.

For Barth, any theological model that suggests that humans can be justified by their faith can only betray itself as "soft on sin." Humans dead in their sins (Eph 2:1, Col 2:13) cannot contribute or cooperate *in* their salvation in any way. It is obvious that for Barth underestimating sin is not the answer to empowering human agency; how then does he propose to do it? As we shall continue to see, Barth intends the *iustus* dimension of Luther's *simul* to be rehabilitated and regenerated as a reference to the Person of Jesus Christ in a way that far surpasses a righteous benefit or standing given to humans. By starting with the Righteous Son of God and his *iustus* humanity shared with every human being, Barth does not attempt to navigate between poles, as if taking the best from both, to determine the proper human agential quotient.

Thus far in this chapter we have sketched how Philippist Lutherans at Concord, uncomfortable with Luther's monergism, modified the Reformer's program through the *praeveaus fides*. The Remonstrants following Arminius spoke of a finished work, but their *fundamentum electionis* proved to be a platform for libertarianism. In face of monergism, these are both evidences of what Barth called an unnecessary "flight into synergism."[29] Protestant theologians continue to write over the same Erasmian scripts in their struggle to define the ideal location for human agency on the spectrum between poles.[30] Glaring amongst all of these efforts is the absence of the human

---

29. CD III/3, 144

30. Modern Wesleyans like William P. McDonald and Randy Maddox, obviously not appreciative of the semi-Pelagian stigma attached to their founder, have attempted with varying success to weight Wesley's synergy more toward divine agency. See McDonald, "A Luther Wesley Could Appreciate?" Asserts McDonald: "Wesley has often been summarized as a synergist who teaches that divine-human cooperation 'seals the deal' between God and believers. To be sure, a pure synergy presumes believers have some fine jewel of virtue to offer God, when in fact Wesley says they have none at all" (55). Of McDonald's assessment we might ask: if a "pure synergy" is to be avoided, what then is the impure synergy he is after? McDonald quotes Wesley to press his point: "The moment the Spirit of the Almighty strikes the heart of him that was till then without God in the world, it breaks the hardness of his heart, and creates all things new. The Sun of righteousness appears, and shines upon his soul, showing him the light of the glory of God in Jesus Christ. He is in a new world. All things around him are become new" (55). With statements like this in mind, McDonald's impure synergy (i.e., his compatibilist modification to Wesley's synergism) is an attempt to posit a role for the Holy Spirit in sanctification that gives full credit to God for everything in the positive direction, while still upholding humanity's freedom to resist. He reasons, "Even though sanctifying grace is a gift, it is a gift that elicits response (and responsibility). Irresponsiveness amounts to a refusal of life with God and the forfeiture of saving grace . . . God effects what God desires in us, and we in turn 'own it'" (54–55). In striving for the best of both poles, one must ask if McDonald has not fallen into the familiar trap of giving us the worst of both instead. From this we can

Jesus Christ as the representative and substitute for all human beings in all human activity of faith and godliness.

Herculean Readings of Deuteronomy 30

If the Garden scenario begins to highlight differences between Barth's view of grace and Wesley's, a reading of Deuteronomy 30 comparing an historic synergist (Erasmus–Wesley) reading and monergist (Luther) reading may perhaps help to further sharpen the contrast between a "Herculean construct" of freedom and obedience and Barth's program for sanctification.

In the Old Testament, it is not unusual to find the people of Israel at the crossroads of decision. In Deuteronomy 30 God's word comes through Moses: "See, I have set before you today life and prosperity, death and destruction" (30:15, NIV[31]). Israel is told that if they respond to God correctly, choosing to "walk in his ways" (30:16), God will delight in them and they will live. If they do not make the right choice, they will bring curses upon their heads. What does walking in God's ways entail? *Only* that Israel "obey the LORD your God and keep his commands and decrees that are written in this Book of the Law and turn to the LORD your God with all your heart

---

only point to Karl Barth's eagerness to take issue with all forms of synergism, including those in monergist clothing. For Barth, to the extent isolated human decisions have a role in establishing the truth about humanity, this "truth" must be doubted. In *Responsible Grace*, Randy Maddox also insists that for Wesley all human activity starts with God's prevenient grace and that human activity is enabled and empowered by God's grace all the way through. It is precisely for this reason that prevenient grace is indistinguishable from what Maddox calls "responsible grace," because it is only by grace that humans may respond and cooperate. But in speaking of human response we must question why Maddox (with Wesley) has largely omitted the only human being who can respond to God. In his theology of "responsible grace," Maddox has failed to articulate the mediation of Christ as the unique context for human response (our response within a Response); he apparently has overlooked the idea of grace as a person, the Son of God and Son of Man. We have argued that Barth's emphasis on the historical and Christo-anthropological mediation proves superior to a spiritual or more ephemeral approach where no real human substitution (Christ's for humanity's) and representation take place in matters of human agency. In other words, the Spirit acting upon and in humanity *sans* incarnational union is not only less concrete, but less personal and human. At bottom, while McDonald's and Maddox's view of prevenient grace could be less than semi-Pelagian when it comes to the *initiating* of human response, it is more difficult to avoid the same charge in regards to the cinching of salvation, where prevenient grace makes room for human cooperation. For Barth, it makes little difference theologically whether the human response starts or ends with cooperation; either is just as dangerous. See *CD* I/1, 211–12.

31. We will rely on the NIV for the remainder of this chapter unless otherwise noted.

and with all your soul" (30:10). Elsewhere the daunting conditions are articulated no less plainly, "when you and your children return to the LORD your God and obey him with all your heart and with all your soul according to everything I command you today, then the LORD your God will . . . have compassion on you" (30:2, 3). Blessings on one hand, curses on the other; it is up to Israel to choose. As the passage concludes: "Choose life . . . for the LORD is your life" (30:19-20).

It should not surprise us that Erasmus, when confronted with the apparently conditional stipulations of Deuteronomy 30, is certain that God would never give Israel, or us, obligations of the law that were impossible for us to meet. Obedience may not be easy, but human beings are adequately equipped to make the free and righteous choice to follow God's law. Indeed, how cruel would it be for God to give us instructions that were impossible for us to fulfill![32] Directly contrary to Erasmus's interpretation of the chapter, Luther insists that the command to love God with all our heart *does not* imply that we can do so; instead, Moses' stipulations in 30:19 show that "by the words of the law man is admonished and taught . . . that he may know sin, not that he may believe that he has any strength."[33] With heavy sarcasm, Luther scolds Erasmus for confusing the Deuteronomic imperatives with indicatives, "you get ahold of an imperative verb [and] take it as implying an indicative, as if once a thing is commanded, it must . . . be done or possible to do."[34] In his ignorance, accuses Luther, Erasmus is unavoidably "singing the old songs of the Pelagians";[35] he is an accomplice to Satan in his attempts to make humans think of themselves as capable of obedience, thereby preventing them from recognizing how bound, wretched, captive, sick, dead and blind they really are. For Luther, while Satan (and Erasmus) pride themselves on the business of foisting a delusional humanism, "the legislator Moses' business is the very opposite," that is "to lay open mass misery to [man] by the law, that, having thereby broken his heart, and confounded him with the knowledge of himself, he may prepare him for grace, and send him to Christ, so that he might be saved forever."[36]

32. Erasmus, *Freedom of the Will*, 49.

33. Cited in Eriks, "Luther and Erasmus," no pagination.

34. Luther, *On the Bondage of the Will*, 191. See 190, even "street urchins" know this rule of grammar, chides Luther!

35. Luther, *On the Bondage of the Will*, 167.

36. Luther, *On the Bondage of the Will*, 169-70. See Luther's comments on "the law as a schoolmaster to lead us to Christ" (Gal 3:24), *Commentary on Paul's Epistle to the Galatians*, 307: Luther describes the law as a "hammer," breaking our hearts so that they might be healed: He also likens the law to a mirror; "a glass that showeth unto a man himself, that he is a sinner, guilty of death, and worthy of God's everlasting wrath

We remember that, for the monergist Luther, justified converts have hope to obey God by the power of the Spirit. However, coming out of a Catholic Scholasticism that he believed engendered a works-based progress in the Christian life, Luther was quite reluctant to speak of sanctification in terms of growth. The *simul* was his way of guarding against the "fanatical" (Luther's word) idea of growing in holiness through our efforts.[37] It is this aspect of Luther's view of the *simul* and sanctification that give it an apparently static character. While on the one hand the *peccatum* aspect of our lives is not lessened, on the other we do not grow in righteousness because it is not really ours; it is Christ's, and Christ is already perfect![38] Our lives may "correspond" in certain instances, states Luther, but we should not be surprised "when afterwards the life does not proceed so strong in its course." Under the guaranty of Christ's perfection, Christians themselves will never attain perfection in the sense that "we shall be without sin," insists Luther, but we "should strive for it."[39]

Predictably, then, Wesley's interpretation of Deuteronomy 30 was very different from Luther's and similar to that of Erasmus. Concerning one of the chapter's loftiest imperatives, the command requiring us to turn to the LORD with all our heart and soul, Wesley finds solace in the next verse, where God explains that what He is asking is "not too difficult for you or beyond your reach" (30:11). Employing the familiar Erasmian logic of God never giving us a law that is impossible for us to follow, Wesley asserts that God's grace "enables us to do our duty, it is near and easy to us, who believe." He cites Paul's own reference to Deuteronomy 30:11 in Romans (10:6) as evidence for his view,[40] which is further detailed in Wesley's response to an inquirer: "This much is certain: they that love God with all their heart and all men as themselves are scripturally perfect. And surely such there are; otherwise the promise of God would be mere mockery of human weakness."[41] As has been

---

and indignation. To what serveth this humbling, this bruising, this beating down by this hammer, the law I mean? To this end, that we may have an entrance into grace."

37. Mann, "Luther's Paradigm of the Christian Life," 216. Mann notes Luther's derision towards the Scholastic understanding of *fides formata charitas*, which can only, asserts Mann, "force people to do good works until they feel no more sin," thereby causing "confusion, distress, despair . . . among the people who are trying to become completely righteous."

38. Mann, "Luther's Paradigm of the Christian Life," 207.

39. Luther, *Luther's Explanatory Notes on the Gospels*, 33. This is part of Luther's exposition of Matthew 5:48, "Be ye perfect as your Heavenly Father is perfect."

40. John Wesley, Deuteronomy 30, Wesley's Explanatory Notes 1754–65, no pagination, Public domain.

41. Wesley letter "To Miss March" cited in McDonald, "Towards Convergence on

well documented, Wesley believed perfection was a promise of God that will eventually come to pass for Christians, and not impossibly in this life.[42]

Deuteronomy 30 without Hercules

When it comes to the demands of Deuteronomy 30, the lofty imperatives to love and obey God perfectly, we might summarize the above interpretations as follows. The Erasmus-Wesley line is that when God gives us a law, he means for us to keep it. Therefore it is possible for the God-enabled believer to achieve what the law demands, advancing towards perfection. Luther's view is the opposite. God gave us the law to crush us and to demonstrate how far short we fall and how needy we are. A third, hybrid version is one even Luther himself acknowledged in commenting on the verse "Be ye perfect" (Matt 5:48, KJV). Even though we cannot obey the law, we should at least try; our effort is the key. Fourthly, and finally, God did not give us the law first and foremost for us to obey, but to point to the only one who can obey. In fact, Jesus Christ is the human substitute who fulfils the law perfectly for each one of us. All of these approaches can be placed on the monergist-synergist spectrum, adjusted according to human capacity or incapacity. The fourth, or last, view is especially problematic, because even though the imperative is apparently given to *us*, it leaves us out all together! Christ does it for us, but where are we? We are not involved. Barth is not interested in any of these approaches.

It bears elaboration that when it comes to view four, Barth's resistance is not as much concerning what it says but what it does not say. Undoubtedly humans need Christ to step in as substitute and to fulfill the imperatives. It follows in this view that because Christ acts instead of us, and we are not involved, we have to *get* involved by faith. The concept of faith is thereby thrust back into the spectrum, devolving into either a monergist or synergist understanding of justification by faith (outlined in the previous section). Barth's conclusion is uncompromising: all talk of Christ fulfilling the law or Christ's "finished work" is irrelevant to the extent that a modicum of human cooperation is required to truly finish the matter. Having deconstructed all synergist options, and dispensing of monergist theologies which can only

---

Sanctification," 57.

42. Wesley's translation of Matthew 5:48 is enlightening, "Therefore *ye shall be perfect, as your Father who is in heaven is perfect*" is a promise of what will happen more than an imperative for Christian living. While Wesley believed this kind of perfection could happen in this life, it was very rare, so even Wesley avoided being too heavy handed with Erasmian logic. *Wesley's Explanatory Notes*, no pagination, Public Domain. Italics added.

quibble regarding the indiscriminate love of God for all persons, what is Barth's constructive way forward in regards to agency and obedience?

In Moses' reminder to Israel of her true subjectivity ("For the LORD is your life"; Deut 30:20), Barth grasps a prophetic allusion to the hidden Person in the imperative: "But we can hardly understand the radical and total nature of what was expected from the people of Yahweh according to the 'Hear, O Israel,' if we do not see in the 'all thine heart, and all thy soul, and all thy might' a reflection of the radical and total intervention of God Himself on behalf of His people."[43] In other words, when it comes to the Deuteronomic imperative to love God perfectly, it is Christ of whom Moses is speaking, exclaims Barth. But lest Barth describe Christ's role as simply "for us" via an external or substitutionary relation to humanity—view number four above—Barth is keen to press forward to Christ's representative role and especially how we are implicated in it. The "curtain of the Old Testament is drawn back," asserts Barth, to reveal Jesus Christ as the hidden, albeit primary human subject informing and determining all human relations with God.[44] In a way view four (which is purely substitutionary) does not, this unveiling includes the mystery that Christ's brothers and sisters are hidden with Christ in God (Col 3:3), intimately enfolded in his High Priestly work on our behalf. On Barth's view, it is only by understanding Jesus as himself the covenant, and "reading from the tablet of this reality," that we can apprehend the possibilities contained therein.[45] To the extent that the law is the covenant, and the covenant is Jesus Christ, Jesus Christ constitutes both the law and the covenant in his person. This enlightens us as to Scripture's meaning about Christ being the fulfillment of the law. God's promise, asserts Barth, "has as its content His own work."[46]

Of course to those whom much is given, much is expected. In this vein Barth connects Deuteronomy 30 directly to Romans 10, noting Paul's chagrin over Israel's failure to recognize God's provision in his gift—the fact that Israel, more than any of us, should recognize Jesus Christ as the long-awaited human intervention of God Himself and that, with God's word already in their hearts and on their lips, they are actually inside the covenant gift in which they are invited to consciously participate.[47] Even

---

43. *CD* IV/2, 780.

44. *CD* I/2, 131.

45. *CD* I/2, 8.

46. *CD* II/2, 244.

47. *CD* II/2, 246. See *CD* III/1, 365: Barth uses Deuteronomy 30 to illustrate the Yes of God to humanity and the Yes of humanity to God. Again, Jesus Christ keeps the covenant from both sides.

if Barth does not make the exact association between Deuteronomy 30:20 ("the LORD is your life") and Colossians 3:4 ("Christ, who is your life"), the implications are unavoidable. But Christ as the life of every human being? Are not these passages pertaining to Israel, and in the case of Colossians, the Church? For Barth the continuing truth of Colossians is instrumental here: "since you have taken off the old self with its practices and put on the new self, which is being renewed in knowledge in the image of its Creator" (3:10), where "Christ is all, and in all" (3:11). Equipped and motivated by the knowledge of who Jesus Christ is as Lord and Creator of all, Christians in the community of faith believe and embody the truth of their "new" life in Christ, empowered by the Holy Spirit.[48] At the same time, they recognize and define their limited and localized experience of reality as it exists within reality's larger scope. The "us-them" paradigm fades away as Christians perceive their own re-creation and renewal in inner connection to the breadth of creation, the image, and Christ. On Barth's view, between believers and unbelievers there is no ontological distinction at any level—anthropologically, epistemologically, pneumatologically, etc. Yet Christians live grateful and worshipful lives in the Spirit; missionally they are given to perceive the Body of Christ as "a provisional representation of the sanctification of all humanity and human life as it has taken place in Him."[49]

Because Barth views all questions of anthropology to be contained within Christology, he returns us time and again "with blind seriousness" to "the basic Pauline perception of Col 3:3, which is that of all Scripture—that our life is hid with Christ in God. With Christ: never at all apart from Him, never at all independently of Him, never at all in and for itself. Man never exists in and for himself."[50] The Epistles therefore provide an opportunity to look through what believers believe about the truth to the truth itself—a truth that includes everyone. In this case Col 3:2ff. functions to establish Barth's fundamental Christo-anthropological premise: the "objective order

---

48. Of Col 3:10–11 Barth notes, "This passage is important because it shows that for Paul 'our' participation in the divine likeness of Christ does not rest on our decision and action but on a transformation which has happened to us, on God's decision concerning us and therefore on Jesus Christ Himself who is the quickening Spirit, so that it is no less than our own decision and action as well, our decisive putting off of the old man and putting on of the new" (*CD* III/1, 204). Instead of conflating the Spirit with Christ here, Barth is properly ensuring an understanding that the Spirit, in moments of existential human decision, is working in correlation with Christ's complete work and not in addition to it. At the same time, as mentioned earlier, any understanding of Christ's work which is not coextensive with the work of the Holy Spirit is to reject the *homoousion* of the Spirit (*CD* I/2, 208).

49. *CD* IV/2, 620.

50. *CD* II/1, 149.

of all things," we repeat, must be "understood in accordance with the existence of the believer."[51]

If, as in Barth's view, Jesus Christ defines every person's existence, the choice between curses or blessings in Deuteronomy 30 is now seen in a completely different light within the context of Colossians 3. In relation to the curses, Jesus Christ defines every human being's death ("You died and your life is now hidden with Christ in God," [Col 3:3]); in relation to the blessings, Jesus Christ defines every person's life ("When Christ, who is your life appears, you will also appear with him in glory," [Col 3:40]).

Two Laws and the Gospel

In speaking about the Deuteronomic imperatives, it is pertinent to recognize Barth's recalibrated approach to the law and to consider what he means about Jesus Christ being the tablet of reality from which we are meant to interpret God's purposes for humanity. As with Barth's intimate coupling of covenant and creation (the covenant being logically prior),[52] Barth posits "an original and ultimate unity" between gospel and law (with the gospel being prior to law) in a manner largely unanticipated by Luther.[53] Within the gospel the "real Law,"[54] rightly understood, is the good news of Christ's life *for* humanity. This "law of the Gospel"[55] is synonymous for Barth with Paul's law of the Spirit of life (see Rom 8:2). In one of his more provocative remarks, Barth asserts that the law of the Spirit of life is the law of the human's "own free act apart from which he has no freedom to choose any other."[56] As should be obvious, the inseparable unity of law and gospel (but

---

51. See *CD* III/1, 205: Barth sees a profound linkage from Col 3:10–11, cited above, back to Col 1:15 "He is the image of the invisible God." Thus Barth asserts that for Paul, the "christological equation" of Col 1:15–18, culminating in Christ as Head of the Body, "has at the root an inclusive character, so that it is also an ecclesiological and therefore even an anthropological equation." See also *CD* III/1, 205: Barth also notes Col 3:10 is paralleled by Paul in Eph 2:10: "we are created in Christ Jesus." See also *CD* III/1, 34: "We have to do with God the Creator no less in our pardon than we do in our creatureliness."

52. *CD* III/1, 44.

53. *CD* I/2, 311. It follows that the law (the law and the prophets) is meant to be a witness to the Law of the Spirit of Life, from which it derives. To the extent it is co-opted by the flesh, Paul has a conflicted relationship to "the law" (e.g., 2 Cor 3:6).

54. *CD* I/1, 457.

55. *CD* IV/1, 651.

56. *CD* IV/2, 580. See also *CD* II/2, 604, for Barth's direct linkage between 7:14 ("for we know that the law is spiritual") and 8:2 ("the law of the Spirit of life"). The law of the Spirit of life is countered by its parasitic rival, "the law of sin and death" (also

not conflated) in Barth protects him against antinomianism in a way Luther's less nuanced view of the law—pitting gospel against law—does not afford. This issues forth in a more robust ethic, for worse for Barth than any form of antinomianism is an approach that is anti-*Christ*-ian!

Earlier we noted Wesley's unique interpretation of "Be ye perfect," which to Wesley signified a promise that we *will* be perfect, perhaps even in this life ("Ye *shall be* perfect"). Wesley's anticipatory interpretation barely approaches the radical nature of Barth's Christo-anthropological interpretation (i.e., the already actual and ongoing truth of every human's perfect obedience in Christ). In Barth's exegesis of this same text (Matt 5:48), it is difficult to ignore what might very well be passing references to both Luther and Wesley:

> This is not a law which crushes and kills. It would be so only if we were to hear it, not from the mouth of Jesus Christ, from which it comes to us as a law fulfilled by Him, but as a human regulation, which we would have to fulfill. Heard from Him it is indeed the Law, but the Law as the promise and form of the Gospel, the Gospel in the Law. Is there any news more glad and comforting than that God wills this similarity between Him and us and has already created it in Jesus Christ?[57]

We remember Wesley's conviction (shared by Erasmus before him) that when God gives us a command, he means for us to keep it. It now becomes apparent that Barth can qualify this statement, in Christ, and heartily concur.[58] Jesus Christ, Barth declares, is indeed both the command *and* the promised fulfillment; human beings are therefore not left on the margins but

---

8:2). It should not surprise us that Barth's *simul* is intimately associated with and perhaps even directly derived from these two underlying laws in Romans; he applies flesh and Spirit to the one law, which is originally good, in the same way he applies them to the one human being, also originally good. See *CD* II/2, 589: "The law of the Spirit of life," Barth expounds with *simul* logic, is "the Law of God . . . in its inmost concealed substance." It is also "the law of sin and death (Rom 8:2) in its form and effect." I hope to soon publish an essay proposing Barth's *simul* as the key to reading Romans 5–8 most coherently.

57. *CD* I/2, 396.

58. See *CD* II/1, 212: "It is disclosed to us that we do not view and think of God, that we cannot speak of Him; and because it is disclosed to us, it is brought home to us that the very thing which has to happen, no matter what the circumstances, is that we must not fail to do it." Thus, within Barth's framework, we have Luther and Wesley in *nuce*. On one hand, Luther was right that the imperative is impossible for humans and that we should not confuse it with the indicative. On the other hand, the imperative is actual (surpassing Wesley's hypothetical) for humans in Christ, bringing imperative and indicative into closest possible relation.

are "already" positively implicated in Christ's covenantal response. Without this ontology of fulfillment anchoring every human in Christ's free human obedience, any "Thou shalt" inevitably leads to despair.[59] In other words, the command of God would be quite the opposite of good news if it were left up to humans to appropriate or assimilate it. On Barth's view, however, the command and the promise are never meant to be understood separately; they exist together in the Person of Christ—the one mediator in whom all human responses are perfectly secured. "'Thou shalt,'" then, "simply shows to the children of God the future which is definitely before them."[60]

Importantly, and this is what Wesley did not envision, when Barth talks about the future, he does not mean it to be exclusive to the present; what is true in the future is true now. In fact, we could say that for Barth the future is *fully present*—a claim as hidden as it is counterintuitive.[61] It should now be clear that Barth believes every human being, in one exceedingly real sense, participates in Jesus Christ. What the above collectively would appear to suggest is that if the future (or equally, the hidden present) was fully disclosed to us, we would see ourselves in the Spirit—with all of the distinctiveness and diversity of our created glory—freely and perfectly obeying the command to love the Lord with all of our heart, soul, mind, and strength, *and* loving our neighbor as ourselves.[62] In fact, if we were not already and actually obeying the law, in Christ, we could not obey it today or tomorrow. Again, the exception proves the rule.[63]

Free Choosing in Christ

But if Christ is our life, it is still not clear what, on Barth's view, human choosing really means. To put it a different way, what legitimate place, if

---

59. *CD* I/2, 384. As per the first corollary of Barth's actualism: "Certainty of faith," asserts Barth, "has first to be regarded simply in its reality, and only then, and on that basis, in its possibility, and in the various conditions of that possibility" (*CD* I/2, 206, see 238–52).

60. *CD* I/2, 412.

61. See *CD* IV/3.1, 262: by future Barth means the consummation, when this present reality will be fully manifest; until then, it remains outside our "circle of vision."

62. In chapter 13, in the section *"Simul* Shema?," we will take up Barth's provocative interpretation of loving our neighbors as "ourselves."

63. As per my second corollary of Barth's actualism, because "Holy Scripture speaks only of the temporal presence of the eternally present when it speaks of the outpouring and gift, the work of the Holy Spirit," Barth can proceed to remark that "faith is more than all the transformation which follows it" (*CD* II/1, 158). Even in our imperfect faith, believers may "apprehend that we are already perfected" (161).

any, does our choosing have for Barth? Barth knows full well that all human beings, like the Israelites of old, are prone to be stiff-necked. As in the urging of Deuteronomy 30, "Choose life . . . for the LORD is your life," Barth beseeches us to "submit" to "the One who wills and acts for each of us," the Object of our faith who is also the Subject of our faith.[64] Again, when Barth talks about human choosing, it has nothing to do with a Herculean construct. Instead of encouraging his readers with the proverbial "give yourselves to the God who gave himself for you" mantra, Barth summons us to "give ourselves to the God who lives for us and saves us by His life for us."[65] Faith, remarks Barth, "is not an act of reciprocity but the act of renouncing all reciprocity, the act of acknowledging the one Mediator, beside whom there is no other."[66] Faith for Barth, then, does not pertain to humanity's contributive role in fulfilling a truth, but instead pertains to humans freely choosing a truth that already includes their own free choosing and fulfillment.[67] We could call this a "gospel choosing."[68]

The objection is at hand: Has not Barth given us a contrived view of freedom? A choice-less choice? Barth can only reply that God has defined freedom to go along with what is the God-given best for his beloved creatures. Because humans are created (Eph 2:10) and re-created (2 Cor 5:17) in Christ, it is established *a priori* that true human nature has one direction, not two. To proceed in the other direction (via a pseudo free will) would demonstrate the enslavement of the flesh (John 8:34).[69] This enslavement is illustrated in the proposition of a prevenient grace which suggests humanity's capacities are unlocked to maneuver freely in either direction from a neutral spot. Such an insidious Herculean position, states Barth with deference to Luther, reflects for this person a true bondage of the will:

---

64. *CD* II/2, 243. See *CD* II/2, 243: Because the Israelites "do not accept this God for what he is, namely, the One who wills and acts for them," states Barth, "they destroy themselves on the rock of their own salvation."

65. *CD* II/1, 393.

66. *CD* I/2, 146.

67. *CD* II/2, 247.

68. Of course, theologically, even this kind of choosing (a submitting which is more like reposing), occurs already from inside of Jesus' submitting, choosing, and reposing. We can never step outside the mediation of Christ on our behalf in order to objectify God. However, by the Holy Spirit we may be given enough transcendence to see ourselves and others inside of the mediation. We will discuss Barth's epistemology more thoroughly in the next chapter.

69. *CD* IV/2, 159; Barth speaks of the impossibility of neutrality in regards to Matt 12:30: "Whosoever is not with me is against me."

"His starting point is the repudiation of his freedom."[70] Barth's alternative is simple and narrow: "For—this was our starting-point—He, Jesus Christ is the holy God and sanctified man in one. In His person God orders and man obeys.[71]

At this point the massive implications of Barth's theology of humanity's agency, freedom, and obedience are hopefully beginning to emerge: every human being's Spirit-filled keeping of the covenant, all aspects of human personal, free, filial obedience to the Father—these things are all revealed by the re-creation of humanity in Christ and ongoing inside the perfect mediatorship of our ascended brother, "Christ, who is our life." Contrasted to this glorious reality, the evil heinousness of human sin and the brokenness of our fallen world stand in fullest relief.

We have considered some of the elements of synergism in early Protestantism which Barth sees rooted in Erasmus and which later sprout forth in Wesleyanism. In declaring "no Hercules at the crossroads" against all forms of synergism, it should be abundantly clear that Barth does not offer us a pendulum swing towards the typical remedy of monergism. Instead, altogether refusing to operate between conventional poles—what he describes as bouncing from "tyranny to tyranny"—Barth presents us with a third way of understanding without making Jesus and his mediatorship a third party. Barth's construct of agency and election involves the full freedom of humans as derived from the full freedom of God, residing together in One Person. In Christ, a person therefore finds oneself in God's authority *and* freedom, the only freedom that "puts him on his own feet, and lifts him into an air in which he can breathe." If Erasmus and others could see what they are asking for, asserts Barth, they would realize that in the cause for more freedom, they were asking for too little.[72]

Additionally, we have sought to establish that for Barth, any compromise of the vicarious authority of Christ—any short-circuiting of his human mediatorship for all persons—can only affect negatively the certainty of a believer's salvation. This often occurs, notes Barth, when the reality of the Christian's experience "is thought of in such a way that in it God hands something over to man in the sense that it really passes out of God's hand into the hands of men, or from man's standpoint, in such a way that man receives something from God in the sense that it is really put in his hands." In this misconstrued notion, concludes Barth, "a conjunction or synthesis

---

70. *CD* IV/2, 495–96.
71. *CD* II/2, 778.
72. *CD* I/2, 669.

has taken place."⁷³ Can we help wondering if this is at very least an oblique reference to the Erasmian metaphor where God offers humans an apple which they in turn grasp?

In recent pages we have suggested with Barth that the person and work of Jesus Christ risks being instrumentalized on the monergist-synergist spectrum. If in monergism it is apparent that Jesus is used as a means to an end of God's free choosing, then just as apparent in synergism is the potential to use Jesus as a means to an end of human "free" choosing. Instead of these, Barth has proposed that, uniquely in Jesus Christ, a human's free choosing *is* God's free choosing and vice versa, all the while the human remaining human and God remaining God. This framework for articulating freedom stands in stark contrast to the spectrum of monergism and synergism. It is not a hybrid or a compatibilist accommodation, which can only predispose itself towards its originating pole. For Barth, it is simply God's economy of grace as the Person of Jesus Christ—grace that includes humanity in fellowship with God before the fall and grace that pursues and restores humanity afterwards. Finally, it is grace which is expressly *not* contingent on a person's capacity to respond. Barth's view of agency thereby challenges the church in the areas of evangelism and discipleship, not least in providing the same theological anthropology and salvific economy for all people, regardless of intellectual ability.

---

73. *CD* I/1, 212.

6

Freedom to *Be* Transformed

"Whoso means to rescue and preserve the subjective element shall lose it; but whoso gives it up for the sake of the objective, shall save it."[1]

WE HAVE WITNESSED HOW KARL BARTH WILL ALLOW NO INSINUATION OF humanism into grace, no truncating of the total grace required to meet humanity's total need. Short-changing grace to make room for humanity's so-called cooperation is a misguided effort to demystify what must remain a mystery; to Barth it would be tantamount to translating the mediatorship of Christ into an intermediary position, compromising both the divine side and the human side of the *verus Deus, verus homo*.[2] For that reason, any synergism to Barth can only smack of self-justification because in essence it relegates Christ's work to being ineffective until an additional human work—even faith itself!—contributes at some level. This chapter seeks to further demonstrate how Barth champions a grace different from that of monergists and synergists, i.e., one that arguably promotes neither a dehumanizing monergism nor a humanistic synergism, but a humanizing freedom in the highest degree.[3]

In paragraph 16, "The Freedom of Man for God," Barth elaborates on how we as humans are to perceive true freedom by understanding ourselves "in Christ by Christ":

---

1. Barth, *Dogmatics in Outline*, 15–16.

2. *CD* I/2, 3; we might coin this compromise of Christ's mediation "the midway fallacy"—the words are present but not contiguous in the *CD* text.

3. See *CD* II/2, 594: "The command of God sets itself against human free will, not because it does not wish man to be free and happy, but on the contrary, because God does want this, because he cannot really be free and happy in his self-will."

> "In Christ" means that in Him we are reconciled to God, in Him we are elect from eternity, in Him we are called, in Him we are justified and sanctified, in Him our sin is carried to the grave, in His resurrection our death is overcome, with Him our life is hid in God, in Him everything that has to be done for us, to us, *and by us*, has already been done ... That is why the subjective reality of revelation as such can never be made an independent theme. It is enclosed in its objective reality ... Therefore we have to say, and in principle it is all that we can say, that *we are brethren of the Son of God, hearers and doers* of the Word of God.[4]

Note the italicized phrases above. It is one thing to say everything has been done for us in Christ, or even by Christ, but to say everything has been done and is being done *by us* in Christ, that we are already hearers and doers of the Word—can this be real freedom? Can this much actualism, the exhaustively rich *iustus* dimension of our lives that Barth presents, be anything other than monergism? What about universalism?

Alternatively, if our subjective decisions play a role in determining our reconciliation, justification, sanctification, adoption, etc., how in the end can there be any real objectivity at all? How can we avoid the fact that in this persuasion humans are co-determining the truth about themselves by their belief? Theologians may talk of a dynamic objective-subjective "tension," but on Barth's view synergism on any level means "God's freedom is drawn in and sucked up by its opposite pole," with the result that God's freedom is simply reduced to "a more precise establishing of the all-dominating 'freedom from man's side.'"[5]

Set Free for Freedom

There is massive value placed on libertarian, or Herculean, freedom in the synergist program. This is arguably the area where Christians are most prone to exert their mythological independence from Christ, violating the safeguards the *simul* attempts to provide. As counter-intuitive as it is, Barth asks Christians to confess that in and of themselves there exists not a whit of freedom to decide for or against God.

---

4. *CD* I/2, 240; emphasis added. The last line is Christian testimony to the epistemological awakening of believers, by the Holy Spirit, to reality. As we have already discussed, this is a reality in which they already stand (epistemologically and otherwise); even with a different existential perspective, the believer is not a different person (271). The second italicized phrase, therefore, should be understood within the first.

5. *CD* I/2, 209.

In view of God's sovereign authority in Jesus Christ, to start with the question, "How could this be real freedom?," is to head down a self-initiated road of counterfeit subjectivity. Instead, insists Barth, the proper question to begin with is, "Where does real freedom come from?" The other question, that of possibility, is important, but Barth insists it only can be raised secondly, once the christological and pneumatological foundation has been laid. In this framework dictated by God, freedom is fixed *a priori*. God created freedom, and God defines it.[6] A human's personal, individual obedience, therefore, just like all other human activity in Christ, never starts from a neutral or stationary position. In fact, although Barth is always reticent to focus on the individual, his teaching suggests that if one were not already and actually obeying the gospel, in Christ, one could not obey it: "There can be no division between the man I am visibly in myself and the man I am invisibly in Christ . . . It is as the man I am visibly in myself that I am invisibly in Jesus Christ. And it is the fact that I am invisible in Jesus Christ that imposes upon me as the man I am visibly in myself the duty to love."[7]

Barth is intent on communicating the importance of this hidden anthropology in Christ as the content of all Christian ethics. For instance, the Christian's ethical conduct is rooted not only in who Jesus Christ is yesterday, today and forever, but also in who Christians are in Christ, an identity that includes the ongoing activity of each person's true self in him. Repeating Barth: "Holy Scripture speaks only of the temporal presence of the eternally present when it speaks of the outpouring and gift, of the work of the Holy Spirit to and in us . . . of the life of the children of God quickened by the Holy Spirit."[8] It is the ethical, quickened activity that manifests from this root, this ontological location where "the church is what it is," actually and presently, that Barth describes as occurring in the "third dimension" of reality.[9] In fact, says Barth, without this third dimension, there would exist "an ethical vacuum." A person "would have a kind of refuge or holy place with an altar to which he could flee and horns to which he could cling. He would obviously choose, yet would also have no option but to exist there 'privately,' . . . without the duty of obedience, as a neutral abandoned in some sense to chance and caprice."[10]

---

6. *CD* I/2, 204–5.
7. *CD* I/2, 394–95.
8. *CD* II/1, 158.
9. *CD* IV/1, 656.
10. *CD* III/4, 325.

The third dimension is largely hidden and cannot be directly perceived, only believed.[11] Therefore, to the extent Christians discharge their witness, they give "proof" of their "Christian existence in this third dimension."[12] In these instances there is a convergence of existential and actual, what we have seen Barth describe elsewhere as a "special" form of expression. Knowing the rootedness of humanity in the third dimension leads to confident and humble Christian living because of its clear delineation between the new, true, and actual humanity and the old, slothful, and false humanity. In other words, it provides a gospel perspective on judgment anchored in the preponderance of the *simul*: "in respect for His and its own secret . . . the sword of rejection which hangs over all Church life is the protective sword of its election and calling. It lives by the awakening power of the Holy Spirit."[13]

Finally, it is of vital spiritual significance for the Christian that the present-future (or perhaps best, the future-present) tilt to our lives, protected by the sword of the *simul*, not only frees the Christian for future obedience but also frees the Christian from the guilt and shame of past failures. This is the same sharp, two-edged sword of which Revelation speaks,[14] and in fact, even now there is a freeing of the quick from the dead. "From what is really past," proclaims Barth, "from what can disappear and be taken from us, we have to be set free and we are set free." The judgment of Jesus Christ on the cross functions as a dividing point; as Christians remember this judgment, we are freed to "forget what lies behind us." No amount of repentance, notes Barth, will convert bad actions—from the Christian's past—into good actions.[15] He continues: "There must be no yearning to be able 'to do it over again.' This yearning passes by Jesus Christ. For in Him our past is judged,

11. *CD* IV/1, 657.

12. *CD* IV/3, 929.

13. *CD* IV/1, 660. It is crucial for us to continually remember that this anthropological truth is not inherent to humanity but always derivative from Jesus Christ (e.g., Christo-anthropological); it is always a gift of grace, and therefore provisional. See Siggelkow, "A Response to Doerge on Barth and Hauerwas," 128. Siggelkow takes issue with what he perceives as Hauerwas's indication that the church possesses the reality in and of itself, instead of being "a *provisional* witness to what God has done in Jesus Christ and continues to do, in the Spirit, for the sake of the world's transfiguration." Siggelkow rightly assesses Barth's consideration of the church as "special" to the extent that it proves its rootedness in the third dimension; "What one sees when one sees the church's hidden reality in faith is precisely *not* the church as a distinct empirical or cultural form, but rather the world itself transfigured . . . . The church must be ever open to the action of the Spirit to live into what the church is called to be: a gate and signpost to the eschatological reality of the world reconciled to God in Christ, the *new creation*."

14. *CD* IV/1, 219.

15. *CD* II/1, 628; Barth is here expositing Phil 3:13.

but also ended as what is past. It should be completely given over to Him. Anything else is sentimentality, a waste of time, and a secret deception."[16]

Barth's discussion of the third dimension further prevents us from misunderstanding the term ontological as being purely transcendent, as in metaphysical dualism. Barth's ontology is embodied; it refuses to separate vertical and horizontal, justification and sanctification. The incarnation therefore keeps being and act tethered in reality in a way that far surpasses Plato's concept of a transcendent universal and a shadowy particular. On Barth's view, Jesus Christ is the particular "One" in whom the many (the community and all individuals) exist in integrated immanent and transcendent fashion. Concerning Barth's view of the many in the one and the one in the many, Tom Greggs comments, "There is no unhelpful individualism to be found here, but nor is there any form of unhealthy Christomonism at the cost of creaturely particularity."[17]

"Lordship means freedom":[18] Unlearning the Cartesian Lie

Those entertaining Barth's view of human freedom are constantly confronted by what we might call the Cartesian lie.[19] This is the falsehood broadcast by the enemy: *There can be no freedom under mastery.* Aristotelian logic and humanist contrivances reinforce the contention that freedom and mastery are mutually exclusive. In face of this claim, Barth proposes that only in the authority of the God-man himself, and all humanity's location in him, do humans enjoy real, genuine freedom in their created *iustus* identity. This freedom is current and active and uniquely animated by the Holy Spirit. We continually acknowledge just how difficult this concept is for those of us entrenched in Western Christianity and prone to process in spatial and zero-sum categories. Can we really go to the extreme of saying that like Jesus, who only did what he saw his Father in heaven doing, *humanity in union with Christ is doing what he is doing, even as he is doing it for us?* In answer, Barth could not be more clear: "the question as to our presence is already answered by His eternal divine 'for us.' If He is for us, this means—and

---

16. *CD* II/1, 628. See *Heidelberg*: Barth notes that because of what Christ has done, to look back would be akin to living anachronistically (71), or more graphically, to "freezing like Lot's wife" (72)!

17. Greggs, *Barth, Origen, and Universal Salvation*, 32.

18. *CD* I/1, 306.

19. Instead of Erasmus, this chapter introduces a new (perhaps equally overgeneralized) scapegoat in Descartes.

in the last resort this alone means—that with the eternal certainty proper to the Son of God, we too are present, genuinely participating in what He is and done."[20] Incredulously, we continue to ask, is not "participation" what *I* decide? Barth insists that even "participation" can subtly become an enemy of grace if we do not recognize that we have been participating in Christ as long as he has been acting "for us" (i.e., ever since our creation in him).[21] In this Christo-anthropological frame we do indeed participate most personally, but on God's terms:

> This participation of ours in the person and work of Jesus Christ does not have to be added as a second thing. As the one thing which has to be done it is already wholly and utterly accomplished in Him. As that which has taken place in God—in which we are indeed participators on the strength of the nature of the person and work of Jesus Christ—it is in itself and from the very outset something which has taken place to us and in us.[22]

Having considered "participation," what about the word "appropriation?" We may recall C. S. Lewis's comment in *Mere Christianity*: "Humanity is already 'saved' in principle. We individuals have to appropriate that salvation. But the really tough work—the bit we could not have done for ourselves—has been done for us. We have not got to try to climb up into spiritual life by our own efforts."[23] Would Barth agree with this? Or would he spy in it the wrong kind of *de jure-de facto* distinction? In other words, is appropriation the remaining "bit" that is up to us? Predictably for Barth, even appropriation can only be a secondary participation in the comprehensive sufficiency and efficiency of our Great High Priest: "Thus our appropriation of what He has won for us has not first to be executed by us. By the fact that He is for us in eternity in God Himself that man who is ready for God, it is executed in eternity, in God Himself, by Him, in the eternal continuation of His high-priestly office."[24]

If Barth is right, and the implicit meaning of Christ "for us" means by God's power and will that we are "effectually represented by Him,"[25] can we avoid viewing Barth's presentation of God's freedom, absorbing typical concepts of participation and appropriation, as monergistic? "No other master,"

---

20. *CD* II/1, 156.
21. *CD* II/1, 157.
22. *CD* II/1, 157–58.
23. Lewis, *Mere Christianity*, 181.
24. *CD* II/1, 156.
25. *CD* II/1, 156. Note "effectually," not merely sufficiently!

contends Barth, "has the power to subordinate another man to his direction and leadership in such a way that the latter is completely himself and is not a cast, and yet completely represents the form and way of the master and not a caricature."[26] Hopefully it is increasingly clear that for Barth, to be in union with the humanity of Jesus Christ and to be indwelt by the Holy Spirit are not two ontologically separate things. We are beginning to answer the question posed earlier, "How can this much actualism really promote freedom?" To which Barth might answer with another question: Is there another place besides the fellowship of Christ and the Spirit where human freedom is really promoted? "The Holy Spirit," enjoins Barth, "makes the power and lordship of the man Jesus, the fact the He lives, and lives for us, so that we also live in Him, the presupposition which obtains here and now for us. He shows us where we always and unreservedly belong because we are already there and have no other location"; Barth then presses home the point with an allusion to Hercules: "The Holy Spirit does not create the ghost of a man standing in decision, but the reality of the man concerning whom decision has already been made in the existence of the man Jesus."[27] It is significant how sharply Barth contrasts the Holy Ghost to "the ghost of a man standing in decision." Resistance to the Spirit could only mean "allowing other aspects of man besides the christological to continue to play an independent role."[28] Try as he might to war against God's grace, this ghost of a man cannot "acquire substance by his resistance."[29] Not only that, but for Barth, the omnipresence of the Spirit ensures that there is no corner to which humans can flee from their real freedom: "To stand unavoidably under any other master is a sign of sickness. But to stand under this Master is not only the normal thing, it is the only possible thing. The outpouring of the Holy Spirit exalts the Word of God to be the master over men, puts man unavoidably under His mastery."[30] But once again, as exhaustive as this mastery is, is it monergism? Barth expounds: "One is attacking the very foundations if one fails to see that, even if in total subjection to the rule of Him who alone can rule here, there is given to men, to all the men concerned, not merely a place of their own and freedom of movement, but also the freedom of decision, with the commission to exercise it."[31]

26. *CD* I/2, 276.
27. *CD* IV/2, 363.
28. *CD* II/2, 162.
29. *CD* II/1, 167.
30. *CD* I/2, 270.
31. *CD* IV/4, 163.

With these words Barth's whole program rises or falls. Barth presents us with an exquisitely free human being within the sovereign authority of God; the only "wholly free"[32] human response to God can be found under and in the Lordship of Jesus Christ. Humans are notoriously stubborn about clinging to their agency, but Barth chides us with the irony of the gospel, "The freedom of the children of God begins only where the freedom, which we think we experience in our humanity, ends."[33] In Barth's paradigm, human subordination to God and human freedom are one. To claim a contrastive relationship between the two could only call into question the goodness, love and freedom of God: "God's freedom does not compete with man's freedom. How could it be the freedom of the divine mercy bestowed on man, if it suppressed and dissolved human freedom?"[34]

Transformation as Liberating Certainty

We have seen how Barth's conviction that we think no less of the Spirit's work than that of Christ is critical for our understanding of his all-encompassing Christo-anthropological "actualism"; it will not do for Barth to have a finished work on the one hand (Christ's) and a pneumatological *partim-partim* configuration (i.e., a loop to be closed by the Spirit) on the other. But we must train ourselves to think differently about transformation in regards to Barth's non-quantitative mindset for sanctification—especially the difficult notion that change occurs inside of completeness, completeness being logically prior to change (as wholeness is logically prior to healing). At this point it may help to introduce a definition outside of Barth's work in our consideration of the concept *transformation*: "This key term does not merely refer to change in a positive direction, as common usage would suggest. Rather, transformation occurs whenever, within a given frame of reference or experience, hidden orders of coherence and meaning emerge or replace or alter the axioms of the given frame and reorder its elements accordingly."[35] This definition may help us to understand Barth's meaning regarding human transformation under and within the framework of the *simul*. Of the Christian disciple, Barth notes accordingly: "[It] is not a question of what he is in himself, but of the reality of the relationship in which he stands. Again, he has not become another person by receiving the Holy

---

32. *CD* IV/4, 163.
33. *CD* I/2, 405.
34. *CD* I/2, 365.
35. Loder and Neidhardt, *Knight's Move*, 316.

Spirit, and yet he is another person, so far as he stands in this relationship."[36] In other words, when it comes to a person's relationship with God, the reality never changes, but the revelation of a person's relationship to that reality changes the person in his or her existential context in unquantifiable and incontestable ways. We repeat the succinct assertion regarding what could be considered Barth's indirect approach to transformation: "Faith," Barth notes, "is more than all the transformation which follows it."[37] What does he mean? Only that in the object (and subject) of our faith, Jesus Christ, all our human transformation is essentially already built-in and included in the human being who has been transformed for us: "Jesus Christ is our sanctification because we are what we are only in relation to Him, because we owe the reality and essence and continuance of our human life to Him, because He is the life of our life."[38]

It is uniquely because of this ultimate context (i.e., Christ's being humanity's glorious transformation, and Christ's breaking and reversal of the vicious circle in "the great liberation of all men") that we might experience "our own little liberations."[39] Again, even these little liberations can seem few and far between. Barth memorably describes the Christian as existing in the overlap of the ages, caught "between his new but not yet exclusive being" and his "old . . . but not yet excluded being."[40] Unquestionably there will be times of discouragement and even despair in this predicament. The Christian does not need Romans 7, or Barth's description of the "old and rejected but not yet excluded" self, to convince one that there is more to the human situation than one's righteousness in the here and now. If it is true that the ontological truth of a believer's righteousness makes sin impossible, just as impossible is the Christian's ability to live in perfect correspondence with the truth. In fact, what Barth predicts in the following litany could cause one to wonder if Barth believes in sanctification at all. He certainly expresses no surprise over the thought that the Christian life may be inconsistent:

> the continuation, by human judgment, will be a flagrant or secret but none the less real failure, a creeping or drastic declension. Constantly there will be either no obedience at all or

---

36. *CD* I/2, 271.

37. *CD* II/1, 158. To say it another way, to know Christ is literally and actually to know and experience Christian transformation. This is because knowledge far exceeds all notions of cognizance and therefore unavoidably issues forth as Christian ethics in a way that ethics externalized from dogmatics cannot. Also see *CD* III/4, 3–4.

38. *CD* II/2, 778.

39. *CD* IV/3.2, 660–61.

40. *CD* IV/3.2, 906.

only forced and not true obedience. Constantly there will be the arbitrary decision . . . at the cross-roads instead of the simple Yes and No of children of God who choose the will of their Father. Constantly man, even the Christian, will take the liberty of disregarding the right which God has against and for and to him, acknowledging instead the right of another god, and ultimately his own right. Constantly the baptized will be shockingly unfaithful to the community, and the community to the baptized, and hence both to their Lord.[41]

For all that Christ has done, Barth's description of Christians acting "as though nothing had happened,"[42] evokes Luther's disillusioned utterance at life's end: "The people that are called by my name . . . are reformed as to their opinions and modes of worship; but their tempers and lives are the same as before."[43] Indeed, we have recently pointed out once again that for Barth the *peccator* dimension of believers does not diminish during their lifetimes. To wit, this remark in *Church Dogmatics* comes a part-volume earlier: "It is the [temporal and historical] sphere of the 'still' which also determines the life of each individual within it. And if the light of life undoubtedly increases in this sphere, continually growing clearer and brighter . . . we cannot say that the threat and temptation of this sin which has been overcome, removed, abolished and deprived of all power in Jesus Christ, are a threat and power which continually grow weaker."[44] For all his proclamation of light, it is easy to get caught up in Barth's pessimistic forecast. Has Barth gone overboard in his refusal to play zero-sum games with light and darkness? Has the severity of the *simul* hogtied Barth in regards to sanctification as it arguably did Luther? Is Barth's "as though nothing had happened" admission, at the very end of *Church Dogmatics*, the self-confessed failure of Barth's program? Or is it its genius? What Barth describes above is not merely the unsurprising experience of Barthian Christians. If we could see with God's eyes, surely we would know it is an accurate portrayal of professing Christians everywhere. But for Barth there is an implicit link between assurance and empowerment in the sanctified life. While the discouraging description is more apt than we like to admit for the cross-section of baptized converts, Barth appears sure that his keystone for sanctification, the *simul iustus et peccator*, will provide a positive combination of humility and confidence that Luther's version does not deliver.

41. *CD* IV/4, 204.
42. *CD* IV/4, 204.
43. Cited in Cox, "John Wesley's View of Martin Luther," 87.
44. *CD* IV/3.1, 392.

Barth's program, as we have delineated, is focused on the certainty of Jesus Christ on behalf of every human being. Instead of the egocentric Cartesian "I think therefore I am," Barth has flipped the script back to its original order. Because Christ is, humanity is, and because humanity is, I am.[45] This framework is where all the "I questions" must remain encased before, and with drastic import for sanctification, after, conversion experiences.[46] Let us note the unavoidable implication when "I questions" are asked first instead of last: while one desires to enter a bulwark of assurance as a Christian, "I questions" notoriously take one as far into the safe haven as a revolving door, but no further. Luther's *simul* does not feature the benefit of assurance because Luther's *simul* applies only to Christians, not to humanity in general. In fact, it could be argued that Luther's *simul* does more harm than good because the *peccator* element is a non-negotiable universal, while the *iustus* element is negotiable, based on a somewhat arbitrary self-determination of justification by faith. This at bottom can only weight the preponderance of the *simul* on the wrong side, inciting fear and insecurity in the believer. No, it must be admitted, applying the *simul* in Luther's manner (i.e., only for the Christian), leaves the *simul* a toothless semantic, the easy prey of psychologism and no friend of freedom and obedience.[47]

John Wesley was determined to avoid what he perceived as the false comfort of Lutheranism. In reading Luther's chagrined confession over his followers' failure to be holy, Wesley was incredulous and grieved over Luther's failure to insist on "an entire change of men's tempers and lives."[48] Perhaps Wesley was right about Luther's theology fostering antinomianism.[49] But we have also outlined the psychological effects within Wesley's

---

45. This is succinctly summarized by Barth: "God is *pro me* because he is *pro nobis*" (*Humanity of God*, 77).

46. See *CD* III/4, 386: Barth speaks of humanity hiding in the Garden as if independent from God, and how reversing the "I-Thou" understanding of humans' relationship to God to a "Thou-I" understanding provides an anti-Cartesian antidote. He quotes Mark 8:34 about losing one's life in order to find it.

47. I say "toothless semantic" in reference to the *simul* being a useless paradox apart from Barth's Christo-anthropological actualism, and only as strong as one's self-analysis when it comes to assurance (see discussion on psychologism in chapter 1).

48. Cited by Cox, "John Wesley's View of Martin Luther," 87.

49. As alluded to in chapter 1 regarding his Finnish interpreters, to the extent Luther is read less forensically in terms of righteousness (forensic implying a declared "courtroom" righteousness, as in a static or passive justified state) and more in terms of dynamic righteousness in union with Christ, he is perhaps less open to antinomianism. However, even by continually pointing us back to the righteousness of Christ in whom we may actively participate, there is an element of external relations. In other words, Luther does not approach the internal relations of Christo-anthropological

zero-sum program of "progressive" sanctification. Wesley's theological anthropology, ostensibly beginning with grace, essentially functions from lack (lack of full sanctification, lack of Spirit-filling, essentially lack of sanctification ontology) making it virtually impossible to avoid a lack of assurance, undermining discipleship. Wesley's hope for change is based on a journey towards an elusive hypothetical perfection, based on "free" human choosing, while Barth's hope for change is based on Change: change perfected, completed, always new, and fully-realized in Jesus Christ and therefore for everyone *iustus* in him. Barth's change is not arbitrary in the least. Instead, the question is posed to the believer as to whether he or she lives in readiness to receive the "little liberations"[50] of the Spirit as truly touchstones to what is real, anticipating their indelible impact.[51] Again it must be stressed that Barth is not against spiritual experiences; he only believes it is within the context of objective certainty that the subjective aspects of sanctification most vibrantly spring to life. Conversely, one's transformation can only be hindered by the predisposition to think of transformation in gradualist or progressive terms within a zero-sum model.

As Barth never fails to remind us, in the "sphere of the still" I will not move forward because my sinfulness recedes but because by the Holy Spirit I am enjoying the superabundant, non-quantifiable transformation of "glory to glory." Instead of human agential freedom being engulfed and lost in the flood of God's activity, the result is quite the opposite; freedom is particularly enhanced under the yoke and mastery of the Son of God, Jesus Christ, our true human brother, the one who promised "if the Son makes you free, you will be free indeed" (John 8:36).[52] In this light, remarks Barth, "we are given to see ourselves and act as those who have thankfully found the centre of their being in the fact that God lives for them."[53] On one hand, we are not objectified in this epistemological moment; in our awakening

---

actualism we see in Barth (i.e., the idea that what Christ is doing *for us* we are doing *with him*).

50. *CD* IV/3.2, 660–61.

51. *CD* IV/2, 557. Barth variably uses "shocks" and "jolts" as words to describe what we earlier cited as our "little liberations" by the Spirit.

52. *CD* IV/1, 744–45. See *CD* II/1, 208: Barth summarizes the very similar previous verse, 8:32: "If we know the truth, it can happen only by the liberation which comes from the truth itself (John 8:32)." See also *CD* II/1, 247: "The question of faith," notes Barth, "has its derivation in God, who is the source and fulness of its whole answer."

53. *CD* II/1, 392. In relation to Barth's comment that "we are given to see ourselves, and act" we could add T. F. Torrance's comment that what has been fulfilled objectively and subjectively by Jesus Christ is an "objective and subjective" that is "objective to us" and which we participate in by the Spirit; *Theology in Reconstruction*, 160.

to faith we are not supplanted, eliminated, or annihilated, Barth insists, for "this self-illumination does not take place without us."[54] On the other hand, Barth will never allow the miraculous "secondary objectivity" given to humans by the Spirit to be party to humans objectifying God, as if the knower could be independent from the known,[55] or as if humans are given the last word about their faith. "Jesus Christ," says Barth, "is really too good to let Himself be introduced as the last word of our self-substantiation."[56] The vain attempt to extract our subjectivity from the objective truth invariably results in a posture of cooperation in contradiction to grace, a posture from which, racked with anxiety,[57] one can only grasp for the impossible. In Barth's view, the only grasping Christians are freely permitted is the grasping by which they are grasped, "we cannot grasp at the Holy Spirit, or the Church, or Christian experience, or the Trinity, or Christ—not to speak of other supports—in order to try to create certainty for ourselves."[58]

Barth is obviously out to expose a semi-Pelagian mindset that can only produce semi-security in the life of the Christian. Having once acquired one's mythical autonomy as the knower from the known, the Christian has unwittingly replaced the mediation of Christ with a Cartesian counterfeit—the imitation of Christ. "The arbitrariness of all imitation," says Barth, "is also its weakness."[59] Imitation is indefinitely relative and inconclusive; we do not ever know if we have done enough or matched the model sufficiently. Only the certainty of one's perfect subordination to God *in Christ*, one's perfect human subjectivity *in Christ* by the "outpouring of the Holy Spirit," accomplishes "what imitation intends but can never achieve: the master acquires a pupil, a servant, a scholar, a follower, in whom he finds himself again and in whom accordingly he, the master, can also be found by others."[60]

---

54. *CD* I/2, 718. Here Barth makes the humorous comment that people do not become parrots under God's Word.

55. This phrase is adopted from Need, *Human Language and Knowledge in the Light of Chalcedon*, 165–66: "In Descartes, then we already find the basic features of western epistemology . . . the search for an Archimedean vantage point in knowledge brings with it the separation of the knower from the known, alienating the two in the process." Need continues, "In the search for 'objective' the knower becomes 'subjective' and a basic dualism emerges."

56. *CD* II/1, 250.

57. See Need, *Human Language and Knowledge*, 165. Need calls this a "Cartesian anxiety."

58. *CD* II/1, 249.

59. *CD* I/2, 276.

60. *CD* I/2, 276. By mentioning the outpouring of the Holy Spirit in this fashion,

The Burning Question

"I am my true self only in the reality of my own free will,"[61] remarks Barth. If Barth is not monergist, neither does he apologize for the strictness of his christological anthropology within which all human freedom, love, and obedience are located. For Barth, then, *iustus* human beings are one with the "being, will and action"[62] of their Lord; there is simply no disobedience

---

Barth is not speaking of Pentecost except as an indication of the reality to which Pentecost points. In Barth's critique of imitation we should not imagine that Barth is fundamentally against concepts like "What Would Jesus Do?" but only if they chafe against the mediatorial premise of his Christo-anthropological actualism. In other words, imitation ("Be imitators of me, as I am of Christ": 1 Cor 11:1; "Christ also suffered for you, leaving you an example, so that you should follow in his steps"; 1 Pet 2:21) is viewed altogether differently when, as Barth states, it is "normative" for true humans located in Christ's own agency, life and death; the "uniformity" required is thus based on the reality of the prior union, that which is already "operative" in the "law of the Spirit of life." On Barth's view, to imitate Christ can only be to "attest" to grace. To the extent we are "oriented" to the law of our humanity in Christ, we walk in our *iustus* selves; to the extent we "deviate," we walk in our *peccator* selves (*CD* II/2, 575–579). As with prayer, Scripture reading, worship and the sacraments, all manner of Christian formation is beneficial for the community of believers as long as sanctifying practices are not couched (visibly or invisibly) in synergist or *partim-partim* (God does part, I do part) forms. In *simul* sanctification, because the person is already in one sense at the goal, good acts "cannot acquire the character of a 'merit.'" The demand to conform to Christ is "serious, penetrating and inescapable, just because it is so simple, just because it requires and expects of man no more than he can do, just because it is always the demand of grace." Understood this way, the "rigorous" demands of God do not burden us—"my yoke is easy and my burden light" (Matt 11:30)—but instead "stir us to action." The "summons to take up this yoke," concludes Barth, "is identical with the invitation: 'Come unto me, all ye that labour and are heavy laden, and I will refresh you.' The claim which fails to speak of this divine refreshment, or which summons man to create this divine refreshment for himself, is definitely not the divine claim" (579). It is worth noting that John Wesley considered *The Imitation of Christ* by Thomas a' Kempis as an unparalleled resource for discipleship (see preface of J. H. Chadwick, *Imitation of Christ*). In chapter 5 we mentioned Wesley's hypothetical optimism towards fulfilling God's demands; we also referenced the way Barth's Christo-anthropological actualism brings the biblical imperative and human indicative into closest possible relation. The difference between Wesley and Barth on matters of imitation and sanctification could be measured by the gap of Wesley's hypothetical construct, a gap equivalent on Barth's view to the heaviness of the yoke.

61. *CD* III/2, 180.

62. *CD* IV/3.2, 534. A more complete quotation here provides a glimpse into Christ's primal relationship with his creatures: "without ceasing to be the Lord or forfeiting His transcendence, but rather in its exercise, He gives and imparts Himself to him, entering into him as his Lord in all His majesty and setting up His throne within him. Thus His control, as that of the owner over His possession, becomes the most

in freedom.⁶³ Jointly, a Christian can declare "Jesus Christ is my free will" as a testimony to the utmost human liberty and integrity. By bringing all incongruity to my free will in Christ into sharpest relief, this declaration also establishes a built-in indictment regarding all ungodly human actions.⁶⁴ We established earlier in the chapter that because every human is already and actually implicated in Jesus Christ's free and perfect obedience on their behalf, good human action does not exist in a vacuum. In the same way, human wickedness, like that of the elementary school murderer (Introduction), does not occur in a vacuum. Having noted Christ's intimate presence with the victims in the tragic Newtown event, are we forced to think differently about God's presence when it comes to the Newtown assassin? Did Adam Lanza somehow loose himself from Christ's subjectivity when he acted in his own "free will"? Barth has presented us with the claim that Jesus Christ is the free will of every human being.⁶⁵ But can we seriously maintain in the Newtown scenario that Jesus Christ is the free will of Adam Lanza? Indeed, precisely because every human being is included in the perfectly righteous human obedience of Jesus Christ, the evil acts of Adam Lanza are exposed as diametrically opposed to the will of God. Because it is in defiance of the Spirit of Truth who sets us free, Adam's is the most un-free choice possible,

---

truly distinctive feature of this man, the centre and basis of his human existence, the axiom of his freest thinking and utterance, the origin of his freest volition and action, in short *the principle of his spontaneous being*. The gift and work of the Holy Spirit as the divine power of the Word of vocation is the placing of man in this fellowship with Him, namely, with the being, will, and action of Jesus Christ" Unfortunately this passage (CD IV/3.2, 538) has been attributed to the existential moment (e.g., Neder, *Participation in Christ*, 77) when Barth's rules of actualism rather insist on this description being *primarily* about the exquisiteness of creation. As Barth states in describing Christian experience (538, just before selected quote) one can not be awakened by the Spirit to a "spontaneous recognition" of God's election apart from "the principle of his spontaneous being" (added emphasis in selected quote) that is gifted in God's original electing work. Again being and act are inseparable, even if distinguishable. We will take up the discussion on creation more fully beginning in chapter 9.

63. See *CD* IV/3.2, 535: believers living into the truth of freedom acknowledge Christ to be their "inescapable Leader," who leaves "no option but to go after Him on the way which He has chosen."

64. *CD* III/2, 274–75: "It is because the secret of humanity remains even when it is shamed by man that sin is always such an inconceivable revolt, and never loses the character of a crime, or becomes a kind of second natural state which is excusable as such . . . Becoming a sinner, he has not vanished as a man, or changed into a different being, but still stands before God as the being as which he was created, and therefore as the being whose nature consists in that freedom."

65. See *CD* II/1, 219: "[Revelation] does not cease to transcend us, but we become immanent to it, so that obedience to it is our free will."

the destructive choice that can only do violence to oneself and others.⁶⁶ With Barth we can only insist that all of our actions are for or against Jesus Christ; no one can ever escape his real presence, or his judgment.⁶⁷

Whether acceptable or not to his critics, we have suggested that it is precisely Barth's sound internal logic which protects him against universalism.⁶⁸ God the Creator will simply not depersonalize his creatures: It is inconceivable that God's freedom would entail giving human beings the "free" choice to do harm. Why would we praise God, Barth asks, for enabling humans to make "inhuman" choices? He continues, "We then ascribe

---

66. *CD* II/2, 589. See *CD* II/2, 695, where Barth calls the rejection of God's free will a suicidal move.

67. See *CD* II/1, 557: Barth talks about there being no escape from the will of God in which we are implicated, and which we can only go with or against: "We can adopt an independent attitude to the divine Yes and No. We can hate what God loves and love what He hates. We can accept what He rejects and reject what He accepts. This is our sinful will. But it does not lead us to a sphere where we have withdrawn from the will of God or hidden and secured ourselves against its realisation and fulfillment in us and by us . . . There is no neutrality in which we can slip between the divine Yes and the divine No (which circumscribe the area of being)." See also *CD* IV/1, 480–81: Barth states that, contrary to the relief a schoolboy might feel when he is expelled from school, Adam cannot escape from his Lord, and, more than that, from his own righteous determination found in Christ. Barth continues based on Ps 139: "For the man whom God has created and with whom He covenants, there is no corner in which he does not exist for God, in which he is not enclosed by the hand of God behind and before. There is no heaven or hell in which he is out of the reach of God's Spirit or away from His countenance."

68. Again, the key to understanding Barth's avoidance of universalism as a system is not to pull up short on his universal actualism. One must "push through" perceived universalism to emerge on the other side, thereby gathering an appreciation for the internal logic that defies depersonalization. In light of Barth's logic, not only is monergism resisted, but also "the flight into synergism becomes unnecessary" (*CD* III/3, 144). See *CD* III/3, paragraph 49 entitled "God the Father as Lord of His Creatures," especially the sub-section "The Divine Accompanying;" herein are contained some of Barth's most penetrating passages related to the love of God for his creatures and therefore the ground rules for the freedom a sovereign God happily gives to his beloved. For example: "The overruling love of the triune God is light and not darkness. And although the rule of this love confronts the creature as supreme in fact, and externally inscrutable in detail, in itself, and known to be the rule of God, it is still light and not darkness" (118). Here Barth establishes such a thorough view of God's fatherly (and irresistible!) sovereignty that Barth is secure enough to re-introduce potentially threatening words, albeit very carefully qualified, such as "independent" (see 118), "autonomy" (see 91) and "co-operation,"(see 110), to describe human participation within God's perfect and predestined will in Jesus Christ. Barth is even able to commandeer the medieval definitions of primary and secondary cause into his unique non-synergist and non-fatalist theological context (99ff).

to human nature the strange distinction of a freedom for its own denial and destruction. We should not call this freedom nature, but sin."[69] On Barth's view, pitting God's agency against humanity's can only have unfortunate consequences. "What seems to be the burning question of the nature of the co-existence and co-operation of the two factors is a highly irrelevant question," remarks Barth, "God and the human element are not two co-existing and co-operating factors. The human element is what God created . . . Between God and true service of God there can be no rivalry."[70]

Confronted with full manifestation of the twin declarations of our humanity, "Christ is your life" and "Christ is your death,"[71] will it really be possible that a person might indefinitely utter, "No he is not"? The more thoroughly we have outlined Barth's actualism, the more impossible such a scenario seems. But here we find our "Pat humanity" at the crossroads where Pat is given "the choice of a free decision."[72] It is not Pat's *peccator* self that needs to repent (it can't), and it is not Pat's *iustus* self that needs to believe (it already does), but it's simply Pat, *simul iustus et peccator*, who must freely repent and believe. That's as far as we can go, and that's where Barth leaves it.[73]

---

69. *CD* III/2, 273.

70. *CD* I/1, 94. In obvious deference to the *simul*, Barth here includes the comment that "Only in the state of disobedience is [the human factor] a factor standing over against God."

71. See *CD* II/1, 630: "He will judge, and against His judgment is no appeal. It is final. Corresponding to this judgment, all that has been will be before Him what it must be, accepted or rejected, acquitted or condemned, destined for eternal life or eternal death. Everything that has been, everything that was in all completed time, will be what He will be to each, and what is proper to it because of His good will for it . . . This vindication, *involving both the eternal life and the eternal death of what has been*, will be the revelation of the kingdom of God." Italics added.

72. *CD* III/1, 265.

73. I have used illustrations similar to this "Pat" example in other publications, e.g., "Sheep or Persons? What Luke 15 Has to Say about Agency and Persons with Intellectual Disabilities," cited above.

7

The *Simul* as a Matter of Life and Death

*Even regenerate man continually has to recognise himself
as unregenerate man.*[1]

"Two Total Men,"[2] One Person

IN THIS CHAPTER, WE SHALL CONTINUE TO CONSIDER WHAT WE HAVE called "the true and false duality of our humanity" as this is reflected in the above quote. Our concern will be to try to resist an "innate"[3] tendency: to think of ourselves as simply one homogeneous person. We might ask if it is perhaps our penchant for being self-engrossed in this fashion that too often dictates the bare sequential and zero-sum sanctification constructs that we have been questioning in this thesis? Regardless, we could say that Barth's *simul* helps us to go with Nestorius as far as is appropriate.[4] And even

---

1. *CD* II/1, 144.

2. *CD* IV/2, 571. Cited earlier: "In the twofold determination of the man engaged in conversion we have to do with two total men who cannot be united but are necessarily in extreme contradiction."

3. The irony of "innate" is self-evident. Obviously, our *most* innate tendency as uncontradicted persons would be to celebrate, not resist, the homogeneous nature of our God-given, true and righteous humanity.

4. Nestorius, hailing from the theological school of Antioch, championed the two natures of Christ (divine and human) against what he perceived as a monolithic understanding of the person of Christ featured at the school of Alexandria. His use of the word "twofold" in describing the person of Christ was perceived as an inappropriate dualism (as if he was promoting two persons). Cyril of Alexandria's group gained the ascendancy and Nestorius was declared a heretic at the Ephesus Council (431). There are those who believe Nestorius has not been given proper credit for his influence on the subsequent Chalcedonian formula (451), which declared Christ to be two natures,

though we are not addressing the Chalcedonian christological formula as much as its correlate, if we do not entertain with Nestorius-like logic what the true-false duality of Christ's humanity tells us about anthropology, we will be as badly off as Alexandria without Antioch.[5] To know the one human person (our "Pat") is to study the "two men" involved—the "old man" and the "new man." We pursue this course while recognizing the indispensability of the overall subject ("Pat"). Indeed, the *iustus* and *peccator* aspects of our lives considered in abstraction can only be as good in the end as two sides of a fence without a fence. Therefore, for the purposes of grasping the true nature of sanctification we will seek to press the *simul* to the limit towards attaining a critical recognition of just how radically disparate these two determinations are as they come to us in Scripture and in the person and work of Jesus Christ himself.

By occasionally disregarding the "one person," Barth has habitually urged us to recognize the two whole and total "men," the "old man" and "new man," the *peccator* and *iustus* determinations of humanity, as if each of the "men" is a single subject. In the preceding chapters we have emphasized with Barth that the two dimensions of *simul iustus et peccator* are not equally serious. We noted the mind-bending claim regarding *iustus* humanity and inherent to Barth's actualism, namely, that in spite of our wickedness which obscures the truth, every human being in Christ is in fact loving the Lord with all his or her heart, soul, mind, and strength because that is what Jesus has done and is doing for us.[6]

Now it is patently obvious that if everyone in his or her *iustus* determination is already a hearer and doer in Christ, and animated with the Spirit by the grace of God, a terrible dynamic of distortion must be also at play. We have considered Barth's attempts to confront and interpret the brokenness and darkness of our lives without minimizing the *iustus* aspect of humanity. But after several chapters highlighting the power of the *iustus*

---

one person. In Nestorius's words: "There is a division of the divinity and the humanity. Christ, in as much as He is Christ, is undivided; the Son, inasmuch as he is the Son, is undivided. For we do not have two Christs, nor do we have two Sons. With us there is not a first Christ and a second, nor this Christ and another one, nor this Son now, and again another Son; rather, the same one is twofold, not by dignity but by nature"; cited by Jurgens, *The Faith of the Early Fathers*, 203–4.

5. See note immediately previous. Nestorius-like logic is another way of describing Barth's functional dualism in *simul* anthropology, and should be distinguished from the anthropological equivalent of Nestorianism.

6. *CD* IV/2, 780; cited in chapter 5. It bears repeating that for Barth the Deuteronomic imperative points not only to the Person of Christ but to those who are "effectually represented" by him and therefore "present [and] genuinely participating in what He is and has done" (*CD* II/1, 156).

dimension—Barth's Christo-anthropological actualism—at this point we must ask once again: in Barth's insistence that we do not take the *peccator* dimension of our lives overly seriously, has he taken it seriously enough?

Determinations at an angle of 180

Barth calls all sin, and its defacing, distorting negation, "the impossible possibility"—"impossible because it is a possibility excluded by the divine possibility, which is the standard for everything possible."[7] This type of talk regarding the un-reality of sin is likely to be met with incredulity by the casual Christian, he or she being all too familiar with sin's consequences. Yet despite the comprehensive nature of *iustus* humanity derived from Jesus Christ, Barth continually reminds us that the blindness of our *peccator* selves never lessens in degree, even as believers. "Where the Church is," submits Barth, "there also we have always this church which is not the Church, i.e., that in the Church the work of sin and apostasy is always going on as well."[8] Grace is always and actually occurring; sin and apostasy are always going on. These are not static states, remarks Barth, but oppositional movements in each person at the angle of 180 degrees.[9] We would be gravely mistaken, warns Barth, if in our promotion of the ontology of light and life and a real dynamic of grace and truth, we neglected to recognize the counterfeit reality that claims to have its own ontology, a counter-dynamic of darkness, death, and falsehood. To the concrete truth is opposed what Barth calls *das Nichtige*—"nothingness"[10]: "But here it will suffice to recognise real evil and real death. 'Real' again meaning in opposition to the totality of God's creation . . . And as such it is a power which, though unsolicited and uninvited, is superior, like evil and death, to all the forces which the creature can

---

7. *CD* II/1, 532. See *CD* II/1, 503: Barth speaks of the impossible possibility as the creature's "opposition to God and to the meaning of its own existence."

8. *CD* I/2, 213. As with the blind and perfect vision metaphor, this picture of the Church and "not the Church" are obviously allusions to the *simul*, even if the *simul* is not expressly mentioned. And consistent with the *simul*, there is always an asymmetry at play within the relationship based on the fact of the One Person who dictates the preponderance, the One Lord of the Church.

9. *CD* I/2, 305.

10. We are grateful to Jorgenson, and in turn Nicholas Wolterstorff (discussed in Jorgenson), for their elaboration on evil as having its own determination and dynamic. The counterfeit reality is so parallel that it even, like its opposite, provides a place for human agency and responsibility (in this case culpability) without being overwhelmed by objective forces (in this case evil).

oppose to it. As negation nothingness has its own dynamic, the dynamic of damage and destruction with which the creature cannot cope."[11]

Barth usually preserves the word "reality" for the kingdom of God, what he calls the "greater reality"[12] or the "true reality,"[13] but as demonstrated above there are other times he deems it necessary to speak of the non-reality as "reality" in order to communicate that it is indeed deadly and something to be reckoned with. Introducing these two diametrically opposed "realities" brings us back once again to the *simul iustus et peccator* and Barth's pitting of the inescapable aspect of righteousness against the impossibility of unrighteousness. It is the *simul*, with its 180 degree relationship between *iustus* and *peccator*, which raises the stakes for human agency far beyond a "Hercules at the crossroads."[14] The human being is not a free agent making decisions from a neutral standpoint. Indeed, Barth's portrayal of the situation is more reminiscent of Luther's illustration of man as a horse with two rivaling riders, God and Satan, compelling the horse in opposite directions.[15] With Barth's *simul* we are given to see that humanity is under the influence of these driving forces occurring not alternately, nor sequentially, but *at the same time*.

Human beings may make every effort to construct a realm of falsehood, or un-reality, for themselves, but in so doing they cannot re-plot their existence off the grid of reality. Even agnostics are confronted by the fact that their rebellion against the reality of Jesus Christ cannot dilute the truth of Christ and therefore the truth about themselves, that each of them is unavoidably a hearer and doer of the Word in Christ. Barth remarks poignantly that the position of agnosticism is made untenable by the revelation of Jesus Christ. By the grace of the outpouring of the Holy Spirit, everyone knows God.[16] And, revealed by God's disclosure, the agnostic's view of incapacity is exposed as weak in comparison with our actual *peccator* bankruptcy.

---

11. *CD* III/3, 310. We credit Jorgenson with drawing our attention to this quotation.

12. *CD* IV/1, 614.

13. See *CD* IV/2, 227: "The reality of God, omnipotent in His mercy, is set against the obvious reality of death. Which will prove to be the greater, the true reality?" See also "truest reality," *CD* IV/3.1, 250.

14. See *CD* IV/4, 204.

15. See Martin Luther, *On the Bondage of the Will*, 103.

16. See *CD* I/2, 306–7: Because of the omnipresence of the Holy Spirit and his intimate relationship with every person, there is a sense in which every person knows God; this is not an inherent truth. Via the covenant of grace, however, the inner meaning of creation has been made known in Jesus Christ. There is, therefore, an ongoing dialogue occurring between the true human Jesus, in whom we are all included, and

> The agnostic informs us that the upward view is blocked. He calls a man a fool who blinkingly turns his eyes in that direction. The incapacity of which he speaks is dreadful enough, but it is certainly not the radical incapacity which is involved when we state theologically that man is not free for God . . . There can be no doubt that acknowledgement of the reality of the Holy Spirit would necessarily compel the agnostic to speak quite differently . . . Instead of eyes which blink (and blink continually), he would have to speak about our blindness and the healing of the blind. In fact, he would have to surrender his agnosticism all along the line.[17]

In Barth's mind, agnosticism is just another one of humanity's attempts to control divine and human freedom. In Jesus Christ, however, the "180-degree rule" has been revealed and determined. "When the Word of God is acknowledged, it is also acknowledged that man is not free for God. But to acknowledge the Word of God means he is actually free for God."[18] We remember that for Barth genuine freedom "excludes the possibility of sinning." He makes no allowances: "Of the free man it has to be said: *non potest peccare*. His freedom excludes this . . . He 'cannot' sin in the capacity granted to him by God. In this capacity he can only believe and obey and give thanks."[19]

In the same way that the *iustus* dimension of human life is inescapable, in this world the *peccator* dimension of human life is equally inescapable. It is not possible to consider the *iustus* element and leave the *peccator* element behind. In fact, not only is a Herculean neutrality or free-agency impossible, but humanity, by continuing to operate within its mythological capacity, also proves itself to be in bondage to evil. If Barth's view of freedom is "not an empty and formal concept," but "one filled out with positive meaning," his view of fallen human will is exactly the opposite (i.e., empty and negative). Whereas in genuine freedom humans cannot sin, in the flesh humans cannot *not* sin. "[This negation] can be described as a freedom not to be

---

the Father. Everyone therefore by grace has a relationship with God through Jesus Christ and by the Holy Spirit. Barth teaches, quoting Romans 1:18, that ever since the fall unbelievers have "held the truth in unrighteousness" (KJV). But again knowledge of this truth is not natural; it cannot be derived from a remnant of the image, as if humanity could claim possession of the *imago Dei* or of the Holy Spirit.

17. *CD* I/2, 244. Likewise in relation to atheism, Barth states, "There is no ontological godlessness. Even the most rabid atheist cannot achieve this either theoretically or practically" (*CD* III/4, 652).

18. *CD* I/2, 258.

19. *CD* IV/2, 495.

free—which is nonsense," asserts Barth. It is inexplicable, "irrational and incomprehensible" . . . yet it is a "real fact," a "sinister fact."[20] And it is here that for Barth the Hercules figure becomes not only a foil to true liberty but also a paragon of wickedness. It is not that a man struggles to decide what is right, it is that he cannot decide for the right *at all* because he is enslaved to the wrong: "His sin excludes his freedom, just as his freedom excludes his sin. There is no middle position. . . . He has not ceased to be a man. He wills. He is a Hercules, the arbiter of what he does. But he does what he does in the corruption of his will. . . . In a deeper sense than the poet had in mind, it is the curse of an evil deed that it inevitably gives birth to fresh evil."[21]

Iustus clarity and freedom, *peccator* blindness and incapacity—the contrast could not be more stark. And, importantly when it comes to any relationship between light and darkness, reality and unreality, truth and falsehood, there is no dialectic. "The Holy Spirit," says Barth, "is not a dialectician."[22] The truth blows in one direction only, and it is by the Spirit that one may take Jesus' words with utmost seriousness: "Whoever is not with me is against me" (Matt 12:30).[23] Within a revelation construct of freedom, to claim a Herculean standpoint of neutrality, with its subsequent libertarian capacities, belies the darkest un-freedom. The *simul iustus et peccator*, insists Barth, "has nothing at all to do with a Hercules at the crossroads."[24] He asserts categorically (and somewhat contentiously!) that only a pagan extrapolation from the Bible could yield such a notion: "It can only be a false Christian earnestness which causes a man . . . to lay aside for a moment the decision about his salvation contained in God's revelation, and to place himself at the critical point where it is seen that the end of one way is eternal glory and the of the other way, everlasting fire. All heathen eschatology thinks in this symmetrical way, but Scripture never puts these two ways before our eyes."[25]

First John: The Bible in Contradiction?

Barth continually seeks to derive his theology of sin and sanctification from the revelation of Jesus Christ and how the Word is presented in Holy Scripture. In this vein we inquire: Is there a biblical theology, other than one that

20. *CD* IV/2, 495.
21. *CD* IV/2, 495.
22. *CD* I/2, 246.
23. *CD* IV/2, 159; Barth speaks of no neutrality in regards to Matt 12:30.
24. *CD* II/1, 627.
25. *CD* II/1, 393.

The Simul *as a Matter of Life and Death*   143

affirms Barth's *simul*, which can do justice to the apparently contradictory passages of the epistle of 1 John?

In a book that has ensnarled interpreters for thousands of years, the author of the Epistle, (for our purposes John) states in the first chapter, "If we say that we have no sin, we deceive ourselves, and the truth is not in us. If we confess our sins, he who is faithful and just will forgive us our sins and cleanse us from all unrighteousness. If we say that we have not sinned, we make him a liar, and his word is not in us" (1 John 1:8–10). Whole dissertations could be written to cover the many ways interpreters have reconciled this verse internally with the altogether different message apparent in 1 John 3:6, 3:9, and 5:18. The latter we take time to quote: "We know that those who are born of God do not sin, but the one who was born of God protects them, and the evil one does not touch them." Let us be clear about the apparent contradiction: On the one hand, if we say we are without sin, we are liars; on the other hand, if we acknowledge we *do* sin, we are proving that we are not born of God, because those born of God *do not sin*. This is quite the textual conundrum!

Again, Barth knows that if we start by interpreting the epistle with a "one person" mindset, it is doubtful that we shall be able to grasp the extent to which the two components presented to us in First John are radically different and mutually exclusive.[26] At this point, in an effort to harmonize the components, we may compromise the severity of the contrast, adopting a fluid zero-sum interpretation in an effort to navigate the riddle. In this case, the verse "those who are born of God do not sin" (5:18) may be allowed to morph into merely a warning against a *pattern* of sinful behavior.[27] For surely the author does not expect Christians to avoid sinning altogether;

---

26. *CD* IV/2, 371. Barth suggests that 1 John is "like a very short and concise summary" of Romans 6, the latter being a chapter Barth labels "the *locus classicus* for this differentiation, demarcation, and separation of that which is radically impossible of the Christian (in view of his Lord) from the one thing that is alone possible" (370). Paul's original recipients, starting with hearing the sequential and apparently spatial delineation of the two separate slaveries, must have been astounded when Paul put the two together in a unified, simultaneous fashion! At one moment we see the two slaveries as purely sequential; Paul tells them they were slaves to sin, now they are slaves to God. The next minute Paul is telling the saints that he himself is still enslaved to sin, even while he is enslaved to God (7:25). See *CD* II/2, 589: Barth reinforces his teaching on Romans 6 with Jesus' own plain remark that anyone who sins is a slave to sin (John 8:34).

27. Our default translation (NRSV) stays true to the Greek, communicating the positive severity of the *iustus* dimension ("those who are born of God do not sin"). Other less literal translations (e.g., NIV) unfortunately take a conciliatory approach, "anyone born of God does not continue to sin," reflecting a desire to navigate the apparent contradiction between this verse and the above (1 John 1:8–10).

that would be unrealistic! But in this view, where do we draw the line regarding "patterns"? Is lusting over pornography once a week a sinful pattern? Once a month? Once a year? This kind of silly arbitrariness is not based on "Christo-logic," the *iustus* One who assumed our *peccator* contradiction, but on viewing the two determinations via the unbiblical logic of non-contradiction or by an artificial synthesis.

In earlier chapters we discussed how the universal *totus peccator* avoided the kind of arbitrary speculation and judgment based on the gradation of sin. Have we allowed for a potentially more cogent possibility, namely that the 1 John text may be presenting us with a *totus/totus* framework for understanding Christians and humanity in general? From the standpoint of reality, as Barth understands it, and with the perspective of the *simul*, it is categorically impossible for children of God to sin because each one is totally *iustus*. Conversely, it is just as impossible for these same persons *not* to sin; each one is totally *peccator*. As with Chalcedonian Christology, we must take the dualistic elements seriously in positing the anthropological duality. We remember Barth's summation, "I was and still am the old man . . . I am and will be the new man." Putting 1 John in *simul* terms, then, requires firstly the understanding that the "whoever is born of God does not sin" passage refers to the *iustus* dimension of our lives; again this must be contextualized *in the one* who is first and foremost born of God, "Jesus Christ, the Righteous One" (1 John 2:1). It should be clear that this relates to the real, renewed, present but also future aspect of our lives in Christ: "I am and will be the new man." Secondly, the "if you say you are without sin you are a liar" passage is a tacit acknowledgement of the overlap of the *peccator* dimension: "I was and still am the old man." This sinful dimension is ultimately and actually extinguished but is temporally present and deadly. Returning to 1 John 1:9–10, what we might call the author's shorthand for *simul* sanctification, we find both aspects included in the one person: "If we confess our sins, he is faithful and just to forgive us our sins and cleanse us from all unrighteousness. If we claim we have not sinned, we make him out to be a liar and his word has no place in our lives." In other words, we confess our *peccatum* explicitly *because* of the *iustus* context of our present and promised forgiveness gifted by the God who is "faithful and righteous," i.e., by virtue of the Word who *is* in us (v. 10).

Importantly, the *peccator* dimension has no future; Barth, in his reading of 1 John, urges us to understand this with all the emphasis he can conjure up, "It is only as the impossible, the excluded and the absurd, only on the supposition that we are not we, and that Jesus Christ is not Jesus Christ,

The Simul *as a Matter of Life and Death*   145

that sin can be thought of as our future."[28] The Christian can therefore know with utmost certainty that the *simul*'s twofold determination of his present existence will not translate into a "twofold future." Barth asserts, "Those who have heard the Word of God and tasted the powers of the world to come cannot reckon with this bilinear but only with the unilinear future."[29]

At bottom, it is easy to dismiss Barth's christological interpretation, but it is incumbent upon others to propose a better understanding that does more justice to the text. Is there another interpretation besides the *simul* that can allow the contradictions in 1 John to stand within an overall singular purpose? Might it be that a Barthian viewpoint is the only one which can actually take First John literally?[30]

One Person and Penal Substitution

Thus far we have entertained the idea from 1 John that what we have called a "Chalcedonian anthropology" might unlock a more biblically sound doctrine of sanctification.[31] Having emphasized the "two total men" of our "one

---

28. CD I/2, 398–99.

29. CD I/2, 399. These words of Barth are obviously alluding to Hebrews 6:4–6, another passage he cites along with 1 John and Romans 6 to make his point about the impossibility of sin in reality.

30. The light-dark, truth-lie *simul* imagery for John is so stark that we might also ask as to his understanding of the anti-Christ and how it fits into this radical contradiction. Could it be that John views the anti-Christ to be the alter-ego of every human being, so that to the degree human beings exist in correlation to the lie they themselves are antichrists? Is the old man the anti-Christ? This seems to be the sense of 1 John 2:18 and following and 2 John 1:7 and following. If this is the case, then our understanding of the evil nature of the old man is soberly enlarged. The counterfeit runs incomprehensibly deep, even to the point of hijacking creation to image a "likeness" onto humanity, one that Christ himself had to assume (Rom 8:2) in order to defeat, thereby restoring the proper "image and likeness."

31. Romans 5–8 is another of the main scriptural locations where Barth derives his *simul* as the keystone for his program of sanctification. To wit: the themes of First Adam/Second Adam, sin/righteousness, condemnation/justification, disobedience/obedience, death/life, slavery to sin/slavery to righteousness, flesh and Spirit. We could generally say that if we are looking for the universal aspect of the *simul* we find it in Romans 5, the severity and starkly differentiated aspects of the *simul* in Romans 6, the simultaneous nature of the *simul* in Romans 7, and the overall victory and accompanying hope of our rescue from the *simul* in Romans 8. What began as a contrast between sinful Adam and Christ (the Second Adam) continues its course until chapter 8, where the same mutually exclusive determinations are translated *sarx* and Spirit. "To set the mind on the flesh is death, but to set the mind on the Spirit is life and peace. For this reason the mind that is set on the flesh is hostile to God; it does not submit

person," we must continually consider the "one person" of the "two total men." It is incumbent upon Barth to demonstrate how he can responsibly hold to a single subject or one person mindset in theological anthropology, especially in light of all that he has said to animate the two determinations as if they were indeed two subjects. Now again, even starting out with multiple *compatible* distinctions of a single entity risks losing sight of the unity. This is compounded by the radically opposite and mutually exclusive determinations of the *simul*, two forces at 180 degrees moving towards "ever-increasing wickedness" and "holiness" (or "sanctification") respectively (Rom 6:19). To what extent do these elements actually hold together in one person? And slightly adjusting Luther's metaphor, how can a single subject riding two "horses" in opposite directions avoid being torn apart? With Barth we turn not to ourselves, and not even first and foremost to Holy Scripture,[32] but to our suggested original manifestation of the *simul*, Jesus Christ. It appears that Barth wants us to consider the oppositional dynamics of human *iustitia* and human *peccatum* as juxtaposed in the Passion of Christ to be so starkly disparate and radically comprehensive that either we have to submit to dualism or conclude Jesus Christ to be the *simul* incarnate. In continuing to unpack Barth's meaning of Jesus Christ himself as "the sanctification of man for God," it will hopefully become increasingly clear that, through Christ's passion, Barth views our sanctification to be not only a matter of *iustus* and *peccator* but also of life and death: "Between the eternal Father and the eternal Son, and therefore between God and man, there is established in Jesus Christ the order in which man, even though he is a transgressor and sinner, but put to death and destroyed as such, may live for God."[33]

Because of his emphasis on ontology, it is often forgotten that when it comes to the topic of atonement, Barth can speak the language of penal

---

to God's law—indeed it cannot, and those who are in the flesh cannot please God" (Rom 8:6–8). This is not to mention Romans 3:23–24, where the *simul* is couched in a universal symmetry (or asymmetry). See CD II/1, 104; of Romans 3:22–23. Barth inquires rhetorically, "Is there a place between this twofold (but in the wisdom and will of God undivided) determination of man by the wrath and righteousness of God, where it is possible for man in the cosmos as such, and grounded in himself, to stand in an independent relationship to God, i.e., untouched by the wrath and righteousness of God . . . ?"

32. See CD I/2, 457: "The theme of dogmatics . . . is the question of the Word of God in the proclamation of the Christian Church, or, concretely, the question of the agreement of this proclamation with Holy Scripture as the Word of God. To answer this question as such we had first to investigate that form of the Word of God which precedes both proclamation and Holy Scripture, i.e., the revelation of God."

33. CD II/2, 739.

satisfaction as well as anyone.[34] He does not hesitate to accumulate the Gospel's lurid descriptions of judgment as part of Christ's rejection by God: "Here the alienation from God becomes an annihilatingly painful existence in opposition to Him. Here being in death becomes punishment, torment, outer darkness, the worm, the flame—all eternal as God Himself, as God Himself in this antithesis, and all positively painful."[35] Again Barth is keen to honor the scriptural witness and to not hold anything back lest he risk understating the *totus* aspect of the darkness. "Infinite suffering," he notes, "is imposed upon the creature . . . as it deserves."[36]

Before turning specifically to the cross, we take pause. It should be noted that Barth includes in the sinful assumption of Christ anything and everything that is not of true, *iustus* humanity. The effect of this is again to emphasize an anti-relativistic or anti-quantitative measuring of human sinfulness and to establish its *totus peccator* nature against all forms of zero-sum or relic-based (building back out from the relics of the *imago*) sanctification. In his desire to be a biblical exegete, we have seen how Barth implements penal satisfaction language in his description of Jesus' assumption and death. This has led some scholars like Bruce McCormack to contend that Barth's primary category for the atonement is forensic.[37] In our

---

34. See *CD* II/1, 153, 399.

35. *CD* III/2, 603.

36. *CD* III/2, 603. Lest the reader be confused by the words "creature" and "man" as if Barth is not talking about Christ, Barth's point is that while it is the creature, the human being, who deserves God's wrath it is Jesus who becomes these things in our place; "It is, of course true that this man is the Son of God. In Him God Himself suffers what guilty man had to suffer by way of eternal punishment. This alone gives the suffering of this man its representative power" (602–3). See IV/3.1, 413: "But it belongs decisively to this work of God, and therefore to the heart of God's person and essence, that His action in the conclusion of this peace, in the work of atonement and deliverance, in the justification and sanctification of man, should entail severity, pain and terror for the one man who was ordained and who gave Himself to accomplish it." Again these kinds of statements are surprising to Barth readers who have presupposed his approach to the atonement to be more Eastern or purely ontological. However, while Barth's approach keeps him tethered to the Western camp, Christ's punishment is a minor key in comparison to the ontological theme governed by Christ's person (i.e., that which holds his approach to the atonement together and which provides room for the intrinsic consequences of sin). Because these penal themes from Scripture are made centerpieces by Western forensic-minded theologians, one wonders perhaps if by piling on the "pain and terror" here Barth would have all of our human constructs of penal satisfaction to be buried with Christ as well!

37. McCormack, "For Us and Our Salvation," 307. McCormack cites *CD* IV/1, 274: "Barth's view of the atonement still operates—as he himself expressly says—with a forensic framework . . . within the sphere of classical Reformed thought (and its

view, Barth's indisputable heavy forensic language has nothing to do with trumping his overall framework of ontology; we could agree with McCormack only if it could be proved that Barth's emphasis on Jesus Christ as our substitute is more dominant in Barth than his emphasis on Christ's role as humanity's representative.[38]

At the same time, McCormack's assessment of the single subject duality of Jesus Christ (*a la* Chalcedon), is a helpful reminder as to why Barth resisted the typical Lutheran *communion naturarum* in favor of a more indirect *communicatio*, one of articulating either side of the Chalcedonian duality of Christ via the single subject, i.e., the person of Christ, the only vehicle that actually exists. This means that instead of the two natures of Christ communicating directly with each other, "the communication of natures is . . . mediated as it were by the Person of the union." This does not make the person a third party, continues McCormack helpfully, for "the only thing that can be predicated of the person is the natures themselves."[39] Therefore, to quote McCormack elsewhere, "[O]ne is fully authorized to say: what the man Jesus does, God does; what the man Jesus experiences, God experiences."[40] It bears repeating that this orthodox permission is not

---

modified Anselmianism)." What McCormack does not point out is that Barth follows his comment about forensic concepts by saying (275) he is determined not to make the same mistake as the older Reformed, who "slip into" allowing the cultic or sacrificial metaphors to be interpreted solely forensically (i.e, without acknowledging the critical mediatorial and "Representative" nature of Christ's High Priestly ministry). When it comes to themes of the atonement, if Barth in places does want to emphasize the forensic before moving to the more representative concept, we can still hold that Barth's discussion of the Judge judged in our place (substitutionary) is always seen in light of the *being* of the Judge himself (representative), providing ontological depth. It is therefore questionable as to whether Barth sees himself here in *CD* IV/1 as correcting his own slip into an Anselmian penal satisfaction model reflected in *CD* II/1, as McCormack asserts. While it might be difficult to prove that Barth's preference is more related to presentation than to conceptual priority, this difficulty may perhaps be lessened when understanding the type of ontological categories Barth has in mind, especially in regards to the ongoing primal relationship between God and humanity.

38. See *CD* IV/1, 253, where Barth talks about the importance of maintaining the "Representative" aspect as the framework for the atonement.

39. McCormack, "For Us and Our Salvation," 292: "Now to speak of a 'person' as something that can mediate between 'natures' obviously entails some difficulties. It would seem to predicate something of the 'person' which is not predicated of either of the natures." But McCormack adds that something of this kind must exist to protect against the Lutheran *communio naturarum*.

40. McCormack, "'With Loud Cries and Tears,'" 50. I am not aware of borrowing the phrase "single subject" from this article, although it is mentioned by McCormack, 45.

granted because the properties of divinity or humanity spill over into each other, or because they are shared or mixed into one another as in a Lutheran communication of natures, but simply because the single subject, Jesus Christ, gives us the latitude to describe it this way. Now with the single subject latitude is attached a single subject discipline, for it is impossible to get behind the single person to the chemistry in order to explain how this occurs; this could not be explained any more than the incarnation itself. We can therefore only rest in faith on the miracle and its mysterious self-validation.[41]

With this helpful reminder, we may ask whether or not our Christo-anthropological employment of the same single subject economy would have any bearing on McCormack regarding Barth's view of the atonement as being primarily forensic. McCormack does not appear to consider our theme: a single subject duality between *iustus* and *peccator* humanity, both represented in Jesus Christ. But, as we have put forward already, if we rightly discount anything like a Lutheran *communion* between the two *totus* and mutually exclusive determinations in the humanity of Jesus Christ, and if the operating framework of Barth's dueling true-false, real-unreal ontologies is kept in view, is it feasible that we might find a *niche* for Barth's forensic language that is perhaps overlooked by McCormack and which keeps all penal substitution within the ontological frame? In other words, if sin is impossible, false and counterfeit, and if God's vehement destruction of sin is a destruction of what is not ultimately real at all—a nothingness assumed by Christ—then can we question the degree to which any vengeful attitude towards humanity in its sinfulness is determinative of God's real attitude towards humanity?[42]

If Barth has applied the *simul* to the atonement in the above fashion, he is not exceedingly clear about his intentions. We can pose good reasons for Barth's caution. At the very least he will not violate the single subject discipline with anthropology any more than he would with Chalcedon directly, i.e., out of deference to the miracle of the single subject, Jesus, and his assuming and destroying the old man *even while* remaining the new. Within this restriction, all that can be permissibly said is that Jesus Christ is the righteous human and Jesus Christ is the "one great sinner."[43] But what about the question concerning the *peccator* aspect of humanity and the non-existence

41. McCormack, "For us and Our Salvation," 292.

42. It is not difficult to see the import of an asymmetrical false-true relationship versus that of an asymmetrical true-true relationship. Apart from the false-true asymmetry, we are left to wonder over the two "true" sides of a seemingly divine split personality.

43. *CD* IV/1, 239; see also 280.

of the old man? How does it relate to Barth's view of the atonement and Christ's destruction of *das Nichtige*—or nothingness? Firstly, Barth is wary of an under-realized eschatology which presents nothingness as *something*, as if it were not in one sense already eradicated in the atonement. Secondly, Barth is wary of an over-realized eschatology, which presents nothingness as *nothing*. Thirdly and finally for Barth, while "nothingness is not nothing,"[44] the "is" of the phrase "is not" functions critically for Barth. It signifies the present-tense, provisional aspect of nothingness, as opposed to simply a static "negation" that could be dispensed of purely in the past tense. It is not difficult to see how this present-tense view of that which *is* complies with the *simul*. Like the simultaneity of what *is* and what *is not*, the single subject aspect requires that we hold together theologically the *iustus* being of humanity in Jesus Christ and a *peccator* aspect assumed by Jesus Christ. The latter is an aspect that does not exist ultimately, even though it does exist provisionally.[45] That is why Barth can say in his sub-section "The Reality of Nothingness" (paragraph 50) that the havoc and pain evil causes in this world is more than a semblance. This is plainly demonstrated in Christ's passion and his warfare against nothingness.[46] However, nothingness does not ultimately exist because at the final judgment, "when the hour strikes" and the victory of Jesus Christ is fully revealed,[47] nothingness will be "deprived of even the transient, temporary impermanent being it had. Even the truth of falsehood, the power of impotence, the sense of non-sense and the possibility of the impossible" are withdrawn in the manifestation of final judgment at Calvary.[48] The age of the *simul* is synonymous with the overlap of the ages; it therefore provides the outer limit for all that is provisional or temporal. Because Christ's finished work in the judgment of the cross establishes the limit between present and future, Barth can therefore make the astounding claim that if nothingness is not seen in retrospect, "it is not seen at all."[49]

How can we summarize this? While holding to the *simul*, which again protects us against a premature teleological perspective (an over-realized

---

44. *CD* III/4, 439.

45. See *CD* IV/3.1, 252: Barth therefore can describe the darkness Jesus assumes as "supremely non-being" with the caveat that it "does not *exist* as non-being."

46. *CD* III/3, 353. The "warfare" engaged in by Jesus Christ is a major theme of paragraph 69; see *CD* IV/3.1, 239.

47. *CD* III/3, 367.

48. *CD* III/3, 363. "Redemption" on Barth's view is this final consummation of Christ's finished work (i.e., its final manifestation).

49. *CD* III/3, 366.

eschatology), we can at the same time take with Barth an appropriate teleological perspective. Along with the undeniable fact of the *simul*'s existence in the overlap of the ages, it cannot be disputed that for Barth God's wrath is funneled toward one end, to destroy in a retributive and decisive manner the old man, the illegitimate imposter who does not comport with the actuality of humanity's primal adoption in Christ.[50] In view of this, perhaps Barth also reasons that compiling all of the punishment for a false, guilt-ridden humanity onto Christ has no bearing in the end in comparison to his overall ontological purpose revealed in the resurrection.[51] Geoffrey Bromiley corroborates this interpretation of Barth, "The righteousness of the second Adam exposes the unrighteousness of the first. It far outweighs it, too, for even as we hear God's sentence on the man of sin we see that this man no longer exists. God has had mercy on all even as he included all under disobedience."[52]

Now with Barth's categories, he will obviously have to ward off all accompanying suspicions of Docetism in his Christology.[53] But it is our assessment that Barth has accomplished his goal, perhaps even to the point of hyperbole, when it comes to convincing us that the Son of God really suffered. And as for McCormack, we can hope that a *simul* perspective as it relates to the humanity of Christ and the atonement might cause him to view the forensic theme in Barth categorically differently.[54] This is a

---

50. *CD* II/2, 558: "The grace of this God is this. When He took our flesh in Jesus Christ, God Himself undertook in our place to subject Himself to the judgment and punishment that must be executed if we are to be raised up to Him. He Himself renounced and confessed our self-will and godlessness . . . He Himself executed and suffered Himself the necessary slaying of our obstinacy." Note how Barth speaks of the slaying of the *peccator* aspect (the obstinacy) even as it is assumed within the one person of Christ. We will return to this important distinction.

51. *CD* II/2, 558: "In the resurrection of Jesus Christ from the dead as it has already been accomplished, we sinners are already revealed as the righteous who may live by their faith. Death could not hold Him, and therefore it cannot hold us. His life (and His life is our life) had necessarily to swallow up death, and it did swallow it up."

52. Bromiley, *An Introduction to the Theology of Karl Barth*, 187.

53. Barth's descriptions of the old man as a "shadow" or "ghost" are helpful in comparing reality to unreality, possibility to impossibility, but they do not discourage suspicions of Docetism. See *CD* III/4, 201; *CD* IV/1, 568. We will say more about Docetism and its ramifications for sanctification in the next chapter.

54. While Barth lets the single subject *peccator*, Jesus, "take the heat" of God's wrath, it is the unreal-real asymmetry which allows us to see the other determination of the single subject, the *iustus* human, Jesus, preserved. The overall resulting category for the atonement is therefore shown to be overwhelmingly restorative (not retributive) in a way that is not possible apart from the single subject duality of the *simul*.

perspective we will capitalize on when we pick up McCormack again in the next chapter.

The Cry of Doubt?

Having witnessed Barth's severe presentation of sin's misery and its deadly consequences, we turn now to the cross and the sharpest point of the *simul*'s cutting edge. For Barth it is the cross which most poignantly eliminates any semblance of neutrality between the warring humanities of the human being Jesus Christ. Much of Barth's talk about the rejection of the Righteous and Elected One centers around the Savior's so-called cry of derelicition, "My God, my God, why have you forsaken me" (Mark 15:34). This is Christ's "not unjustifiable cry of pain which no arts of exegesis should be allowed to mitigate."[55] And just as no other human experiences the misery experienced by Christ on Golgotha, Christ's abandonment on the cross is also unique:[56] "God has never forsaken, and does not and will not forsake any man as He forsook this man. And 'forsook' means that He turned against Him as never before or since against any . . . But the very fact that He was for Him—for Him as our Reconciler, Savior and Mediator—necessarily entailed that He was wholly against Him."[57] So what are the key elements to deciphering Barth's radical, simultaneous, for-and-against language? And is this merely rhetoric that cannot be distilled? As insinuated above, for Barth to say God is *for* "this man" but against *sin*, or that God is for the "new man" and against the "old man," might be less confusing because it puts the accent on the atonement in the right place, but at this critical juncture of the interpretation of the cross Barth appears even more adamant in maintaining the single subject duality of Chalcedon and in turn the *simul*.[58] Regardless, Barth's "for and against" language in *Church Dogmatics* increases in a manner commensurate with the intensity of Christ's passion.

Before proceeding, it will help briefly to reestablish with Barth the *simul*'s severe ground rules. We have established that for Barth the true human, i.e., *iustus* humanity, has true knowledge of God. This is not merely

---

55. *CD* IV/3.1, 413.

56. We do well to pause here to catch the full force of what Barth is saying without siphoning anything away from the "single subject" principle. As will be explained later in this chapter, Barth can at once assert that Jesus was "abandoned" and "never abandoned." Strict abandonment of Jesus on the cross, as in theories of penal substitutionary atonement, is never in view.

57. *CD* IV/3.1, 414.

58. Again we remember that it is not sin as an abstraction that is crucified, but Christ.

a noetic cognizance, Barth reminds us, but a true knowledge that cannot help but issue forth in true embodiment.[59] Here knowledge and obedience are one. Barth decisively states, "True knowledge of God is not and cannot be attacked; it is without anxiety and without doubt."[60] Certainty and uncertainty, Barth continues, are "circles that do not touch each other but are mutually exclusive; and therefore a direct transition from one to the other is impossible. Uncertainty will never be possible in this constraint of the Word of God."[61]

Interestingly, by posing the *peccator* falsehood of enslaved humanity in sharpest relief against the *iustus* and holiness of true and free humanity, Barth has put the biblical expositor assessing Jesus' passion into an interesting predicament. That is, what does one do with the passages in Gethsemane and Golgotha where Jesus apparently expresses doubts? Again, the true human being as Barth has established him is *totus iustus*; he is not a Hercules at the crossroads. The true human cannot and does not waffle at the point of his decision, but is perfectly and unquestionably obedient, responding to the Father with an unequivocal "yes." But do we not see here not only original sin assumed by Jesus but also the activity of willful sin as articulated by Barth?

Habitually we do not consider doubt to be sin. It typically falls in the neutral category or even on the righteousness "side of the fence," which is true especially if, *after* doubting, one chooses rightly! We are not aware of a time when Barth calls doubt sin, but he does cite Jesus' chastisement of the disciples for doubting[62]—their doubt is not a positive or even a neutral occurrence. If they had eyes of faith, they would not doubt. In his passion Jesus Christ certainly questioned (Mark 15:34). But can we suggest that the Son of Man doubted, or that he waffled in the midst of his struggle (Matt 26:39–42)? Can we say that he sinned? If "he who is not with me is against me," then neutral is *against*, a product of sin.[63] If we blindly refuse to say Jesus sinned, how do we explain his doubts? This is a tougher task to explain as compared to thinking of Jesus being made sin, as if sin were something he passively accepted and suffered. Why, for instance, when Jesus doubts in the Garden, do we not have permission to say, "Ye of little faith, why do you

---

59. See *CD* I/1, 188: "Knowing, they are affected by the object known . . . Face to face with this truth they can no longer withdraw into themselves in order to affirm, question or deny it thence."

60. *CD* II/1, 7.

61. *CD* II/1, 8.

62. See *CD* III/1, 35.

63. *CD* IV/2, 159; as related to Matt 12:30.

doubt?" (Matt 8:26, KJV); or perhaps we should quote "ask in faith, never doubting, for the one who doubts is like a wave of the sea, driven and tossed by the wind" (James 1:6).

Barth does not seem overly interested in pursuing this course of Jesus' apparent susceptibility, at least if it means jettisoning the traditional view that Jesus did not sin.[64] At the same time, Jesus is described by Barth as "He who trembled and shrank back in Gethsemane."[65] Perhaps the prospect of Jesus sinning does not appear to trouble Barth because he views any challenges in that direction as a consequence of the *peccatum* flesh Jesus has assumed, not as the eternally true, *iustis* human being that he ultimately and actually is. At this monumental juncture of Jesus' life, attempting to discern the degrees of the *peccator* dimension of Jesus is not helpful and can only be akin to positing gradations of total darkness. But we do have to confront the situation in Gethsemane and Golgotha as is and to see in Jesus' passion the interplay of two mutually exclusive determinations. If we fail to do so, how can we avoid short-circuiting Jesus' solidarity with us, he who went at least to the extent of meeting us at the nub of all sin—the point of unbelief?

More than the amount of sin Jesus assumed, or the passive or active nature inherent in his being made sin (2 Cor 5:21), what is at base most important is the severe delineation between the two mutually exclusive determinations. We have sought to establish that the wall between the two is infinitely high, so no amount of sin can ever spill over to create an admixture with righteousness. And while the false piled up high against this wall has no meaning and cannot exist without the true, the true *can* and *does* exist without the false. Henceforth, regardless of Jesus' passive or active association with sin, we must continue to remember the true, *iustus* humanity of Jesus Christ—that which, while so shrouded in the trauma of his passion, remains hidden in God. This is the humanity of the Righteous One, Jesus Christ (1 John 2:1). Congruently with the Epistle we can maintain that Jesus Christ is uniquely *the One born of God*: "those who are born of God do not sin, but the one who was born of God protects them" (1 John 5:18). This Jesus is not the Jesus Christ who is the "greatest sinner," and not even the Jesus who doubted. We can therefore suggest that *this* is the sinlessness of Jesus that Christians can still hold to in orthodox Christian belief, regardless of the implications of Jesus Christ's assumption of *sarx*, regardless of his doubt or even unbelief. Perhaps *this* is the Jesus Christ who was tempted in

---

64. See *CD* I/2, 152: Jesus was "without sin of His own." See also *CD* I/2, 152; *CD* III/2, 51; *CD* IV/1, 131, 258; *CD* IV/2, 92.

65. *CD* IV/3.1, 390.

every way as we are but did *not* waver?⁶⁶ We could hold to this view even as we confront the possibility that our formal view of Jesus' sinlessness has been too simplistic. Regardless of our verdict with respect to the nature and extent of Jesus' sinfulness, the implications of the New Testament witness point to the human being Jesus Christ as the archetypal guarantee of the promise that we are righteous in Christ in the midst of our unrighteousness. In other words, Barth presses us to see that Jesus' passion demonstrates more than any other time the fact that Jesus Christ in and of himself is representing *peccator* and also *iustus* humanity.

In this connection, if we hold to Barth's line that in reality there is no room for doubt, no uncertainty and "no fluctuation" under the slavery of righteousness,⁶⁷ it is clearly apparent that we cannot therefore chalk up Jesus' doubts to a weak moment in his true *iustus* humanity. A low ebb in the fluidity of his singly pure humanity would not indicate true humanity, but some kind of hybrid of true and false humanity—a synthesis. Alternatively, should we then choose to describe Jesus as fallen humanity, singly *peccator* in his assumption of corrupt flesh? How then could we explain Jesus choosing rightly in the end? What kind of theological anthropology could result if we give Jesus a corrupt humanity and in the end default to his divinity? This would indicate a battle not between human natures but only between his corrupt human nature and God.⁶⁸ It would belie anything but Jesus being tempted in every way that we are (Heb 4:15). Not only that, but God's decision to go forward to Calvary then occurs over the head of the human Jesus; it is in fact not a human decision at all!

From the beginning of our study we have argued that the *simul*, derived from the christological and biblical witness, prevents us from having to choose between Jesus assuming a fallen humanity or a pre-fall, pristine humanity, nor do we have to resort to a third option, a zero-sum combination of the first two. Perhaps we tend to favor the latter (zero-sum) concept because that is the preconception we have of ourselves, but only the *simul*

---

66. See *CD* III/4, 401, where Barth puts Jesus' request for the cup to pass in a more positive light: it "is not to be understood as an inclination to disobedience but as an element in the obedience of Jesus." In contrast to a waffling Jesus, is this, for Barth, the *iustus* Jesus?

67. *CD* III/1, 350: "In the realm of reality and the covenant faithfulness between God and humanity there is no room for doubt or uncertainty, because there is no choice between hypotheticals."

68. See Kevin Chiarot, *The Unassumed is the Unhealed: The Humanity of Christ in the Christology of T. F. Torrance*. Chiarot makes the argument that T. F. Torrance is at risk in this direction, i.e., in couching the hypostatic union in such a way as to fail to give the *true humanity* of Christ the focus it deserves.

helps us to characterize Jesus biblically and accurately as both spotless lamb and scapegoat. In derivative fashion, and because Jesus is our human substitute and representative, we are given to see ourselves as *simul iustus et peccator*.

The Cry Revisited

Jesus' behavior in the gospels is ambiguous; we might give him the benefit of the doubt that, for instance, his rejection of his family (Mark 3:31) was not sin because he is God and God cannot sin. Case closed. But we perceive in Gethsemane and Golgotha a pinnacle of intensity in Jesus' struggle where the two human minds of Christ, that of *totus iustus* and *totus peccator*, are engaged in fiercest warfare. Because Barth establishes his *simul* as the key to sanctification, his whole program of what we have called "Chalcedonian anthropology" is placed on trial in the light of what happens in Jesus' passion. Here we ascertain whether or not the dualities we have articulated collapse into dualism. In our continuing investigation we return to *Church Dogmatics* and Barth's insight below:

> He finally hung on the gallows as a criminal between two other criminals, and died there, with that last despairing question on His lips, as One who was condemned and maltreated and scorned by men and abandoned by God . . . And in the passion he exists conclusively as the One He is—the Son of God who is also the Son of Man. In the deepest darkness of Golgotha He enters supremely into the glory of the unity of the Son with the Father. In that abandonment by God He is the One who is directly loved by God.[69]

Abandoned and loved? Darkness and glory? Condemned by God while unified with the Father? With the logic of Chalcedonian anthropology we have noted Barth's theological refusal to separate too soon what must be separated in the end (sin from humanity), lest he separate those things which should not and cannot be separated (God from God, humanity from God).[70] Because untruth and truth are both dimensions of humanity, and because the parasitic is lethally insinuated into the real, the whole human must die

---

69. *CD* IV/2, 252. Barth also remarks, "the darkness of a criminal execution . . . was in a sense His coronation as this man."

70. To clarify, humanity is always distinguished from God but never separated from God. Humanity cannot exist apart from God even though God can exist apart from humanity.

to be preserved.[71] But when it comes to separation, vouchsafes Barth, this does not entail the deepest separation of humanity from God, or especially of the Son from the Father, any more than the infinite and eternal depth of sin can trump the infinite and eternal depth of grace. Explains Barth, "We are dealing with sin itself and as such: the preoccupation, the orientation, the determination of man as he has left his place as a creature and broken his covenant with God; the corruption which God has made his own . . . In the place of all men he has wrestled with that which separates them from Him. He has Himself borne the consequence of this separation to bear it away."[72]

Have we tired yet of Barth's "playing both sides of the fence" on the *simul*? How can Barth, in different sections of *Church Dogmatics*, variably describe Jesus in his cry of dereliction as rejected and abandoned, abandoned and loved, never abandoned by God,[73] and even "never less abandoned by God"?[74] Every theologian can be excused for a few inconsistencies, but Barth would have to be the worst of systematicians to contradict himself consistently on this matter. Instead of contradicting himself, we could suggest he is heightening our awareness of the contradiction of righteousness and sin in the *simul* of Jesus Christ and therefore in our own lives.

Barth asks us to see Jesus' "dereliction" in nuanced fashion. On one level it is real, it hurts, it is the darkest of ontologies that cannot and will not be exposed as counterfeit until later. But on another level it does not indicate the "true reality," and for that reason, Barth can actually say Jesus' cry of dereliction is comforting. This is especially true for those of us who both believe, and doubt:

> What are our doubts and despairs, disguised or acute, compared with His dereliction, which was also suffered by Him in our place? . . . Unless we are to evade our own sanctification at

---

71. *CD* II/2, 690: Barth speaks of God's judgment as "the light which falls from above upon the tangled skein of your life," and continuing in first person from God's perspective, "Condemning you, I exonerate you. Judging you, I accept you, slaying you, I make you alive."

72. *CD* IV/1, 247.

73. *CD* II/2, 741. Jesus was only "on the brink of dereliction, because for our sakes God did not will to abandon Him and did not in fact do so."

74. *CD* II/2, 740. See immediately preceding note. Barth is more reticent to use the word abandoned here in *CD* II. He says Jesus was "threatened" with abandonment, and he draws a line between rejection and dereliction; here in II/2 rejection "does not mean" dereliction. Barth seemed to lose his reserve as time went on, perhaps because of the critique of Docetism or again because he realized that even erring on that side would be inconsequential to his overall program, as long as the line was clearly drawn between the two mutually exclusive dimensions of *iustus* and *peccator*.

the decisive point, we have to bear it, to see it through, in this character. The only thing is that in so doing we are not forsaken by the One who raised and answered the question whether He was not forsaken by God. At this point, then we find ourselves in the deepest fellowship with God.[75]

Barth has constructed for us a powerful picture of our own rejection in Christ, and the death of the "old man" in us, all in the context of the divine embrace. Because at bottom righteousness proves deeper than sin, so as insolent sinners humans find themselves in "the deepest fellowship" with God.

---

75. *CD* IV/2, 612–13. That Christ "raised and answered" the question of forsakenness brackets a similar cry of humanity in Rom 7:24–25. Barth makes this derivative correlation (IV/1, 591), describing the Christian as one who is a person of the Question and simultaneously a person of the Answer: "He could not do the one if he tried to refuse the other . . . he can only be both at once."

8

A New Perspective on the Cross

"And the pardon of man, declared in the promise concerning him, the reality of his future already in the present, is not less than this: totus iustus."[1]

WE HAVE PASSED THE MIDPOINT OF OUR STUDY. IN THIS CHAPTER, ACCOMpanied by Barth's treatment of Job, and armed with Barth's introduction of the pure and impure forms of humanity, we will press into my contention for a christological *simul*. The accumulated ideas above will ideally provide continuation for our discussion on the atonement and buttress my early (Introduction) suggestion that Barth is a theologian of the cross with an Eastern, dimensional mind. It is fitting that this chapter provides a turning of the corner into the rest of the book; my hope is that the pivotal conclusions reached here will launch us forward into the rest of the book with a deeper appreciation for Barth's theological anthropology in light of the cross, i.e., his hidden dimensional vision that what is "new" about humanity reconciled to God is simply what is true, continually fresh, and inherently transformative.

Job and Jesus

Job is one of Barth's best illustrations of how we, like Christ, are never less abandoned than when we are "abandoned"—and I am using quotation to mark the asymmetry between the two infinite determinations. In fact, in Barth's extensive treatment of Job we find him presenting the ancient saint as "a type of Jesus Christ,"[2] comprehending all of the suffering passages of

1. *CD* IV/1, 596.
2. *CD* IV/3.1, 388.

the Old Testament.³ Barth is obviously inspired by the parallels between Job and Jesus. It is our contention that Barth's lengthy excursus toward the end of *Church Dogmatics* IV/3.1 provides him with a sort of license to speak about Christ indirectly in a way that he would not typically afford himself to do directly out of reverence for the paschal mystery. For example, could the following description of Job be anything less than an oblique reference to Jesus on the cross?

> There can be no question of God abandoning him. He does not abandon him, but keeps him inescapably in his grasp. Yet Job finds it impossible to see or understand in what sense he experiences this unbreakable clasp of His hand, or can understand it as His will and accept it as His work. He firmly sees his God and not another in what overwhelms him. But he does not understand him in it. He does not recognise his God any more. He sees . . . a God who does not have the true features of his own true God, who had become his Partner in free faithfulness, and whose partner he had similarly become, in blessing on the one side and righteous obedience on the other. He does not doubt for a moment that he has to do with this God, but it almost drives him mad that he encounters Him in a form in which He is absolutely alien. He suffers from the very faithfulness which means that God will not abandon him nor he God . . . And he has to experience the fact that all his crying and beating and attempting to escape, all his questioning and doubting and protesting, is powerless against the iron fact that God does encounter him in this form.⁴

Again, is Barth here giving himself permission to probe not only into Job's but perhaps also into the "questioning, doubting and protesting" of Christ's agony, including what we earlier cited as "His not unjustifiable cry of pain which no arts of exegesis should be allowed to mitigate?"⁵ Now if Job's and Christ's sufferings are not to be mitigated, it can only be in view of the bigger frame, the frame which the human beings Job and perhaps Jesus lose sight of, but without which there is no gospel.

In light of this, the Job excursus potentially provides us with at least three affirmations from Barth concerning Jesus' suffering. The first and

---

3. *CD* IV/3.1, 401.

4. *CD* IV/3.1, 402–3. See 403 where Barth lists all of Job's complaints in his persecution, possibly alluding that they could just easily fall under Christ's cry of dereliction; for instance, "you have turned cruel to me: with the might of your hand you persecute me" (30:21).

5. *CD* IV/3.1, 413; cited earlier.

already mentioned is that while Barth does not hold back from penal language, it is always meant to be kept within an overall framework of ontology. A non-ontological approach could simply claim that Jesus was separated from God; that he became God's hated enemy and was punished by God instead of us, as our substitute, so that we would not be subjected to those things. This type of simplistic substitution forces or dictates the separation in exactly the wrong place (i.e., between Jesus Christ, Son of God, and the Father). It is the biblical witness to the *simul* of Jesus Christ which arms Barth for a different perspective, one in which the separation in view must be between the true and false natures of humanity, of which Jesus encompasses both. As quoted earlier, Barth insists it is the *peccator* determination of corrupt humanity, "the determination of man as he has left his place as a creature,"[6] that Christ is out to separate and carry away in his person. In bearing the consequences of our sinfulness, Christ in his "separation from God" destroys the un-creature in himself while preserving the creature in himself. It is the *simul* which allows Barth to position the one person Jesus Christ be "two different men" in atonement—simultaneously the "old man" and the "new man." Consequently the only thing that we can say, and that Barth does say, is that Jesus was abandoned, but he was not abandoned, the latter reflecting the bedrock truth. It is only this knowledge which makes us sure that when Jesus asks us to love our enemies, he is not saying we should do so in contradistinction to a God who does not love his enemies! God loves his enemies, even if, where they are crucified with Christ, God's love is a slaying grace within the context of a saving grace.[7]

Secondly, from Barth's excursus on Job we learn that Job's sufferings were allowed by God, but that the real active agent for all of the nasty sicknesses and persecutions that came upon Job were foisted upon him by Satan. Barth notes that God "can give Satan, within a limited but very large sphere, a free hand in relation to Job. He can do so to such an extent that God Himself can and actually does appear to Job to be an enemy and persecutor."[8]

6. CD IV/1, 247. See Rom 6:6: "For we know that our old self (*anthropos*) was crucified with him so that the body of sin might be destroyed, and we might no longer be enslaved to sin."

7. CD III/2, 336: "The human existence of Jesus is in its totality . . . this conquest and renewal of the flesh, its slaying and displacement in the old form and its quickening and coming to life in the new." Partially quoted in chapter 3.

8. CD IV/3.1, 387. See 393–94 where Barth elaborates on sin being allowed "in the very presence of its Conqueror. Since it is directed as evil against God, it does not take place without Him that within its solidly and definitely described limits it can rage violently and lash out around it. But if it does not take place without God, does it mean that it takes place with Him?" Barth makes very strong qualifications in answer to this, which in turn qualifies all talk of Jesus being "smitten and afflicted by God."

Satan's wiles involve taking advantage of the misery and torment that God mysteriously allows, in order to tar the face of God, deceiving human beings into thinking that God must be unequivocally against them. Job's confusion is so deep, and unmitigated while in the midst, that he cannot know his afflictions *from* Satan, nor the faithfulness of his God obstructed *by* Satan, as anything but the final word.[9] He cannot know that the No of God's "rejection" is the penultimate word, except in retrospect.[10] As Barth concludes, "God Himself will intervene between Himself and Job. He will not justify him without humbling him. But He will not humble him, as he had not been humbled in all his misery and affliction, without also justifying him."[11]

This brings us to the third and most important point we learn about Job from Barth's multi-part excursus on Job, and again the associations with Jesus can hardly be avoided. Even while Job is acting in *peccatum* ignorance, he is still the righteous man that he was in the opening of the book—and the righteous man who emerges at the end of the book. He is the righteous man of knowledge throughout. Barth exegesis concludes that, even if the truth of Job's righteousness is mostly obscured in the large middle portion of the book, and only rarely emerging, it is there all the time. The occasional right statements by Job do not make his wrong, ignorant statements any less wrong, but Barth describes the *iustus* knowledge of Job in the middle portion of the book—his righteous appraisals in the midst of ignorance and darkness—as "meteors descending from another world." It should not be surprising by now that Barth also surmises them to be "exceptions confirming the rule."[12] We shall soon see the implications Barth draws out concerning Job's righteousness even in the midst of contradiction.

In the middle of his crisis, however, without the perspective (or retrospective) of the end, Job has lost sight of the rule. In his checkered existence Job "rightly maintains his righteousness before God," but at the same time, "he blatantly sets himself in the wrong by arrogantly advancing this righteousness as a claim that God should be righteous before him."[13] If the "profound knowledge" of Job arguably exists throughout his complaint, it is at the same time so entangled with his "no less profound ignorance" that to extract any statement he makes in order to define it as purely *iustus*

---

9. *CD* IV/3.1, 400. Barth notes the conflation of good and evil in Job's mind in Job 16:9–10. Echoes of Jesus' passion are unmistakable.

10. *CD* IV/3.1, 407.

11. *CD* IV/3.1, 408.

12. *CD* IV/3.1, 406.

13. *CD* IV/3.1, 406.

is absolutely impossible.[14] We might say it is here where, tucked into the fine print of IV/3, Barth places a hidden key meant to unlock humanity's sanctification from the inside (and which provides welcome corroboration of our thesis).

> In Job's complaint as such we cannot distinguish between right and wrong in such a way as to fix on any of his utterances and say this is right or this is wrong. In their own way they all point both to the right and to the left, both above and below. It cannot be otherwise that Job—*simul iustus et peccator*—is right in all his sayings as the servant of Yahweh, and in none of them as fallible man. We thus see him everywhere under the law which he has accepted and on the way of the expression and repetition required of him, yet everywhere, too, as a blind and deaf and lame man who can only stumble and fall and rise and stumble and fall again on this way.[15]

Job as *simul iustus et peccator*! To our knowledge this is the closest Barth ever comes to attributing the phrase directly to the person of Jesus Christ himself. Without getting too carried away by this discovery, let us return to one prior point where our comparison may shed some light on Christ's passion. Earlier we talked about how the severity of the *simul* provided the sharpest of edges between *iustus* and *peccator* so as to eliminate any grey area or harmonization. We asked how this related to Jesus' doubts as the man of Gethsemane and Golgotha. If with Barth we classify Job's doubts and questions as unfaithful, manifestations of *peccatum*, should we do likewise with Jesus? If doubt is sin, because it is not strict obedience, i.e., if there is no room for waffling in *iustus*—then we can at least say doubt is also the kind of sin God condemns by empathizing with us, not by penalizing us. Only by the severity of the *simul* can we actually find freedom to call doubt sin, knowing at the same time the consolation of Christ, the one who shared all human doubts in order to bury them. Moreover, this viewpoint overwhelmingly weights God's justice to its restorative purpose and away from a fundamentally retributive one, for who can penalized for doubting?

---

14. *CD* IV/3.1, 401. It is not because Job is right that he is qualified to come out righteous in the end, but "because God Himself throws His own weight into the scales, dispelling the fault of Job, causing him to give up the conflict, and enabling him to experience, see and know to what extent he has to do with Him . . . For the moment, however, we see this knowledge and ignorance of God in headlong collision and unbearable tension. This is the depth and essence of the suffering of the suffering Job" (401).

15. *CD* IV/3.1, 406. Importantly Barth adds "If he were not on the way, he could not stumble and fall" (407).

Do we decide to doubt? Doubt therefore reveals itself in sharpest relief to its opposite, another involuntary occurrence—belief. Perhaps the simplest *simul* prayer for persons in the realm of sanctification is, "I believe, help my unbelief!"(Mark 9:24).[16]

In this section we have put forth not a straight up correspondence between Job's sufferings and Jesus', but perhaps a closer one than is normally entertained. It is hopefully already apparent that Chalcedonian Christology can only take us so far when it comes to anthropology because of its ambiguous definition of the type of humanity Christ assumed. We contend that a double duality perspective, that of a "Chalcedonian anthropology," better helps us to understand Jesus in his passion and during the greatest points of struggle. Unequipped with Barth's *simul*, it is doubtful we could compare Jesus' and Job's humanity very realistically, much less see the strong echoes between them that Barth seems to appreciate. In fact, it must be asked if Barth's apparent indication of Jesus as *simul iustus et peccator* does not better safeguard against Docetist insinuations into the conventional Chalcedonian formulation, especially as we contemplate the Temptations,[17] the Garden of Gethsemane, and Golgotha. At the same time, Barth knows that the more seriously we take Jesus' cry of dereliction, "the stronger becomes the temptation to approximate to the view of a contradiction and conflict in God Himself." This temptation must be rejected. To separate God from God, as if Jesus' suffering dictated a separation between the Trinitarian persons, is for Barth "the supreme blasphemy."[18]

---

16. Barth quotes what we have called the '*simul* prayer' in *CD* I/1 (24) and *CD* IV/4 (42) and many times in between in *Church Dogmatics*, describing Christian vacillation between the two determinations of belief and unbelief.

17. See *CD* I/2, 158: "The temptation narrative (Mark 4:1ff) obviously describes the very opposite of a mock battle." Versus those critics who would want to describe the temptation of Christ as merely an "external molestation by Satan," Barth presents it as an "inward temptation and trial." Barth continues, "The point is that, faced with God, Jesus did not run away from the state and situation of fallen man, but took it upon Himself, lived it and bore it Himself as eternal Son of God. How could He have done so, if it His human existence He had not been exposed to real inward temptation and trial, if like other men He had not trodden an inner path, if He had not cried to God and wrestled with God in real inward need? It was in this wrestling, in which he was in solidarity with us in the uttermost, that there was done that which is not done by us, the will of God."

18. *CD* IV/1, 185.

A New Perspective on the Cross 165

One Person—"Two Men"—One Spirit!

We have observed just how seriously, almost dualistically, Barth takes the two determinations of the *simul*. The *iustus*, true humanity, and the *peccator*, false humanity, can have no reconciliation or compromise with one another; the severity is marked by utter and complete disparity, and no relationship between the two humanities involves a receding of one in favor of the other. There is no negotiation between the two determinations, only incessant warfare. Implementing his twofold anthropology, Barth exercises the latitude to use "the One" with each descriptive side of the duality, reckoning either dimension of the duality as the one whole entity. We have argued that Barth's employment of the Chalcedonian principle includes the Son of God's prerogative to be not only God and human but also both *iustus* and *peccator* human. We have proposed that our old humanity and new humanity do not exist independently any more than Christ's. In Barth's language, the "old man" exists only in the one, and the "new man" exists only in the one; there simply is no "new man" or "old man" apart from the "one man."

Because of this christological dictum of the "one," the alien factor that needs removal, the *peccator*, cannot be extracted prematurely. It cannot be extracted in the positive sense any more than in the negative sense Solomon could resolve the true and false mothers' squabble by cutting the child in two. In other words, when Barth says God is wholly against Jesus, he means against the old man of sin, yet because this abstract dimension of sin cannot itself be crucified, it necessarily means Jesus. The Righteous One therefore has to die in order to take the *peccator* down to be deposited in the grave. But again, the One God-man, the One *simul iustus et peccator*, can do this simultaneously as the immanent and transcendent One. "In this humiliation," states Barth, "God is supremely God, that in this death He is supremely alive."[19]

In sum, Barth can say Jesus Christ died, but he can also say Jesus Christ did not die. He can say because Jesus Christ is God the Son, God died, but he can also say God did not die.[20] Likewise, and only because of the mirror Christ's revelation provides, we can say in Pauline terms "I am a sinner, and I am a saint"—"I am a slave to sin, I am a slave to God." We have demonstrated the influence of Holy Scripture on Barth in relation to employing this single subject latitude. Without the theological discipline of the single subject principle, *simul* sanctification can only lose its legs. Barth is sure, however, that the more I know who I am, seated with Christ in the

19. *CD* IV/1, 247.
20. See *CD* I/2, 108: Barth speaks of "God Himself" suffering the judgment.

heavenly places, the more I will realize on this earthly sojourn who I am *not*. By virtue of *simul* sanctification and empowered by the Holy Spirit, the Christian might be one who more habitually, in Barth's words, "turns his back on himself, and away above himself 'seeks those things which are above' (Col 3:1)."[21]

> Therefore life in the Holy Spirit means "already," even in the midst of the "not yet," to stand in the full truth of what, considered from our "not yet," is pure future, but on the strength of this "already," pure present, in which we can already live here and now, expecting the annulment of the duality.[22]

Again, the Christian's assurance about the annulment of the duality of the *simul* is rooted in his or her confidence in Christ's own work and with the accompanying knowledge that even as one duality ends, the original Chalcedonian duality remains, held together by the single subject, Jesus Christ.[23] In the incarnation, Barth assures us that we observe the work of the *God* Jesus Christ, "He does not become estranged from Himself by the fact that in doing this work He is one with God, and in this oneness of being with God."[24] Likewise Barth assures us that throughout the work of the *man* Jesus Christ, he remains in the bosom of the Father (John 1:18).[25]

Of course, for Barth it is the Holy Spirit who is the antidote to our depraved adherence to spatial categories—our refusal to allow for two things to operate simultaneously in the same space or for one person to be in two places at the same time. Lest we resort to the preposterous notion that Jesus stopped being God for a few days or hours in order "to be sin," Barth gives us reason to hold to the testimony that Jesus became sin and the old man in a way only God could accomplish. The Holy Spirit is the One who provides the unity where unity is required and joins together what no person can tear asunder.[26] Just as the Spirit maintains the Trinity at the point of deepest

---

21. *CD* II/1, 159.

22. *CD* II/1, 158.

23. See *Heidelberg*, 135: Barth speaks again of the assurance of the Holy Spirit, who "puts under our feet new ground on which we can confidently walk; ground from which we can catch sight of an eternal, true, and indestructible life; where since God is with us, we may participate in God's own true life."

24. *CD* IV/2, 63–64.

25. *CD* III/2, 65.

26. *CD* IV/3.2, 761: note Barth's Chalcedonian language again in the pneumatological realm: "of the divine working, being and action on the one side and the human on the other . . . [the Spirit's] work is to bring and to hold them together, not to identify, intermingle, nor confound them, not to change the one into the other nor to merge

A New Perspective on the Cross 167

contradiction in Christ,[27] Christians can already know that they, in the "sphere of the still" and conflicted in the *simul*, are risen with Christ, hidden with Christ in God, where they are seated at the right hand of the glory of the Father.[28] While Christians groan here, there is no groaning there, in humanity's uncontradicted *iustitia*—in the One who is humanity's righteousness, sanctification and redemption. While there, seated with Christ, believers are also here, bolstered with the confidence that Christ "lives to intercede" (Heb 7:25) for them as they prayerfully participate in Christ's name.[29]

As sojourners, Christians draw their greatest comfort from the Holy Spirit's permeating presence, evidence of God's oneness with *simul* humanity, and engendered especially in the fact that the Comforter is groaning in them. Undoubtedly these non-verbal groans existed even under the articulated cry of Jesus, and therefore the Spirit's groaning is an implicit indication that God is always with us in both locations of our already but not yet existence, a constant reminder of Christ's ongoing solidarity with humanity. If we are convinced that Christ's work as *simul iustus et peccator* forces all the right separations in the right places, it becomes exceedingly clear that, just as nothing can separate Jesus from God and nothing can separate humanity from Jesus, "nothing can separate us from the love of God in Christ Jesus our Lord" (Rom 8:32).[30]

---

them one into the other . . . but to bring them into harmony and therefore to bind them into a true unity."

27. Who we are as persons is dependent on who we are in Trinitarian Persons, i.e., human identity is both in Christ and in the Spirit even if we don't know the second without the first or the first consciously by the second. We are spiritual beings in Christ. The unseen Spirit, then, is in his own way just as foundational to human being. So to say the Spirit held the Father and Son together, as well as the Son and humanity, is not to instrumentalize the Spirit. Clearly, in regards to the latter, to make the Spirit into a "magical third" (*CD* IV/2, 343) at this point would be to lay the groundwork for instrumentalizing the Spirit elsewhere, as in conversion.

28. *CD* IV/3.2, 761.

29. In chapter 13 we revisit the topic of prayer and how Barth understands praying in Jesus' name.

30. See McCall, *Forsaken*, concerning the question of Trinitarian relations and the cross. McCall helpfully contends that there is no rupture of the Trinity, and as cited in Rom 8:34 above, that we can therefore not be separated from God ourselves. McCall's interpretation of Rom 7 is less helpful. In relation to that oft-contested chapter, McCall apparently fails to consider the simultaneous *peccator* and *righteous* dynamic derived from—and congruent with—the one who was made sin (2 Cor 5:21) while also being Righteous God. McCall's reading of Rom 7 therefore evidences a purely sequential conversion logic, opining that Paul was not speaking of a typical Christian experience. One would have instead expected McCall to see the *simul* connection to Romans 7 because of his christological perspective and his mutual commitment with Barth against

168   *Simul* Sanctification

The Pure Form and Docetism

What more can be said about Barth's assertion above, that in Christ's death he is "supremely alive?" Barth understands the importance of allowing Jesus' rejection, abandonment, suffering and death to have their full force. Failure to do so might cause us to look past "the man of Gethsemane and Golgotha" to another, pure form of humanity, as if in a Platonic Ideal. Barth does however assert, as a provocative prelude to his discussion on the dereliction of Christ, the existence of a pure form of humanity revealed in Him:

> We must consider the man Jesus Christ, who comes as the true Witness in the promise of the Spirit, first of all in his pure form; and we must never forget this in what follows. Yet it would be a kind of Docetism to stop here, or to be content with what has been said. This pure form is certainly the meaning and power of the existence of this man and His witness to the truth . . . This does not mean, however, that He is revealed to us men, and may be perceived and apprehended by us, in this pure form as such.[31]

In sum, there is a pure form of Christ's humanity, but even though it is "the secret of His existence"[32] it remains concealed in "this man," and knowledge of it is always, therefore, indirect; it is the kind of disclosed knowledge "which arises when the person or object to be known makes itself known."[33] It is no surprise so many have failed to acknowledge the pure form of Jesus' humanity, because it comes to us in a form that is "alien and quite dissimilar to it," or as Barth continues, "only in a form which is hidden, obscure and puzzling."[34]

Now with talk of a "pure form" of the Sanctified Man, Barth knows the charge of Docetism is at hand.[35] We remember his pre-emptive strike:

"the supreme blasphemy" (referenced earlier).

31. *CD* IV/3.1, 388, 389.
32. *CD* IV/3.1, 388.
33. *CD* IV/3.1, 389.
34. *CD* IV/3.1, 389.

35. It is questionable whether Barth can stem the tide of opinion that he is somehow promoting Docetic concepts. The challenge is to prove otherwise when he acknowledges sin and death to be "that which is not" and in the end eradicated falsehoods, part of the lie. See *CD* IV/1, 46: Barth states humanity's sin "takes place only as the powerful but, of course, before God absolutely powerless irruption of that which is not into the fulfilment of His will." We have already foreclosed on the spurious notion to Barth that uncontradicted reality includes hurt. Yet in the midst of our contradiction, and far from making light of hurt, could we not actually claim with Barth just the opposite? Could we not also claim that the reason falsehood hurts so badly and

"it would be a kind of Docetism to stop here." Yet even while bracing for this criticism he will not back off of the resurrection perspective we are given in Scripture—that the secret of Christ's existence is his pure form, even though he comes to us in his incarnate "alien form." Notes Barth, "It is in this form of suffering, as the wholly Rejected, Judged, Despised, Bound, Impotent, Slain and Crucified, and therefore as the Victor, that He marches with us and to us through the times, alive in the promise of the Spirit."[36] The fact that the pure form of Christ is thoroughly hidden is evidence of the deceptive and distortive nature of the alien form, but the hiddenness of what is truly real does not diminish the truth of its presence. Barth wants us to know that in the "Victor of Gethsemane and Golgotha" we have the simultaneous existence of both forms, the pure and the alien: "elected by God as rejected of Him; judging the world as judged by it; superior to all men as despised by all: free as bound; mighty as impotent; eternally living as dead and buried; completely victorious in complete defeat."[37] *Eternally living as dead and buried*? No wonder, notes Barth, that Jesus Christ in his alien form is foolishness to the Greeks.[38]

To be faithful to the revelatory biblical witness, God incarnate, the one in whom "the whole fullness of deity dwells bodily" (Col 2:9), must be anchored in both spheres of the so-called overlap of the ages. In Chalcedonian fashion, Barth insists we must distinguish but not separate the pure form from the alien form of Jesus Christ:

> ... distinction does not mean separation. It is as the Word and Son of God that he exists as the man of Gethsemane and Golgotha. It is in His pure form that He is the secret, power and meaning of His form of suffering. He exists in this unity, and not otherwise. And in this unity He does not exist merely for us, as though He were a spectacle arranged for our benefit behind which there stands another reality.[39]

Two things must be said concerning Barth's comment above. First, we mentioned the import of warding off all separation between God and Jesus

---

wounds so deeply is precisely because it is *not* real? Barth knows he cannot prove, only posit, this counterintuitive position. He cannot prove it any more than he could prove the incarnation, death and burial of the Son of God. His confidence to hold this line is founded in his belief that, regardless of the real hurt we experience in this world, what is being removed and extinguished by Christ's death is actually less real in the end.

36. *CD* IV/3.1, 390.
37. *CD* IV/3.1, 390.
38. *CD* IV/3.1, 390.
39. *CD* IV/3.1, 396–97.

Christ, Son of God. To do otherwise would "carry the frightful implication that the mercy in which Jesus Christ comes to us as our Brother here and now in our world of sin and misery has nothing whatever to do with the mercy of God Himself." Just as the Christ event is described as anything but a spectacle or charade, we must refuse all thought that "God does not participate, or does so only from a divine height and distance as a Spectator." No, insists Barth, "God himself suffers as we suffer."[40]

The second thing we must note concerning the above excerpt is that in describing Christ's unity, Barth is including in the One Person of Christ not only the pure form of his divinity, and not only the corrupt human nature he has assumed, but also and less obviously the pure form of his humanity. Just as his pure form is, as above stated, "the secret, power and meaning of His form of suffering," so too his "pure form is certainly the meaning and power of his existence of this man and His witness to the truth . . . as the Mediator between God and us men in His prophetic work."[41] It could hardly be accidental that this description of Christ's pure form and alien form as a human being comes one page previous to the excursus where Barth portrays another human being, Job, as *simul iustus et peccator*, noting Job's "pure form" and his "different form."[42]

How exactly does Barth's discussion of the pure and alien forms correlate to the two determinations of the *simul*? Here we take pains to make a very careful distinction, because with all of Barth's emphasis on unity as it applies to both types of couplets (that of the forms and the determinations) it might be easy, mistakenly, to equate the impure or alien form with the *peccator* determination. Instead, the impure or alien form describes Christ and derivatively all human beings in their overlapped or contradictory form, i.e., in their form as experiencing the *simul*. It follows then that even though the impure form is not equivalent to the *peccator*, the pure form *is* equivalent to the human being as *iustus*. In other words, while it is true that apart from the unity of the single subject, the *simul*'s determinations fall apart as

---

40. *CD* IV/3.1, 397.

41. *CD* IV/3.1, 388.

42. *CD* IV/3.1, 398: "In relation to Job, too, we cannot stop at the pure form in which we have learned to know this typical witness to the truth. He appears as such only at the beginning and ending of the Book. In the main central section . . . he takes on a different form. It is not that he does not remain the same. As the same both in God's relationship to him and his to God, he will later reappear in the pure form which for the moment is concealed, and is thus in some way maintained and demonstrated even during the concealment."

abstractions, also true is that in the pure form the true predicate 'finds its home' with the true subject.[43]

If real incarnation is an antidote to Docetism in Christology, a point so powerfully articulated in First John (e.g., 4:2), then Barth's christological-anthropological derivative, the *simul*, is a corrective preventing realized eschatology from spilling over into one that is over-realized. Contrary to the remotest shades of metaphysical dualism, Barth contends that the Creator who visited this world in Jesus Christ is still actually here by the Holy Spirit, not simply on the other side of the veil. He is Victor, but always the Victor of *Gethsemane and Golgotha*. Jesus, says Barth, has not triumphantly left us as a butterfly leaving its cocoon behind.[44] The reality of Christ is a present, personal reality as demonstrated in the incarnation and the outpouring of the Holy Spirit. As humans confess the present, personal reality of the Incarnate One to be fully here in his pure, albeit hidden, form, so too they posit their pure form as human beings in him, fully present yet hidden. With our own eyes, we can only see our alien form, but by revelation the true Witness proves to be the only one who can parse the two forms: "Hence in relation to what each individual still is, He is a Witness to what he no longer is in Him. And in relation to what he is not, He is a witness to what he already is in Him."[45]

We spoke earlier of the end of the *simul*, positing that day when there would be no contradiction, but Barth wants us to remember that while the *simul* is not over for humanity, neither is it over for Christ, *until* it is over for humanity. He does not leave us behind without his solidarity, by the Holy Spirit, in his pure *and* alien form. Because of the incarnation, the temporal and provisional sphere for Barth cannot be classified as categorically unreal, only penultimate, but when created time evaporates into God's time, temporal and provisional will lose their meaning and all secrets will be made

---

43. See *CD* III/2, 336.

44. *CD* IV/3.1, 395. See 394, where Barth asserts Christ's ongoing compassionate solidarity in humanity's immanent plight, including the almshouses, etc.

45. *CD* IV/3.1, 394. As the Apostle Paul teaches (1 Cor. 15:35ff.), our mortal bodies are only seeds of our real selves not yet disclosed, but they are seeds, not shadows. Lest we get caught up in spatial concepts, we remember that the "seed" is the single, whole, *totus iustus* determination and definition of our lives, a concrete totality just as fully present here as on the other side of the veil, albeit hidden like a seed by our mortal bodies. That Barth says our false selves ghost around (*CD* IV/1, 568) or that Paul or the writer of Hebrews calls the things of this world shadows in comparison to reality should not dissuade us from the overall Christian meaning. The reality, after all, is found in Christ (Col 2:17), the one who descended and ascended in order to fill the whole universe with his real presence (Eph 4:10).

known, all tears wiped away (Rev 21:4).[46] In the meantime, asserts Barth, humans carry their respective crosses, knowing, at times even joyfully, that their suffering is delimited by Jesus: "The dignity of the cross is provisional, indicating the provisional nature of the Christian existence and all sanctification." Continues Barth, "It is not our cross which is eternal, but, when we have borne it, the future life revealed by the crucifixion of Jesus."[47] We should not miss Barth's meaning; "the time of sanctification" is identical to "the time of the cross."[48] It is the middle portion of each human story, when our *iustus* humanity is largely concealed—we might call it the time of *"simul* sanctification."

Reconsidering the Atonement in Light of the "Truly Real"[49]

Perhaps we noticed Barth's comment above concerning "the future life revealed by the crucifixion of Jesus." How are we meant to understand this? Is not the resurrection where humanity is born again and the new creation emerges? What more can be said about the pure and impure forms of the humanity of Jesus Christ, and therefore what more can be said about the idea of humanity's own pure form in him? Again, Barth would have us to remember that it is human misery that Jesus took on in his impure, alien form. Therefore it is to the cross we again turn for a deeper investigation.

Earlier we suggested that Barth is able to keep the forensic and penal approach to the atonement within his overall ontological framework, the latter able to contain the former, whereas the former cannot contain or take on board the latter. If readers introduced to Barth through the likes of T. F. Torrance have imagined Barth to be exceedingly Eastern in his theology of the atonement, they may be surprised to find that the cross is so central to Barth, and not in the least overshadowed by the resurrection. An "ontological" atonement motif puts the emphasis on the Second Adam and thereby the restoration and recreation of all human beings through the death and resurrection of Jesus Christ.[50] While Barth relishes the truth of these themes,

46. *CD* IV/2, 613.

47. *CD* IV/2, 613.

48. *CD* IV/2, 613.

49. *CD* III/2, 120.

50. Advocates for the ontological atonement motif may include the phraseology "birth, life, death, resurrection and ascension" of Christ to helpfully communicate that there is no part of human being (or the universe!) that Christ has not recapitulated in his soteriological, ontological, inversion. There are different ways that this model can

he also believes the cross accomplishes all that is required to ensure human salvation.[51] Of course it is only in light of the resurrection that one can know such a thing. For those readers who were hoping Barth would dispel all matters of penal satisfaction, their fears can only be assuaged by the fact that Barth does not allow a theory of the atonement that commits "the supreme blasphemy," as do most penal theories. But still, what is Barth on about concerning the cross as being all that is required to accomplish human salvation? Far from trying to move us simply from Anselm to Abelard (i.e., from a legal theory to a moral theory of the atonement), it at least appears Barth is subverting the typical polarity which pits the atonement motif of penal satisfaction against that of a resurrection-heavy or ontological view. Yet if Barth is indeed endeavoring to maintain all atonement theories inside of the overriding ontological motif, what could be meant by his emphasizing Jesus' "It is finished" in a manner which appears to comport more to a forensic view—i.e., the sacrifice complete, the penalty paid?

At least two initial things can be said in response. One, while it is true that some Western forensic views threaten to make the so-called transaction involving the cross more important than the person of Jesus himself, Barth refuses to make the opposite error of marginalizing the cross on the way to a resurrection emphasis. This includes Barth's constant guard against Docetism. Secondly, Barth certainly does not view Christ's death as first and foremost a means to satisfy a legal penalty to be paid, but he does not hesitate to use the word "satisfaction" to denote that God will not be satisfied with less

---

be parsed; on one extreme there is universalism, on the other end there is a backing up from the actualist ontology (Christo-anthropological actualism) to "make room" for human decisions of faith, i.e., to turn the "new humanity" into a hypothetical (inevitably bringing objective-subjective, *de jure–de facto*, passive-active bifurcations back into the picture). It should be continually clear that neither of these extremes represent the view we are espousing.

51. See *CD* IV/1, 343: "We have thought of the resurrection of Jesus Christ as God's proclamation and revelation. But what can it proclaim and reveal, what can it disclose, but the act of reconciliation and redemption once and for all accomplished in His death, in the judgment fulfilled in Him." Barth consistently speaks of reconciliation being "accomplished" in Christ's death and "revealed" (*CD* IV/2, 112) or "manifested" (III/2, 500) by his resurrection. See also *CD* IV/1, 328: here Barth talks about the resurrection being *a revelation* of "the situation which has been radically and irrevocably altered in the crucifixion of Jesus Christ." To exactly what extent salvation is "accomplished" at the cross in Barth's view has been challenged by scholars such as Alister McGrath, who has claimed that for Barth "the death of Christ does not in any sense change the soteriological situation." See Alister E. McGrath, *Iustitia Dei: A History of the Christian Doctrine of Justification*, 405. While there is a grain of truth to McGrath's claim, we opine that it is a severely limited view in light of the context we are providing in this and the next chapter.

than the erasure of all evil without remainder—the radical removal of *peccator* humanity.[52] We remember scriptural attestations that the Savior entered the world to destroy sin and death; this he accomplished, or finished, by virtue of his own death. The question above concerning "It is finished!" is now distilled: To what extent is Barth promoting Christ's resurrection as the revelation of an ongoing and incessant reality for *iustus* humanity, instead of the genesis of it?

It is pertinent here to consider what may potentially be a new way of looking at the "salvation" narrative. If the human Jesus remains, as Barth insists, "in the bosom of the Father"[53] throughout his suffering and death, then where are we as humans located during Christ's suffering and death? We understand Christ's immanent solidarity with *peccator* humanity and that our "old self was crucified with him" (Rom 6:6), but does the thoroughness of Christ's representation entail for Barth that even while humanity is crucified with Christ, humanity's *iustus* self remains transcendent in and with Christ in the bosom of the Father throughout suffering and death?

We made reference earlier to Bruce McCormack's analysis of the atonement and what he considers to be Barth's predominantly forensic category for Christ's work. We add here that McCormack furthermore argues that Barth adjusts his atonement theology between *CD* II/1 and IV/1 to avoid pitting God against God in regards to the penal vengeance imposed on the smitten Savior.[54] In other words, Barth's category is still forensic in *CD* IV/1, even if less penal. We offered the perspective earlier that Barth's undeniable forensic and even penal emphasis can be explained by the *peccator* humanity (old) and *iustus* humanity (new)—the duality of the *simul*—in the human being Jesus Christ, for it provides a *niche* whereby Barth can, with all the force of the scriptural witness (Isaiah 53 for instance) destroy or extinguish the old, false humanity with necessary harshness. We suggested that Barth's reticence to explain this more overtly is because he wants to honor the "one person" component of the duality, i.e., Jesus Christ, even though he could be criticized for "playing fast and loose" with the single subject latitude it allows. But again, this is not problematic for Barth because

---

52. See *CD* IV/1: "For the sake of this best, the worst had to happen to sinful man: not out of any desire for vengeance and retribution on the part of God, but because of the radical nature of the divine love, which could 'satisfy' itself only in the outworking of its wrath against the man of sin, only by killing him, extinguishing him, removing him. Here is the place for the doubtful concept that in the passion of Jesus Christ, in the giving up of His Son to death, God has done that which is 'satisfactory' or sufficient in the victorious fighting of sin to make this victory radical and total."

53. *CD* III/2, 65.

54. McCormack, "For Us and for Our Salvation," 305–6.

the single subject human duality of the *simul* does not need to be maintained in the end as does the Chalcedonian one directly. At the point of Christ's death Barth can allow for, even insist upon, what appears to be an unsustainable double-subject anthropology, all within the sustainable single subject Christology/anthropology.[55] If this is the case, there is no need for Barth to apologize or to adjust his approach to the atonement in CD IV/1, even if he gives more breadth at that point to his argument. It does, however, bring us back to our current question, which is to ask what is behind Barth's forensic perspective on the atonement as the extinguishing and removal of the "old man"—or what does his perspective say about the single, uncontradicted, human subject that does remain, i.e., the "new man"? Let us turn to *CD* IV to see perhaps if Barth's forensic approach and his finished work perspective regarding the cross, instead of diminishing the ontological view of the atonement, can actually enhance it. To what degree is Barth pointing to the possibility of an eternal, ongoing pure form of humanity?

Barth describes the atonement made for humanity by Jesus Christ as the event whereby "The man of sin, the first Adam . . . was taken and killed and buried in and with Him on the cross."[56] It cannot be emphasized enough that for Barth it is the "old man" who needs to be removed, the "man of sin," not us; or perhaps we have to add that it *is* us to the extent that we are the "old man."[57] For this purpose, "[God's] Son willed to go into the far country, to become one with us and to take our place as sinners, to die for us the death of the old man which was necessary for the doing of the will of God, to shed our wicked blood in His own precious blood, to kill our sin in his own death."[58] In this sacrifice Jesus "wills and demands as the man of

---

55. A most poignant example of this occurs where Barth uses the same phrase to designate that he is both the new man and the old man; "And in this way, *not by suffering our punishment*, but in the deliverance of sinful man and sin itself to destruction, which he accomplished when *he suffered our punishment*" (CD IV/1, 254; italics added). Barth is saying at once that Christ is delivering or rescuing the man of righteousness who does not need to be punished even while delivering the sinful man to destruction and punishment.

56. *CD* IV/1, 254.

57. See *CD* III/3, 304: God "in his Son gave and humbled Himself . . . He did so in necessary and righteous wrath, not against His creature but against its temptation and destruction, against its deviation, defection and consequent degeneration . . . That which rendered necessary the birth of His Son in the stable at Bethlehem and His death upon the cross of Calvary, that which by this birth and death He smote, defeated and destroyed, is that which primarily opposes and resists God Himself, and therefore all creation."

58. *CD* IV/1, 280. Note Barth's phrase "to kill our sin"; again this is perhaps Barth's way of creating some distance between the true identity of persons and their alter-egos

sin he should abandon his life . . . that as this man he should go up in flames and smoke." This unique sacrifice, says Barth, is "the meaning and end of sacrifice . . . the judgment that is not fulfilled in any other sacrifices."[59]

> It has the power of a real offering and taking away of the sinful man, the power to bring about his end and death as such, and therefore to create a new situation in which God no longer has to do with this man, in which His own faithfulness will meet a faithful people and a faithful man. In the sacrifice of Jesus Christ the will of God is fulfilled in this turning, in this radical conversion of man to Himself which posits an end and therefore a new beginning.[60]

Now we must assess Barth's words above very carefully for what they do and do not say. Barth asserts that there has been fulfilled a radical turning in this sacrifice, a "new situation" created, "an end and therefore a new beginning." But here there is no mention of resurrection. At first glance the requisite sacrifice Barth describes can certainly fit into the typical forensic format for the atonement; the penalty has been paid. But if Barth's purpose is all the time ontological, as we have suggested, what are we missing? Unless we are to capitulate to McCormack, there must be something more. Could it be that Barth's lack of mention of resurrection in describing the finished work means again, "a new situation in which God no longer has to do with this [old] man?"[61] If so, it is a situation which, again, is not actually new, but which we can only call new because of the radically oppressive nature of the old. Perhaps this is Barth's intent when the calls Christ's atoning death on the cross "the birthday of a new man?"[62] Indeed, Barth will even go so far as to say elsewhere that Christ's cry of dereliction is "*at once* the death-cry of the man who dies in Him and the birth-cry of the man who comes to life in Him." Undoubtedly Barth describes Christ's suffering within a penal construct, "it is God's will to cause this one man to pay the price . . . in accordance with the deserts of all." But in this one man's death the purpose is that "the old man should be expelled and the new man introduced once and for all in the place of all, to His glory and to the salvation of all."[63]

---

as *peccator*. See CD IV/1, 254, where Barth notes similarly that Jesus Christ "caused sin to be taken down and killed on the cross in His own person (as that of the one great sinner)."

59. *CD* IV/1, 280.
60. *CD* IV/1, 280.
61. *CD* IV/1, 280.
62. *CD* IV/1, 259.
63. *CD* IV/3.1, 413.

In this vein Barth continues, "In [Jesus Christ] He does that which has to take place to set aside sin and remove the conflict." Renewal or conversion, in this view, occurs when the contradiction of the *simul* is removed by he who is "pure and holy and sinless" even when consenting to be "the greatest of all sinners."[64] That the new man is always present, only suffocated by the old, seems to be indicated by Barth in the following: "[Jesus undertakes] the bitter reality of being the accused and condemned and judged and executed man of sin . . . in order that in place of this man another man who is pleasing to God, the man of obedience, may have space and air and be able to live."[65] In other words, the removal of the one, the old human, does not leave a vacuum; the new human, the now renewed human, is revealed; the truth of this to be made manifest on Easter morning.[66]

At this juncture we are quick to add to our discussion that the forensic motif and Barth's focus on the cross is contextualized and rooted in the ontology of who Jesus Christ already and always is in his transcendent human form. The implications of this assessment are that, even if we agree with McCormack in regards to Barth's emphasis on the forensic theme, this does not preclude in any way an overriding ontological interpretation concerning Barth's view of the atonement, or what we have referred to as the Eastern motif. Barth can at once describe Christ's death as "a new beginning" (as we have seen) and the resurrection as "a new beginning"[67]—for Barth the two motifs run concurrently and interpenetrate one another, as per justification and sanctification. As we shall elaborate on upcoming pages, this is the pattern Barth derives and traces from his christological interpretation of the

---

64. *CD* IV/1, 280–81.

65. *CD* IV/1, 281. An almost identical phrase is found on the facing page: "God wills and demands . . . to make an end of him, so that the new man may have air and space for a new life." There is perhaps some intentional irony here on Barth's part, as surely his comment about the new man having "room to breathe" is not completely disassociated from von Balthasar's charge that Barth's theology does not give humanity room to breathe. Von Balthasar made this claim in *The Theology of Karl Barth*, published in 1951 just previous to *KD* IV/1 (1953). See Kenneth Oakes, *Karl Barth on Theology and Philosophy* (Oxford: Oxford University Press, 2012), 220. I thank my friend Joey Sherrard for reminding me of von Balthasar's critique. The hypothesis of Barth's oblique reference to von Balthasar is my own.

66. If not a vacuum, then where exactly does this "new man" exist during his death, and what is his constitution? This concern will be addressed in chapter 12.

67. See *CD* III/1, 28: "His death reveals the end of all creatures, and at the same time their new beginning in His resurrection." See also *CD* IV/3.1, 300, where Barth speaks of the resurrection as the new creation. Interestingly, Colin Gunton has called Barth "above all a theologian of the resurrection, rather than of the incarnation or cross." Gunton, "Salvation," in *Cambridge Companion to Karl Barth*.

two creation sagas in Genesis. But how then, if the two motifs are concurrent in this fashion, can we give priority to the ontological over the forensic view? The answer lay in what we will call the "before-before," i.e., the being of humanity in Christ before the fall.

Two chapters ago we began our review of the *simul* and the atonement questioning to what degree Barth's perspective fits into a more Western (forensic) or Eastern (ontological) model. Barth's comparison of the sufferings of Job and Jesus, along with his insight into the pure and impure forms of humanity, have led us to revisit the possibility of a christological *simul* and therefore a Chalcedonian anthropology, not to mention an altogether different way of perceiving the atonement (can we call it the *new* perspective?).[68] Now we are given to see that Jesus' dying words "It is finished" can be taken literally, not first and foremost because of a penalty paid, and not even as a foreshadowing of the resurrection, but because of a full stop at the end of the sentence that includes sin, death, and the devil. Instead of fulfillment referencing what is previously incomplete, with Barth we can speak of humanity's fulfillment as the revelation of that which has always been complete, yet up to this point hidden, until a "setting aside" takes place. Words like "new" and "birth" and "conversion" in this light take on a new meaning: "In the person of His Son there has taken place the . . . conversion of man to God, and in the conversion the setting aside, the death, of the old rebellious man and the birth of a new man whose will is one with his."[69]

---

68. To be clear, I mean "new" not in view of time (as in more recent) but in spite of it.

69. *CD* IV/1, 282.

9

When Is the *Simul*?

"The day of His death was revealed on Easter Day to be the day of their life."[1]

THE REVELATION OF THE CROSS DEMONSTRATES THAT SEQUENTIAL AND spatial tendencies cannot be allowed to reduce the severity of the *simul*'s grade into a gradual hill for humans to climb. Along with asserting the boldest demarcation between the *iustus* and *peccator* determinations, Barth has considered the incomprehensible depth of the *peccator* dimension of humanity, a depth only to be overmatched by the righteousness of the One person who defines *iustitia* and delimits *peccatum* in his resurrection life and atoning work.

We have observed our two Chalcedonian dualities under the strain of Christ's passion. We established that for Barth, the first duality, that between divine and human natures in the incarnate person of Jesus Christ, is inviolable. The second duality, that between the true humanity of Jesus (our created humanity in which we are adopted) and the false humanity of Jesus (our fallen humanity which he assumed), remains intact only until the death of the Savior who carries all falsehood to the grave. Christians anticipate the final manifestation of this annulment while still existing in the present within the overlap of past and future dimensions. As in the quote above, Barth constantly reminds us that it is only in the light of Easter that one may obtain the resolution to the contradictory aspects of humanity. In this chapter we turn to look at the *simul*'s duality from another angle. By continuing to establish with Barth the *simul*'s eventual end, over the next

---

1. *CD* III/2, 469.

two chapters we will be increasingly free to entertain another critical question—when does it begin? In other words, when is the *simul*?

Creation and Perversion: Discovering the "Before-Before"

Barth's adherence to "Very God-Very Man" is definitive for anthropology and for his articulation of the proper, single, "original" human determination (*iustus*).[2] Again and again, Barth returns us to the premise that the truth of humanity is unavoidably wrapped up in the true humanity of Jesus Christ. Human participation in Christ is far from being hypothetical: "God's Yes to this man, like this man's Yes to Him, is not abstract but concrete."[3] This concreteness goes "all the way through," extending to all levels of human activity in relation to God. In other words, inside of the true human Witness—the unique human hearer and doer—there is a real sense in which all humans already hear what Jesus hears and do what Jesus does as he shares his humanity with them.[4] In this truth, *iustus* humanity enjoys in Christ's mediatorial righteousness the "reciprocal freedom" of humanity's created existence.[5] Humanity is at home in the mediation of the one human Jesus Christ: "For in this relationship to this man God is the true God . . . God as He is. And in this relationship to God man is true man, i.e., man in faithful confession of His humanity, man as he is. The meeting of this revelation of God and this confession of man is truth in the full sense of the term. For both, i.e., both God as He is and man as he is, are the one, whole truth."[6]

With proleptic permission, that which "acquires its proper sense only through the message of the resurrection,"[7] we continue to inquire about the pure form of humanity revealed by Jesus Christ and hidden under the perversion he assumed. Perversion is a very intentional word for Barth. Perversion, even "radical perversion," does not mean total ruination of the one person (i.e., as if the person could be *totus peccator* without remainder). It is a word that complies with the parasitic nature of sin and its counterfeiting obfuscation of what is real and true:

2. *CD* III/2, 29.
3. *CD* IV/3.1, 381.
4. *CD* I/2, 240.
5. *CD* IV/3.1, 381.
6. *CD* IV/3.1, 379–80.
7. *CD* I/2, 487.

> We do not see deeply enough if we think and say that there is here *only* darkness, want, shame, impurity, sadness, temptation, curse and perdition. In the strict sense, the misery of man is a ... history in which there can be no abstract "only." Thus the light is still there, but quenched; the wealth as it slips away; the glory as it turns to shame; the purity to impurity; the joy to sadness. They are all there in this movement from the right to the left, from above to below, in their perversion and corruption.[8]

No matter what form of expression his perversion might take, man is "the good creature of God." This never changes, insists Barth, "All the features which make him a man still remain. He has not become a devil ... Even in his misery he is not half a man, but a whole man. His misery consists in the corruption of this best."[9] References to "half" and "whole" are crucial for understanding Barth. Even while acknowledging the *totus peccator*, Barth refuses in any way to depreciate the *totus iustus*—true human nature.[10] As hidden as righteous man is after the fall, insists Barth, the "secret of his humanity" remains intact: "But rightly to appreciate this corruption brought about by man, and therefore the sin of man, we must quietly consider what is corrupted, and calmly maintain that all the corruption of man cannot make evil by nature the good work of God."[11]

But how does Barth know that the secret remains intact? How does he know the secret is underneath, so to speak? Barth acknowledges that, after the fall, we as fallen humans have no direct view to humanity in its reality as *iustus*; "we do not have in any case the direct vision of a sinless being of man fulfilling its original determination."[12] For Barth, therefore, humanity's natural determination can only be grasped indirectly, through the eyes of faith, or through the revealed knowledge of the primary and original human, Jesus Christ.[13] In the same way that we spoke of Jesus' pure form being "the secret of his existence,"[14] we may derivatively speak of Jesus Christ as

---

8. *CD* IV/2, 488–89. Italics are original. Again, the *totus* determinations are both immeasurable but not coextensive. Human hope is anchored not in our ability to measure the immeasurable, but in knowing the ultimate asymmetry between determinations.

9. *CD* IV/2, 488.

10. *CD* III/2, 29: "In the radical depravity of man there is necessarily hidden his true nature; in his total degeneracy his original form."

11. *CD* III/2, 274.

12. *CD* III/2, 28.

13. *CD* III/2, 29.

14. *CD* IV/3.1, 388; cited above.

the secret of our existence—"the secret of humanity."[15] Jesus Christ, then, shares his "open secret"[16] with every human being, and believers are those who recognize it as such.[17] "That there is a human nature created by God and therefore good and not evil," notes Barth, "must be accepted as we see man against the background of the man Jesus."[18] Jesus Christ, Barth insists, is "the one Archimedean point given us beyond humanity, and therefore the one possibility of discovering the ontological determination of man."[19] In light of authentic anthropology, the provisional nature of "Chalcedonian anthropology" (our proposed second duality between Christ's true and false humanities) becomes increasingly clear. Also clear is that Barth is comfortable using *iustus*, original, natural, and ontological all as synonymous adjectives for humankind's truest, albeit hidden, determination.

At this juncture several questions arise; for instance: What does Barth mean about us ignoring grace that is present to us even in our corruption? Did we not fall from grace? Are we now saying that Barth believes in a remnant of grace or at least relics of the *imago Dei* in fallen and corrupt humanity? Have we not already put this idea to rest when we spoke of Barth's resistance to all *partim-partim* or zero-sum progressive sanctification themes? In answer we must reemphasize that Barth does not demur from the *totus peccator*; saints are absolutely incapable of building back out from any foundation, even so-called "relics." Against all traditional notions of a point of contact, Barth, perhaps not coincidentally, describes humanity as corrupt "at every point."[20] However, we should also interject that while Barth categorically dismisses the relics system, he does promote a point of contact of sorts, very carefully qualified: the human always exists, despite being *totus peccator*, as *totus iustus*.[21] He comments, "the good

15. *CD* III/2, 274; cited above.
16. *CD* IV/3.2, 712.
17. *CD* III/1, 36.
18. *CD* III/2, 274. It is massively unfortunate when Christian anthropology devolves to a simplistic approach which equates humanity to depravity without remainder; in this view, opposite of Barth's, we are directed to recognize how wicked humanity is against the background of the human Jesus, without recognizing how his true humanity applies to us.
19. *CD* III/2, 132. Barth continues, "Theological anthropology . . . is not yet or no longer theological anthropology if it tries to pose and answer the question of the true being of man from any other angle."
20. *CD* IV/2, 489.
21. See *Heidelberg*, 131: Barth insists there is no point of contact that can be equated to a "spark covered over by the ashes," which could only introduce a *partim-partim*, i.e., an incomplete *iustus and* an incomplete *peccator* humanity. Instead, Barth

which remains to man as a sinner is not merely a 'relic' but the totality of His God-given nature and its determination."[22] This is what Barth calls the *character indelebilis* of humanity which is as invisible as it is indelible.[23] A person's sinfulness, then, "does not mean that he is below and in darkness in everything he is and does. On the contrary, in everything that he is and does he is above. But he is not merely above . . ."[24]

Such reference to true humanity being simultaneously "above," even when it is "below," can be dizzying, but obtaining the full breadth of the *simul*'s importance at this juncture requires us to consider Barth's mention of sequential movement from above *to* below. States Barth, "the slothful man is and exists . . . in the sequence of such events, in this sinister history. It is the history of his impotent ignoring of the grace of God present to him."[25] It is plain that Barth's usage of 'sequence' differs from our prior usage, because up to this point we have emphasized the sequence from below to above or from death to resurrection. We have spoken of the import of loading the sequence into the present tense of the *simul*, so that via the dynamic salvation history of Jesus Christ the *simul* maintains the preponderance necessary to keep it from being a static paradox. But now we are investigating the sequence from creation to death via humanity's "fall." And in the same way that we spoke of the death-resurrection sequence as within the *simul*, we must inquire concerning how the creation-fall sequence relates to the *simul*. In other words, what does "sequence" have to do with Barth's prognosis that we are always above, only to continually sink below?

Barth asserts rather provocatively that even though human beings are exiles away from "home, 'in Jesus we are all back home again.'"[26] This of course invites the question, if we are always at home above, only to continually sink below, what can be said about where we began in the first place? And, if we started at home and now we are back at home, what is the difference, if any, between home now and home in the beginning? Barth's failure to delineate clearly the difference between home (i.e., creation) and home (i.e., re-creation), causes us to ask, "To what degree did we ever leave home at all?"

---

predicates a point of contact "on the basis of the completed relationship of man to Jesus Christ!"

22. *CD* IV/2, 489.

23. *CD* III/4, 652. Again this indelible "character" of humanity (dimensional) must be distinguished from some kind of "core" (spatial).

24. *CD* IV/2, 489.

25. *CD* IV/2, 488–89.

26. *CD* IV/2, 488.

Earlier we asked if Barth sees the resurrection as a revelation of an incessant and ongoing reality and not the genesis of something new *ex nihilo*. Barth appears to be suggesting the idea that, if the resurrection reveals re-creation, then re-creation reveals creation, properly understood. If so, it remains a challenge to discern how Barth can avoid conflating creation and salvation. It indeed sounds as if Barth is advancing the position that all human beings, as included in the true humanity of Jesus Christ, are full participants in the truth of the Triune God—and this before any human has the Holy Spirit experience of being "born from above" (John 3:3,7) in this world. Barth has insisted that it is only and precisely *because* of a prior and actual truth that humanity can by the Spirit of Truth avoid existential expressions of the lie, but how far back does this truth go?

Barth has given us a bigger frame in which to view humanity's relationship with God. Instead of simply a before-and-after sequence of death to life, or sin to salvation, Barth has led us to consider what we might call "the before-before," which involves perceiving God's grace as humanity's primal inclusion in the life of God, adoption in the One God loves (Eph 1:6) by the Holy Spirit. Barth speaks of the Spirit as the divine *conditio sine qua non* of the creation and preservation of the creature.[27] Grace then is not a reaction to human sin as much as it is the very life breath of human existence in created dependence on our brother and Savior Jesus Christ.[28] God's love and grace is self-giving, so when humanity inexplicably rebels against God, grace in the person of Jesus Christ pursues humanity, i.e., grace responds in keeping with God's character, engaging in a "war of grace against [humanity's] enmity against grace."[29] In this light, where grace does as grace is, salvation serves grace; it is therefore fitting that Christ's victory over and against rebellious humanity includes the ultimate self-giving of the cross. Again this pursuit of grace is in keeping with creation. In Barth's

---

27. See *CD* III/1, 57; Barth cites Ps 104:29, "Thou send forth thy Spirit and they are created," noting that this verse "undoubtedly refers to the first creation."

28. See III/2, 35: "The whole witness of the Bible shows that sin does not originate in the void, as the transgression of a universal law, but in rebellion against the concrete reality which sums up all the divine laws (i.e., that God is gracious to man and that man is the being to whom He is gracious). Sin originates in wanton rebellion against the God who has given Himself to mankind in the person of His Son. To this extent it has to be said that sin is impossible without grace; that it has its perverse origin in the grace of God"; and III/2, 41: "divine grace is primary and sin secondary . . . we cannot contradict the order . . . We are forbidden to take sin more seriously than grace, or even as seriously as grace."

29. *CD* II/1, 166.

mind, the covenant of grace established between God and humanity is the internal basis of creation itself. Grace, he insists, "is not a sequel."[30]

But creation as grace? Does Barth want us to include creation, so often viewed as a means to an end, as part and parcel of salvation reality? Do we have biblical permission to add to humanity's resurrection rebirth, and our experience of being born from above by the Spirit, humanity's creation too—all as part of the proleptic picture of this one transformational reality? At this point we will not leave the *simul* behind, but we will concentrate on filling out the *iustus* determination, that of true humanity, before reintroducing its contradiction as we continue on our way to proposing an answer to the question, "When is the *simul*?" In view of Christ's assumption of *sarx*, the true humanity of the incarnate one can be easily overlooked (much like Volume III of *Church Dogmatics*), so it is fitting that we now turn to Barth's Doctrine of Creation.

The First Adam?

Before moving into the final stages of our study, it will be important to establish or reestablish some foundational tenets related to Barth's theology of creation. For Barth, as we have seen, all talk of humanity begins with Jesus Christ: "all anthropology should be based on Christology and not the reverse."[31] On Barth's view, it does little good if we speak of humanity being created in the image of God unless we understand Jesus Christ to comprehend each anthropological aspect. Firstly, Jesus Christ himself is uniquely the *imago Dei* (2 Cor 4:4). All other human beings are created in Christ (Eph 2:10), created *in* the image; they are therefore image bearers in a derivative fashion, by grace alone.[32] Barth relates thusly: "Our human nature rests upon His grace; on the divine grace addressed to us in His human nature. It is both His and ours, but it is His in a wholly different way from that in which it is ours . . . It is actualised in Him as the original and us as the copy."[33]

Secondly, according to Barth, not only is Jesus Christ the image of God, but he is also the original Adam, the first born of all creation (Col

---

30. *CD* III/1, 97.

31. *CD* III/2, 46; see *CD* III/2, 47: "The human nature of Jesus Christ forbids us our own."

32. *CD* III/2, 225. See III/2, 219: "The humanity of Jesus is not merely the repetition and reflection of His divinity, or of God's controlling will; it is the repetition and reflection of God Himself, no more and no less. It is the image of God, the *imago Dei*."

33. *CD* III/2, 50.

1:15), the epitome of "our natural condition as willed and planned by God and pleasing to Him."[34] Barth obviously claims the high ground in calling Christ's original Adamic humanity "natural." He states: "In this way Paul regarded the man Jesus as the real image of God, and therefore as the real man created by God."[35] Precisely because of the intimate connection between Christ and the glory of created man "in his original righteousness,"[36] Barth is adamantly opposed to humans coopting this honor as if to bestow righteousness on themselves. God's covenant with humanity can only be first and foremost a covenant with the human being Jesus Christ. "We are not created the covenant partners of God, but to be His covenant partners," insists Barth. Humanity's "rightness, goodness, worth and perfection spring from its correspondence" to Jesus Christ and to Him alone.[37] Creation and covenant are inextricably bound to each other, but because of the primary and unique covenant relationship between Father and Son, it is more accurate theologically to say that "creation follows the covenant" than the other way around.[38] Within the covenant of grace mediated by Jesus Christ, Barth can make the astounding biblical claim: "Creation is understood and apprehended as grace in faith in Jesus Christ."[39]

But if grace precedes sin, and is not merely a reaction to it, how are we to explain the fall? For Barth to claim that the *iustus* determination of humanity never recedes in any way can be quite alarming, especially for those not familiar with his reliance on the *simul* and the *totus/totus* framework as he sees it reflected in Scripture. But if there is no diminishment in the created *iustus* determination of humanity after the fall, this raises the age-old question as to whether there was something lacking in creation that made humanity susceptible in the first place? How else could the fall be explained? After our discussion of "Hercules at the crossroads" (chapter 5) it should not surprise us that Barth refuses to introduce a deficiency in humanity in order to "make room" for the possibility of the fall. In other words, the fact that

---

34. *CD* III/2, 519. See III/2, 598: ". . . what is natural to man is his endowment with the life-giving breath of God which constitutes him as the soul of his body, not his subsequent loss of it. What is natural to him is the fact that he is and will be, not that he has been. What is natural to him is his being in the land of the living, not his being in the underworld. What is natural to him is life, not death."

35. *CD* III/1, 202. See *CD* III/1, 50–51: Barth is careful to note that according to Col 1:15–16 the fact that Jesus is the "firstborn of all creation" is not mutually exclusive, as Arius would have it, to Jesus Christ being God and Creator.

36. *CD* II/2, 163.

37. *CD* III/1, 370.

38. *CD* III/1, 44.

39. *CD* III/1, 40–41.

the fall is quite inexplicable is not a problem for Barth because it comports with his conception of sin as irrational and absurd. Barth calls humanity's rejection of God an "incomprehensible fact."[40] Even if incomprehensible, humanity's "mortal conflict with itself is not ruled out"; there is always for the creature the impossible possibility of self-destruction. However, critically for Barth, and most pertinent to the present discussion, "The fact that the creature can fall away from God and perish does not imply any imperfection on the part of creation or the Creator."[41]

For Barth, as we have seen, sin and apostasy can be described, but they cannot be explained. Therefore Barth holds adamantly to the idea that there was nothing at all lacking in creation. "It is a part of the history of creation that God completed His work and confronted it as a completed totality. The true and finished world in its actual constitution."[42] A page later, Barth expresses with certainty that God "did not need to have any regrets . . . He did not need a better world, nor, after the creation of man, did He need in this world any higher or more perfect beings."[43] Simply put, for Barth, God was supremely satisfied when he looked upon his finished work. "The history of the covenant," he insists, "was really established in the work of the seventh day."[44]

We have seen how Barth will not allow for the fall to be rooted in a human flaw related to humanity's creation; it cannot be explained by a human shortcoming or even a susceptibility to temptation. Then what more can be said about sin's presence? Barth comments as follows:

> Sin is undoubtedly committed and exists. Yet sin itself is not a possibility but an ontological impossibility for man. We are actually with Jesus, i.e., with God. This means that our being does not include but excludes sin. To be in sin, in godlessness,

40. *CD* II/1, 504.
41. *CD* II/1, 503.
42. *CD* III/1, 222.
43. *CD* III/1, 223.
44. *CD* III/1, 217; Barth speaks of the seventh day of creation as a convergence of God's work and rest. In the seventh day, God has "united Himself with the world He created . . . in His rest He associates Himself with it in the fullest possible way. In this historical event He repeats no less nor other than His own perfect being, and declares Himself as such to belong to what He has created so entirely different from Himself." In human creatures, Barth continues, God "was satisfied with what He had created and had found as the object of His love. It was with man and his true humanity, as His direct and proper counterpart, that God now associated Himself in His true deity." Note how Barth, employing covenantal language, names humanity the counterpart of God, and in the block quotation names God the Counterpart of humanity.

is a mode of being contrary to our humanity. For the man who is with Jesus—and this is man's ontological determination—is with God. If he denies God, he denies himself. He is then something which he cannot be in the Counterpart in which he is. He chooses his own impossibility.[45]

Should we take pause over the implications of Barth's argument? If sin is categorically excluded from our created identity, if sin is not rooted in an innate weakness of any sort in God's original humans, and if there is not "an improvement" to be made on creation, i.e., an improvement made on humanity via redemption, then how could we posit any difference between creation and redemption? To begin with, perhaps we should consider with Barth that there might not be as much difference as is normally assumed. One thing is clear, the fall happened, and even if God allowed the "alien" Adam to pose as the first Adam, Barth speaks of Jesus Christ putting himself under the "fallen" and "fatal Adam" to put him away.[46] Thus the reconstitution of humanity is accomplished in the Second Adam, who proves himself to be the real first and original Adam in the process. But let us continue to pursue the relationship between the constitution and reconstitution of humanity. Just how far do we want to take Barth's assertion that "since the constitution of man is from God, it is a saving fact"?[47]

Creator and Deliverer

Now for Barth all talk of the relationship between the constitution and re-constitution of humanity returns us to assess the relationship of Creator and Deliverer. Hopefully we have moved past the idea that creation simply exists to make redemption possible. But more positively, what is the nature of the relationship between the two? We begin with the scriptural attestation that, in Barth's words, "the Creator and Deliverer are one and the same." Barth continues, ". . . the whole world and I with it—everything that is actual—must serve the work of God the Deliverer because it owes its existence solely to the work of God the Creator."[48]

This intimate connection between God the Creator and God the Redeemer is important for understanding how Barth views reality and what, if any, differences are made in reality by its being "delivered" or "redeemed." What do we make, for instance, of Barth's potentially startling assertion

45. *CD* III/2, 136.
46. *CD* III/2, 214–15.
47. *CD* III/2, 347.
48. *CD* III/1, 45.

below—that the seventh day of creation is in closest theological relation to the *eschaton*? Here Barth borrows a comment from a friend before adding his own, "On the seventh day God was well pleased with His Son. He saw creation perfect through Christ; He saw it restored again through Christ; and He therefore declared it to be finished, and rested." Adding Barth, "There is no avoiding the eschatological explanation of this rest."[49]

It is the divine rest, the integrated inclusion of the Sabbath as belonging to creation,[50] which for Barth designates creation as "the sphere of grace."[51] The sphere of grace is therefore not a sequel to creation any more than the seventh day itself, and even though the world's "history is in order" from this point, God is pleased to manifest his finished work over time "as a sequence of divine self-attestations with their revelations, miracles, signs and new creations."[52] Barth wants us to know that on the one hand, God does not create anything new or different from what he has already completed, yet on the other hand God as Creator is free to express renewal in fresh ways: "In every new creation it will be partly a question of the gracious preservation and confirmation, and partly of the gracious renewal, of the creation which in itself is ready and finished."[53] Importantly for Barth, it must be emphasized that this finished work has nothing to do with a static quarantining of God's glory, as if it could be "enclosed in the reality of the creaturely world"; it is unconscionable, asserts Barth, to imagine God enslaving himself in this way.[54] Instead, the fathomless manifestations of again-and-again renewal reflect the radiance of God's inner glory. In relation to God's work of creation Barth can say, "His celebration when it is finished is in reality the coronation of His work . . . When God celebrates the completion of His work, this totality becomes the festive hall and man His festive partner." The "radiance" and "illumination" of God's glory abounds.[55] "Revelation may be new when it comes," Barth suggests, "but it will not be absolutely new. When its time comes, it will fulfil that which must be fulfilled because creation commences and culminates in light."[56]

---

49. *CD* III/1, 222. The first quotation Barth attributes to Hermann Friedrich Kohlbrugge.
50. *CD* III/1, 223.
51. *CD* III/1, 225.
52. *CD* III/1, 223.
53. *CD* III/1, 182.
54. *CD* III/1, 225.
55. *CD* III/1, 223.
56. *CD* III/1, 119.

Undoubtedly, in Barth's view Jesus Christ is the royal man in his exaltation at the cross as well as post-humiliation, but what do we make of this arguably premature evaluation of Barth's concerning what appears to be the exaltation of Christ and his heirs at *creation*? We know Barth better than to come to the conclusion that "all is light." At the same time we might admit that thus far our presentation of Barth's doctrine of creation has perhaps done little to dissuade the reader that Barth tends to conflate creation and salvation. Here three points of clarification are in order. First, it must be noted that Barth's association of the seventh day with the *eschaton* does not mean he is claiming a direct likeness between the two. Barth can speak confidently of the comparison because he believes God is not only celebrating the finished creation in front of him, but because he is in a sense looking from creation to its future, or to its restoration and re-creation.

> God does not only look upon the present of His creation, nor does He only look back to that which He did in creating it. God knows its future. And He knows more, and more gladdening things, about the future of the work which is finished before Him, than is to be seen in the present state of the things themselves . . . God rests when He completes, and celebrates when he has finished, because in relation to His work He knows what He has in view; because He looks forward to a completely different fulfilment and completion of its relationship to Him, and therefore of its own reality.[57]

But if God's view of the finished work is simply based on foreknowledge, is the "finished work" of creation really finished? This brings us to our second clarification—Barth's view of foreknowledge is carefully, and unusually, defined. We remember that Barth's view of time allows him to hold past, present, and future together in the One who is the same yesterday, today, and forever. When God looks ahead, unlike our own human viewing, God is looking ahead to new iterations of his finished work, what Barth calls a "correspondence and repetition."[58] In other words, when Barth says (in the above block quote) that God can look forward to "a completely different fulfilment" of creation wrought by redemption, he expressly does not mean the finishing of a work that was not previously finished. Barth can thus maintain at once that the history of the covenant and salvation inaugurated in creation is completed in the resurrection, but also that the "completion"

---

57. *CD* III/1, 222.
58. *CD* III/1, 225.

the resurrection provides is a confirming witness, a new revelation, of what is already complete, revealed in glorious new ways.[59]

The third pertinent point to this fear of conflating creation and the *eschaton* regards the role of the Holy Spirit. For Barth, the Spirit "creates new facts only to the extent that the revelatory character of reconciliation is confirmed in it."[60] In other words, for Barth, God's unveiling of his truth in human history is a process whereby "something old is again and again shown to be old, and something new to be new."[61] By the Holy Spirit we understand the resurrection to be not only the revelation of the righteousness of God but the "the revelation of our righteousness" in him.[62]

Barth acknowledges that in looking at the sordid history of the human race, we are constantly confronted by "a state of affairs which cannot possibly explain God's rest in face of His completed work."[63] That is why the opposite perspectives of looking from redemption to creation, and from creation to redemption, must be held together. Again they are held together uniquely by the Redeemer and Creator—the Creator and Redeemer.[64] It should be increasingly clear that Barth's understanding of God's foreknowledge is different from our own "futuristic" perspective. But it raises the question whether Barth, by endeavoring to demonstrate that the Redeemer is the Creator, is not compromising the Godhead. Does not the fact that God is Redeemer presuppose what humans are redeemed from? In other words, if redemption has already happened in the One who is eternally present,

---

59. *CD* III/1, 228.

60. *CD* IV/3.1, 10.

61. *CD* III/1, 114. The quote in full shows Barth is referring specifically to prophetic testimony in the OT: "When the "Thus saith the Lord" re-echoes from the lips of Moses and the prophets, history is made, i.e., something old is again and again shown to be old, and something new to be new."

62. *CD* II/1, 404. Here Barth is certain, in view of Romans 4:24 and following, that even our personal awakening to faith is included in the righteousness of Jesus Christ revealed in his resurrection, and, because Jesus was "raised to life for our justification" we can know it is not our faith which justifies us.

63. *CD* III/1, 222.

64. See *Heidelberg*, 57: Nowhere is Barth more clear on this coinherence than in his lectures on the Heidelberg Catechism, where he states, "the doctrine of creation . . . is the backbone of all Christian doctrine. It does not stand somehow apart from the truth of our redemption through righteousness. It is not a preliminary, first word which is to be heard and understood by itself to begin with; it stands in immediate connection with the knowledge of our redemption in Jesus Christ. The doctrine of creation points to the one true God who is also our Redeemer." This interpenetration of creation and redemption anticipates our discussion regarding Barth's view on the two creation sagas (chapter 11).

then does it not follow that the sin and darkness from which mankind are redeemed are eternally present as well? Should we not be concerned about a Christ who is eternally *simul iustus et peccator*? Barth's comment below offers little consolation:

> In respect of His Son who was to become man and the Bearer of human sin, God loved man and man's whole world from all eternity, even before it was created, and in and in spite of its absolute lowliness and non-godliness, indeed its anti-godliness. He created it because He loved it in His Son who because of its transgressions stood before Him eternally as the Rejected and Crucified. And again, in respect of His Son who was to become man and the Bearer of the divine image, God attributed to man and his entire world from all eternity, even before he created it, enough glory, as a likeness of future glory, to cover and indeed obliterate its misery because He thought of it in His own Son, who for its justification stood eternally before Him as the Elected and Resurrected.[65]

The Original Antithesis

At this point our investigation turns to the fallen nature of Christ and how *peccator* humanity relates to eternity. What does Barth mean, for instance, when he uses the phrase "from all eternity" to describe Jesus Christ, the Son of God, as Rejected and Crucified?[66] In order to assess this, we must first lay some necessary groundwork from Barth's exegesis of Genesis. According to Barth's interpretation, when it comes time for God to create, he does so in the face of darkness, chaos, or what Barth calls "nothingness" (Gen 1:2). Barth does not attempt to explain the origin of darkness and chaos, but he asserts that creation was an act whereby God declared "Let there be light" and thereby "separated light from darkness and being from non-being."[67] Does this mean that nothingness is the necessary stuff from which he created light? Not in the least. Barth can hold to the traditional "creation *ex nihilo*" and the protections it offers; in other words, even with light being "the first creation of God, and therefore the first work of His Word," Barth does not want to advance the misunderstanding that light came *from* the darkness any more than the opposite misunderstanding that created light is an essential emanation from God's being. Notes Barth, "The uncreated light

---

65. *CD* III/1, 50–51.
66. The phrase "from all eternity" appears over 300 times in *Church Dogmatics*.
67. *CD* III/2, 143.

which is God Himself and His Word is one thing; the light whose creation is spoken of here is quite another."[68] That is why created light is not God Himself but a sign—a sign "of the divine covenant of grace, of the faithfulness which God will maintain and acknowledge to His creature."[69] In other words, while created light is not God, as a sign it does point to "the true and original antithesis ... between God and darkness" (i.e., between God and *das Nichtige*—nothingness; this "darkness" should not be confused with its derivative). In this way created light "enters into this antithesis and serves it in correspondence with the divine will of the Creator."[70] What can we say about this negation of darkness? Like created light, the negation of darkness also derives from the original antithesis; Barth describes it as a "shelter" of nothingness.[71] It functions as a type of witness to nothingness; we could say it is as darkness is to Darkness, or the "non-divine,"[72] in similar fashion as light is to Light, or God. Let us take one more look at Barth's subconcepts of light and darkness as they reflect the greater antithesis: "It is light that *is*. Of darkness it can only be said that, as long as light is, it is also, but separated from it, marked and condemned by it as darkness, in opposition to it, as its antithesis."[73]

How dangerous is the threat of this "deep chaos of nothingness"—"the abyss of evil"[74]—in the face of what God has created perfect and good? If, by their creation in light, humans are entering into a primal conflict—the original antithesis between God and chaos—to what extent in Barth's mind does God make provision in advance to deliver his creation from this threat? Obviously, if God creates human beings without also protecting against such a threat, it might be asked if God himself is actually good.

> No man, no creature has within himself the power to overcome this threat. Of course, the world created by God is light. Of course, the only ontological possibility of man is the being which his Creator has imparted to him. But it does not lie in

---

68. *CD* III/1, 119.

69. *CD* III/1, 118–19. Barth goes on to say here that light is a sign that God is more committed to the creature than the creature can be to God, i.e., "in face of its sin and apostasy, in face of the death to which it has sold itself, in face of hell which opens up in consequence."

70. *CD* III/1, 120.

71. *CD* III/3, 305.

72. *CD* III/1, 119. We will elaborate on Barth's distinction between darkness and nothingness in the next chapter.

73. *CD* III/1, 123.

74. *CD* III/2, 143. Both phrases are cited from this page.

> the power of the creature to maintain the distinction which God drew when He separated light from darkness and being from non-being . . . And so the will of God for His creation is to preserve it from the nothingness to which it would inevitably succumb apart from the divine initiative, to save the creature from the threat which it cannot overcome of itself. The fact that it cannot overcome it is shown by the wholly irrational and inexplicable fall of man. But sin itself is only man's irrational and inexplicable affirmation of the nothingness which God the Creator has negated.[75]

Barth presents us with a fall of mankind that is as inevitable as it is inexplicable. While allowing the creature to be threatened by darkness and even to succumb to it, Barth hastens to add that God effectively saves humanity in Jesus Christ even before it falls; "for the fulfillment of this aim He bound Himself to His creation from the very act of creation." Barth continues, "Thus the fall of man, while it formed no part of His intention, was not outside His foresight and plan. From the very first He was determined to be the Preserver of that which He created, of that which He separated as being from non-being." Just when did this deliverance and preservation occur? It was "resolved from the very beginning," says Barth, "even before the foundation of the world." Barth elaborates in his own forceful way that the contradiction has been "resolved before all things . . . before man fell into sin, before light was separated from darkness or being from non-being, and therefore before there was even a potential threat."[76]

In the next chapter we will return to Barth's idea that Christ delivers humanity even before the fall, but is Barth also suggesting that humanity is effectively fallen as the implicit back side of its creation? What happened to what we customarily understand as the fall? Even with Barth's positing of Christ's assumption of the twofold determination from the outset, he does not altogether ignore what is typically called the fall. Instead, it appears that Barth views the fall as a manifestation of the *peccator* determination of humanity, a humanity that at the crossroads of decision can only choose wrongly. Barth does not seem to be concerned about whether or not the fall is an actual historical event; "the fall" appears to be simply a confirmation and recurrence in the negative sense as acts of obedience are in the positive sense. In other words "the fall" is a premier illustration of a habitual matter—that of humanity over and over again choosing the wrong.[77] In this

---

75. *CD* III/2, 143.
76. *CD* III/2, 144.
77. *CD* III/3, 352.

view, the *simul* situation for humanity has already been established before "the fall." Remarks Barth on the history of humanity: "It began in and with this history . . . It is continually like it. With innumerable variations it constantly repeats it. In constantly re-enacts the little scene in the garden of Eden. There never was a golden age. There is no point in looking back to one. The first man was immediately the first sinner."[78]

How shall we summarize Barth's picture of Eden? Adam is created perfectly righteous (*totus iustus*) in Christ with no room for error, but in Genesis 2 he also arrives on the Garden scene *totus peccator* from the very beginning. Barth therein makes clear his astonishing claim of the *simul* in relation to Christ and humanity, "Thus the heavenly man is also the earthy, the righteous man the sinner. In other words, Adam is already Jesus Christ, and Jesus Christ is already Adam."[79] The fact that humanity is already united with Jesus Christ does not safeguard the first humans from making wrong decisions any more than it safeguards the modern day Christian. Adam, "not acting as a free agent but as a prisoner," chooses the impossible.[80] As Barth notes, "We remember that this can happen. The creature can be so foolish. It can become guilty of the inconceivable rebellion of looking past the Word of God and the ground and measure of its own reality . . . to this darkness and therefore to this state of chaos; loving what God hated in His love as Creator."[81] Again and again Barth reminds us that it is by revelation only that we might recognize clearly, in the Creator who became the creature, the *iustus* and *peccator* determinations of humanity. And again it is the good and righteous humanity that is original and prior: "the self-revelation of God the Creator, in confirming and transcending the two concepts of being and the corresponding judgments, discloses the perfection of being, the divine good-pleasure resting upon it, its justification by its Creator, and therefore that it is right as it is, that it is good in its totality, indeed that it is best."[82]

We are hopefully beginning to grasp Barth's bigger picture for who Jesus Christ is as Creator and Deliver of the cosmos, aside from simply what we perceive in the frame of his earthly, historical narrative. The question

---

78. *CD* IV/1, 508.

79. *CD* III/1, 203.

80. *CD* III/3, 356: "The creature sinned by thinking, speaking and acting in way alien and adverse to grace and therefore without it. We are certainly not to say that man was capable of sin. There is no capacity for nothingness in human nature and therefore in God's creation, nor is there any freedom in this direction as willed, ordained and instituted by God" (356).

81. *CD* III/1, 108.

82. *CD* III/1, 378.

that Barth never answers is a precursor to the theodicy question: Why does it *have* to be the case that to posit God's being means there is also a mirroring non-being, a non-divine? Why does Barth make so much of the "reality" of nothingness? The immeasurable and indescribable potency of God's adversary (nothingness) is reflected in Barth's comment about the lengths God went to combat it: "God willed Himself to become a creature in the creaturely world, yielding and subjecting Himself to it [nothingness] in Jesus Christ in order to overcome it."[83] It becomes more and more clear that the reason Barth takes the *peccator* determination of humanity so seriously in comparison to the *iustus* determination is because of the seriousness of *das Nichtige* in comparison to God. In this chapter we have attempted to demonstrate from Barth's view that God is good, that God came first (Light before darkness), and that God does not need to include evil in his creation, nor is he party to it. Even though we have not been able to answer the Why? question—why evil exists—Barth has gone to great lengths to convince us that God would never create us unless he had already defeated evil in his own death. Still, we are in a sense unresolved in our quest to discern "When is the *simul*?" Is the fact that Christ's death and resurrection somehow establishes the victory from "the outset" somewhat confused by Barth's own inference that both determinations in the two-fold *iustus* and *peccator* are both present in the eternity of Christ, i.e., that the *simul* exists from "the outset" as well? Barth's proposed mutual interpenetration of Creation and Fall, *iustus* and *peccator*, are meaningless to the extent they are endless in *either* direction. In other words, any consolation derived from the belief that the *simul* ends in the death of Christ is severely mitigated by the idea of a mutual beginning. Has Barth painted himself into a corner theologically with an eternal *simul*; if the *peccator* determination is not logically primary, is it at least co-eternal with Christ? If the *simul* is eternal, how do we know that the death and resurrection of Jesus Christ would not be better fitted as themes in a Manichean paradigm? In the face of excruciating human suffering, these concerns of a cosmic tug-of-war cast doubt on Barth's proposal of a matchless Maker, a good, all-powerful and loving God. In the upcoming chapter, we will probe further what Barth has to say about creation and suffering in view of the simul.

---

83. *CD* III/3, 305.

10

The Darkness Shall not Overcome It

"He has utterly destroyed death, i.e., not merely dying, but the nothingness which threatens and lurks behind it, and brought life and immortality to light (2 Tim 1:10)."[1]

IN OUR PRESENTATION OF BARTH'S ARGUMENT FROM VOLUME III WE HAVE thus far sought to establish the priority and preponderance of what *is* to that which *is not*. What he makes abundantly clear is that there can be no synthesis between darkness and light any more than there can be a synthesis between the opposing ontologies of being and non-being—these stemming from the original antithesis between God and nothingness. However, even though one is not the other, light and darkness do exist in the same "space" even as different "spheres." Therefore, when God creates what *is*, already included "within" his creation is what *is not*. Again, this does not mean God actually creates darkness or evil,[2] but that as negations they are unavoidably present.[3] It should also be critically reinforced that Barth does not wish to confuse the "shadowy side" of creation with nothingness itself.[4] It is this

---

1. *CD* III/4, 594.

2. *CD* III/1, 123. Here Barth deems the meaning of Isaiah 45:7 to be along these lines.

3. *CD* III/1, 128. Barth calls the implicit backside of creation a "dreadful encroachment." At the same time, Barth notes that we can actually take solace in the fact that evil is "included" in creation because it is a loving and all-powerful God who includes it and who is committed to extinguishing it.

4. *CD* III/3, 296–97. Barth continues to elaborate on this theme in great depth in *CD* III/3; Barth states that nothingness hides behind the negation, the latter of which could be termed a more neutral antithesis to God's good creation. Nothingness is aggressive in character, an active evil in the truest sense of the word privation, a "negative

nuance which arguably contributes to Barth's avoidance of a theological conflation of evil with creation. Nonetheless, indicative of his practice as we have already acknowledged it, Barth has introduced a logjam impossible for us to parse other than by revelation. With this is included a hidden vision for humanity via a point of contact that does not show up on any zero-sum spectrum! Barth is so committed to running the *totus-totus* to the "nth" degree that there are times when the contrasting elements of light and darkness, *iustus* and *peccator*, look like a straight never-ending parallel. For instance, in spite of the fact that by virtue of creation we are already one with Christ, in the preceding chapter Barth has opined that we enter the world, before the fall, as sinners. In this chapter, as we continue to ask "When is the *simul*?," Barth reminds us that even if we enter this world *simul iustus et peccator*, this world is not all that there is.

"A dualism which is dissoluble"

For the gatekeeper guarding God's reputation against all connotations of evil, Barth goes uncomfortably far to describe the negation as included in creation—to the point where, out of context, one might think that Barth believes God created it; "Hence the joy and the misery of life," Barth contends, "have their foundation in the will of God."[5] By now we know that Barth can say this because of his undying contention that the one eternal person Jesus Christ, Creator *and* creature, is himself the upholding principle of humanity and the revelation of God's will for his beloved creatures. "Since everything is created for Jesus Christ and His death and resurrection," asserts Barth, "from the very outset everything must stand under this two-fold and contradictory determination;"[6] Jesus Christ therefore comprehends and in a sense defines both the joyful and miserable, *iustus* and *peccator*, dimensions which is more than the mere complement of an antithetical positive" (302). When God steps past nothingness to create (353), the negative aspect of creation is bordered by and contiguous to nothingness (350). This articulation allows Barth to maintain that God does not create evil, even while allowing it. Of course, because evil crosses this boundary to make humanity a victim, and because humanity steps across the boundary as itself an agent of evil (350), the negation is immediately consumed by nothingness in such a way that the two might thereby be perceived as one and the same (306). Barth asserts that God knows the fall will occur because it is inevitable humanity is no match for evil and sin as "the concrete form of nothingness" (310). And, if it can be said God allows evil, it can also be said that God destroys the evil he allows by himself becoming "a lost creature"(304) and a "victim" (356) of it, entering into nothingness to eradicate it and the "shelter" (305) of negation along with it (327).

5. *CD* III/1, 376.
6. *CD* III/1, 376.

of humanity in order to delimit the latter and prove the asymmetry. Again, apart from resurrection revelation we do not see the asymmetry; we cannot excavate below the *simul*'s eternal contradictions to an answer to the *simul*'s origin or to find the secret of a created *iustus* foundation. This is something we can only discover with the eyes of faith: that Jesus Christ is the one and only foundation (1 Cor 3:11) and that he is in his *iustus* humanity more foundational to our existence than the *simul*.

On Barth's view, then, as the "Bearer of our contradiction," Christ's is the "original participation in the twofold nature of our being."[7]

> The secret, the meaning and the goal of creation is that it reveals, or that there is revealed in it, the covenant and communion between God and man . . . which is so far-reaching that the Word by which God created all things, even God Himself, becomes one of His creatures . . . like all the created reality distinct from Himself, *and thus making His own its two-fold determination,* its greatness and wretchedness, its infinite dignity and infinite frailty, its hope and its despair, its rejoicing and its sorrow. This is what has taken place in Jesus Christ as the meaning and end of creation.[8]

Note Barth's use of symmetry once again—"infinite dignity and infinite frailty"—in describing the asymmetrical determinations assumed by God Himself, again appearing to suggest Jesus Christ as *simul iustus et peccator*. Obvious also is the uniqueness of Christ's experience compared to his human sisters and brothers. "What," Barth continues, "are all the severity and relentlessness of its contradiction as known and experienced by us in comparison with the relentlessness and severity which He caused to be visited on Himself, on His own heart, even before He acted as Creator?"[9]

But to allow for Jesus' intimacy with God as His Son to be maintained, and to determine Jesus' taking on of human corruption in himself, can we avoid the fact that for all Barth's insistence, what we have called the "duality" of Jesus Christ's humanity is nothing but a dualism that runs right through to its source in the very being of God? Surely our hopeful inquiry into the "before-before" has not ended with the somber realization that the "before-before" is simply more of the same? Barth's way through may not be

---

7. *CD* III/1, 382. In connection to Bearer of our contradiction, note Barth's description of Christ as "the Bearer of the divine image" and "the Bearer of human sin" (both cited above, see *CD* III/1, 50–51). With these labels he appears to suggest Christ as the *simul* incarnate, as well as the Subject of both determinations.

8. *CD* III/1, 377. Emphasis added.

9. *CD* III/1, 381.

satisfactory to some, but at the very end of Volume III/1 he appears to suggest that the two mutually exclusive determinations of the *simul* are "both grounded in an eternal dimension."[10] In other words, these opposites do not exist together *ultimately* in eternity, but they do coexist in a *dimension* of eternity—a dimension that is not merely of this world, because Jesus Christ is not merely of this world. We will return to this otherworldly dimension. For now, we take note that Barth takes eminently seriously the scriptural testimony that before the foundation of the world Christ died for the ungodly (Rev 13:8); "from all eternity God has determined upon man's acquittal at His own cost . . . God has ordained that in the place of the one acquitted He Himself should be perishing and abandoned and rejected—the Lamb slain from the foundation of the world."[11]

It should not surprise, us, therefore, that Barth can claim the chaos of Genesis 1:2 to be most poignantly reflected not in Genesis itself but in the darkness of Jesus' cry of dereliction.[12] In fact, later Barth will say that the judgment and reconciliation wrought by the event of Jesus' death is "in exact correspondence with what He did as Creator when he separated light from darkness and elected the creature to being and rejected the possibility of chaos as nothingness."[13] In this act of separation, states Barth, God declares "His Yes to the real and his definitive No to the unreal."[14] And, true to form, Barth equates the separation of light from darkness, this Yes and No of creation, to "the divine Yes of Easter Day," a Yes which by its very nature requires a "divine No" to all that opposes God's righteousness.[15] Lest we mistake God's No as being opposed to anything that he has created, Barth asserts that the No revealed in the judgment of the cross is "never addressed to creation as such but to the nothingness by which creation is surrounded and menaced, to the sin and death by which it is mastered."[16] We take note of how this statement comports with our earlier conjecture as to the proper target of God's judgment and why Barth can employ the harshest penal language to that which is not (i.e., "the old man").

---

10. CD III/1, 413. The German phrasing of "an eternal dimension" here is *einem jenseitigen Zusammenhang*, which is the only occurrence of it in *KD* (*KD*, III/1, 475). *Jenseitigen* can also be translated "otherworldly."

11. CD II/2, 167.

12. CD III/1, 109.

13. CD IV/1, 349. See III/2, 51–52.

14. CD III/2, 52.

15. CD II/1, 394.

16. CD III/1, 386.

Returning to God's primal decision, it is God's rejection of nothingness that gives the dark sphere its "reality" in "its absurd way, very different from the world willed and created by God." And in this first act of creation God "passed by this lower sphere without a halt," assuring that chaos has no future and can only be past, "originally and definitively superseded and declared to be obsolete."[17] In fact, Barth affirms 2 Cor 5:17 as reflective of this very first creative act of God: "Gen 1:2 speaks of the 'old things' which according to 2 Cor 5:17 have radically passed away in the death and resurrection of Jesus Christ. It tells us that even from the standpoint of the first creation, let alone the new, chaos is really 'old things.'"[18]

It is pertinent here to consider Barth's radical assessment of 2 Cor 5:17, a verse which might well be commandeered to describe the existential experience of a Christian's faith event as opposed to, or at least in isolation from, the ontological rootedness of all new experiences of faith. Barth considers that the extravagance of creation itself is often overlooked in talk of "new creation," when instead creation should be given a more prominent view. For one thing, revelation and reconciliation cannot claim a *creatio ex nihilo* as can creation proper. Barth continues: "The new or second creation presupposes the old or first, not as a reality familiar to us in its nature and at our disposal, but as one given beforehand, presupposed by God, i.e., as the existing reality to be freshly enlightened and shaped by judgment and grace."[19]

Purely from the perspective of our human experience, darkness appears to be at least coeternal with light, and the fact that "God is light and in him is no darkness at all" (1 John 1:5) is not self-apparent. Barth acknowledges that juxtaposed against the reality of perfect creation is the distortion of what Barth calls "this monstrous world."[20] It is therefore only by the revelation of Jesus Christ in his death and resurrection that we can know the difference between darkness and light, falsehood and reality. Only by virtue of the one who has shared our plight and overcome "the sphere of non-grace" are we given to know there can be "no symmetry or equilibrium" between light and darkness; there can be "no question of an absolute dualism" but only an "impassable barrier" between these two "mutually exclusive" elements.[21] Henceforth, notes Barth, we can be assured of the proper relationship between the two elements: "Whatever else may take place between light and darkness, light will never be darkness and darkness will never be light. It

17. *CD* III/1, 108.
18. *CD* III/1, 110.
19. *CD* I/2, 186.
20. *CD* III/1, 109.
21. *CD* III/1, 123–24.

is also to establish an inviolable hierarchy."²² We would suggest that all of this talk from Barth about the original antithesis mirrors exactly Barth's economic description of the *simul* assumed by Jesus Christ and derivatively affecting all humans. We therefore have an "archetype" of the relationship "between Holy God and sinful man in the covenant of grace," states Barth, "the antithesis which in Jesus Christ became an antithesis in unity."²³

Because of the tendency to think of eternity in unnuanced fashion, it may strike us as strange that for Barth some things in eternity are still relative to one another. As a corollary to our aforementioned discussion of God's freedom and his prerogative to absorb evil and still remain himself, Barth reasons that if eternity is God's time, he can parse it into "moments" as he desires. Indeed, Barth asserts with resurrection perspective that Christ's "participation in this negative aspect of existence became only a transient episode. It was the affair of a moment. The moment has now passed."²⁴ It is in knowing by faith the verdict of the Victor of Gethsemane and Golgotha, the "after" of the historical "before-after" sequence of the Christ event, that we can postulate with Barth concerning "the before-before." For Barth the "justification of creation" involves "looking at creation through the message of Good Friday and Easter."²⁵ In this light, creation follows reconciliation. There is no other way, even in our best exegesis of Genesis, to find the preponderance in the *simul* that we find in the revelation of Jesus Christ. In Barth's words, we hold to

> the divergence between the two aspects of existence in the one work and living action of God; the asymmetry and disproportion, the polarity between the two determinations of created reality at the level of the covenant between God and man which is the meaning and end of creation . . . It is clear that from this point of view it is impossible to speak of an eternal dualism of aspects, but only of a dualism which is dissoluble.²⁶

---

22. *CD* III/1, 123.

23. *CD* III/3, 106.

24. *CD* III/1, 384. Again, nothingness is not technically the negation for Barth, but for all practical purposes for humanity the negation is nothingness.

25. *CD* III/1, 413. See III/1, 76, where Barth discusses reconciliation being "before" creation.

26. *CD* III/1, 384.

The Original Intervention

We return to the idea that it is only the death and resurrection of the incarnate God that makes what is otherwise a dualism the revelation of a duality—a duality which is dissoluble. The *simul* annulled. Barth invites us to look forward to the *eschaton* not because of an essential newness to creation, and not because of a strengthened humanity less susceptible to the fall, but because of the full manifestation of the eradication of evil and the threat of wickedness altogether. In the meantime, even if we can assert with Barth that Good Friday and Easter prove the superiority and priority of one aspect over the other, we continue to live in the *iustus* and *peccator* determinations simultaneously. And in this "strange battle," we suffer. Admittedly, Barth's description of Christ's suffering in the flesh as a "transient episode" may not sound serious enough to be commensurate with our suffering in this world. Lest we remain skeptical of Barth's proposal of the otherworldly or "eternal dimension," i.e., in case we see it as a poor substitute for traditional categories of impassibility and the like, we are now brought to a most positive and concrete significance of God making evil his own. Barth has warned us against "a static perfection of God beyond and above creaturely imperfection" and invited us to perceive "the contesting and overcoming of the imperfection of the creature by God's own intervention on its behalf."[27]

Barth insists that the pain and suffering of our world is "not in vain" and "not without purpose."[28] He cannot explain exactly how this is the case, but Barth believes God gives us the answer in himself: God suffers, God is crucified. By giving himself, God thereby gives integrity to our suffering to hold us over until the day when all becomes clear. It must be emphasized that in spite of Barth's similarities with Platonic themes, it is the revelation of the suffering God is what takes us past metaphysical dualism and all forms of Docetism. But it really has to be God who suffers, declares Barth; "A surrogate cannot perform for us the service which is necessary if we are to achieve a positive attitude to creation."[29] In the compelling quote that follows, Barth claims that it is the incarnation which reveals God's character most acutely; he suggests that God was already affected by humanity's sin and struggle even before any of us was born. Because God was affected in this way, we can be certain there was never a time when God was not compassionately disposed towards humanity.

---

27. *CD* III/1, 385.
28. *CD* IV/2, 192.
29. *CD* III/1, 379.

> For the real goodness of the real God is that the contradiction of creation has not remained alien to Himself. Primarily and supremely he has made it His own, and only then caused it to be reflected in the life of the creature. His rejoicing and sorrow preceded ours. For before light could gladden us and darkness torment us, He was aware of them both, separating and thus co-ordinating them. Before life greeted us and death menaced us, He was the Lord of life and death, *and bound them both in a bundle*. And He did not do all this in such a way that it was alien and external to Him, but in such a way that in the full majesty of His Godhead He participated in these antitheses and their connexion, in eternal mercy causing them to be internal to Himself, and to find their origin in His own being.[30]

If it had not been addressed in previous pages, Barth's last phrases might cause one to pause, but now Barth's conviction comes to the fore, namely, the consolation of knowing we have a God in truest solidarity with us—one who understands his creatures' personal pain and who embraces us at our very worst (1 Tim 1:15). Because for Barth reconciliation in a sense precedes creation,[31] he is confident of God's eternal compassion—"from the very outset."[32] What is Barth inferring by the phrase translated "and bound them both in a bundle"[33] above? Might we suggest that it points to the babe of Bethlehem, he who was born the *simul* incarnate out of love for the world?

---

30. *CD* III/1, 380. Emphasis added. Barth forbids there to be anything but the boldest line of demarcation between good and evil, in God's being or in the world; Barth will never give us permission to call good bad or bad good. In this view, suffering cannot be viewed as a gift, but it is Jesus who is the gift to us in the midst of our suffering, sometimes in such acute ways as to prompt us to name the suffering itself as a gift.

31. *CD* III/1, 76.

32. *CD* III/1, 376. See *CD* II/1, 370 and following for a very similar passage to the indented quotation above concerning the "personal God" who "has a heart." A God who "can feel and be affected. He is not impassable. He cannot be moved from outside by an extraneous power. But this does not mean that He is not capable of moving Himself." Barth states that in Himself God "is the original free powerful compassion . . . from the very outset" (370). For the Son of God to take alien form does not mean that our suffering is alien to God. In fact, "so much greater is His sorrow on our behalf than any sorrow which we can feel for ourselves" (373). Here Barth bemoans the practice of lament when it is not contextualized properly in union with Christ. As Barth asserts elsewhere, God is "the supreme sufferer and partisan of all" (*CD* IV/2, 191).

33. See *KD* III/1, 436: Barth's exact German phrase for "and bound them both in a bundle" is "und hat er die beiden miteinander verbunden."

> The incredible and real mystery of the free grace of God is that He makes His own the cause of the creature which is not even the equal of nothingness, let alone its master, but its victim ... God is not too great, nor is He ashamed, to enter this situation which is not only threatened but already corrupted, to confess Himself the Friend and Fellow of the sinful creature which is not only the subject to the assault but broken by it, to acknowledge Himself the Neighbor of the sinful creature stricken and smitten by its own fault.[34]

> He might have been a majestic, passive and beatific God on high. But He descends to the depths, and concerns Himself with nothingness, because in His goodness he does not will to cease to be concerned for His creature. He thus continues to act in relation to nothingness with the same holiness with which He acted as the Creator when He separated light from darkness. He continues to be the Adversary of this adversary because His love for the creature has no limit or end.[35]

So, we ask once again, when is the *simul*? We might abridge accordingly: If the *simul* begins at the very outset, and even before creation, it appears conclusive that Barth is saying the *simul* for humanity is indirectly reflective of the primal conflict—"the original antithesis"—between God and nothingness. In Barth's estimation, Jesus Christ, as the God of the original antithesis between God and nothingness, would never consider the creation of humanity without first entering in to the original antithesis from below, putting himself under the derivative contradictions light and darkness, righteousness and sin.[36] As a single subject within the Chalcedonian definition, Jesus Christ in his divinity allows him to deal with the threat posed to humanity even before creation; at the same time it is his humanity that uniquely puts him in solidarity with his creatures. Christ then, while always with humanity, is also always ahead of humanity, suggests Barth, acting as the unique "penetrating spearhead" of humanity.[37] It is precisely the distinction between the spearhead of humanity (Christ) and humanity in general which provides Barth credence to claim that the original antithesis

---

34. *CD* III/3, 356–57.

35. *CD* III/3, 357.

36. See *CD* II/1, 517: Barth makes a case for the Philippians 2 hymn as describing Christ's humiliation as occurring *before* creation. Christ therefore proves himself to be *Kyrios* not in spite of his humiliation but because of it.

37. *CD* III/2, 143–45; Christ's role is primary, even if humanity in general "shares in the battle fought and the history of triumph inaugurated by Him" (146).

is resolved even before creation—this along with the fact that in his one person Jesus Christ is at once Creator, Reconciler, and Redeemer. On Barth's view, it is by God's becoming the first born creature, and entering into the original antithesis in a different way (i.e., from below) that nothingness is drawn out and fully exposed.[38] Jesus does not enter into the primal conflict without the sword of the Spirit. It is the Spirit, asserts Barth, who "discloses the antithesis which dominates this life in its necessity as the antithesis which is first in God because it is first opened up, but also overcome and closed again, in the will of God."[39]

Within this "antithesis which is first in God" nothingness seeks to maximize its foothold, making every attempt to "defraud God of His honour and right and at the same time to rob the creature of its salvation and right." Again, it must be emphasized that, while it is true that nothingness feasts on creation through the shelter of the negative side of creation, it is most directly the antithetical enemy not of the creature but the Creator God himself. Instead of evading the theodicy question, then, Barth heightens it. On Barth's view God never abdicates his sovereign responsibility. Instead, preemptively intervening—the original intervention into the original antithesis—Jesus Christ's incarnate passion demonstrates that the "controversy with nothingness, its conquest, removal and abolition, are primarily and properly God's own affair."[40] And, continues Barth, "because nothingness is *His* enemy, because it is He who allows it to be this, because He has made the controversy with it *His* affair,"[41] God will act to ensure that "nothingness has no perpetuity."[42] God in Christ "throws Himself"[43] against chaos, he "casts Himself into this conflict."[44] Because it is primarily his affair, God faces the threat by becoming the "primary victim" even as the primary "foe of nothingness"[45]: "Nothingness could not master this victim. It could neither endure nor bear the presence of God in the flesh. It met with a prey which it could not match and by which it could only be destroyed as it

---

38. *CD* III/3, 366.

39. *CD* IV/2, 352. See also *CD* IV/2, 365, where Barth speaks of the Spirit of Truth as dividing truth and falsehood.

40. *CD* III/3, 354.

41. *CD* III/3, 362.

42. *CD* III/3, 364.

43. *CD* III/3, 352.

44. *CD* III/3, 357.

45. *CD* III/3, 360.

tried to swallow it. The fulness of grace which God showed to His creature by Himself becoming a threatened, even ruined and lost creature, was its undoing."[46]

What we see then, is that while the war is primarily between God and nothingness, this war takes place in the human arena for the sake of the humanity that God desires to save. Could God not have done this another way? On Barth's view, God deems that humanity have "a real part in the conflict with nothingness." Again, humanity's participation happens in a secondary way, but in an authentic way nonetheless; the creature is "no mere spectator."[47] We might ask for less! But those who suffer can at least know their Brother Jesus Christ is not "the Physician who prescribes a medicine for the patient with no intention of testing or taking it Himself."[48]

Because of Jesus Christ's original human journey from Light through *das Nichtige* and darkness to created light—from Life through death to resurrection—while humanity shares Christ's sufferings, that same humanity can be assured that it will share the glory (Rom 8:17).[49] Indeed, notes Barth, just as true as to say "man is dead even while he lives"[50] is to say "even in the midst of death we are not only in death but already out of its clutches and victorious over it."[51] Believers can know in Christ that nothingness is not itself primal, and that it cannot perpetuate. "If Jesus is Victor," declares Barth, "the last word must always be secretly the first."[52]

---

46. CD III/3, 362.

47. CD III/3, 359. As we shall see in chapter 12, while angels can in one sense give us an indication of the activity of *iustus* humanity, Barth (citing 1 Pet 1:12) recognizes that angels do not suffer like humans in this cosmic struggle and are therefore inferior to humans who share Christ's incarnate sufferings (CD IV/3.2, 732).

48. CD III/3, 329.

49. See CD II/1, 422: "The sufferings of this present time, which reflect both the light and shadow of this moment, are nothing in comparison with the glory that shall be revealed in us (Rom 8:17f.). If we suffer with Him in this hope, and we believe according to God's Word that we have to suffer with Jesus Christ in this hope, we can and may suffer in patience: answering His patience with our patience; giving the right answer to the waiting of His wrath with our waiting for redemption."

50. CD III/2, 601. Barth cites Matt 8:22; Luke 15:32; Eph 2:1; 1 Tim 5:6.

51. CD III/2, 610. Barth repeats "already out of its clutches and victorious over it" three times in two pages.

52. CD III/3, 364. This Origenist phrase is repeated shortly hereafter; "our final word must really be the first" (366). See CD IV/3.2, "the final thing," states Barth elsewhere in Origenist language, "is already the first thing." Again renew is not re-do: "Man is . . . rescued from destruction and renewed in the being assigned him by his Creator."

Christ the Victor: Not Over Our Heads

With the focus on Christ inviting humans into his earthly sufferings, is Barth suggesting that Jesus' passion is primarily not in order to address the sin and guilt of humanity,[53] but instead that his work is especially directed against "the resisting element" (the devil) victimizing humanity?[54] Without absolving humanity of guilt, if Barth comes down on the side of human beings as victims more than as perpetrators we could hardly argue that we are discovering something fundamentally new in a theologian whose "God is for us" is always deeper than his "God is against us."

Barth assures us of God's unchanging attitude, whether it be towards humanity corporately or the human person. The human, Barth writes, "is dark and in darkness, and darkness is in him. He loves darkness more than light (John 3:19). This is bad enough. But he is not darkness. The Word of God speaks of the grace directed to him. But God has no grace at all for darkness. He has not reconciled darkness to Himself, not made any covenant with it. He attacks it in His Word, not to spare and preserve, but to destroy. He does not attack man. He attacks the darkness which envelops and indwells him for man's sake, for his good, for his salvation." God has sworn to keep faith with humanity, Barth concludes, and he follows through as evidenced "in the attack against darkness mounted in His Word"; God's love for the world is thereby proved "in the giving of His Son."[55] In this light one could contend that Barth's preferred motif for the atonement is "Christ is victor," rightly understood.[56] For Barth *Christus victor* provides a central place not only to the resurrection but also to the cross, all the while within an ontological context. It is in Barth's subsection "Jesus is Victor" in paragraph 69 that we find the plentiful allusions to Luther's hymn *A Mighty Fortress is*

---

53. See Jorgenson, 460. Jorgenson arguesthat the use of *das Nichtige* as a comprehensive theme to describe evil, and including sin, may have been Barth's way to soften human culpability to the degree of placing more blame on the forces of evil.

54. See *CD* IV/3.1, 261: Barth prefers "the resisting element" to "the devil," who he also describes as the "hypostatised falsehood." Regardless of label, Barth notes, "What is essential is simply that his power and malignity as the alien force which dominates, seduces and deceives man, but is absolutely subject to God, should be known and revealed in the limits in which, as the light shines in the darkness, it may be seen and known in its encounter with Jesus the Victor."

55. *CD* IV/3.1, 251.

56. Traditionally viewed, *Christus victor* is completely untenable for Barth because it typically speaks of Christ's arrival and rescue of humanity without an ontology which relates it *internally* to humanity in general. The typical external relations of *Christus victor* speak of a cosmic victory over the forces of evil by Jesus Christ long ago, which is then somehow appropriated to believers' lives today.

Our God. "The ancient foe, or however we might describe him, cannot alter the justification and sanctification of man actualised in Jesus Christ. But he still has space to resist the Word of reconciliation, to hinder its understanding, acceptance and appropriation on the part of man."[57] So again we ask, does Barth's *Christus Victor* motif absolve humanity of all responsibility? Barth demurs, God does not handle evil "over the heads" of humanity[58] any more than God sanctifies humans over their heads.[59] In other words, even if God is responsible for allowing evil into the world, humans are responsible for living in correspondence to darkness, says Barth: "It is man who is responsible and guilty and in mortal peril at this point." But even though it is "man" who "makes himself the battlefield,"[60] there always exists distinction between the real identity of humanity and the darkness humanity has capitulated to. Walking by faith and not by sight, the Christian may know by virtue of the justification and sanctification in Christ that "man, whether he realises it or not, is objectively alienated, separated and torn away from this resisting element in him, because he is already set in the liberty of the children of God."[61] Obviously, the "before-before" nature of *iustus* humanity—what we have presented as Barth's Christo-anthropological actualism—is critical to Barth's ontological enhancement of *Christus victor*; Christ's victory is perceived not as an establishing of our *iustus* human identity but as a reestablishment of an ongoing truth and a validation and preservation of his perfect creation.

It may involve a reschematization of our categories for us to think rightly about our death being "behind and beneath us" even before we are born. Even more challenging perhaps is to think in this fashion about the babe born in Bethlehem. But that appears to be exactly what Barth is asking us to do.[62] For Barth, it is by looking through "Johannine Christology"[63] that we discover most pointedly the proper definitions for both Christ *and*

---

57. *CD* IV/3.1, 260.

58. *CD* IV/3.1, 251.

59. *CD* IV/3.1, 332: "He does not will to go over our heads, because He wills to give us a share in His work . . . He wills to give us time and space for participation in His work." Again "share" for Barth is very carefully qualified (the following in regards to a person in prayer): "It is a share which is quite incomprehensible from his own standpoint. He cannot deduce it from his own capacity or volition or activity. It is not in any way effected or conditioned. Yet it is still a genuine and actual share" (*CD* III/3, 285).

60. *CD* IV/3.1, 251.

61. *CD* IV/3.1, 269.

62. *CD* III/2, 611–15. The phrase "behind and beneath us" appears four times in five pages.

63. *CD* III/2, 65.

humanity. From this standpoint (and again rife with allusion to the *simul*) Barth asks concerning "the riddle of the existence of Jesus Christ":

> What is it that we beheld? Flesh of our flesh? And therefore the judgment of God fulfilled on all flesh in Him? And therefore His own and our misery? No, we beheld His glory—"the glory as of the only begotten of the Father, full of grace and truth" (John 1:14). What is it that we heard? That no man has seen God at any time? That we are so far from God, so godless and god-forsaken? No, for although we did hear this, we hear also the declaration of the One who is in the bosom of the Father, and "of His fulness we have all received, and grace upon grace" (John 1:16). This is paradoxical, not merely because it is said of the man Jesus, of the eternal Word which became flesh, of the humiliated Son of God as the Son of Man . . . but also because this man was so superior and exalted, so genuine and glorious a man.[64]

In this same human's existence, comments Barth: "There is in it not only night, but also day, not only confusing darkness but also—no less and perhaps even more strangely—blinding light; the sharp light of contrast, but genuine light." As always, Barth appears adamant in his conviction that what is true of the human Jesus Christ is true for humanity, and that in this "riddle" we are given to see not only a "god-forsaken" human but one in the "bosom of the Father," not only the true nature of God but also "the glory of man as it is present in Him." Barth notes that it is "inconceivable" for us to grasp the goodness of this "new beginning of our human being," yet by faith we might indeed acknowledge "this royal man, to the glory of the Son of God revealed in His human majesty, to His human life and therefore to the exaltation of our life as it has taken place in Him."[65] It is the "It is finished" of Calvary that Barth sees as one with the "it is finished" of creation; this is where humiliation reveals exaltation, and the "lifted up" of the cross converges with the "lifted up" of the King.[66] And what of the resurrection? For Barth it is "the revelation of our righteousness, the revelation of the fact that God's righteousness has prevailed," and that we have become born anew to what we are, "the righteousness of God."[67]

We began this chapter with Barth's mysterious statement that "everything is created for Jesus Christ and His death and resurrection." Barth

---

64. *CD* IV/2, 353–54.
65. *CD* IV/2, 354.
66. *CD* IV/2, 255.
67. *CD* II/1, 404. Barth notes that this is the correct understanding of Romans 4:24–25.

has expressly *not* asked us to blindly deduce that 1) if God is good, then 2) creation meant for the purpose of the death and resurrection of Christ must be for an overall good; however Barth *has* asked us to view the first things (regarding God's love, goodness, and power) through the second (regarding God's solidarity, suffering, and self-sacrifice). He has not encouraged us to dig under the foundation of Jesus Christ to discover the answer to "When is the *simul*?" as if we could discern it by reading Genesis apart from 2 Cor 5:17. Instead, he urges us to interpret the original antithesis by means of the original intervention. At the end of chapter 9, I stated that "Barth's proposed mutual interpenetration of Creation and Fall, *iustus* and *peccator*, are meaningless to the extent they are endless in *either* direction . . . any consolation derived from the belief that the *simul* ends in the death of Christ is severely mitigated by the idea of a mutual beginning." Hopefully we have recognized that to set out on a direct journey to find the "before-before" is like chasing the end of the rainbow. There are surely as many creation theorists as there are what Robert Capon called "eschatology junkies"; the answer is not found on either of the two ends, but by doubling down on humanity's central history. Indeed, Barth presents us with the "riddle of the existence of Jesus Christ" and the accompanying punchline—that to be sure of the asymmetry on the resurrection "end" of the story *is* to be sure of the asymmetry on the creation one. In a sentence worth repeating, Barth remarks: "If Jesus Christ is Victor, the last word must always be secretly the first."

The theodicy question may continue to haunt us, but on Barth's view, we may proceed knowing that God's revelation will not let us define suffering without himself; God and suffering cannot be defined apart from God *in suffering*. Without the eye of faith, we can only see dualism—whether it be related to the *simul*, the opposite dynamics of the atonement, or concerning creation and the challenges of good and evil, flourishing and suffering. However, Barth points us to the proclamation of the duality of Jesus Christ and him crucified, under the sound of which he is sure the preponderance of the asymmetry will continue to speak for itself.

11

The Humanity from Heaven and the Humanity of Earth

"Even in the sowing, the passing, the dying and the burying of our temporal life we are a new creation, born again, the children of God, justified, partakers of the Holy Spirit. But this reality of our being in and with Christ is not visible in this sowing."[1]

WHEN BARTH GAVE UP HIS PLAN TO COMPLETE *CHURCH DOGMATICS*, LEAVing glaringly absent his proposed Volume V on redemption, he suggested he had already written everything he wanted to write on the topic.[2] Is there ground for thinking that the reason Barth seemed relatively unconcerned about finishing Volume V (and an incomplete Vol. IV) is because he had already written Volume III? Creation on its own does not have gospel value; Barth would readily concur. Creation imbued with the Reconciliation of Jesus Christ is a different story. Regardless of age or infirmity, if Barth was not keen to finish his *Church Dogmatics*, it may suggest Barth's concern to distance himself from Origen—he who first insisted that "The end is always like the beginning."[3]

---

1. *CD* IV/1, 330.
2. Come, *Introduction to Barth's "Dogmatics,"* 60. Barth stated this in the author's presence.
3. Origen, *De Principiis* 1.6.2.

The Humanity from Heaven and the Humanity of Earth 213

Two Sagas, One Covenant

I have begun making the case for Barth's belief in the transcendence of the new person in Christ even in the midst of the destruction of the old. Lest the critic chalk up my reading of Barth to so much proof-texting, I would like at this point to set a firmer foundation for my trajectory by expounding upon Barth's "two sagas" argument in *Church Dogmatics* III/1. My purpose in this excursus is to corroborate my prior indication that Barth indeed operates with a human transcendence or human immortality narrative from creation forward. We turn once again to John, and to a verse handpicked by Barth,[4] in order to frame Barth's discussion of the truth of creation in light of redemption. It is Jesus' apparently enigmatic remark: "I am the resurrection and the life. Those who believe in me, even though they die, will live, and everyone who lives and believes in me will never die" (11:26). What does this statement tell us about the truth of creation?

To begin with, Barth believes the two creation accounts, or "sagas,"[5] in Genesis are from two distinct sources that cannot and should not be harmonized. If the goal is to construct a purely "historical" synthesis of the two creation sagas, says Barth, one will have to do violence to the text. Indeed, "The older expositors who attempted a 'historical' harmonization of the two accounts did not adhere too closely to what is actually written."[6] Not only is it problematic for Barth to synthesize the Genesis 1 and 2 accounts, it is also an injustice to "Genesis 2" (which technically runs from 2:4 and through chapter 3) to relegate it to a purely complementary role or to present it as merely a supplement to Genesis 1. "Our best course," advises Barth, "is to accept that each has its own harmony, and then to be content with the higher harmony which is achieved when we allow the one to speak after the other." By refusing the goal of literal historicization, Barth believes that the perspective of the two sagas taken together will provide us with the fullest biblical history.[7]

We have already elaborated on the first creation saga and its completion or finished work over seven days. As Barth would remind us below,

---

4. *CD* III/2, 621. Barth mentions John 11:26b ("everyone who believes in me will never die") as spoken from the above, or transcendent, standpoint, versus the below standpoint, and he again speaks of Christians knowing that death "is behind them."

5. See *CD* III/1, 78–81. For Barth, the creation accounts have "pre-historical" *and* historical meaning, but since we cannot always decipher the extent to which they are purely historical, he prefers the word "saga" to history. In other words, Barth necessarily contrasts saga to myth but not to history.

6. *CD* III/1, 80.

7. *CD* III/1, 229.

"the Creator . . . has accomplished the *creatio*": "The statement that God has created heaven and earth speaks of an incomparable perfect, and tells us that this perfect is the beginning of heaven and earth. It is also true that this beginning does not cease . . . To the uniqueness of this perfect there belongs the fact that it also contains a present. But this does not alter the fact that it is a perfect, referring to something which has happened once and for all."[8] The first saga presents us with a perfect creation that cannot become imperfect, a good that cannot be anything but good, a complete that cannot be incomplete. But what does the second creation saga tell us? And how does it relate to the first? Instead of being presented as a completed picture, Genesis 2 demonstrates for Barth the more directly historical realm in its narrative form. Noticeably, Barth points out in Genesis 2 the beginning of Adam's creation is not in the Garden; the Garden is not Adam's "home," but he is placed there subsequently by God who has prepared it for him. For Barth, Genesis 2 thus pictures a creation still on the way to completion—to the point where Adam is completed by a helper, Eve.[9] If the "Garden" of Genesis 1 presents us with a finished work of creation perfect and complete, the Genesis 2 Garden includes more obvious themes of light and darkness, good and evil, and what we might call abnormalities to God's perfect creation, even before the fall. Remarks Barth: "from the very first this place is not without serious problems."[10] Therefore Barth sees Genesis 2 as a separate testimony of humanity from Genesis 1. Genesis 2, with its tree related to the knowledge of good and evil, signifies retrospectively the historic sequence: the conception, birth, life, death, resurrection, and ascension (homecoming) of humanity in Jesus Christ. How then do the two sagas with their apparent disparities inform one another? How does the imprecise movement from incompletion to completion in Genesis 2 correlate with the primal completion of Genesis 1?

As noted in the introduction, Barth describes eternity as having three forms: pre-temporal, supra-temporal, and post-temporal. Importantly, Barth's concept of time has everything to do with his disavowal of Platonic dualism. Time is shot through with eternity, even to the point where Barth can say that within time is found the hidden centre of eternity, the center in time.[11] For Barth created time is also supra-temporal eternity, the form of eternity that is perfectly consistent with pre-temporal and post-temporal

---

8. *CD* III/1, 13.

9. *CD* III/1, 251: "[Adam's] creation does not begin in the Garden but is completed in it."

10. *CD* III/1, 250.

11. *CD* II/1, 626.

eternity.¹² These forms of eternity, says Barth, "are not to be played off one against the other, as if God could be better known and were able to be taken more seriously under one of these forms."¹³ Barth admits his hesitancy to use the description "supra-temporal"; he does not want the term mistakenly to suggest that "supra" means above or parallel to time.¹⁴ Eternity for Barth, then, is not timeless, but by virtue of the incarnation eternity is shown to be "the element which embraces time on all sides." Because time is not a "self-enclosed middle," the truth which Jesus Christ reveals to us in time (i.e., in supra-temporal eternity) accurately indicates what is true in pre-temporal and post-temporal eternity.¹⁵

Of course we are most conscious of our existence as lived in supra-temporal eternity, and it is there where we perceive transformation to be most apparent.¹⁶ But as we have discussed, Barth's view of transformation cannot be understood in a vacuum (i.e., apart from the Christ's actualizing context or by means of gradualist progression). Instead, transformation in the supra-temporal is to be understood only in light of, and in consistent correspondence to, the reality of the other aspects of eternity (as revealed in the resurrection). In other words, the manner of transformation which is revealed to us in the "time of the *simul*" is consistent with the transcendent truth which has been in less than plain view all along—God's economy of transformation and super-abounding glory which does not rely on the contrast of the *simul*. It appears that Barth's juxtaposition of the two creation

12. *CD* II/1, 634. Barth describes his view as a realized eschatology which assures God's presence in time (*CD* II/1, 626). "God's eternity is in time. Time itself is in eternity" (*CD* II/1, 623).

13. *CD* II/1, 623.

14. *CD* III/1, 70: In view of "supra-temporal," Barth here submits that "co-temporal" might be a better term to avoid encouraging the Neo-Protestants from their a-historical view that the believer's connection to the "above" occurs only in the existential faith event of the believer. Elsewhere Barth also warns against the pre-temporal imbalance of the older Reformed view, which sought to establish a limited atonement template of double-predestination in which to fit supra-temporal revelation (*CD* II/1, 634).

15. *CD* II/1, 623. See *CD* II/1, 625: "We must speak of the supra-temporality of God the Father, Son and Holy Spirit if under the title of eternity we are not to speak secretly of a timeless God and therefore of a godless time, again taking refuge in a desperate hypostatizing of the 'now' of our time which cannot be hypostatized."

16. Previously we have made the argument with Barth that a contrast is not necessary for transformation to occur because of God's unique economy of super-abundant glory. In fact we might even say that it is exactly the contrast between sin and righteousness, with its accompanying temptation toward zero-sum categories, that prompts our misguided views of transformation as the wrong kind of "becoming"—i.e., becoming something that we are presently *not*.

sagas of Genesis 1 and Genesis 2 is consistent with a duality (not dualism) between transcendence and immanence where the later, as Barth states earlier, cannot alter "the perfect" but can only reveal it. While not to be separated, it follows that Genesis 1 correlates most closely with pre-temporal and post-temporal eternity, while the Genesis 2 saga correlates most closely with supra-temporal eternity.

Supra-temporal eternity, then, is the time of the *simul iustus et peccator*; it is the time where Jesus exists simultaneously in the provisional unity of the two mutually exclusive spheres. In Barth's words: "It is he who draws the distinction between disobedience and obedience, sin and righteousness, guilt and freedom from guilt, fate and freedom, death and life, alien lordship and the kingdom of God, damnation and blessedness."[17] Barth does not want us to confuse the simultaneity of the spheres with their contemporaneity, as if each sphere has the same present and future. As the incarnate Christ, Jesus sets out to dissolve the sphere which is basically past (sin) in order to reveal that which is basically future (righteousness)—the latter sphere making up the hidden centre of eternity. Asserts Barth, "In His death on the cross Jesus Christ slew and buried the old man of the first sphere. He destroyed in Himself the disobedience of Adam . . . in His resurrection Jesus Christ brought to light and life in Himself the new man of the second sphere."[18] It is not difficult to see how Barth's view of time and the two spheres comports to his conceptualization of the two sagas and to our prior discussion of the pure and alien or impure forms. Christ's work in the second sphere, represented by the second saga, "brought to light" the finished work of the first sphere and saga.

How are we to summarize Barth's conclusions? In the first saga of creation, God in Christ has already "passed by" the chaos of nothingness in order to create.[19] If not already plain from the last chapter, this move by Barth is critical to understanding how God's good and perfect creation is not reflective of, or negatively affected by, the original antithesis (between God and nothingness).[20] The first creation saga therefore gives us, with revelatory permission, the clearest view of salvation and redemption. In the second saga, as suggested above, the struggle with nothingness is waged in

---

17. *CD* II/1, 626.

18. *CD* II/1, 626. In regards to drawing a distinction, can we avoid Jesus' allusion that he came not to bring peace but a sword?

19. *CD* III/1, 108.

20. See *CD* III/3, 331: as a parasitic "reality" relative to God's reality, Satan cannot create, he can only react. Barth continually reminds us the chaos and nothingness of Genesis 1:2 are "not endowed with invented negative qualities, but with the specific and authentically evil character of the antithesis to the grace of God."

what appears to be a typical chronological narrative of creation and fall, the redemptive end accomplished (or as Barth might say, brought back around to the beginning) when Christ humbles himself unto death, only to rise and ascend victoriously. There is no glimpse of the christological-anthropological truth of the first saga without the retrospective perspective of the second, but the second saga is not possible without the actuality of the first. Both creation sagas exist inside the one covenant faithfulness of God.

In the end, then, where does this leave us regarding the "framing verse" from Lazarus's grave? "Those who believe in me, even though they die, will live, and everyone who lives and believes in me will never die." The second saga obviously signifies the first part of the verse; it is the history of death and resurrection and therefore it is the eternal God meeting humanity in the sphere of the *simul*. The reconciliation accomplished in the center of revealed time (supra-temporal eternity) points to, and through the resurrection reveals, post-temporal eternity, which in turn witnesses to pre-temporal eternity or what we have called "the before-before." It follows then that the creation saga of Genesis 1 and its accomplished perfection comports to those who "will never die" and the saga of Genesis 2 points to those who "will live, even though they die." Thus what is good by creation is re-created in reconciliation and again renewed in redemption. To put it another way, John's verse encapsulates in itself the two creation sagas, again suggesting that Barth views the resurrection to be a new revelation of creation itself.

For Barth, the death, resurrection and ascension of Jesus Christ has revealed to us the truth of the first creation saga—the "before-before" of Christ's eternal life and ours. Again, we are trained to think of life and death as sequential instead of simultaneous, while Barth is asking us to consider eternal life and human immortality to be just as real now as they will be later, or, more pointedly, as real as they have always been. This is the incessant and "truly real" truth of every human creature which no amount of sin or death can affect.[21] In *CD* III/3 Barth speaks of the non-negotiable truth of God's preservation of his beloved creatures in their primal *iustus* determination: "On this living and trustworthy basis in God Himself, it is decided, and continually decided, that the creature may have permanence and continuity . . . Because of God it cannot not continue; it cannot perish."[22] This is

---

21. *CD* III/3, 90: "This is the eternal preservation of God. It is not a second preservation side by side or at the back of the temporal. It is the secret of the temporal. It is a secret of the temporal which is already present in the fulness of truth, which is already in force."

22. *CD* III/3, 71. As with John 11:32 regarding Lazarus's tomb, Barth's realist interpretation of creation (the creature "cannot perish") also puts John 3:16 "those who believe in him will not perish," in a new light; i.e., the hearer is, by believing,

presented in glaring contra-distinction to life in the time of the *simul*, where the creature can and does "perish."[23]

The implications of Barth's exegesis of Genesis 1 and 2 are massive, especially when coupled with Barth's treatment of the creation "of heaven and earth." As with the two chapters in Genesis, Barth refuses to separate God's creation of heaven from the creation of earth (i.e., he does not allow the duality of the upper and lower cosmos to be split into a dualism).[24] To wit, Barth notes the internal biblical testimony to the coinherence—"heavens and the earth" and "the earth and heavens"—in the two sagas.[25] The correlation of these two dualities expounded by Barth—Genesis 1 and 2 (*CD* III/1) and heaven and earth (III/3)—would appear to suggest that for Barth, Genesis 1 is related to human creation and pre-existence in heaven, while Genesis 2 is related to the birth of humans into the world and therefore into the *simul*. In other words, I am proposing that on one hand Barth views Genesis 1, heaven, and human *creation* as going together, while on the other hand he groups Genesis 2, earth, and human *birth*. Again, these two groupings must not be separated nor indiscriminately merged.[26] To view humanity in this way is vitally related to Barth's insistence on the one Jesus Christ being the man from heaven and the man of the earth, thereby representing humanity in heaven simultaneously to humanity on earth.[27] For Barth, this theological construct can only give deepest meaning to Jesus' instructions

---

encouraged to live into a reality that already exists. Obviously, this perspective of God's unconditional preservation also magnifies the universalism charge against Barth.

23. See *CD* II/1, 503.

24. Barth establishes that, while we typically think of God "in heaven," God is distinct not only from earth but also from heaven as the creator of both (*CD* III/3, 421). Thus the first "frontier" is that which "separates God and creation." The second frontier is between that which is visible and invisible, but, critically, this is "not co-extensive in the Bible with the frontier between heaven and earth." Heaven and earth are therefore posed by Barth as dimensional, even though there is a "hierarchy," or "superiority," of the former over the latter (426). The "kingdom of God comes to earth as the kingdom of heaven . . . in a concentrated multiplicity of revelations . . . which have their constitutive centre in God Himself, namely, in Jesus Christ as very God and very man" (448).

25. *CD* III/3, 428–29: Gen 2:1 and 2:4 respectively.

26. Again, the second saga provisionally interpenetrates the first saga and bears relative witness to it. As per this relationship (the "earth and heavens" of Gen 2 interpenetrating the "heavens and earth" of Gen 2) it is notable that the reconciling activity of God in the immanent, historical, sphere is described in Col 1:20 from the Gen 2 perspective: "God was pleased to reconcile to himself all things, whether on earth or in heaven, by making peace through the blood of his cross." Emphasis added.

27. *CD* IV/2, 167: It should not surprise us that in one of the few pages in *CD* where Barth specifically mentions the heavenly and earthly man of 1 Cor 15, Barth asserts, "In Him the will of God is done on earth as it is in heaven."

that we pray for God's will to be done on earth as it is in heaven.[28] Knowing the simultaneity of our lives in Christ in heaven as on earth provides rootedness towards living into our true humanity in day to day sanctification—the depth of actuality which precedes possibility. In complementary fashion, and pertaining to our false humanity, Barth continually urges us in the time of the *simul* to turn our back on ourselves and to seek that which is above.[29] It is this perspective, which I will attempt to articulate in the closing pages of this book, which highlights the theological anthropology of Karl Barth as being nothing short of "dimensional." If Barth's anthro-dimensional understanding that each person has two simultaneous and opposite determinations (*iustus* and *peccator*) is to truly be "*simul* sanctification," it is only because of its inmost Christo-anthropological basis (i.e., created human participation in Christ apart from sin).[30]

Hidden with Christ

Towards the beginning of our engagement with Barth I noted George Hunsinger's analysis that Barth was one to give more ontological weight to certain passages of Scripture than has been granted for centuries. Now with ontology implicitly and unavoidably comes a certain nod to pre-existence. Barth was not shy to mention the pre-existence of Jesus Christ, but he did not do us the favor of overtly unpacking the implication, especially when it comes to Christ's relationship with his human brothers and sisters. When it comes to transcendence and immanence, we have ascertained from Barth that these aspects are not mutually exclusive for God and that Jesus Christ is always the exalted human even in his humiliation. We have also suggested that in one sense Barth sees humanity's exaltation as complete in Christ, even from creation. Of course, as we have demonstrated, Barth can point to passages of Scripture that very clearly emphasize the ontological truth

---

28. *CD* III/3, 445: When praying this prayer, we remember that heaven is where God's will "takes place already, and has always done so." See *CD* IV/3.1, 165: Just as with Gen 1 and 2, heaven and earth interpenetrate each other; the perfection of heaven cannot be allowed to affect the integrity of history on earth. On Barth's view, the "is" of the phrase "on earth as it *is* in heaven" must be understood in "dynamic rather than static terms."

29. See *CD* II/1, 159, cited above.

30. See CD III/2, 205: We "do despite" to the Creator, Barth submits, "if in relation to the human creatureliness of his covenant-partner we begin with the actual antithesis, making the contradiction in which he exists a basic principle, and thus overlooking or contesting the fact that he exists originally and properly in an inner connexion and correspondence between his divine determination and his creaturely form."

that we died with Christ and are at this very moment risen and ascended with Christ and already seated with him in the heavenly places; we are "secretly present" there "above," even as we live our lives in this immanent sphere.[31] That is transcendence enough. Or is it? What more can be said about Barth's view concerning the eternal and pre-existent nature of this human exaltation?

When speaking of the pure form of humanity, we continually acknowledge that "the above" and "the inner man" are not meant by Barth to be spatial terms. The inner man, for instance, has for Barth (and for Paul as Barth would argue) nothing to do with a pure core at the heart of humanity in contradistinction to some kind of corrupt outer wrapping, or layer, of flesh.[32] For Barth, "above" and "the inner" simply mean "hidden." In other words, all of these above terms are meant to signify first and foremost the hidden, pure, *totus iustus* determination of Jesus Christ and derivatively those same truths about humanity—a humanity that is simultaneously above and below with Christ. If, as Barth asserts, heaven is where Christ is,[33] then can we go so far as to say humanity is immortal, since wherever Jesus Christ is, humanity is there too? For Barth, while we must never stray from the derivative nature of human immortality, neither can we deny God's freedom to give us at creation (as revealed in redemption) what is proper only to him.

> If a creature is to have immortal life, i.e., the life which defies and overcomes death, which leaves it behind, which is no longer threatened by it, then . . . [i]t can be only its new life from God and with God. It can be only the eternal life which is given it by God after the manner of His own life. Its corruptible and mortal, therefore, must as such, as that which was between birth and death, put on the incorruptibility and immortality which are proper only to God (I Cor 15:53). Its *present form* is not, then, dissolved or done away or destroyed, which would mean death, or a future without God. It is taken up into the *new form* which is not proper to it in its creatureliness but is given to it as that of God its Creator. The past state which it enters with death, and which is manifest in death, is thus taken away from it by the fact that God, who was its only but true future even in its corruptibility before death and its corruption in death, is present to it in

---

31. *CD* III/3, 438: "The saying in Col 3:1 may well be regarded as the normative biblical definition of heaven . . . where we ourselves are secretly present. Where is this heaven? The answer is that it is where Christ is."

32. *CD* IV/1, 494.

33. *CD* III/3, 438, 441.

death itself. As what it was before death, it may thus be present and live eternally even after death in the power of His presence, i.e., not of itself, but in the power and presence of God.[34]

This beefy quotation holds great import for our study, for without bowing to Platonic dualism it substantiates our theme phrase for Barth's theological anthropology: "I *was and still am* the old man . . . I *am and will be* the new." Firstly, having established the derivative aspect of immortality, we notice (designated by italics) that Barth is elaborating on what we have previously noted as the impure and pure forms of humanity—the "present form" and the "new form." These forms, again, are "the two forms of the one factor." The "present form" (impure form), Barth insists, is not done away with or destroyed, as if in dualistic terms it was purely unreal. But why? Because it is only partly "unreal"; to dissolve it would be dissolve not only the corrupt and mortal *peccator* dimension of the one person but the *iustus* dimension as well! The *iustus* person would then have "a future without God." Instead of the totality of the person being dissolved by death, it is the *totus peccator* humanity (the "old man") that is dissolved and that has no future. In death, referenced primarily by the death of Christ, humanity loses its "past state" and is "taken up into the new form" with a "true future." Again, this "new form" (pure form) is only given by grace and expressly not somehow inherently deserved. The kicker regarding the "new form" of what we have called *iustus* humanity is that it does not exist relative to death but is always present, even in the midst of it.

Secondly, just as pure and inner mean "hidden," it appears obvious that for Barth the gifts of "new life" and "eternal life" are synonymous—eternal life is life that is continually renewed or refreshed by the Holy Spirit. By virtue of God's intimate and undying presence, God in Jesus Christ shares his immortality with his creatures, and humans are given to see that our lives are always lived "from God and with God and for God."[35] Moreover, if the *parousia* for Barth is what he calls "the effective presence,"[36] it can only signify the final revelation or manifestation of what is already real and actual. We should not be confused by Barth's statement that "the victory of Jesus the Victor is not yet consummated"—by this he merely means that it is outside "our circle of vision."[37] All talk of humanity "putting on" immortality, then, as if merely a future occurrence, must be recalibrated in light of the

---

34. *CD* IV/3.1, 310–11; emphasis added.
35. *CD* IV/3.1, 316.
36. *CD* IV/3.1, 292–93.
37. *CD* IV/3.1, 262.

present kingdom; here Christ is already "all in all."[38] Comments Barth, "For the kingdom of God consists in the fact that in some sense He is all in all. It is only in revelation that the kingdom of God is post-temporal and lies in the future . . . After time, in post-temporal eternity, we shall not believe in it. We shall see it."[39]

Transposition: A Sacred Order

This book has been largely anchored on Barth's claim that Jesus Christ himself is humanity.[40] We have noted Barth's rather curious statement locating the "opposite" determinations of humanity in an otherworldy "dimension of eternity," held together in eternity by none other than Jesus Christ.[41] In view of this, two critical delineations must continually be reinforced between 1) Jesus Christ and sinful humanity and 2) Jesus Christ and humanity in general.

First, Barth's quotation below might lead one to think Barth is promoting the existence of the *simul* (and therefore *peccatum*) as co-eternal with Christ:

---

38. Such a recalibration would suggest that Paul's words in Corinthians: "this perishable body must put on imperishability, and this mortal body must put on immortality" (1 Cor 15:53) and the words of Ephesians (4:24) and Colossians (3:10) about putting on the "new self" are of no material difference. Instead of content, the difference is related to the contradiction; in Corinthians Paul is speaking of finally ascending out of the contradiction, away from the perishable and mortal, whereas in Ephesians and Colossians Paul (arguably) is speaking of living the transcendent life (the imperishable and immortal) even while still ensnarled in the *simul* overlap of this immanent sphere (see Col 3:1–2). As shorthand for participating in Christ and the Spirit, to "put on"—to be who you are—is inherently transformational, without or with the presence of the "resisting element." For Barth, Romans 13:14 has the same sense: "Its final word, that Christians should put on the Lord Jesus Christ, is obviously the first as well. It amounts to this—that they all have reason first and foremost to become what they are" (CD II/2, 729).

39. CD II/1, 630–31. Barth is referencing Ephesians 1:23.

40. See CD IV/2, 519: "Thus the humanity of Jesus in the particularity in which He is this one man is, as the humanity of the Son of God, humanity as such, the humanity for which every man is ordained and in which every part already has a part in Him."

41. CD III/1, 413 (cited above); speaking of these dimensions being held together in eternity, it is fitting that Barth's phrase *einem jenseitigen Zusammenhang* ("an eternal dimension") could also be translated as "an otherworldy connection." For the remainder of our study, I will refer back to this otherworldly (*jenseitigen*) "dimension of eternity," which I posit to be the "second heaven" and theologically located between Barth's supra-temporal and post-temporal eternities.

> We have already heard what it means that Jesus Christ is man. It means that the only begotten Son of God and therefore God Himself, who is knowable to Himself from eternity to eternity, has come in our flesh, has taken our flesh, has become the bearer of our flesh, and does not exist as God's Son from eternity to eternity except in our flesh. Our flesh is therefore present when He knows God as the Son the Father, when God knows Himself. In our flesh God knows Himself. Therefore in Him it is a fact that our flesh knows God Himself.[42]

Again, asserts Barth, Christ assumes *sarx*, the flesh connoting "man as the enemy of the grace of God . . . He, the pure, holy Son of God, obedient to the Father from eternity to eternity, has Himself become a man like this."[43] We have seen the importance Barth places on Christ's assumption of *sarx*: "If His human essence were sinless as such, how could it be our essence? How could he really be our Brother at this decisive point? How could there be any solidarity with us in our lostness?"[44] Just as important for Barth as Christ's solidarity with us is the fact that Jesus Christ is different from us; otherwise he could not function as a mediator to help us, being in the exact same straights as lost humanity apart from him.[45] Is this salvific distinction simply related to maintaining the *deity* of Christ throughout his incarnate work? On the contrary, insists Barth; it is also vital to maintain the humanity of Christ, or more specifically, the two humanities in the one humanity of Christ. States Barth, "To say man is to say creature and sin . . . Both of these have to be said of Jesus Christ."[46] This returns us to my original assertion of Jesus Christ as *simul iustus et peccator*. In light of this human duality, we have seen how Barth will honor the nuances of the word "flesh." On the one hand it means "a perverted essence and lost as such," while on the other hand flesh also means without contradiction, i.e., flesh unmarked by sin in its "created and unlost goodness."[47] As Barth insists above with character-

---

42. *CD* II/1, 151. See *CD* IV/1/131: "Jesus Christ is man."

43. *CD* II/1, 151.

44. *CD* IV/2, 92. Noted in the last chapter, Barth elaborates on the idea of Christ as himself "lost" in *CD* III/3, 303–4: "The Word became a creature which had fallen under the sway of a possessive and domineering alien, and was therefore itself alienated from its Creator and itself, unable to recover or retrace its way home . . . The the word became flesh means that the Word became a creature of this kind, a lost creature."

45. *CD* IV/1, 131. Even as Very Man there can be "no reservation and no diminution" in regards to Christ being Very God; this could only be "an immediate denial of the act of atonement made in Him."

46. *CD* IV/1, 131.

47. *CD* IV/2, 92.

istic symmetry, both of these mutually exclusive determinations are "from eternity to eternity."

Yet for all Barth's posturing about the apparent co-eternal nature of true (*iustus*) and false (*peccator*) humanity, and in spite of Barth's comment above which apparently promotes a conflation of Christ's pure and impure forms, we must now point out Barth's first critical delineation, that between Christ and sinful humanity. We have witnessed that true humanity is created by and in God's Word in Genesis 1, but note how Barth describes God taking his place amongst the transgressors in what we have already alluded to as the second creation saga:

> This time there takes place something which had not happened even in God's utterance in Genesis I. God's Word itself, the Word by which everything was created, becomes a creature amongst others . . . In this way it makes the world created by it its own—its liability to temptation, its actual temptation, its corruption and need. In this way too, the world for its part is made a partaker of the Word of God by which it was created; a partaker of its triumphant vitality, of its holiness and glory.[48]

As suggested earlier, Barth here is presenting a strong nuance between not only Genesis 1 and Genesis 2 but also between the Word of God becoming a creature and the Word of God becoming a *corrupt* creature. Is this in direct conflict with his statement about the co-eternity of our contradictory determinations? Apparently so, yet we might take the co-eternal language in context with Barth's typical use of symmetry, knowing that Barth has shown prior confidence that the weight of the dispute will do the work of delineating between "infinite determinations." Perhaps Barth has not delineated the two determinations earlier or more clearly because of his reticence to introduce a greater evil, the idea of human brokenness and suffering not affecting God in God's inmost being. But, regardless, it is very plain that he wants to present Jesus Christ as the Word—*Logos*: the Word became incarnate; the Word became something the Word had not been before. The Word became the flesh of the good creature logically prior to becoming the flesh of the sinful creature.

If we can assert a logical priority of Christ's association with *iustus* humanity over *peccator* humanity, if the *simul* is not co-eternal with Christ, do we at least have permission from Barth to claim *iustus* humanity is co-eternal with Christ? This brings us to the second delineation introduced above, and again I will first introduce an apparently incongruent quotation

---

48. *CD* III/1, 115.

from Barth which might lead one to believe that Christ does not exist apart from his brothers and sisters.

> What he is in Himself He is not to be for Himself alone. He is to be the Firstborn among many brethren, among many who are like Him. God's will for Him from the very outset, as the will of Him who had created Him in his image, aimed also at these His future brethren. Who are these brethren of whom God thought simultaneously with His Son, who for His sake are as precious to Him as the latter Himself, who He wills to liken to His Son without detriment to His uniqueness?[49]

Barth's comment certainly supports the contention that his brothers and sisters are never without Christ, but it does not clearly support the idea that Christ exists as Son of God apart from his brothers and sisters. What are the implications of this? If it is the case that Jesus Christ is the God who elects Jesus Christ, then this might imply the idea that the Son of God actually came into being as the vehicle for creation instead of existing apart from that decision (i.e., as the One who made the decision). On Barth's view, for Jesus Christ to be the firstborn of the human family (Rom 8:29) means he is "first of all the bearer of the image in and after which God created man according to Gen 1:26f."[50] But it seems clear that, in Barth's view, Jesus Christ is God—he is the Word—before he is God's image, which he also is. In other words, for Barth to posit that God thinks "simultaneously" of Jesus Christ's "brethren" when he thinks of his Son (as stated above) is not to say Jesus Christ does not exist without his "brethren." Barth would not want to theologically eliminate order or priority any more than he would posit the "brethren" are themselves God. As a result, Barth can emphasize "this One, the pre-existent Son of God, is the One who exists for us," while at the same time claiming "Jesus Christ does not first become God's Son when He is it for us."[51] Undoubtedly for Barth, Jesus Christ eternally represents humanity, but also "[a]s against all other men and the whole world of creation" Jesus Christ is "the Representative of the uniqueness and transcendence of God."[52] For Barth, God—Father, Son, and Holy Spirit—elects "man in general" from a position *distinguished* from humankind. Barth presents us with the fact that Jesus Christ exists before "man in general," even if, "vis-à-vis the

---

49. *CD* III/1, 204.
50. *CD* III/1, 204.
51. *CD* I/1, 426.
52. *CD* III/2, 144.

Word of God, there is no man in general."[53] Simply stated, Jesus Christ exists without humanity, but humanity does not exist without him.

For Barth the nuanced manner of God's revelation makes theological demarcations a paramount necessity for the orthodox theologian. We have demonstrated two lines in particular—between Jesus Christ and sinful humanity and and between Jesus Christ and humanity in general—which are incredibly thin but sharp. Barth comments, "Thus in spite of the almost confusing richness of the forms of divine immanence we are led to recognise a hierarchy, a sacred order, in which God is present to the world."[54] What this means for us theologically is that we view the history of humanity in conjunction with Jesus of Nazareth in all his forms, as like a prism. We see Jesus Christ as God, as the *imago Dei*, as created humanity (original Adam), as fallen Adam (the "first Adam"), and as the Second Adam. Subsequently, we are to exegete our own lives accordingly as they exist in this prism of human reality and existence according to the true witness, Jesus Christ. With Barth, then, we can first posit that the Second Adam (1 Cor 15:45) is logically prior to the "first Adam" of Genesis 2 and 3; Jesus Christ is therefore "the first and true Adam," the "unknown of the Genesis story"[55] (beginning in Genesis 1) until the revelation of the Second Adam. Secondly, while created apart from the *simul*, we can posit that every human being, including Jesus Christ, has been born into the *simul*—into the dimensional matrix of *iustus* (created) and *peccator* (corrupted) humanity. Jesus' own birth in Bethlehem was a manifestation of this very descent into the shadowlands, the descent that Jesus assumed before he was born and "from the very outset." At first glimpse, we regard Jesus himself from a fleshly point of view (2 Cor 5:16); like all earthly humans, he is "a man of dust" (Gen 2:7; 1 Cor 15:47), his heavenly humanity to a degree obscured in perishable "flesh and blood" (1 Cor 15:50). Only after dust returns to dust (Eccl 12:7) will the relative witness of our *simul*-wracked material bodies fully give way to the glory of our spiritual material bodies.

In this chapter we have investigated Barth's understanding of the nature of true humanity and human transcendence. We have considered Barth's admonitions against flatly defining earthly existence. Instead, humanity is in Christ, and therefore is where Christ is. By virtue of the resurrection and ascension, and in light of the first creation narrative, Barth posits a human origin before the garden and before any potential problems. Indeed, it is only from this transcendent origin and destiny that human life on earth

---

53. *CD* I/1, 196.
54. *CD* II/1, 317.
55. *CD* IV/1, 513.

derives its meaning. Real human beings, as centered in the true humanity of Jesus Christ of Nazareth, are perfectly obedient in their own loving response to the love of God. This free obedience—initiated as a Spirit movement from above to below, and from within to without[56]—is as dynamic, ongoing and real as that of the continuing high priestly ministry of Jesus Christ, the true human from heaven who is also the heavenly human of earth.

---

56. *CD* III/4, 491.

12

A Kinship of Being: How Far Can We Go?

"The general definition that man is with God as he is with Jesus thus acquires a content of almost unfathomable range and significance."[1]

IN THIS CHAPTER WE WILL CONTINUE TO LOOK BACK THROUGH OUR Christ-informed prism to see what might be "under" the perversion of human corruption, assessing more carefully the transposition of the inner layers (i.e., the nature of the relationship between God and humanity apart from sin). To some this theological enterprise into the sanctified spaces of the Christo-anthropological might appear only slightly less threatening.

Arius Revisited

In his articulation of the original, single *iustus* determination of humanity, Barth presents *Jesus Christ as true humanity* with utmost force. We have distinguished the *Logos* from humanity in general to protect theologically against conflation and emanation, but can we say more about humanity's pre-existence in the pre-existence of Christ? We asked earlier about the location of transcendent *iustus* humanity, in the context of considering Barth's view of the transcendence of the human Jesus as constitutive of our human transcendence. We put forth the idea that there is no "vacuum" left by our death because of our ongoing *iustus* humanity that does not die. But if that is true, where exactly are we when we are not in the immanent sphere, and what is our constitution? This is one of the few places in *Church Dogmatics* where Barth speaks directly about the pre-existence of humanity in general: "But there is a real pre-existence of man as the one summoned by God . . .

---

1. *CD* III/2, 145.

A Kinship of Being: How Far Can We Go? 229

because it brings us face to face with the positive determination—namely a pre-existence in the counsel of God, and to that extent, God Himself, i.e., in the Son of God, in so far as the Son is the uncreated prototype of the humanity which is to be linked with God, man in his unity with God."[2]

We have noted Barth's delineation between the *Logos* and humanity in general. But exactly *how* does the human being exist in the transcendent realm? Barth answers, "We may say in a word that it is in God the Holy Spirit that the creature as such pre-exists."[3] Barth is plainly advancing the idea that humanity exists in the spiritual realm from all eternity. But again, Barth is careful to avoid conflation or in this case a Hegelian articulation of a human being as "spirit." Human beings exist in the Spirit, but they are not spirits; they are souls. Human beings are souls of their bodies and bodies of their souls.[4] Importantly, stresses Barth, "It is by the Spirit that the soul and body are sustained in their interconnection."[5] As souls, even as pre-existent souls, they have a material nature; might we say they are material souls? Again, for Barth, "man has spirit. We can and must say that he is soul; and from this we go on to say that he is body. But we cannot simply say that he is spirit."[6] From this standpoint, then, what is the difference between what we have called material souls, our perfect incorruptible flesh, and our spiritual bodies? Are they all one and the same? In light of Barth's realized eschatology, could the "redemption of our bodies" (Rom 8:23), for which we eagerly await, describe anything less than the unveiling of our spiritual bodies? Is this pre-existent form of humanity not unlike that of the risen Jesus in the

---

2. *CD* III/2, 155.

3. *CD* III/1, 56.

4. See *CD* III/2, paragraph 46, 344–436 which includes "The Spirit as Basis for Soul and Body" (46.2), "Soul and Body in their Interconnexion" (46.3), "Soul and Body in their Particularity" (46.4), and "Soul and Body in their Order" (46.5). Despite the reciprocity of this interconnection of soul and body, Barth insists that the soul is logically primary, even though it cannot exist without a body (417). Barth communicates this unity and differentiation with use of italics: "That man is the soul of his *body* is the secondary fact which is no less indispensable to real man than the first, namely, that he is the *soul* of his body" (418).

5. *CD* III/2, 429. Cf. Price, *Karl Barth's Anthropology*, 276–77: "Apart from the Spirit, there is nothing but a constant and puzzling duality of immortal soul on the one side and mortal body on the other." Might we take it a step further and ask concerning the connection between immortal soul and *immortal body* of said soul? Can Paul have spoken of our new bodies and of putting on immortality if our souls were immaterial?

6. *CD* III/2, 354. See McLean, *Humanity in the Thought of Karl Barth* regarding Barth's hesitancy to identify the Spirit with the human. "[Spirit] does not merely become the human subject . . . [Spirit] is the principle which makes man into a subject" (45).

forty days?⁷ Is it possible that for Barth we as humans live in several dimensions of existence at once, all informed in our earthly perspective by the revelation of God and humanity we witness in Christ?

The negative stigma of pre-existence is quite daunting in orthodox dogmatics, to the point where it is rarely entertained. But again, do we not already speak of pre-existence to the extent that we speak of ontology? In Barth's serious adherence to Scripture's attestation that when Christ died, all humans died, and when Christ rose, all humans rose, is Barth gently nudging us in the direction of understanding true humanity to be as pre-existent as Christ's humanity?⁸ This would explain even more fully how Barth's view of the atonement, in spite of extant penal themes scattered throughout *Church Dogmatics*, functions essentially within an ontological death and resurrection frame.

Perhaps we passed over in the last chapter Barth's mention of humanity partaking in the Word of God through Christ coming to us. We cannot see "partaker in the Word" without immediate associations with the Scripture phrase most often quoted by proponents of *theosis*, "[God] has granted to us his precious and very great promises, so that through them you may become partakers of the divine nature" (2 Pet 1:4, ESV). Yet if we think of the comparable terms *theosis*, divinization, or deification at all, it is certainly not in association with Karl Barth! Time and time again Barth vociferously rails against the idea; he is keen to protect the boundary between God and humanity at all costs.⁹ And yet, have we accounted for the fact that, keeping intact the demarcation between God and humanity, what Barth gives us is surprisingly close to some forms of *theosis*? Might we even say it complies to some variations of the term?¹⁰ There are variations of "*theosis*" that, in

---

7. Because for Barth supra-temporal eternity begins with Christ's birth and ends with his death, the "forty days" (without at all denying the bodily resurrection) represent Christ's humanity in a kind of post-temporal form *in the midst* of what is still for us a supra-temporal existence. Therefore, because the resurrected Christ is witnessed by the disciples in the supra-eternal realm, it would be a mistake to project the different humanity they see for Jesus as Jesus' post-temporal body (or as a model for ours). While certainly appearing more post-temporal than before his resurrection, because Jesus is straddling dimensions, there is still a degree of refraction at play.

8. To include as Barth does (see chapter 11) Christ's ascension as part of the ontological "narrative" (i.e., that all humans died, rose, and ascended in Christ) obviously tilts towards pre-existence, "ascended" having more interconnection to our "before-before" than simply "rose."

9. CD IV/2, 79–82.

10. A comparison may be made to the *analogia entis* controversy, where Barth relents once definitions are redefined.

spite of the fact that they betray their name, do not involve conflation of humanity with God. To wit, T. F. Torrance remarks,

> At this point let me plead for a reconsideration by the Reformed Church of what the Greek fathers called *theosis*. This is usually unfortunately translated deification, but it has nothing to do with the *divinization* of man any more than the Incarnation has to do with the humanization of God . . . *Theosis* describes man's involvement in such a mighty act of God upon him that he is raised up to find the true centre of his existence not in himself but in Holy God, where he lives and moves and has his being in the uncreated but creative energy of the Holy Spirit.[11]

Torrance will say that Jesus as mediator is not only *homoousios* (of one being) with God but also *homoousios* with humanity.[12] As discussed above, if Barth is uncomfortable with such an association, it is out of concern that humans might reverse the initiative by claiming a status of *homoousios* with God. But Barth did go so far as to affirm an intimacy between God and humanity in strikingly Athanasian fashion, as Barth himself advances: "As in Him God became like man, so too in Him man has become like God."[13] Having noted his warnings against conflation, is there more to Barth's concern? With such an emphasis on likeness, one can only ponder whether Barth ever entertained the idea that, if not *homoousios*, humanity in general might perhaps instead be better described as *homoiousios* (of like being) with the Father? Might we now fashion a *niche* in theological anthropology designating true humanity by the term *homoiousios*? In other words, if a distinction between Jesus Christ and humanity in general must be posited, might we say that the distinction is the same as that between *homoousios* and *homoiousios*? If so, we might assert that Arius had the wrong man! Does Arius' intense focus on Jesus not being *homoousios* perhaps cause us to overlook the fact that our true humanity *in* the original human is *homoiousios*? Now if this is the case, we must quickly return to an acknowledgement that Jesus Christ is both *homoousios* and *homoiousios* with God in advance of assuming our corrupt flesh (*sarx*). All three of these aspects of Christ's humanity—*homoousios, homoiousios,* and *sarx*—can then be implied by the Chalcedonian formula. We locate humankind's original human determination in the second of the three, in Christ, who comprehends them all. It follows that Barth's *simul* is the result of combining the last two elements,

---

11. Torrance, *Theology in Reconstruction*, 243–44.
12. Torrance, *The Trinitarian Faith*, 203.
13. *CD* IV/1, 131.

again, only in Christ. Hereby we arrive at our provisional term "Chalcedonian anthropology."

If Arius was irredeemably wrong about the *homoousion*, might we acknowledge that he was partially justified in saying that Jesus, in his human nature, was "like God"? This only plays to Barth's desire to keep some form of demarcation; he wants to maintain that humanity was created *in* "the image and likeness," and that humanity therefore could only be described *as* "the image and likeness" in an indirect sense or derivatively. Should it surprise us that Barth's interpretation of this original human blessing as God's likeness obtains from the first creation saga (Gen 1:26)?[14] It therefore makes sense that Barth could derive meaning from *homoiousios* while still holding the all-important *homoousios/homoiousios* line.[15] In what could only be a sideways allusion to Arius himself, Barth states: "The creature was not from all eternity like God. There was a time when it was not."[16] For Barth, therefore, mankind is not *homoousios* with God, but in Christ and by grace "we are children in the Father's house, just as [Christ] is by nature."[17]

Regardless of whether Arius is in view, it is difficult to argue against the idea that Barth's standpoint on the unity of God and humanity certainly reflects the closest association possible without affirming essential correspondence: "What is entailed in the simple exegesis of the fact indicated in Emmanuel, namely, that God has accepted man in Jesus Christ, that in Him He has become man and that He is revealed in His unity with this man."[18] Could we say Barth's position is to postulate humanity as one with God, one step removed? The statement below certainly substantiates *at least* that much.

> If it were not wholly proper to it, how could it be compatible with the essence of God to give Himself to solidarity with man as He has done in making the covenant with Himself the meaning and

---

14. *CD* III/1, 190; Barth here describes humanity as both *the* image and likeness and created *in* the image and likeness; mankind has hope as "God's image and likeness . . . because he was originally blessed and is still blessed in spite of the fact that the blessing has been turned into a curse."

15. See *CD* III/1, 200–204: Barth holds that scripturally the creature is not the image of God directly, but the creature is conformed to it, and sometimes therefore even defined as the image. Barth notes scriptural attestations to this, including Rom 8:29.

16. *CD* III/3, 73. It appears that Barth has not only commandeered Athanasius (*theosis*) into his program, he seems to enjoy rehabilitating (to an appropriate degree) Origen and Arius as well, not to mention Nestorius! We have proposed the latter throughout our study.

17. *CD* I/2, 240.

18. *CD* III/1, 25.

purpose of its creation and therefore the determination of its humanity, in Himself becoming man in Jesus Christ? For all the disparity, there is here presupposed a common factor, a parity, not merely between Jesus and other men, but, because between Jesus and other men, between God and man generally.[19]

While staunchly guarding the gate against the wrong brand of *theosis*, perhaps Barth's promotion of a "kinship of being" allows a more Torrancian version to sneak in the back door.[20] And, if a Torrancian *theosis*, or what could be otherwise labeled entire sanctification, is arguably a proper category for Barth, then we could also posit that what John Wesley is looking for as a culmination of sanctification is really found in Barth where he least expects it—front-loaded from the beginning! Might Wesley's heart be strangely warmed by a concept of sanctification that not only moves towards perfection but also from it? Again it is perhaps laughable to think of Barth himself being an advocate for any variation of *theosis*, but we should also inquire, using Barth's own words about another topic, "may it not be the greater formal difference betrays the greatest material agreement?"[21]

As per his warnings about the *analogia entis*,[22] Barth is obviously aware that discussion of *theosis* can quickly devolve into categorical statements about essence and substance, which proves no more helpful than speaking of static forensic righteousness. Without forcing a marriage of the so-called "energies" of Trinitarian essence and the dynamic relationship of *iustus* humans united to Jesus Christ, we can at least say that without the understanding of Barth's actualism which we have put forth in this book, consideration of the concept of righteousness together with any accommodated version of *theosis* would be completely untenable. In the Introduction I maintained the advantages of describing the *iustus* and *peccator* aspects as either dimensions or determinations. If "dimensions" helps us to understand the simultaneity of the *simul*'s opposite aspects (as well as the simultaneity

---

19. *CD* III/2, 225.

20. *CD* IV/1, 600. Barth here describes the "kinship of being" between adopted humanity and God. Cleverly, while Barth holds the line against a unity of essence, "the divine sonship of man is not his divinity," Barth will still maintain that "the right of sonship is the essence of every right of man." In this passage the difference between Barth and a Torrancian *theosis* is not obvious.

21. *CD* III/1, 202.

22. It should be clear from our study that Barth's understanding of humanity as *totus peccator* protects against natural theology and all misunderstandings potentially introduced by the *analogia entis* wrongly understood. In other words, Barth's *simul* protects against all human acquiring of, or possession of, an inherent or intrinsic capacity to know God or to know of God.

of other, distinct, but compatible aspects, e.g., *homoousios* and *homoiousios*) just as true is that discussion of *ousios* can overlook the ongoing *activity* of the *iustus* "determination"—the human's derivative but invariable participation in Christ's incessant being-in-act in God. Only in such a vein (outside their respective traditional Western and Eastern contexts) can we imagine the concepts of righteousness and *theosis* as compatible, and only in this vein can we imagine how the heavenly perspective of a "front-loaded" *theosis* (undiminished from creation) might drive the Christian to righteous, sanctifying activity on earth. It is in Barth's vision of the seventh day of creation that the inner basis of *simul* sanctification is proven to be Sabbath sanctification: "From this point of view man after this day was not set on the way to a Sabbath still to be sanctified, but on the way from a Sabbath already sanctified; from rest to work; from freedom to service; from joy to 'seriousness' of life. Rest, freedom and joy were not just before him. He had no need to "enter" in them. He could already proceed from them"[23]

The Angels of Our Better Nature?[24]

On Barth's view, it should be clear that to be an ambassador of Christ on earth is to first be a citizen of heaven. The will of God, asserts Barth, is "first done in heaven, and then on earth."[25] Apart from our awareness of the integral relationship between heaven and earth in his theology, we might be tempted to dismiss Barth's full scale discussion of angels, tucked away at the end of *CD* III/3, as a strange one-off. Instead, I believe it provides an intra-*Dogmatics* proof of sorts for our grasp of *simul* sanctification, and not simply because Barth reminds us angels will come at the end of the age "to separate the righteous from the wicked."[26] Paragraph 51.3, "The Ambassa-

23. *CD* III/1, 228. Barth's continuation is worth repeating, if for no other reason than that it exposes just how contrastive will be the relationship of work and rest after the fall: God's beloved creature "had already sat at the divine wedding-feast, and having eaten and drunk could now proceed to his daily work. The 'Lord's Day' was really his first day . . . Each week, instead of being a trying ascent, ought to have been a glad descent from the high-point of Sabbath."

24. This is a rephrasing of Abraham Lincoln's memorable comment in his first inaugural address (1861). By appealing to "the better angels of our nature," Lincoln expressed hope in a common ground of friendship under the un-reconciled factions within the Union (which would soon turn against each other in mortal combat). As has been clear throughout this book, my rephrasing is not meant to communicate that humans have, at bottom, two natures.

25. *CD* III/3, 462.

26. That angels function as the reapers who separate the wheat from the chaff or as the helpers who separate the good fish from the bad fish does not mean angels are

A Kinship of Being: How Far Can We Go? 235

dors of God and their Opponents," is a means by which Barth presents—in a way he insists is not purely speculative[27]—a glimpse of the hidden nature of *iustus* humanity in its unadulterated heavenly form. In other words, by ostensibly delineating the differences between angels and humans, Barth is showing us how much they have in common (beneath the *simul*, so to speak). This is where a unique combination of what we have considered the *iustus* determination (emphasis on act) and *iustus* dimension (emphasis on being) come together in *CD* to comprehend Barth's actualism, or what we have called his Christo-anthropology. It is this view of a *iustus* humanity which Barth suggests is just as present and actual in the supra-temporal realm of eternity as in the pre- or post-temporal dimension.

Exactly to what extent, then, does Barth want to compare angels to humans? Barth describes angels as heavenly creatures; they visit earth,[28] whereas *iustus* humans in Christ dwell simultaneously on both sides of the veil. As heavenly witnesses, without worry of *simul* contradiction, angels hear and see perfectly in a way humans will not see and hear until the *eschaton*; when it comes to obeying God's will, angels have "no room," and "no option" for a "deviation."[29] Indeed, they cannot be considered proper angels if they are tempted by "whatever lies on the right hand or the left" of the will of God.[30] Because they are *purely* heavenly creatures, angels are in one sense

---

superior to *iustus* humans, but it does mean that in one sense they are well-suited for the task, not having any struggle of discernment (as have *iustus* humans in their present impure form). See Barth's comment on wheat and tares in *CD* IV/3.1, 112–13; Barth states that parables such as this are not meant to apply to individuals, as if the readers are meant to recognize themselves in the stories, but are instead fundamentally about the revelation of the Kingdom of God and the final separation of righteousness and wickedness in the day of redemption. Perhaps Barth planned to speak more in Volume V to how a christological *simul* applies exegetically to the apparent "righteous and the wicked" dualism of the parables and Psalms, but regardless, I believe it is a worthy pursuit which we have only touched on in this study.

27. *CD* III/3, 459. After surveying biblical references to angels, Barth remarks, "we must be on our guard against thinking we know too much, but also against the stupidity which refuses to know what is to be known"; of the service of the heavenly host, he continues, "the answer to the question in what this service consists is so obvious that no speculation is needed to see it."

28. *CD* III/3, 497.

29. *CD* III/3, 498.

30. *CD* III/3, 514. It should be obvious that Barth does not adhere to the idea that Satan was an angel gone awry (see 531). Barth would not want to provide Satan even the backhanded compliment of ever existing in the third heaven, although we certainly could imagine Satan "falling" from the second heaven, the realm of judgment (i.e., the cross). A discussion of what I consider Barth's three heaven cosmology awaits in chapter 14.

higher than humans who are saddled with *simul* contradiction. This aligns with the comment in Hebrews that Jesus himself "for a little while was made lower than the angels" (Heb 2:9), which Barth takes to mean that the Word made flesh shared the plight of the *peccator* determination. On Barth's view, when Christ assumed fallen humanity, he entered a territory that the angels could not comprehend. They could accompany Jesus to a degree, but of God's inmost love and glory demonstrated on earth, they could only "watch and learn."[31] Jesus' entry into the depths of human depravity constitutes at once his highest glorification. Barth can therefore claim that, while humans are in one sense lower than the angels, in another sense, by the extent of Christ's humiliation, humans derive a higher standing even than of angels.[32] It is as if angels are somehow external to the most acute expression of God's glory shared in by the sons and daughters of God; angels do not share in God's suffering, and so they do not share God's glory in the same way (see Rom 8:17).

Barth has turned us again to the wondrous incarnation to understand God's economy and inmost being. Jesus became a little lower than the angels in order to reveal that human beings have always been the pinnacle of God's creation. All creatures, including angels and animals, exist in Christ, but humans are different from these because of God's sojourn on earth as a human being and because of every human being's existence in the "one man" who lived in the "human sphere."[33] It is therefore understandable why Paul would describe human beings as forming the vanguard of redemption, when all creatures—indeed all of God's creation—will be "brought into the glorious freedom of the children of God" (Rom 8:19–21).

In his discussion of angels, Barth is obviously reconfirming human beings in their created glory, but it is clear that he has additional purposes as well. The perfect witness of angels, he states, "forms the necessary presupposition for the human witness with which the doing of God's will on earth

---

31. *CD* III/3, 501. See 500–501: "Even when God has appeared in the flesh and in the Spirit, they [the angels] have much to learn." Barth cites Ephesians 3:10 and 1 Peter 1:12 to support his view: "In this phenomenon," Barth continues, "they are again surprised as if it were by something new." Barth understands the revelation of this incarnational occurrence to be dimensionally equated with the Son's taking of the scroll in Rev 5:7 and the resulting angelic chorus (see 467–68): "For it is in heaven that the occurrence originates which then takes earthly form as cosmic and eschatological occurrence. The angels in heaven do already what will also be done on earth by earthly creatures."

32. *CD* III/3, 498.

33. *CD* III/2, 158.

begins."³⁴ Not only that, Barth claims that the angel of the nativity story is "archetypally" what the two humans Mary and Zacharias will be "at the end of the story," and indeed, Barth continues, "what all those will be after them whom the coming One Himself will call and gather to his community."³⁵ Taken together, Barth is suggesting in these statements that the human witness, in a way not possible on earth, will be revealed at the consummation to be perfectly consistent with the perfect heavenly witness. Furthermore, the implications of this appear to suggest that Barth understands what we have called *iustus* humanity, humanity in its pure form, to be virtually synonymous with the supreme witness of angels. "If" on occasion a human being is "the messenger of God with this supreme authority," writes Barth, "we can only say it is an angel who speaks and acts through this man."³⁶ In other words, when it comes to *simul* humanity, the existential exception (humanity's true witness) is proving the rule (humanity's *unerring* witness).

Thus far we can establish with Barth that 1) humans in their *simul* experience are lower than the angels, as was Christ in his humiliation of the flesh; 2) because of the hidden glory of the incarnation, humans in *simul* solidarity with Christ are actually revealed to be, in their pure *iustus* form, higher than the angels, the pinnacle of God's creation; and 3) there is the closest correspondence between human beings in their heavenly (and earthly albeit hidden) *iustus* nature and in the being of heavenly angels. But are we making an overstatement to claim that Barth describes the two types of creatures—*iustus* humans and angels—as virtually synonymous with one another?

In chapter 7 we discussed the 180-degree opposition between the *iustus* and *peccator* determinations of humanity as Barth lays them out. The *totus peccator* person is a slave to sin and cannot hear and obey, whereas the *totus iustus* person is a slave to righteousness (and freedom) and cannot *not* hear and obey.³⁷ With this in mind, consider Barth's words about angels. Angels live out God's will

---

34. *CD* III/3, 499.
35. *CD* III/3, 504.
36. *CD* III/3, 513.

37. See *CD* III/3, 520. Barth considers angels and demons to be cosmologically correlated to the *simul* in their radical, diametrically oppositional and mutually exclusive missions: "Angels and demons are related as creation and chaos, as the free grace of God and nothingness, as good and evil, as life and death, as the light of revelation and the darkness which will not receive it, as redemption and perdition, as *kerygma* and myth." Barth describes both angels and demons as plenipotentiaries of God and the devil, respectively.

> exactly as He wills it to be done... The possibility of deviation or omission does not arise. Their obedience does not have to come into being, and it has no limit. Their creaturely freedom is identical with their obedience. Their heavenly nature consists and expresses itself in the perfect willingness and readiness, but also in their capacity to speak and act from and with and for God. We can thus have unlimited confidence that their speech and action is always and in every respect that of God Himself... The divine action is not exhausted in theirs, but theirs is in the divine. God is not bound to them, but they are to Him.[38]

We remember that for Barth, the heavenly is the earthly, but the earthy (because of the fall) is not *merely* the heavenly. The unity and distinction of heaven and earth must be maintained. When it comes to angels, they are distinguished from humans of the *simul* because they do the will of God without the slightest question of Cartesian autonomy.[39] Angels give perfect testimony to the reality of Christ, which is "present in all its fulness"[40] (and yet "concealed" in its "distinctive invisibility").[41] Because of Barth's understanding of the interrelation of the heavenly and earthly spheres, and because he correlates the ministry of angels to "the whole participation of heaven in earthly occurrence," Barth posits an underlying unity between the operation of heavenly and earthly creatures (humans): "The angels are remarkable only in the fact that in distinction from all earthly creatures they stand first and perfectly in the service which forms the determination of all creatures... They live and move and have their being in preceding and accompanying and following this action."[42] The oblique reference to Acts 17:28 could hardly be incidental. Angels and *iustus* humans may not be synonymous, but they are virtually synonymous in the way they live and move, i.e., in their righteous and obedient movements. Indeed, angels provide "a cosmic contour and concreteness" for humans, reflecting the hidden reality of humanity's *iustus* determination, "in the deity of God, in His mystery."[43]

Twice Barth remarks of angels that "their freedom consists in their obedience."[44] Could not the same be said of *iustus* humanity as we have defined it throughout this book? As with angels, humans are not given the

---

38. *CD* III/3, 493.
39. *CD* III/3, 493.
40. *CD* III/3, 509.
41. *CD* III/3, 511.
42. *CD* III/3, 493.
43. *CD* III/3, 493–94.
44. *CD* III/3, 498; see also 493.

freedom of choice, but a free choice. The signal difference between humans and angels is that humans in *simul* contradiction can inexplicably resist the free will of God—posing like Hercules at the crossroads, deviating from the path of God's will. Is it then possible that in these back pages of *CD* III/3, Barth is giving us his clearest indication of what true humanity—humanity apart from the *simul*—is like? Barth appears to suggest that angels and humans (in their pure form) are dissimilar *not* because ultimately humans do not measure up to angels, or are categorically unlike them, but quite the opposite. Barth's posited dissimilarity is grounded in God's action to stoop down lower than the angels and to reveal in resurrection light what was hidden—the superior glory of humanity in Christ. This appears to be how Barth can hold together passages that speak of Christ descending below the angels to the sphere of human flesh, while at the same time taking seriously Paul's teaching that humans will ultimately judge even the angels (1 Cor 6:3).[45] It might seem that, with their "undeviating consistency" being the bar, it would instead be angels who judge humans, unless of course angels and *iustus* humans both invariably share the attribute. Having established that this is indeed the case for Barth, it is again apparent that it is the election of Christ as played out on earth, and humans as elected in him, which sets humans apart from the angels while giving implicit worth to the earthly sojourn.

Having surveyed the internal evidence, it is the corroborative force of Barth's discussion of *iustus* humanity in Volume II (paragraph 35) that in my view proves Barth's section on angels to be more than a "one-off." Indeed, Barth's teaching concerning the angels in *CD* III/3—his confidence in the perfect consistency of their speech and action as representative of God's own—is remarkably similar to his teaching concerning the elect in *CD* II/2, where he couches humans in even higher terms. Like angels, humans do not emanate from God, they are distinct from God and yet bound to him. However, the human elect, states Barth, "do not stand in a merely external and formal but in an inner and actual relationship to God. As created beings they are completely and utterly other than God, completely and utterly dependent upon Him, and therefore made by Him alone into what they are; but as the elect of God they are not strangers to Him, but possess a definite affinity with Him and a definite share in His kingship. The elect of God, in fact, gives us a picture of God in the midst of creation."[46] In God's sovereign decision, Barth continues, the elected human

---

45. *CD* III/2, 158.
46. *CD* II/2, 344.

is marked by constancy. In virtue of this constancy he is just as necessarily this or that person, completing the corresponding course of action, as God Himself is always the same and faithful to Himself in all His attributes and works. In him therefore, and what he represents, and what happens through him, what he suffers, his succour and salvation, the peculiar continuity of this existence, a legitimate testimony can be given to the constancy and therefore to the sovereignty and therefore to the will of God. Not of himself, but as an elect man, the elect is an authentic witness of God.[47]

Never mind for the time being that the *simul* existence of this same elect person clouds his or her perfect obedience. Barth wants us to know that humans on earth can still be called trustworthy ambassadors of Christ—to the extent that they are! To put it another way, for the testimony of angels, there is no contradiction, no *simul*, and therefore no "to the extent"; a "to the extent" rule is not needed for angels because, unlike earthly humans (who in *simul* existence cannot claim pure speech or action), heavenly angels "never speak in half truths or do things in halves."[48] Again it is not that the witness of humans is less genuine in content than that of angels, but it cannot be taken as genuine or pure in the same way because the earthly witness is not "unalloyed with alien elements" which are unavoidably present "in even the best and most sincere and fitting witness." The mere earthly witness can therefore "have its full truth only in that which it attests and not in itself." Even a prophet or apostle cannot claim the genuine witness of the angels, but to the extent that earthly witnesses are genuine, they are accompanied and ministered to by the angels who in a sense envelop them. Christian testimony, remarks Barth, "like all earthly witness to God . . . draws its strength directly or indirectly, consciously or unconsciously, explicitly or implicitly, from the fact that before, above and beside it there is the pure witness to God which it can never be even as the best of earthly witness."[49]

We cannot miss Barth's meaning. He maintains that humans are, presently and in the most concrete dimension of existence, just as constant as are angels in maintaining the will of God without deviation. In fact, we should not be puzzled by Scripture's witness that persons—not just angels—are enabled for the ministry of reconciliation in this broken world; it is precisely *because* these persons are elect that they are so enabled. The actuality

---

47. *CD* II/2, 344–45: if not clear, this significant passage comes just after Barth's acknowledgment of 1 Cor 6:3, that humans will judge angels.

48. *CD* III/3, 513.

49. *CD* III/3, 484.

precedes the possibility. "The elect are," concludes Barth, "those who walk before God and find His good-pleasure. How can it be otherwise when they are His, when they are His friends, His children?"[50] As God's children they function in perfect "expression of their election";[51] they exist *only* in obedience and with an exclusively "truthful" witness. More than free angels could ever be or enjoy, elected humans live as "free children of the household."[52]

In sum, in spite of the startling similarities between Barth's descriptions of angels and the pure form of humanity, we could say that while angels are authentic witnesses—what Barth calls "crown witnesses"—of God, *iustus* humans are not only authentic witnesses but also share in God's actual "kingship." Angels are superior witnesses to humans, therefore, only in a relative sense, relative to humans ensnarled in the *simul*. In the sense that God's work moves from heaven to earth, angels have "primary and original knowledge of God's words and actions. However, angels "do not know the Father as the Son knows Him, or the Son as He is known by the Father."[53] Angelology, insists Barth, is only an "annexe" to Christology. In other words angelology is not, as is anthropology, "a consequence and analogy of Christology. For God did not become an angel in Christ."[54] As stated of Christ in Hebrews, "it is not angels he helps, but Abraham's descendents" (2:16). To the extent humans have deviated from their original, purely "angelic" nature, they need saving. As the horrific death of God crucified reveals, they need it quite a lot.

Rethinking Inclusion

That God's will "should be done on earth as in heaven," asserts Barth, "necessarily implies that it should be done on earth in a heavenly way."[55] The angels' announcement of Jesus' birth in Luke 2:14 properly begins, Barth reminds us, with the heavenly sphere: "Glory to God in the highest heaven," before transitioning to "and on earth peace among those he favors."[56] But

---

50. *CD* II/2, 344–45.
51. *CD* II/2, 345.
52. *CD* II/2, 347.
53. *CD* III/3, 497.
54. *CD* III/3, 500.
55. *CD* III/3, 478.
56. *CD* IV/1, 212. Barth speaks not only of the connection between these two phrases but also of the import of their theological sequence. God in his glory does not need humans but does not want to live without humans. This gives Barth another opportunity to assert that God, "in being *pro se* . . . is also *pro nobis*, and therefore *pro me*."

who again are those whom God favors? Barth explicitly connects the "favor" of Luke 2:14 with the similar wording at Jesus' baptism (Luke 3:22). By calling Jesus the "first" of the favored of God, Barth is thus signifying the representative inclusion of all humans in "God's beloved Son . . . the Son of Man upon whom God's good-pleasure rested."[57] As the one fulfilling the covenant from both sides—that is, from the side of God and from the side of humanity—Jesus is "identical with the glory of God in the highest" and "identical on earth with peace among men as the object of the divine good-pleasure." Again, the incarnation and the cross (in its disposal of wickedness) reveal the good-pleasure and love God shares with humans in the highest heavens as well as on earth through "the royal man Jesus." Like earth from heaven, the supra-temporal sphere is not to be separated from the pre- and post-temporal spheres. In fact, Barth calls Luke 2:14 "the most accurate description of God's supra-temporality . . . God's love and therefore His freedom, His holiness, righteousness and wisdom, are to be measured in all their immeasurability by His supra-temporality."[58] This is consistent with Barth's elevation of humans over even the angels, the latter being unable to relate to the accentuated glory of the supra-temporal realm in the same way. Thus Barth makes an internal connection from the announced peace to earthly humans, given via the heavenly Jesus in his incarnation and atonement, and the glory of humans as heavenly beings in the same resurrected and ascended Jesus. "God does not will to be great and glorious apart from man," Barth asserts, "As God is glorious in His own way, so is man in his. The being of man is thus fulfilled as presence and implication in God's self-glorification."[59]

On Barth's view, the characteristic of humans as God's beloved children is as certain as the resurrection glory of Jesus Christ. Again, it is not as if humans are legally righteous due to the righteous mantel of Christ, all the time corrupt underneath; this could only entail humans being hidden *by* Christ *from* God! Instead, Barth's understands humans to be hidden *with* Christ *in* God, hidden as true and righteous persons in *the* Person, colorfully enhanced as creatures, not in the least diminished. Heaven is where Christ is, asserts Barth, and humans are in Christ, who is as genuinely

---

57. CD IV/4, 66. See also *Humanity of God*, 47, "God's glory shines in the heights and thence into the depths, and peace on earth comes to pass among men in whom He is well pleased."

58. CD IV/2, 158: Barth here makes two elaborations pertinent to our study: 1) the good-pleasure or favor of God to humans in Christ is derivative, not by nature, but purely by grace and 2) the peace of God and his good-pleasure in humans is "realised and fulfilled" not only in the incarnation but also by the cross.

59. CD III/2, 183.

present on earth as he is in heaven.⁶⁰ In their announcement from heaven, then, it is as if the angels are highlighting the deepest reality of humankind, from God's perspective; God is thereby calling every human under heaven to their true heavenly, and therefore earthly, selves—participants in Christ as sons and daughters of God. If we have learned anything in our study thus far, it is that human identity in Christ is not a static state of being. It follows that to describe someone as a favored child of God or as a person "of good will" in Barthian fashion without recognizing that every child is also *doing* God's will, i.e., without recognizing the depth of Barth's actualism, is a gross objectification.⁶¹ On one hand, it could be pointed out that a more technically correct reading of the angels' announcement (Luke 2:14) renders a Christmas message addressed—quite exclusively—to only those individuals "of good will" (*contra* the traditional "good will to all" individuals). On the other hand, viewed with Barth's actualism, such a narrow translation of the angels' announcement ends up being the most inclusive of all—by identifying every person as a righteously active individual of good will in Christ, it provides a deeper, more commanding (i.e., more accountable) inclusion than does a "blanket" generic version.

---

60. See *CD* III/3, 438, 441: Barth connects Luke 2:14 with Col 1:1–3 in speaking of Christ's simultaneous immanence and transcendence. Barth comments in the same way that heaven is "higher than earth, which distinguishes it as the upper cosmos, and yet which also sets it in indissoluble union with earth." Jesus is at once true God, true human "our flesh in heaven," and "the one true God who became one with our poor flesh." Again in describing glorious flesh and corrupt flesh Barth makes plain the duality of Jesus' humanity (441). Our "flesh in heaven" apparently connotes our spiritual bodies, for, as Barth understands it, the soul is never without a body, whether on earth or not.

61. It should go without saying that categorizing all people as children of God because of having a common Heavenly Father is indistinguishable from the sloppy inclusiveness of Protestant liberalism which Barth disavowed. Alternatively, to categorize people as children of God because of their inclusion specifically in the Son of God, and therefore with a common Heavenly Father, is better, but apart from Barth's actualism it is indistinguishable from abject universalism because of its static state.

13

Taking Scripture with *Totus* Seriousness

"The imperative: 'Ye shall be holy,' is simply the imperative indication of the irresistible dynamic of the indicative: 'I am holy,' i.e., I am holy, and act among you as such, and therefore I make you holy—this is your life and norm."[1]

As is apparent, it is Barth's Christo-anthropological actualism as we have described it that provides the fullest expression possible to the imperatives of Holy Scripture. Conversely, commands received apart from Christo-anthropological actualism create frightening distance between imperative and indicative and leave us with arbitrary and "relative" quibblings regarding the nature of God's command and what can really be expected of humans in "living up to it."

The Reality of "if" in John's Gospel

Barth is constantly coupling the command of God to humans with an active human ontology (determined participation in Christ's *iustus* being-in-act). Barth is quick to point out the multiple Johannine passages expressing the non-negotiable connection of love and obedience, for example 1 John

---

1. CD IV/2, 501. The phrase "irresistible dynamic" connects well with our last chapter and our understanding of Barth's Christo-anthropological actualism. On this page Barth goes on to say: "It is not the glory of any man or creature, not even of Israel, but that of Yahweh Himself, which sanctifies the tent of meeting (Exod 34:53) . . . The 'name' of God is the holy God Himself, who is present as such in His holiness, present to His people as the Lord, to sanctify it, and in so doing to sanctify Himself." As if from the inside-out, Barth speaks of the starting point of Christ's reconciling work from Yahweh, to Israel, to the church, and indeed to include all of humanity.

5:3; 2 John 6 (these he calls "a recurrence of the Deuteronomic formula"); John 14:15, 14:21, and 15:10. The latter verse, for instance, "if you obey my commands, you will remain in my love," does not set up a contractual relationship, avows Barth, but instead describes the covenantal reality that in Christ humans do actually and freely love and obey God, and therefore it is possible that they may freely do so.[2] Again Barth's actualism, as derived from Scripture, provides motivation *and* accountability; these imperatives, Barth insists, "do not allow us to sink back into an idle contemplative enjoyment."[3] As with our other explanations of the importance of the third dimension, Barth here notes again that only a Christo-anthropological understanding of actualism avoids a theological or ethical "vacuum." In other words, it is this already fulfilled relationship that is happening between us and God in Christ—a relationship that refuses to separate love from action—which precludes ideas of empty space still needing to be filled, as in a contractual relationship (where we supply our part). Thus imperatives such as the above, which come across as hypotheticals because of the word "if," are actually descriptive of what Christo-anthropological reality looks like—a reality in which we are meant to "remain." We could call this window into the third dimension "the reality of *if*" in John's gospel!

The question is at hand: If, as true to Barth's vision for human transformation, our proposed Christo-anthropological actualism means that Jesus Christ is the subject-self of every human being, does that mean that if I am kindly opening a door for someone at a department store, then can I reason that somewhere Jesus is opening a department store door too? If I start with myself, I can only go around the circle of analogy in the wrong direction. Christo-anthropological actualism does not mean that Jesus is in the pulpit preaching, and therefore I am (this paradigm also starts with me, even though in the phrase I put Jesus first); it could not mean this any more than imagining the Father was building a fire for Jesus on the beach, and therefore Jesus builds a fire for his disciples on the beach. Jesus did not say of his work that the Father was doing what he (Jesus) was doing, but instead that he (Jesus) was doing what the Father was doing (John 5:17). Positively speaking, however, if we go around the circle of analogy in the correct fashion, John's transferable (we might say semi-analogous) sentences *are* critical to our understanding of Christian sanctification; they demonstrate the unidirectional movement of the Holy Spirit from the source to and through

2. To communicate that our *iustus* determination is not slavishly coercive (as is the *peccator* determination) Barth notes that this obedience is not a case of "must" but "may." However, he follows this without marginalizing our slavery to righteousness, which includes our freedom: "Our 'may' is our 'must'" (*CD* II/2, 593).

3. *CD* IV/2, 799.

the participant, the fruit of the Spirit being consistently active in Christ (and humans) in multiple dimensions of eternity. It is this fruit that manifests or expresses itself in sundry ways as it is translated through dimensions into the particular physical and temporal expressions of contemporary existential life (in the pulpit or the department store doorway). This uniquely Trinitarian double movement of grace—from the Father to the Son in the Holy Spirit, and from the Son to the Father in the Holy Spirit—provides us a theology of personalized non-segmented work where it is difficult to tell where the vine gives way to the branch (because even as the laws of nature teach us, it never does!).

If we go around the circle of analogy properly, then why the term semi-analogous (above)? The term simply protects us against promoting ourselves into a conflated relationship with Christ, even if, apart from that realm which no eye has fully seen (1 Cor 2:9), one could not know just how semi-analogous is the analogy! We mentioned above the "if" of reality in John's gospel. Perhaps we should step back and again inquire: What is this reality and how does it apply to us? Jesus said he is at work because his Father is always working (John 5:17). Does that imply that we are always working too, in Christ (i.e., always actively participating in the one who is always working in the Father)?[4] Comparing Jesus' work to the Father's (the fundamental level), we might say that the work is not only correlated but also identified, whereas our work (as derived) is not identified with Jesus' and his Father's but intimately correlated.[5] As is obvious in Jesus' utterance

4. See CD III/3, 34: Barth comments that a preliminary obstacle to this kind of analogical deduction is that even the first level of identification—that between Jesus and the Father—has not traditionally been taken seriously enough. If an equivalence (A) between Jesus' work and his Father's is not granted, we will have trouble imagining a derived form (B). However, having secured an anchor of equivalence on this first level, it must be continually stressed that Barth is not after a theological equivalence between humans and Christ. He instead seeks to maintain a semi-analogous relationship between the two even while maintaining our creaturely "kinship of being" with Christ.

5. CD III/3, 67. See CD III/4, 486: "Especially in John's gospel it [Jesus' work] is described as an operation and work in the light of God's work, and in relationship and even identity with it." The first two descriptors fit a derivative human format of participation, but not the third (identity). Following John's analogic the identification (A) "I am in the Father and the Father is in me" (John 14:11) leads into its corollary (B) "On that day you will realize that I am in the Father and you are in me and I in you" (John 14:20) but is not contingent upon it. As mentioned in the above footnote, Barth knows the power of the derivation (B) is only as strong as its anchor (A). It is not surprising then that John (and later Barth) would make a simple statement like "Jesus is the Christ" (1 John 2:22) the centerpiece of his gospel to human beings so that they would know that when it comes to the gospel (not to God himself) the anthropological

about always working (even, in this case, on the Sabbath), the Sabbath is meant to remind us of the derivative nature of work and that we are not God. For us to stop working, Barth insists, is to remember that God never stops working.[6] We are in a sense inside the superior work, relates Barth, such that we can never step outside and objectify it (as in the wrong kind of "participation" outlined in chapter 4): "God created the conditions and pre-conditions, and pre-pre-conditions of all creaturely working. God gave them to the creature. All the preliminaries of creaturely activity were the effect of God's activity, of His friendly activity in the sense and to the end revealed and active in Jesus Christ, and in the history of his covenant of grace, of His activity as it was determined and controlled by his saving will."[7]

Not surprisingly, Barth is again pointing to a grace given to humanity in Christ at creation *and* as revealed in the atonement. As a man on earth, even Jesus himself (as we also discussed in chapter 3) is participating in the already finished work of the covenant; it is this very fact which gives integrity to his statements related to doing the Father's will and finishing his work (John 4:34). Thus, whether with the life of Jesus or with our own lives, "the distinction of a human work is to declare the occurrence of a good work of God." In fact, asserts Barth, we must start with "the completed good work of God if we are to see what is the possibility and actuality of good works on the part of man." It is true in our conflicted existence that we can only discern such good works to the extent that we can, but even without quantifying the extent, we might discern enough to declare that the good work is there. Again, Barth notes that if an emergence or expression of God's good work can happen through the human being Jesus Christ, he who most

---

statement (B) is intrinsic to the statement of divine identity. (A). Oppositely stated: "No one who denies the Son has the Father; whoever acknowledges the Son has the Father also" (1 John 2:23).

6. See *CD* IV/4, beginning on page 47: Barth speaks of the "radical importance, the almost monstrous range of the Sabbath commandment" (57) which is meant to keep derived truth as precisely that, derived! From Barth's discussion on the Sabbath (see *CD* III/1, 218–220) I understand the Sabbath to be a sort of caveat related to our *simul* existence, because it's in our *peccator* determination that we, in our hubris, are prone to cast ourselves into self-idolatry. Past the *peccator* dimension, however, work and rest are not contrastive; we are not meant to be "always working" here on earth, but this does not necessarily mean that we take breaks from "working" there in unconflicted heaven, where we see clearly who God is and who we are, and where there is no temptation to think otherwise. As discussed in chapter 9, our life with Christ starts and ends with the unadulterated (but not inactive) "rest" of creation and redemption that we share with God now and which we may "enter" into fully (without contradiction) later (see Heb 4:3–11).

7. *CD* III/3, 119.

mightily struggled in *simul* contradiction (to what extent we do not pretend to know), then it can also be a true experience for believers: "The man Jesus did the good works of his Father as He lived and died in our stead, in the place of sinners, in the flesh, in our character. We conclude that even a sinful man in his sinful work—and we are all sinners and all our works are sinful—may declare the good work of God, and therefore, even as a sinner and in the course of sinning, do a good work."[8]

We might think, in speaking of himself as the true vine (John 15:1), Jesus is speaking of his divinity, or at least of his true humanity. But the line that follows is full of sordid humanity: "My Father, the gardener, takes away *every branch in me* that bears no fruit" (v. 2).[9] Jesus is obviously saying the branches in him which bear no fruit are cut off to wither before they are gathered up, thrown away, and burned. It seems probable that Jesus understands himself at once as the true vine and also as the rebellious vine of Israel[10] (and more deeply as he who "gathers" up false humanity in himself). Jesus is cut down, and with him the fruitless branches, but in Jesus' *life*, the branches are nothing but fruitful.[11] By now we know that Jesus' life informs his death, not the other way around. Not only is this the incarnational economy which informs our existence, but also it is quite obvious that the purpose of Jesus' words about pruning or cleaning have nothing to do with treating the bad branches. The bad (unfruitful) branches are cut off; only the good (fruitful) branches are pruned/cleaned. Instead of restrictive or disciplinary words, pruning and cleaning have expansive connotations: they are related fundamentally to the superabundant and non-quantitative economy of the Holy Spirit which proceeds from completeness to completeness (v. 11) or from fruitfulness to fruitfulness (not from unfruitfulness to fruitfulness). "Every branch that bears fruit he prunes [also *cleans*] to make it even more fruitful" (v. 2), and indeed, the branches are already clean, Jesus says,

---

8. *CD* IV/2, 589.

9. In view of John 15:1 ("My Father, the gardener, takes away every branch in me that bears no fruit") is it possible that the author sees Mary's words at the tomb as an ironic identification of the divine Jesus with his Father when she, mistaking Jesus with the gardener, says (John using the same Greek root) "they have taken my Lord away"? If so, in this one physical space we have represented Jesus' divinity, his true, risen humanity, and his false humanity, i.e., himself as a former corpse (the body of sin which has been "taken away"), the bracketing of the false self reinforced by the empty tomb.

10. See Ps 80:8ff.; also Jer 2:21.

11. Anticipating our discussion in the final chapter, we could say the "Thou-I" relationship (*CD* III/4, 386) is the healthy true relationship of vine and branches, but the fruitless branches are the "abstract I" (388) or "bad subjectivity" (389). Our own single-subject duality as branches is thus described within the single-subject duality of Jesus' humanity.

before they are cleaned (v. 3). It is from this standpoint that we are meant to understand Jesus' comments about bearing fruit: "This is to my Father's glory, that you bear much fruit, *showing yourselves* to be my disciples" (emphasis added). "You did not choose me but I chose you and appointed you to go and bear fruit, fruit that will last" (vv. 8, 16). When it comes to the Spirit, fruit is fruit; it has a genuine and lasting permanence, regardless of dimensions of existence, and even if it is manifest in different ways.

To start sanctification with Christo-anthropological reality does not mean we can fully apprehend it or live in perfect congruence to it in this age; this appears to be something "John" understands full well. John 14:23–24, for instance, is ripe with the congruity-incongruity language of the *simul*: "If anyone loves me, they will obey my teaching. My Father will love them, and we will come to them and make our home with them. Those who do not love me will not obey my teaching." As in our discussion of 1 John (chapter 7), to take statements like "if you love me you will obey my command" (14:15) in a contractual manner can only question the *reality* of our obedience and our love; we therefore oblige ourselves to diminish the force and integrity of this passage and to grade ourselves "on the curve." By using "if" in a non-contractual sense John is simply employing the Christo-realist logic that Barth would later apply as the "to the extent" principle of his actualism. The *assumption* of the above passage, then, is that we are already home with Christ in the Father's love, and in Christ, loving the Father. To read accompanying statements like "if you obey my commands, you will remain in my love" (15:10) apart from our proposed Barthian reading of John cannot help but throw a heavy yoke of futility on the Christian disciple.[12] Conversely, under a realist interpretation full of revelatory character, we might read Jesus' words in John 15:10 (above) as follows: "to the extent you obey my commands, you are demonstrating the reality of our union." Here the disciple stands to be empowered within the dynamic Christo-anthropological relationship where obedience and love, like authority and freedom, are one.

If a contractual emphasis breeds disillusionment due to unmet conditions or the failure to meet expectations, the covenantal basis of *simul* sanctification breeds promise and anticipation: Jesus Christ is the way, the truth and the life of every person; reality is therefore happening, reality is going on. Where will the kingdom of God emerge from its hiddeness to testify to the truth?[13] Where will the subjectivity of the human Jesus Christ spring

12. In J. B. Torrance's words, the great "sin of the human heart" is "to try to turn God's covenant of grace into a contract."

13. See CD II/1, 606: "For He Himself is the kingdom of God which is destined to come but still hidden, and the being of this kingdom is simply His own being. Therefore to believe in Him means 'to taste the powers of the world to come' (Heb 6:5), as is

forth as human life and act and speech?[14] Where will the Spirit blow today? The evangelical message inherent in *simul* sanctification is, borrowing the Johannine theme, as follows: In the Son of God you *are* a child of God, born from above in the Father's love and the life of the Holy Spirit; may you *be* born from above today! In Jesus' own words, "Very truly I tell you, no one can see the kingdom of God unless they are born from above" (John 3:3). As gospel proclaimers, we have the privilege of putting words to the music that is playing everywhere; if we might have permission to momentarily side-step Barth's Mozart for the sake of a pun, we could call it the music of *are* and *be*.

Which "himself"?

In speaking about the work of a sanctified disciple, Barth has continually driven us back to the one who has established a kinship of being with us—the one who sanctified himself for our sakes. Everything begins with Jesus and Jesus' relationship with his Father. Because of the authority of the Father, Jesus does not have to self-authenticate his works and words (even though it is Jesus' divine prerogative). Jesus typically describes his authority as coming from beyond himself, and in this sense Barth can describe Jesus' humanity in close correlation to our humanity in him, a "real" humanity which can only lapse into nothingness upon deviation from the determined course:

> He would not be accomplishing His own work, but would become alien and unfaithful to Himself, if He were to do any other but the work of God. And it would not be His own but an alien being which did not consist in His oneness of being with God. He is Himself as He does the work of God . . . it is in this way,

obviously done by those who do not fail to notice the meaning and purpose of those signs, but learn from them what they have to indicate beyond their character as acts of mercy and miracles."

14. See *CD* IV/1, 35–36: note how replete is this passage with Barth's principles of actualism: "In Him God Himself enters in, and becomes man, a man amongst men, in order that He Himself in this man may carry out His will. *God Himself lives and acts and speaks and suffers and triumphs for all men as this one man* . . . But the final thing that takes place here—just as it cannot be something provisional—cannot be a second or later thing. It can only reveal the first thing. What takes place here is the accomplishment and therefore the revelation of the original and basic will of God, as a result of which all the other works and words of God take place. What *breaks out* at this point is the source of all that God wills and does" (emphasis added). See also Col 1:5: "the faith and love that spring from the hope stored up for you in heaven and about which you have already heard in the true message of the gospel."

in the doing of the work of God, and therefore in His oneness of being with God, that He is Himself, this man. It is in this way that He exists as a creature, which cannot be dissolved in its Creator, which cannot itself be or become the Creator, but which has its own reality and worth in face of the Creator, deriving its own righteousness from the Creator.[15]

Jesus would not have been himself, Barth relates above, unless he invariably engaged in the work of the Father. Likewise, God desires that in obedience the human person "should come to himself and always be himself."[16] Conversely, humans operate in the alien dimension of their existence (the *peccator*) when they leave "the way, the truth, and the life" ascribed to each person.[17]

In John 14:10 we read Jesus' words, "Do you not believe that I am in the Father and the Father is in me? The words that I say to you are not my own; but the Father who dwells in me does his works." Again, it is as if in such hierarchical descriptions Jesus—as the true human within the *simul*'s contradiction—is pointing to a higher dimension, the glorious dimension he has continually shared with the Father since before the world began

---

15. CD III/2, 64.
16. CD III/4, 386.
17. Speaking of Jesus as the "way," Jesus' parable about the narrow and wide roads (Matt 7:13–14) can be used to illustrate the reality of "if" and the unreality of "as if." To grasp the sanctifying epistemological power of the narrow road we must grasp its universal scope. In other words, the narrow road is not the exception to the rule, but the exception which proves the rule; it is the authoritative (therein powerful) rule of the real road going in the *iustus* direction. In radical opposition is the wide road, which can only be tread in falsehood; i.e., "as if" the person in question is not in and on the narrow road. Existentially speaking, it is the narrow road that appears to be the exception, yet ultimately speaking, it is the wide road which is the exception to the rule. The end result of this is that there is only one real road—Jesus Christ "the way"—but two directions. Where the narrow road (right direction) is inside the wide road, it is the road "for those who are being saved." Where the wide road (wrong road) is inside the narrow road, it is "for those who are perishing" (1 Cor 1:18). The tragic irony is plain. Failure to repent is to insist on the wide road and yet be met by the narrow gate; the new self accompanied by the old self simply won't fit through (see 2 Thess 1:9)! The gate "Jesus Christ and him crucified" is an implicit judgment. Of course Scripture (e.g., 2 Pet 3:9) provides a proper Christian hope that the ultimate result will manifest an even better picture than the inversion of Jesus' parable. We do not want to find ourselves in Kierkegaard's story of the traveler who was informed that he was indeed on "the road to London" but never arrived (because he was on the right road but going the wrong direction!).

(John 17:5).[18] As "real man,"[19] Barth reminds us, Jesus never did any work or spoke any words which were "just" his own. The work and words were his own, but also his Father's: "My teaching is not my own, it comes from him who sent me . . . He who speaks on his own does so to gain honor for himself, but he who works for the honor of the one who sent him is a man of truth; there is nothing false about him" (John 7: 16, 18). In the same way, humans in Christ have their own distinctive and personalized good works and words, but these works and words are never "just" theirs. That is the nature of personalized participation the way the Creator has set it up. Taken alone, it is not at all clear if the statement above (John 7:18) pertains to Jesus himself or to his disciples. Later Jesus will make the semi-analogy imminently clear, it is *both* he and his disciples who are in view, maintained in their proper order: "As the Father has sent me, so I send you" (John 20:21; see 17:18). This once again begs the question, if the statement "he who works for the honor of the one who sent him is *a man of truth, there is nothing false about him*" (emphasis added) is meant to apply to Jesus and his disciples, then how can these words maintain any integrity at all unless they indicate the uncompromising *iustus* determination of the *simul*?

Barth is certain that our humanity, like Jesus', is never dissolved by this relationship with God.[20] But in his humanity Jesus also models the abject dependence that comes from the empowering authority outside of ourselves. Barth is not hesitant to draw the parallel between Jesus' words in John 5:19 to those of John 15:5: just as Jesus can do nothing except what the Father is doing, we can do nothing except what Jesus is doing.[21] The "Christ of the New Testament," asserts Barth, "not only has this power of His as something that comes to Him from the outside, flowing in Him, and received and therefore exercised by Him. He has it only to the extent that as the Son He can do and does nothing without the Father. But to that extent what he can do and does is also His own power belonging to Him as the Son of the Father."[22] Even apart from divinity, it is this Spirit power in the human

---

18. In the sense that these hierarchical descriptions are remindful of Jesus' solidarity with humanity, Calvin's quote is quite apt: "The Son of God . . . became man in such a manner that he had God in common with us." Cited in Hart, "Humankind in Christ and Christ in Humankind: Salvation as Participation in our Substitute in the Theology of John Calvin," 73.

19. *CD* III/2, 64: the omission of "the" preceding "real man" is intentional in keeping with Barth's fuller phrase here: "He is real man."

20. *CD* III/2, 64.

21. *CD* II/2, 106. See Jesus' words in John 5:30: "by myself I can do nothing."

22. *CD* II/1, 607.

Jesus which is active in those in the Vine. That is why "to remain" in the Vine is to be and to go with the truth of our already active participation in Christ.

The subject-self of Jesus Christ provides the center of Barth's actualism as we have articulated it. What we have called variably the force field of our subjectivity, or the ground of our being-in-act, or the vine of human vitality, all provide pictures of what Barth elsewhere calls the perceptible or imperceptible "substratum" of our activity in Christ's life and the source of any good fruit. But how does what Barth describes above as the flow—identifiable to us as the words and work of Christ in the Spirit[23]—translate from the Vine into our specific existence as citizens of cities and states in this century? To say crudely that the "fruit" is general and to be applied to specific situations is to capitulate to our sight; more precise might be to describe fruitful acts as even more specific in the third dimension than could ever be crystallized by our earthly perception.[24] Again, Barth's program for human sanctification is in keeping with the roots revealed in Jesus' earthly life; his was "an active life" to the extent that it is invariably orientated on the living Word and work of God. As Barth suggests, "Both in the Fourth Gospel and elsewhere, however, it is evident that this central, atoning and saving operation of God is His work as the Lord of the covenant of grace, which Jesus faces, by which He sees Himself governed and determined, and which He adopts and fulfils by His own *working*."[25] This active life of Christ on earth was "neither indolent nor active only in the sense of pious contemplation," assures Barth with apparent sharpness! Likewise, disciples of Christ are called to "the act of his life" which issues forth "full of realistic content." There is one governing criterion to the derived "active life" of the Christian: it "must first and decisively take place" in the Christian's "relation to the centre of this action and therefore in his relation to Jesus Christ," insists Barth. He continues, "Here it has a name. Here it takes place truly and properly.

---

23. Again, note the derived correlation of human knowing this time as issuing forth from all three Persons of the Trinity: John 8:28, "I do nothing on my own but speak just what the Father has taught me," and John 14:26 "But the Advocate, the Holy Spirit, whom the Father will send in my name, will teach you everything, and remind you of all I have said to you," and John 15:15, "instead I call you friends, for I have made known to you everything that I have heard from my Father."

24. CD III/4, 333: in terms of actuality always preceding possibility, even at the specific level, Barth writes, "Does not the command always demand specific human decisions, attitudes and acts? Yet, however these actions might be conditioned and directed, there can be no doubt that none of them can become an event without the substratum of a specific life-act. That man is obedient always includes in itself the fact that he lives. Therefore the command, whatever its form, always contains the demand that he should live in his acts."

25. CD III/4, 486. Italics represent translation from Barth's original Greek.

Here the will of God has the form and outline in which it may be recognised elsewhere as His will. Here His Word becomes audible, articulate and intelligible. Here it is to be heard first in order that it may be heard elsewhere, demanding obedience and in its singularity distinguishable from all other words and voices." Only then, in decisive relation to the "centre," can this lived content be described as realistic content which pierces "dimensions" and proves to be just as real in any contemporary setting, taking different forms in its specificity, remaining consistent with itself.[26]

The Command to Pray

Real, concrete human action derives from the center of human action, Jesus Christ himself, states Barth, "here it has a name." Nowhere is this more true than in the life of prayer. Indeed, we are commanded to pray in Jesus' name. So how does the *simul* relate to meaning-full prayer, in Barth's words, prayer "full of realistic content"? First, we are to recognize that our prayer begins with the mediation and intercession of Jesus Christ and the Holy Spirit, "in both cases it concerns the one event of laying a foundation for prayer, i.e., for the cry, Abba, Father." By now we have moved past the idea of a foundation as a static state of being without act—the foundation is a person Jesus Christ, and as our subject-self Jesus Christ is praying *our* prayers to God. This actuality makes it possible for us to pray. Again, this should not be thought of as a segmented exercise, where Jesus either gets us started and leaves the rest up to us, or where he takes our prayers and cleans them up to present to God. Because of Jesus' prayer for us, from the human "side," and through his Spirit, "we for our part may and must pray." Contextualized in our Creator and brother, this "must" is a word of pure gospel. The word "must" could only introduce a coercing element if our prayer was not intimately related to God's best on our behalf, the good already being done for us (and therefore implicitly by us).[27] Jesus' and the Spirit's prayers for us are impeccable, but obviously ours under the *simul* are not. While we "might ask God for anything," Barth remarks, the "whole of human egoism, the whole of human anxiety, cupidity, desire and passion, or at least the whole of human short-sightedness, unreasonableness and stupidity, might flow into prayer . . . as the effluent from the chemical factories of Basel is discharged into the Rhine."[28] Even when we have obediently examined our requests be-

---

26. *CD* III/4, 486. Barth concludes: "The divine action includes other spheres, and therefore the active life as man's obedient answer to it will exhibit other dimensions."

27. *CD* III/4, 94.

28. *CD* III/4, 100–101.

forehand, even when we have couched our prayers in an attitude of "thanksgiving, repentance and worship," we can never claim a pure prayer.

Why then are we commanded to pray in Jesus' name? "Whatever you ask from the Father in my name," Jesus said, "it will be given to you" (John 15:16; see 16:23; 14:13); this theme is repeated four times in three chapters! What can this mean? It is plain that tacking on the phrase "in Jesus' name" does not guarantee procuring the desired response. "In His name," remarks Barth, "means under His leadership and responsibility, in the unity of our asking with His . . . with the support of His power as that of the Son, of His unity with the Father."[29] Jesus' prayers are always heard and always answered, and it follows that so are ours in our *iustus* determination—it is this fact that maintains the integrity of Jesus' promise that all our prayers in his name will be answered. Existentially speaking, it is easy to deduce that many of our prayers are not prayed in Jesus' name! This proves the depths of our *peccator* determination. However, to the extent our prayers from our *simul* contradiction are prayed "in unity" with Jesus, they will be answered as they are asked, made manifest in this dimension in God's way and in accordance with God's will, on earth as it is in heaven. As always, this "to the extent" is in God's hands and cannot be captured by us. It is in this sense only that we can understand God as cleansing our prayers: "it need hardly to be said that there will never be a human request which does not need to be effectively and definitively rectified" by God's "pure hands." Again this is not meant to be a segmented description—as if our prayers were not of Christ and then they were—but that God brings out from sinners' prayers "the cleansed meaning, which it did not have in our hearts and mouth." In correspondence with our exploration of John 15, above, Jesus takes our earthly prayers and cleanses them because in the deepest sense our prayers in Christ are already invariably clean—this is sanctifying prayer. The result is that we can pray "fearlessly" says Barth, knowing the true freedom of prayer where there is not "the smallest interval" between asking and answering.[30] In other words, where the command to ask and pray in Jesus' name and where the Father hears and responds is where "the Gospel and the Law are not twofold but one."[31]

29. *CD* III/4, 108.
30. *CD* III/4, 108.
31. *CD* III/4, 109.

Simul Shema?

Having considered Barth's interpretation of the command to pray, what can we say about the *simul*'s relation to the greatest commandment, Jesus' shema?[32] It is the appendage of the shema, to "love thy neighbor as thyself," that is especially pertinent here because of our consideration in this section about the self. Barth eviscerates every idea that in this command we are meant to love our neighbors as much as we love ourselves, as if our self-love is the reference point.[33] Barth is adamant about the fact that when it comes to obeying the command to love our neighbor in this world, we can "only bungle" the attempt.[34] We in our sinful selves simply have no love to give, to ourselves or to anyone. Barth is obviously redirecting the ethic once again to its living center, Jesus Christ; the love of our neighbor, insists Barth, "will be His business, not mine, and however badly I play my part, He will conduct His business successfully and well." Again, when it comes to not only the context but the content of Christ's obedience (i.e., him doing it *for* us), we are not uninvolved! He continues, "We have to rely on the fact that it is Jesus Christ who has given me a part in His business; that He has not done so in vain; that He will make use of my service, and in that way make it real service, even though I do not see how my service can be real service." My love for neighbor in 2018 is real because it is real in Christ in eternity, full stop. It could not be real love otherwise. And, as with prayer, I cannot quantify the extent of the real love I dispense, although I can give proper credit for it. With an exact reference to the *simul*, and the inner-connection of the imperative and the indicative, Barth expounds, "That we have the commandment is our true being, with which we can and should be satisfied, leaving it to God to decide what will come of our doing and fulfilling of the commandment in view of that other fact which is simultaneously revealed to us, that it is a being of sinners."[35]

In concordance with the practice of prayer, then, Barth's model of *simul* shema obedience can be expressed as follows: 1) In my false self I cannot love God, myself or my neighbor, 2) Jesus Christ can and does perfectly love God, me and my neighbor for me, 3) In Christ's perfect obedience, I,

---

32. I say "Jesus' shema" to acknowledge that the second part of Jesus' shema commandment (Lev 19:18) is actually not a core shema passage as is Deut 6: 4–5. My use of shema here means both parts, with special attention to the second.

33. *CD* I/2, 452.

34. *CD* I/2, 453.

35. *CD* I/2, 452. Note Barth's use of "that other fact" (i.e., "fact" as opposed to truth) to describe the counterfeit ontology in what otherwise appears to be a symmetry: "our true being" vs. "our being as sinners."

in my true self, am perfectly, really and truly, loving God, myself and my neighbor. In this way, my "self" is not the reference point at all, but Jesus Christ. So that when we think of loving our neighbor "as ourselves," we are to think not of us loving them as much as we love ourselves, but of us loving them as we ourselves truly love them—as we ourselves already and actually do love them, in Christ! Finally, 4) when this truth manifests itself in our day to day lives, it is only by the Spirit of Truth, i.e., it is as miraculous as it is poignantly transformative. It is therefore *simul* sanctification that puts most emphasis on the concrete depth of Spirit power because it is rooted in the deepest place of human activity, the *de facto* being-in-act of Jesus Christ *for* and *in* every human united to him. It should not surprise us that Barth views our life in the Spirit as synonymous with a sense of "urgency" in prayer, "the urgency is that of the Holy Spirit pressing, driving and impelling the one who prays, and continually leading him to more radical and serious depths and fresh turns and aspects of the fellowship with God grounded in Jesus Christ."[36]

When it comes to the shema, Barth makes his actuality-before-possibility claim exceedingly clear below, along with a reminder that the *simul*'s claim connotes judgment (separating our false selves from true). Again, it is the authority of Christ's human life lived in perfect obedience as the Son of Man (or Second Adam) which carries judgment within itself (John 5:27). We will all be judged on the basis of *who* he is and *therefore* who we are in him. With this awareness, it is a judgment we should welcome as gospel: "We have to see that we can obey the commandment only as those who are judged by the commandment, that it is the Gospel within the commandment that we should obey as those who are judged by the commandment. When we do, we shall cease trying to hide from each other. There is nothing to hide: we can and should love our neighbor only as the people we are, and therefore 'as ourselves.'"[37] Three times in two pages in his discussion of the shema Barth notes that we must keep "the Gospel within the commandment." Here, thousands of pages and seven part-volumes previous to his discussion on *simul* prayer, Barth is making the same claim about the oneness of Gospel and Law. It follows that we are ourselves when we are obeying the gospel. Even Christ would not have been "himself" if he had

---

36. *CD* IV/3.1, 110. Note Barth's discussion of the shema ends with the importance of prayer (*CD* I/2, 453–54) even though this citation is from the section of IV/3 previously mentioned (above).

37. *CD* I/2, 452–53.

done otherwise. Borrowing from Paul, then, the *simul*'s application is as follows: it is I, yet not I, who love my neighbor.[38]

As we discussed earlier (chapter 8) Barth's notion of sanctification is that the Christian is meant to turn "his back on himself" and seek things which are above.[39] Unless we grasp Barth's meaning in relation to the latitude afforded by the *simul* (i.e., to his theology of a single-subject duality), we might view turning our back on ourselves as a contraction to Barth's comments above—those pertaining to Jesus being "himself" and to Christians being most themselves when living without deviation from the Word. Two comments are thus in order: One, Barth would never ask one to turn "his back on himself" unless there was another "himself"! And two, to turn one's back on oneself could only be a heavy obligation if Christians were thrown back on themselves, as if called to make their own "arbitrary renunciation." It is clear that Barth means the false self is powerless to make a renunciation; can we then take Barth to mean that in acts of faith, we *are* in a sense thrown back on ourselves, our true selves? Can we understand the single-subject in *that* manner (the false self as incapable, but the true self as capable)? Such a self-centered understanding would unravel all that we have said before about the all important prefix of *Christo*-anthropological sanctification. Even the true self is nothing, and completely incapable, apart from Jesus Christ. Indeed, it is Barth's view that on the day of "judgment and consummation" the derivative dependence of true humanity that the Sabbath is meant to teach us now will be unobscured. It will be plain that, in regards to each human,

> God has taken his case into His own hands and therefore out of those of man, and that the last and final thing which man will experience about himself as he enters eternity is that his self-positing, self-affirming, self-expression, self-help and self-justification will be spread out before God who will then in His grace make a sovereign decision concerning him, and that man will then be wholly and utterly the one who stands there in the revelation of this sovereign divine decision, not as that which he would like to make and has actually made of himself, but as that

---

38. In both cases, concerning prayer and shema, Barth's teaching reflects that of Christ, who asks us to deny ourselves, our wrong selves, in order to find ourselves (Matt 10:39). In a way the original disciples could not yet anticipate, to take up one's cross (Matt 16:24–25) is to recognize that our old selves have been crucified with Christ and therefore we may and must follow Christ.

39. *CD* II/1, 159.

which he will be on the basis of the will and according to the judgment of God.[40]

The judgment demands that humans allow their "self-understanding in every conceivable form be radically transcended" so that the only true knowledge they have of themselves is as true believers in God. It therefore demands that the believer, on earth as in heaven, "work and express himself only in this imposed and not selected renunciation, and that on the basis of this renunciation he actually dare in it all to be a new creature, a new man."[41]

But finally, as we close this chapter, we must inquire: is Barth leading us into an esoteric realm of mysticism with his "two-himself" notion? Barth finds corroboration in at least two places to debunk such an idea. For one, his ideas concerning renunciation of all self-renunciation certainly find roots in Calvin: "*the only entrance to salvation lies in neither knowing nor to willing anything by oneself, but simply to follow as God leads. Let this then be the first step in a person deserting himself.*" But more importantly, in response to the question of mysticism Barth points directly to Scripture. Citing Gal 2:20 ("I live, yet not I, but Christ liveth in me"), Barth enjoins: "Well, if and so far as it is mysticism, then Paul too was a mystic ... If this is mysticism, then mysticism is an indispensable part of the Christian faith."[42] In sum we might say that to follow Christ in this way, i.e., when we take following to mean finding ourselves in Him, then with Barth's premise it stands that we might also find ourselves newly refreshed in reading Holy Scripture.

---

40. *CD* III/4, 58.

41. *CD* III/4, 58.

42. *CD* III/4, 59. The italics represent translation from the Latin in *CD*. Barth here notes Calvin's dependence on Bernard of Clairvaux, but describes it as a positive association: "Bernard's mysticism, with its strong christological character, is not to be regarded as mysticism in the more dubious sense."

14

Seeing through the *Simul*

"That this is not a direct vision, but a seeing through, makes it a struggle—the struggle in which the decision fulfilled by God may be continually recognised as fulfilled by us. Yet the fact that on this basis it can be and may be a true seeing, makes it a free and lighthearted struggle untainted by any toil or self-will."[1]

BEGINNING IN CHAPTER 8 I INTRODUCED A SOMEWHAT SCANDALOUS ASsertion, namely, that for Karl Barth, human life, both Christ's and ours, transcends our death and even more bracingly our birth. If what is, at the very least, a strand in Barth's thought represents the thrust of what he is saying, then this has profound implications for how the *simul* can be implemented for the church and as a framework for Christian sanctification. Some of these implications will be outlined below, but the foundational basis of sanctification for Barth is always before us: the more belonging and love a person knows in God the Creator as revealed in Jesus Christ by the Holy Spirit, the more motivated to obey God the person will be. It follows that the more deeply anchored this belonging and love is, the better. This book has attempted to clarify Barth's discontent with an obedience founded upon the experience of Christians who think they belonged to God merely from the point of their existential conversions. Instead, Barth insists that we belong, and are beloved, as manifest uniquely in the historical "before and after" sequence of Jesus Christ's death and resurrection long ago. Yet deeper still, as I have argued, Barth wants us to know that this belonging and belovedness as God's children, revealed to be humanity's "new creation," is not an exception to the rule; instead, it is actually a fresh expression of creation in which each

---

1. *CD* III/1, 380.

creature's belonging and belovedness *has always been* the rule. Therefore, to the extent one knows the "before-before" of one's bedrock identity (i.e., the created and eternal *iustus* determination of his or her life in Christ), one will be best equipped to address the desperate challenges of the false *peccator* self in the midst of the overlap of the ages, the time of the *simul*.

Having practiced considering the "two subjectivities" of the *simul* throughout this book, I want to reemphasize in this final chapter the single subject of the *simul*. If, in our emphasis on the two total selves, we forget the one person, we will allow our "Chalcedonian anthropology" to lapse into the equivalent of Nestorianism. To borrow Barth's words related to Christology, it will be as if we have lashed two planks together with a rope and called it a unity.[2] Why is this so problematic? All that we have said above about the love of God for each person is at risk if somehow it is communicated that God loves only the true self of each person. Instead, God loves the whole person, God loves the sinner (Rom 5:8), God loves the broken person.[3] Does it follow, then, that God loves the false self? As we reviewed in chapter 8, in light of Barth's theology of the cross, Barth can claim God's overall love for the person with the false self without pledging his love *for* the false self. God does not love evil; in fact, he hates evil because of what it does to his beloved creatures.[4]

Like any new paradigm, the theological precision that goes along with practicing *simul* sanctification can be tiresome. Would it not be easier if we just went back to speaking of the one person in a zero-sum manner (as in Wesleyan or Arminian thinking)? Do we have to think about one person in *simul* fashion, with two total selves? Ironically, I have found that an effective approach towards understanding the import of the *simul* version of the one person is to press to the limit the mutually exclusive nature of the duality. By interrogating the apparent dualism in Jesus' teaching on the two trees (Matt 7:17–19), for instance, we may expose objectionable alternatives to Barth's

2. See *CD* IV/2, 70.

3. As my friend Alan Torrance is fond of reminding us, when it comes to having a sick pet, we do not say, "I hate the sickness but love my dog," but instead, "I love my sick dog."

4. If we start from the predicate (false self) and move to the inseparable subject (inseparable in the sense that the false self cannot exist in abstraction), can we then say that, because God hates our false selves, he therefore in a sense hates us, the subject of the false self? In one very specific sense, Barth is forced by his logic to admit this (see *CD* II/2, 452), although he does not and cannot put legitimate stock in any theological assessment that starts with the false predicate. Nothingness, which has no ultimate root or future, can never be a proper starting point; its present tense destructive power must be acknowledged, and seriously, but also parenthetically, for God never ceases to love the sinner (see *CD* IV/1, 406).

position. Only three succinct internal principles derived from Jesus' word picture are necessary to present the question: 1) a good tree cannot produce bad fruit nor a bad tree good fruit—this appears to designate people as *either* one or the other, righteous or wicked; 2) the designations are apparently intractable since there is not the least insinuation of an ability to cross over from one column to the other; and 3) there is absolutely no indication that a person could be composed of some of each tree, producing a zero-sum mixture of good and bad fruit. The cumulative rhetorical question is this: If, in fact, people do indeed produce a mixture of good and bad fruit, what could be the intent of Jesus' teaching? Does Jesus (as we briefly proposed in the last chapter) want us to have eyes to see him as the one person who is simultaneously both trees, the righteous one without fault, and the bad one who is cut down and burned, and in turn to consider that humans in Christ might also be both trees in their undeviating fullness (*totus*) of each determination? Derived from Christ's narrative, such a perspective maintains the internal logic of a *simul* anthropology, which 1) preserves the strict premise of like producing like;[5] 2) keeps the two determinations mutually exclusive;[6] and 3) allows for absolutely no admixture, and yet at the same time maintains that these good and bad dynamics all exist within one subject.[7]

Backwards as the New Forward

Undoubtedly the time of the *simul* is equivalent to what Scripture calls "the present evil age" (Gal 1:4), yet hopefully our consideration of the *simul* has edified our understanding that the age of humans' earthly pilgrimage is not *purely* evil, despite the prevailing darkness. Because of the oft-hidden nature of righteousness, however, this age, if not pure chaos, is certainly a time of confusion. As we look around us, there is much evidence to the contrary to what Barth has posited as a third dimension of human being and act in

---

5. See John 3:6: "flesh gives birth to flesh, Spirit gives birth to Spirit."
6. See 2 Cor 6:14: "what fellowship is there between light and darkness?"
7. I consider the first verses of John 15 (briefly exposited in the previous chapter) to be similar in theological reasoning to our Matt 7:17–19 text, only described from the one person to the duality instead of the other way around. The Father (gardener), Jesus says, "cuts off every branch *in me* which bears no fruit" (emphasis mine). As for Matt 7:17–19, even if our exegetical reasoning explodes any notions of an Arminian zero-sum framework, we must admit that at least one other view, isolated from our christological, *simul*, interpretation, may be legitimately be drawn from this isolated text. The hyper-Calvinist (Dortian) interpretation, painting a swath of people (reprobates) as completely evil and impossibly relegated to producing nothing but bad fruit (despite "good" appearances) is obviously another exegetical consideration.

Christ, *sans simul*. The remainder of this final chapter will examine what Barth may mean when he exhorts believers to live their lives "*from* the third dimension"—citizens of heaven living penetrating lives on earth, people empowered "from above" by the Holy Spirit.[8] Christo-anthropological revelation urges us, in faith, to begin with the end in mind. In fact, all talk of purely immanent earthlings "going to heaven" is nonsense. No one dies and "goes to heaven" who is not *from* heaven.[9] Our recognition of the "before-before" may have had the effect of framing our typical understanding of the "end" less linearly, but even though the *simul* urges the sanctified to think dimensionally—to live as those who have already died and to face death as those who are already alive—we still must take our cue from the orders of historical revelation. Eschatologically informed from this resurrection-revealed standpoint of "no contradiction," we in our current worldly existence can move forward by looking backward—we could say from the *eschaton*, through the cross, and to the crib. In other words, the clarity needed to interpret our confused world comes from the final judgment implicit in the *simul*—the gospel of Jesus Christ and him crucified.[10]

8. Webster, *Barth's Moral Theology*, 24. Quotations here are Webster's quotes from Barth's Tambach lecture, "The Christian's Place in Society," (1919), which Webster notes is Barth's first lecture after his definitive emergence from nineteenth-century German liberalism. Even if the theme of immanent human subjectivity within the divine subjectivity of the fully human Jesus Christ is not as pronounced as it would be later (e.g., "the humanity of God"), there is still an obvious line of consistency related to the third dimension from Tambach and through *Church Dogmatics*. "New life," quotes Webster from the Tambach lecture, is "from the third dimension which penetrates and even passes through all of our forms of worship and our experiences; it is the world of God breaking through from its self-contained holiness and appearing in secular life; it is the bodily resurrection of Jesus Christ from the dead." The movement of the third dimension, although always initiated from "above" to "below," is not like an isolated lightning bolt which retracts after intersecting earth.

9. In our new economy, it is the idea of starting on earth and going to heaven which is backwards, as the incarnation shows, see John 3:13: "No one has ascended into heaven except the one who descended from heaven, the Son of Man." Obviously our interpretation rides on the question distilled from Matthew 16:13, "*Who* is the Son of Man?"

10. The judgment of Jesus Christ and him crucified is another way of expressing God's love. Here John 3:16 and 1 John 3:16 ("This is how we know what love is: Jesus Christ laid down his life for us," NIV) speak clearest to the truth that God's self-offering proves that God loves us more than he loves himself. John's use of "world" ("God so loved the *cosmos*") which typically has evil connotations, reveals the import of the world as a single subject in its own "impure form," i.e., under the sway of the prince of this world. Like humanity, the world is "groaning" in *simul* contradiction until "set free from its bondage to decay" (see Rom 8:19ff). Like humanity, the world is not purely evil or God would not love it. The implicit side of Rom 5:8 ("while we were

Hopefully we have grasped that Barth's retrospective understanding of Jesus' own historical sequential narrative is the key to our own forward movement. Contrary to the typical adage, Barth would therefore have Christians be so heavenly minded that they *are* much earthly good! But can we say more about what it means to be "heavenly minded" in this world? Even in the realm of confusion, the fullness of God's unadulterated, incarnational, Spirit-presence dictates that humans of the 21st millennium are already (as per Luke 17:21) permeated by the kingdom of heaven—we could call it the first heaven. Having introduced us to more theological dimensions than meet the eye, Barth obviously does not mean us to live from a limited first heaven perspective.[11] If the third dimension is, unlike our current existence, the realm of no contradiction, could we then be so bold as to posit the third dimension as comparable to Paul's third heaven? If so, in turn we might consider the second heaven to be comparable to Barth's otherworldly "dimension of eternity." This is the dimension, we remember, where the contradiction between righteousness and wickedness still exists, but where the duality is finally manifest (on that Day) in perfect delineation. To summarize, then, our final quest towards heavenly thinking will be to develop a framework of *simul* sanctification that involves living *from* the third heaven (the realm of no *simul* contradiction) and living *under* the judgment of the second heaven (the realm of perfect *simul* clarity), in order to live sanctified lives *in* the first heaven (the realm of *simul* confusion)—and in doing so we will be developing a mindset that will arguably best equip us to deal with what we might call first heaven problems.[12]

---

yet sinners, Christ died for us") is that "sinners" is not all we are. Still, by virtue of the single subject, the fact remains that God loves sinners *as* we are.

11. Likewise, Jesus, in granting that the kingdom of heaven is "in you" or "amongst you," did not leave his hearers under the impression that that is all they needed to know!

12. By presenting (with revelatory permission) a prospective view beginning with our current existence (and within the overarching simultaneous perspective, viewed retrospectively) I hope my three heavens theme will provide a nice complement to Barth's three dimensions of eternity. The first heaven is loosely equivalent to supra-temporal eternity, the time of the *simul*. Again, this is what Barth called "the fatal middle stretch between creation and consummation" (*CD* III/2, 304). Like the supra-temporal, inside the retrospective view, our first heaven should not be thought of as a "self-enclosed middle"; like the pre-, supra-, and post-temporal, the three heavens can be distinguished but not separated. To reiterate our mapping, if Barth's post-temporal is loosely equivalent to the third heaven, it follows that the second heaven is comparable to Barth's otherworldly "dimension of eternity" between the supra-temporal and post-temporal.

Blurring the Lines?

As per the logic of this book, if the third dimension is the reality where the church is truly the church, then the church on earth, as a microcosm of the human race, is indeed meant to be a witness of Christ-revealed reality. It follows, then, that even if not everyone is a so-called Christian (an existential term) in this world, at least everyone is a hearer and doer of the Word. Rooted in the most foundational dimension of human existence, what we have coined Barth's Christo-anthropological actualism is what Bonhoeffer called the "Law of the real," the content being a "who" and not a "what." This is the intersect of imperative and indicative in the person of Christ; the law that every human may freely participate in precisely *because* it is their bedrock truth and binding in Christ. In other words, "the law of the Spirit of life," in a way to which the Jewish law could only bear relative witness, posits all persons as hearers and doers of the "real law"[13] and *therefore* accountable (Rom 2:12–16). Our consideration of angels with Barth has reinforced the jealous love inherent in the command of a God who is the creator of exquisite human freedom and distinctiveness. As followers in "the Way" (Acts 24:14), believers aspire to "live into" the will of God uniquely defined and delimited by the salvific history of the Redeemer. The road is narrow for a reason, as Barth relates: "the community and its members necessarily cease to be what they are if they are guilty of any arbitrary deviation from His history."[14] On one hand, to the extent we deviate, we are party to nothingness, as if trying to sustain the old self. On the other hand, to the extent we participate in the Spirit, we enjoy the fruit of the Spirit, even in the midst of life's challenges. When asked if we have deviated or not deviated today, in answering "yes" we have taken ourselves appropriately seriously. At the same time, instead of welcoming a quagmire, we can be confident that there is a best course for us to take. This approach should not be misconstrued as posturing wrong as right and right as wrong, but the overall quotient of whether an action is considered right or wrong must continually be discerned in the wisdom of the Holy Spirit, the Counselor of righteousness and truth, as he moves in and through the Body of Christ. The call of the church is to hold people to grace, to hold brothers and sisters accountable to

---

13. *CD* I/1, 457, cited also in chapter 5. As for the law bearing relative witness to the law of the Spirit of Life, i.e., the law of Christ, see 1 Cor 9:20–21. Paul declares not the separateness but the superiority of "Christ's law" where it is not rightly represented by the so-called "law and the prophets." Again, Barth is never after a blind replacement of Torah by "gospel," even if paramount to his concern is to "obey the gospel" (see 1 Thess 1:8; a phrase also used by others, see 1 Pet 4:17).

14. *CD* IV/2, 277.

who Christ is and who they are in him, or we could say to hold them to the law—the law of the real.

The question is at hand: If everyone is in truth an unmitigated person of good will, and if everyone is in one sense a child of God enjoying the undeviating goodness of creaturely freedom and abundance, then what difference if any does Barth see between a Christian and an unbeliever? Sin is irrational and absurd. Christian belief is miraculous. Once we get comfortable with the fact that neither belief nor sin can be explained and rationally controlled, Barth has given us in the *simul* a template for Christian living that applies to any person and any situation. However, it is indisputable that the universally stark lines of the *simul* also have the effect of blurring the line between Christian and non-Christian before clarity can re-emerge. Barth elaborates, "believing man is the one who will find unbelief first and foremost in himself." When it comes to the relationship between believers and unbelievers, "believers . . . are in no way less sinful men than their unbelieving partners in the conversation," and so Barth concludes, "in this way they can and will meet unbelievers sincerely, in the humility of a full and honest solidarity with them; but also confidently . . . they are not superior to them."[15] As we near the conclusion of our study, Barth's statements reflect the first words of this book's Introduction and how *simul* sanctification is meant to inspire both humility and confidence. Barth's *simul* insists that human beings see themselves, with all humans, standing under the judgment of Jesus Christ and him crucified. It follows that these same humans need not (and should not) judge each other; neither should they judge themselves. God alone is judge.

How does Barth propose that we move ahead without judging our neighbors? Firstly, says Barth, we must resist the temptation to make distinctions between one another—believer, unbeliever; elect, reprobate, etc: "We become entangled in these distinctions only if in our definition of the Church we look abstractly at the men assembled in the community rather than at the Lord and His action. But who tells us to do this?"[16] Secondly, what do we observe when we look at the Lord Jesus? Barth's answer is that we see that each person gathered in Christ, in the church or out, as a "a *justified* and *sanctified* sinner, yet also a justified and sanctified *sinner*."[17] Thirdly, having asked us to see every person as under the *simul iustus et*

---

15. *CD* II/1, 95.

16. *CD* IV/3.2, 783. It is not always clear when Barth is speaking of the church or humanity in general, which is probably purposeful, especially when he is warning against making distinctions.

17. *CD* IV/3.2, 784.

peccator—"all qualified and all unqualified"[18]—what then is the difference to Barth between a Christian and non-Christian? Does "Christian" retain any meaning to Barth?

Barth's statement in *CD* IV/3 is one of his clearest on the subject: the Christian "sees what others do not see." Barth continues, "What makes him a Christian is that he sees Jesus Christ, the Son of God, in the humiliation but also in the exaltation of His humanity, and himself united with Him, belonging to Him, his life delivered by Him, but also placed at His disposal."[19] To put it in expressly *simul* terms, Barth views Christians as those who know that they are justified and sanctified sinners, and who know by the history of the Original Subject of the *simul* that there is an asymmetry at play, i.e., a relationship between *iustus* and *peccator* "not in equilibrium, but in a definite order of superiority and inferiority."[20] So does a person have to understand the *simul* to be a true Christian? Hopefully we have moved past the idea of "knowing" as merely noetic intellectualism. Indeed, as introduced in chapter 3, it is apparent that Barth views everyone as participating in Christ, consciously or unconsciously; Christians are simply those who in adoration and gratitude acknowledge the righteous Person in whom they are inherently and personally being transformed.[21] Knowing grace as more than an extrinsic gift (i.e., "God's riches"), but an intimate gift fleshed out by the loving embrace of the Savior himself, the believer is motivated to worshipful obedience: "The grace of God has appeared, bringing salvation to all. It [grace] teaches us to say no to ungodliness and to live self-controlled, upright and godly lives in this present age" (Titus 2:11–12). Again, persons may participate in various ways, but a misguided focus on who is participating more directly or more indirectly returns us to the first point about making unwise distinctions. Barth comments about the futility of this line of thinking: "In the ongoing common history of the community, there may

---

18. *CD* IV/3.2, 784.

19. *CD* III/3, 241.

20. *CD* IV/3.2, 784.

21. While both the Gentiles and Jews fail in this regard, according to Romans 2, by not giving credit where credit is due, it is the Jews who are more culpable. The Jews prove themselves faithful, true people of God, to the extent they follow the real law, which cannot be conflated with the "Jewish law" but to which the Jewish law bears relative witness. The Jewish law is therefore, in one sense, the real law, but only to the extent that it is. The relationship is derived and therefore cannot be reversed. Ironically, it is the Gentiles who may prove to live more congruently to the law of God, i.e., bearing witness to the law of a humanity "circumcised" in Christ, the law "written on their hearts." This is the "real law" according to Barth, where all humans are already implicated as "hearers and doers" in Christ.

have arisen yesterday, and there may arise to-day, a juxtaposition of those who participate more directly and those who participate more indirectly in its mission, but this may also reverse itself and become very different to-morrow."[22]

By rightly calling our behavior (undeniably inconsistent) and judgment (invariably skewed) into question, Barth is recalibrating our definition of "Christian." To begin with, these arbitrary factors make it impossible for persons to truly know they are included in the life of Jesus Christ unless they know everyone is included.[23] It follows that for Barth Christians are nothing less than those who, by the revelation of Jesus Christ, know humanity in general and *therefore* themselves as grateful participants within the ongoing human mediation of Jesus Christ—participants in Christ's death and his life—and therefore human beings under the definition of *simul iustus et peccator*. "Above all," counsels Barth, "it is obvious that the elect man cannot possibly receive this witness if he gives it only to himself, if as he gives it to himself he does not also give to his 'rejected' neighbour, if he does not permit the contradiction of the rejection that threatens him to benefit this other man as it has benefited him."[24] But what of those who attempt to restrict what Christ has accomplished for the world, trying "to make private an event which is so essentially public"? Barth issues a stern warning: This person needs "to be told quite bluntly that he definitely loses the prospect of his own personal participation in this event."[25]

If Barth's position on sanctification is awry, we must ask what is the better biblical, theological explanation for sin and addiction in a believer's life, or for the good things in an unbeliever's life (could we so bold as to say the fruit of the Spirit in unbelievers?).[26] To put it differently, if Barth's *simul* is the way forward for believers, it must at least be entertained as the

---

22. *CD* IV/3.2, 784.

23. See *Heidelberg*, 89: "Faith is the confidence in which a member of the Christian community believes that in the death and resurrection of Jesus Christ God's righteous action has achieved its goal for all men and *thus also* for him." Emphasis added.

24. *CD* II/2, 340.

25. *CD* IV/3.2, 932. In terms of our proposed nomenclature, there is no advance beyond the second heaven for such recalcitrant persons. Asserts Barth in *CD* IV/3.1: "To the man who persistently tries to change the truth into untruth, God does not owe eternal patience and therefore deliverance" (477).

26. See IV/3.1, 335: Barth speaks of God being the only judge as to whether our lives are "fruitful" or "unfruitful." This has nothing to do with us calling ourselves Christian, especially based on a mistaken notion that "fruit" refers to our spiritual qualities and not to the Spirit himself. Taken as an objective genitive, fruit refers away from itself (i.e., the Spirit himself is the fruit itself).

template for grasping the best theological anthropology in general. The *simul* is not meant to be applied merely to Christians because Jesus Christ himself is not applied merely to Christians; Barth simply will not let us have the paradigm without its defining Person. This universal context is just the concession Barth's pundits are not willing to make, and so they are at risk of discounting the one program of sanctification that actually has the authority of reality behind it.

Irresistible Grace?

Speaking of authority, and in light of Barth's phrase above that Christians see themselves "at Christ's disposal," a final note here about Christian ethics (as opposed to what Barth calls special ethics) is in order. It cannot be stressed enough that all ethics, on Barth's view, are rooted in the Lordship of Christ's freedom. Barth makes plain that the divine authority of freedom granted to humanity (i.e., Christ's human life as the life of every human), is an ethical imperative in and of itself. Instead of a static category, or simply a forensic imputed righteousness, it is the ongoing life of Christ's inseparable being and act—the union and communion in which we are personally implicated—which provides all humans the irresistible freedom to live in the truth by the Spirit, blessing God and others. As Barth constantly reminds us, actuality always precedes possibility. Since Christ is acting for us in his incessant, high priestly intercession, we *are* freely acting in, with, and through him. This dynamic union assures that we cannot love and obey God unless we are already doing so in Christ, but at the same time the *iustus* dynamism of grace means intrinsic and destructive consequences for all humans to the extent that we, as Barth chagrins, choose falsehood and "unfreedom."[27]

27. CD II/2, 589. See *Heidelberg*, 32, where Barth equates "anti-divine" with "anti-human" (i.e., human violation of God's will in the flesh is self-violation). I have chosen to turn often in this last section of our study to Barth's *Learning Jesus Christ Through the Heidelberg Catechism* as a complement to *Church Dogmatics* because of its concern for sanctification and discipleship and because it reflects in microcosm some of Barth's same desires to move past Lutheran categories in his reformulation of *simul iustus et peccator*. In filling out the *iustus* dimension of humanity, as per the paragraph above, Barth is adamant about what he calls the comprehensive "He-I" relation between the subject Jesus Christ, and all human subjects. Of *Catechism* Question 1, "I belong not to myself . . . but to my faithful Savior, Jesus Christ." Barth remarks of the representative nature of Christ's agency, "All further statements are relative clauses added to this subject, 'my faithful Savior, Jesus Christ': '. . . who makes me wholeheartedly willing and ready from now on to live for him.' These are all statements about Jesus Christ. They concern me because he acts for me. The whole content of this catechism is to be understood as an explanation of this He-I relationship. I am included in what is said

Barth continually forces us to consider just how Cartesian is our perception of ourselves and our world. Instead of judging God from the standpoint of self-understanding, Barth calls us to glorify God for making irresistible the most imaginable splendor of humans fully alive. God has created humans—corporately and individually—for himself, granting them pure freedom in their pure form. "Again, the world-rule of the fatherly good-will of God, if it is known to be such, does not bear any relationship to caprice. And since its activity is the activity of grace, its almightiness does not in any sense destroy the free activity of the creature. On the contrary, we have to think of the majesty and absoluteness and irresistibility of the divine activity as the confirmation and continually renewed basis of the singularity of the creature to whom God is gracious, and of its worth, and independent activity."[28] Barth again clearly lays out the terrain of created glory. If we deviate from the majesty of our irresistible freedom, we are simply not "ourselves." We hear like expressions in multivarious forms from those around us and in the news, those who in their confessions declare "it wasn't me," or "that's not who I am," or "those actions don't represent the real me." Without the judgment of the *simul*, such alibis lose their steam

---

here because he acts for me" (124). Barth also insists that there can be no severance of being and act: "I cannot simply observe this heavenly-earthly drama of Christ's priestly and kingly work. I myself am involved. If it could be simply observed, this would no longer be what it is" (137). In other words, the potential ethical vacuum (otherwise filled theologically with the vicarious humanity of Christ) would reemerge. Of the fact that existential experiences of faith are not exceptions to the rule but actually prove the rule, Barth acknowledges the non-generic aspect of faith. Christ's faith is always *my* faith or *your* faith. When faith is there, *we* are there" (137). This is obviously an ongoing critique of Barth's on Bultmann, who did not ascribe to the idea that actuality precedes possibility, or that our real faith precedes our experience of it. The fact that both our personal faith and works are both already actual *in Christ* testifies that faith and works are not and should not be divided: "It is not so that I believe in Jesus Christ and then confess, thank, fight. Believing is not something different from these things. Faith itself is our participation in Christ and thus in his action. *Faith involves us in this action*. If we are not involved in this *action*, we do not *believe*. One has falsified the Christian life as soon as he separates faith from life. There is no such thing as a believer which is not confessing, thanking, fighting. There is no life of confessing, thanking, and fighting which is not the life of faith. *In Jesus Christ there is no such separation*" (137–138). Finally, as a reinforcement of our implication in Christ's subjectivity Barth comments on the Catechism: it speaks of Christ as the subject of "this thankfulness, of good works and the Christian life," notes Barth, but it also "speaks of me ... insofar as I share in Christ! It is in this closed circle of this He-I relationship that *this* thankfulness, *these* good works, the *Christian* life, take place. I am involved in his prophetic, priestly and kingly office and now on my side I confess his name, offer my life as a sacrifice of thanksgiving, with free conscience fight against sin and the devil" (140).

28. *CD* III/3, 118.

for two basic reasons: firstly, to the extent that the real person meant to be understood in contradistinction to the false is not solidly established (and I would argue, cannot be solidly established apart from Jesus Christ); and secondly (even when identity in Christ *is* firmly established) to the extent that confessing persons dodge culpability, as if pretending that their false selves are not intimately related to their single subject self in this world. Still, the "those actions are not me" claims can provide educational moments, especially if culpable persons are striving to understand the dark forces underneath what may be, even to them, genuinely puzzling behavior.[29] The *simul* continually teaches us that we can know who we are *not* only when we know who we *are*, in Christ. If, as we quoted Barth in chapter 3, "I am my true self only in the reality of my own free will,"[30] then with Galatians Barth can say the opposite, "if he who is called to freedom . . . follows the lust of the flesh he necessarily does that which he does not will."[31] Barth's *simul* gives the most robust meaning to the words of an old country saying, "Be who you are, because if you ain't who you are, you are who you ain't!"

Too Little Grace and Too Little Judgment

We have seen that for Barth Christian transformation must be very carefully qualified away from typical progressive or zero-sum constructs, and while it has nothing to do with humans judging one another, it has everything to do with the judgment of the cross. Nowhere more than in the sacrament of baptism are we reminded of the good news of Calvary. "When Jesus died and was buried," proclaims Barth, "my old self was also buried in and with him, so that I might begin to live as a new self. I, the subject of my sinful existence, died then. And as a sign of this . . . I am baptized." It is interesting and instrumental to our study that Barth does not mention resurrection in this description of baptism. Instead, it is "the washing away" of the old self which is stressed, signifying the freeing and renewing of the true self.[32] It follows that in Christian sanctification all transformation, even the responsibility of hating and fleeing from sin, is met rather counterintuitively:

---

29. À la Paul in Romans 7. Interestingly, without adapting "the devil made me do it" perspective, and holding to an overall single subject economy, Paul does say twice that it is "not I who do it, but sin living in me" (7:17, 20).

30. *CD* III/2, 180.

31. *CD* IV/2, 370. Galations 5 is another Barth favorite to highlight the *simul*.

32. *Heidelberg*, 100. See 68: God gives himself in Christ "to kill and bury the old sinful and wrong man, and . . . to bring again into being the new obedient man who is pleasing to him and who is the goal of all creation." Again because it is revelatory in nature, re-creation is not, like creation, creation *ex nihilo*.

"it means humbly and seriously, but above all joyfully and thankfully, to let happen what *has* happened in Jesus Christ." Barth concludes, "This is how the old self dies. *He dies from joy at the new self!* The whole 'art' of the Christian life is to learn to repeat: *thou* has borne all sin."[33]

As in the comments directly above, we have recognized in our study that Barth understands the human person as one subject with two subjectivities. He has urged us to consider these two subjectivities as "two total men," old self and new, lest blinded by the one subject, we miss the point. Our false subjectivity, what Barth calls "the abstract I,"[34] haunts us. Our true subject-self is Jesus Christ. No one can find oneself by plumbing the depths of one's self, as if that were even possible. Instead, insists Barth, it is in looking to Jesus Christ alone where we find our true selves. Because he is the real subject-self of every human being, remarks Barth, our knowledge of ourselves is always derivative.[35] Again, just as true as who humans are in Christ is who humans are in the Spirit, which pertains especially to our spiritual bodies that are always present, albeit hidden. We can even posit that what we have called our "material souls" actually signifies our most concrete existence.

We have already noted that transformation does not need a contrast; accordingly, Paul's comment that while our outer *anthropos* is in decay, our inner *anthropos* is being renewed day by day (2 Cor 4:16) indicates that even *in spite of* the corruption of the flesh, renewal is happening in the Spirit.[36] Unless we fall back to zero-sum calculations, this cannot but evidence the existence of two mutually exclusive dimensions in one person. Even though presently blinded by the distortion of sin and evil, in our sanctified imaginations we can visualize every person, created perfectly in Christ: alive, distinct, diverse, free, and in communion with the Triune God and each other in the unadulterated Kingdom, the "inner" dimension of humanity in its pure form. In this created dimension of humanity transformation has always been happening in the Spirit, and as part and parcel of eternity in Christ, always will. Anything less is too little grace!

It should be plain that the objective (width) and subjective (depth) extent of Barth's Christo-anthropological actualism is so radically enormous as to erect critical, albeit under-appreciated, scaffolding for comprehensive

---

33. *Heidelberg*, 132. For Barth, there is no greater sign of Christian sanctification than gratitude: "Thankfulness is the attitude of the man who lives by grace and does not plunge again into the abyss from which he has been saved" (138).

34. *CD* III/4, 388.

35. *CD* I/1, 94: as revealed in Christ's true humanity, notes Barth, "God is the subject from whom human action must receive its new and true name."

36. *CD* IV/4, 7.

judgment. In Barth's view, there is no difference between persons ontologically, and there is only one true ontology: the being and act of Jesus Christ as he has established it for all people.[37] However, there is also a false, unexplainable ontology: the old self, the anti-self. That is why intrinsic to a life of *simul* sanctification is a willingness to live under the good news of God's severe judgment. Returning to our purview are Scripture passages which have been marginalized for centuries by Christians with a static view of grace, i.e., with a wrath-less grace that avoids judgment and does not bring all humans to account (such passages include Matt 12:36; John 12:48; Rom 14:10–12; 2 Cor 5:9–10; and Heb 4:12–13).[38] Assisting our reading of Scripture through Jesus Christ and his crucifixion, the *simul* ensures us no one will "get off the hook" when it comes to judgment. I would argue that even the Old Testament passages of judgment, when subsumed under the cross of Jesus, can be read more coherently.[39] Barth himself takes seriously

---

37. *CD* III/4, 651–52.

38. When it comes to the gospels, we should not be surprised at Barth's favoritism of John. Like First John, John's gospel gives stark oppositional precision and unforgiving exactness to language which congeals Barth's *simul*. For instance, "Those who believe in me will never walk in darkness" (John 11:32); "Those who love me obey my word . . . those who do not love me do not obey my word" (John 14:23–24). Without the *simul*, these oppositional statements have to be interpreted as either permanently concretized categories of people or as on-again off-again categories; either alternative leads to deep confusion and inevitable subterfuge. For instance, if I determine that I love God, yet walk in darkness or disobey him, do I not love God? If I tell people about my sin, will they think I do not love God? The *simul* allows us to securely acknowledge that we are both believers and unbelievers, and our "to the extent rule" describes how we may manifest the reality of our lives in Christ (the reality that I perfectly love and obey God) in my current existence.

39. In a way reminiscent of the Psalmist, "If you, O Lord, should mark iniquities, Lord who could stand?" (130:3), Malachi declares, "But who can endure the day of his coming? Who can stand when he appears? For he will be like a refiner's fire or a launderer's soap." Malachi asserts that not only the people, but also, and perhaps especially, their representatives (the priests), will be purified and refined (3:2–3a). The theme of judgment is revisited at the beginning of the next chapter, "the day is coming, burning like an oven, when all the arrogant and all evildoers will be stubble; the day that comes shall burn them up, says the Lord of hosts, so that it will leave them neither root nor branch" (4:1). The people judged by God are those specifically listed as "sorcerers, adulterer, and perjurers . . . those who defraud laborers of their wages, who oppress the widows and the fatherless, and deprive aliens of justice"? Considering these texts, is there a person who has not committed adultery according to Jesus (Matt 5:28), or who at least has not been indirectly complicit in the unjust systems mentioned? Apart from the *simul*, we are back to the same interpretive problems we faced in 1 John: we would have to say the wrath and judgment of God is not universal, while favoring an apparently arbitrary judgment which parses shades of adultery, murder (*contra* Matt 5:21), etc. The theme of God's universal and all-inclusive judgment is corroborated

the Old Testament theme that the so-called "day of vengeance" *is* the day of redemption.[40] Thankfully, just as Christ represents us with his life, he also represents us in his death. Everything that is not of righteousness and life is actually destroyed and ultimately done away with by our death in Christ's. This includes all evil we have perpetrated on others. and all evil that has been perpetrated on us. Far from being let off the hook, asserts Paul, we were crucified with Christ, that the body of sin might be done away with (Rom 6:6). Just as Jesus Christ is every person's life (Col 3:4), he is also every person's death (Col 3:3). Anything less is too little judgment!

Simul sanctification involves a "be ye separate" mentality which is rooted in the *simul* before it is ever meant to be implemented as a dictate for physical, spatial separation. Fundamentally, spatial separation of humans from Christ or humans from each other has never been the question, but ultimately a spatial separation of false from true.[41] This apparently is what Paul is on about in First Corinthians: in our terms Christians were forgetting the

---

elsewhere in the minor prophets. Zephaniah 1:18 speaks of "the day of the LORD's wrath": "In the fire of his passion the whole earth will be consumed, for a full, a terrible end he will make of all the inhabitants of the earth." The universal judgment presented in Zephaniah includes an unmistakable christological tenor: "The whole world will be consumed . . . *then* I will purify the lips of the peoples, that all of them may call on the name of the LORD. . . . The remnant of Israel will do no wrong; they will speak no lies, nor will deceit be found in their mouths" (Zeph 3:8–9, 13; NIV). The entirety of Zephaniah 3 is arguably a gospel picture of the judgment of grace in Christ. The interpreter who prefers to see the remnant in strictly an exclusionary and I would argue non-christological sense must grapple with the comprehensive and universal nature of destruction in this and other Old Testament judgment passages.

40. See Isa 61:2: "to proclaim the year of the Lord's favor, and the day of vengeance of our God, to comfort all who mourn." The "vengeance" motif was discussed in chapter 7. If, in his synagogue debut in Luke 4, Jesus stopped reading Isaiah 61 after v. 2a ("the year of the Lord's favor"), as Luke could be indicating, it may perhaps be because his hearers were not yet equipped (without the revelation of the cross) to understand the day of vengeance and day of redemption as a piece. See also Isa 63:1–4. In Barth's gospel light, Jer 46:10 can also be understood as keeping all retributive aspects of the atonement inside of an overriding restorative motif ("But that day belongs to the Lord, the LORD Almighty—a day of vengeance, for vengeance on his foes. The sword will devour till it is satisfied"; NIV). Again, as discussed in chapter 7, Barth's view of "satisfaction" communicates a different kind of satisfaction than a God needing to be mollified, as in many penal substitutionary theories.

41. To the extent the testimony of Israel served the latter, its intentions towards cultic purity is a positive witness. Without the *simul* (via the revelation of Jesus Christ and him crucified) however, Israel was easy prey for a dualistic understanding of the righteous and the wicked which could only breed self-righteousness. Paul thereby attempts to reappropriate dualist understandings from the Psalms into language of the universal *simul*, e.g., Romans 3:23–24.

simul, failing to claim the distinctiveness of the old self from the new, living as if there was no right and no wrong.[42] In other words, they were living as if there was no past, present or future judgment. This is where Jesus' words in his high priestly prayer—"for their sakes I sanctify myself"—ring truest. That these words are words of judgment would be borne out in the imminent death of the Savior, enlightening his earlier announcement: "I came into this world for judgment" (John 9:39).[43] Barth speaks of God's judgment as "the light which falls from above upon the tangled skein of your life," and continuing in the first person from God's perspective, "Condemning you, I exonerate you. Judging you, I accept you, slaying you, I make you alive."[44] Here new light is shed on the word sanctification (*hagiazo*) itself, which can mean to purify *or* to separate. With progressive schemes of sanctification, purification can only be gradual. Equally deficient is separation in non-*simul* terms, which can only be spatial. The result is a judging of the

---

42. CD IV/2, 370–371. The believer is meant to mutually recognize that what Barth calls "(the subject of sin), the old man, is done away . . . in the death of Christ, so that they can no longer serve sin." The "can no longer" is meant to be taken as fully literally as Christ's death and resurrection; if disobedience occurs, it is expressly *not* because there are legitimate grounds for it. Regarding 1 Corinthians 6:14ff (the "be ye separate" passage) this necessitates that between righteousness and unrighteousness, light and darkness there can be "no *sharing*, no *fellowship*, no *harmony*, no *common ground*" (italics are translated from Barth's original Greek). The delineation is so stark that Barth does not consider the one person who is the overall subject of the old self and new self to be the "common ground," as in some kind of third entity. Any attempts at harmonizing light and darkness into such a false third word (Christ being the only "third word") would cause both to lose "their absolutely distinctive antithetical character," inevitably resulting in an "intermingling" which blurs creation, makes goodness parasitic to evil (*CD* IV/3.2, 704–706). Accordingly, Barth sees a Christo-anthropological understanding where faithfulness really and truly is the faithfulness of *God* shared with *iustus* humanity. The identifier "the faithful," for instance, is meant to be grasped in "absolute" terms (nothing but faithful), before any "substantive" (what we could call a "to the extent" meaning) or general adjectival meaning (the faithful as meaning the category Christian) is given (*CD* IV/1, 749). By starting with what is real, the Corinthian church should refuse any softening of the *simul* antithesis (see *CD* IV/3.2, 488), any efforts to compromise the mutual exclusivity of the oppositional determinations (IV/3.2, 510).

43. In the words of John 9:39, Jesus arguably identifies himself less as the judge and more as one putting himself under judgment. In John 12:47 he states, "I came not to judge the world, but to save the world." Together these are encapsulated in John 12:48, "The one who rejects me and does not receive my word has a judge; on the last day the word I have spoken will serve as a judge." In other words, Jesus does not come to judge, but by unity of his person and work, he is an implicit judgment in and of himself—he is the Word that will prove to be sharper than any two edged sword (Heb 4:12–14).

44. *CD* II/2, 690. Quoted also in chapter 8.

other according to self-assessed comparisons of purity, as if purity (*totus iustus*) is not already fully intact for all people in Christ, or as if a single human subject could be *sola totus peccator*. Only in *simul* parlance (i.e., by the testimony of Jesus' Christ's death) can both of these words have their fullest complementary effect: to purify is to separate, to separate to purify. In extreme examples where the church has chosen to accommodate "the old self" and ignore the ontological distinction between new and old, right and wrong, it is apparent Paul can endorse physical spatial separation (1 Cor 5:11–13, 2 Cor 6:14–15). Again, spatial separation (as if one subject could be classified as distinctly wicked) only serves the overriding commitment to *simul* separation—to the theological separation of the old self from the new self in the one subject, to which Christians are supposed to hold one another, and upon which all of Barth's ethics are built.[45] As believers walk in newness of life together, albeit inconsistently, the light points to a greater brilliance than the sum of its parts, so that Paul can even exhort his flock with the unflickering indicative: "be blameless and innocent, children of God without blemish in this midst of a crooked and depraved generation, in which you shine like stars in the world" (Phil 2:15).

The Prince of Darkness Grim

Part of the purpose of this book has been to provide Barth's biblical and theological basis for raising humanity into its proper heavenly sphere via the gospel of Jesus Christ and him crucified. At the same time, and with the same biblical and theological foundation, the constant desire is to bring the heavenly reality back to bear on humanity's earthly struggle. Barth's study of angels helps us grasp the *simul* by filling out the heavenly and earthly reality of *iustus* human existence. If Barth is correct, and all humans remain in their original glory (created in Christ, as in Eph 2:10) throughout their *simul* existence; and, if, to quell all doubt, the reconciliation of the world by God means all creation is reconstituted in Christ; and, if who we are in Christ is "the basic and comprehensive determination" of our "true being";[46] then the contrasting forces we face in this fallen world spur us to

---

45. Against the idea that physical spatial separation from less holy people is Paul's primary, general concern, he clarifies: "I wrote you in my letter not to associate with sexually immoral persons—not at all meaning the immoral of this world, or the greedy and robbers, or idolaters, since you would then need to go out of the world" (1 Cor 5:9–10).

46. *CD* III/2, 158.

acknowledge just how bad sin is and how darkly shrouded in darkness is our existence in this "present evil age."

If we are to take seriously with Barth the gospel as the anthropological revelation of Jesus Christ and him crucified, it is only the *simul* derived from this Word which can assist us in embracing the indicative truth of a humanity *totus iustus* without falling prey to an over-realized eschatology. In other words, in view of the human *totus iustus*, anything less than the opposition of *totus peccator* cannot provide a sane estimate to the theological concerns of Docetism, Gnosticism, and other concepts which invariably keep humans (contrary to the theme of this chapter) so heavenly minded that they are no earthly good. Refusing to dull in any way the "sharpness of the antithesis" between the spheres of light and darkness, Barth will also not allow (any more than he will entertain the supra-temporal as a "self-enclosed middle") any suspicions of dualism which seek to artificially posture his view "as a kingdom of spiritual truths and eternal ideas" or as "a static backdrop to world history."[47]

Barth has continually put forth the claim that "the objective ground of our knowledge of nothingness is really Jesus Christ Himself."[48] Only with the right starting point—only with the one who "made himself nothing" (Phil 2:7)—can anyone apprehend the gravity of sin and its abhorrent consequences:

> When seen in the light of Jesus Christ, the concrete form in which nothingness is active and revealed is the sin of man as his personal act and guild, his aberration from the grace of God and its command, his refusal of the gratitude he owes to God and the concomitant freedom and obligation, his arrogant attempt to be his own master, provider and comforter, his unhallowed lust for what is not his own, the falsehood, hatred and pride in which he is enmeshed in relation to his neighbor, the stupidity to which he is self-condemned, and a life which follows the course thereby determined on the basis of the necessity thus imposed. In the light of Jesus Christ, it is impossible to escape the truth that we ourselves as sinners have become the victims and servants of nothingness, sharing its nature and producing and extending it.[49]

---

47. *CD* III/3, 468.

48. *CD* III/3, 306.

49. *CD* III/3, 305–6. Note in this quotation Barth's acknowledgement of humans as both "victims and servants" of sin. This section of *CD* III/3, "The Knowledge of Nothingness" (especially 302–311) is a critical section for Barth to lay out human sin not as the result of a passive defect, but as an offence to God in which each person is

If an over-realized eschatology fails to take sin seriously, what of an under-realized eschatology? Ironically, in a way the *simul* avoids, an under-realized eschatology has in common with its opposite an underestimation of sin. Under-realized eschatological proposals (*partim-partim* schemes of progressive sanctification which debunk the idea of humanity as *totus iustus*) simply have too small a frame to consider the unfathomable extent of humanity as *totus peccator*.[50] To put it another way, progressive sanctification models, utilizing a zero-sum perspective, pride themselves on paying attention to what is before them in the immanent sphere; unfortunately in their hesitancy to compare the "reality" of sin to an already established (non-hypothetical) transcendent reality, they can only grasp the degree of sin and evil that their sight will allow.[51]

If symptomatic to the loss of real transcendence is the taking of sin and evil less seriously than the *simul* demands, this inevitably leads to an increased susceptibility of humans to be deceived by transcendent evil powers. We are "unconcerned in face of it," Barth warns in relation to satanic activity; we ignore the designs of nothingness, we "persuade ourselves that there is nothing in it, that there is no devil . . . no evil and demons" who have power in our "nations and societies," or in the "psychical and physical" realm of human lives and relationships. "Nothingness," Barth continues, "lies also and supremely by trivializing and concealing itself, spreading abroad a carefree optimism. . . . Nothingness rejoices when it notices that it is not noticed, that it is boldly demythologised, that humanity thinks it can tackle its lesser and greater problems with a little morality and medicine and psychology and aesthetics, with progressive politics or occasionally a philosophy of unprecedented novelty."[52]

Of course Barth also warns against the opposite, giving evil too much due, i.e., allowing the pendulum to sweep past the the semi-parallelism of Barth's *simul* into a dualism: as though evil, jibes Barth, could really "found and organise a kingdom, as though its powers and forces were really agents which could contradict and withstand the grace of God and the salvation of the creature . . . Let us only admire it for its independent truth! Let us

---

complicit, even while acknowledging the work of the adversary who victimizes us.

50. See *CD* III/3, 307; Barth calls this frame the "objective basis": "Unless Jesus Christ is their objective basis, our own knowledge and acknowledgment will bear no real relation to the alien and adversary here involved, nor to the insult which it is his very nature to offer to God; and we ourselves shall certainly accept no responsibility for this insult."

51. See *CD* III/3, 307: "No abstract law of God . . . could reveal this to me"; and 309; "The sickness is disclosed with the cure. How else could we see it?"

52. *CD* III/3, 525–26.

only integrate the devil and the kingdom of demons and evil into the same system in which elsewhere and according to their different character we also treat of God and Christ and true man and the angels!"[53]

Paul tells the Corinthians not to be "outwitted" by Satan's schemes or "ignorant of his designs" (2 Cor 2:11). When it comes to perceiving our lives and the world, the *simul* helps us maintain a keen sensitivity to evil, to not be surprised by it, and to take it deadly seriously without respecting and fearing it as ultimately true and real. By the revelation of Jesus Christ, and with the "sword of the Spirit," believers together learn can learn to separate and distinguish light from darkness.[54] In the armor of God—which is effectively the "true reality"[55] of their union with Christ—believers in the "breastplate of righteousness" (Eph 6:14) and assured of their *iustus* humanity in the Savior are trained in readiness to face "all the flaming arrows of the evil one" (6:16). When it comes to the "illegitimate and perverse demonic powers which imitate and rival the heavenly," remarks Barth, "although we still have to fight (Eph 6:12) we do not need to fear them (8:38f.)."[56]

Actualism before Activism

In this chapter I have suggested exegeting our lives most accurately by looking back through the prism of Christ's humanity, which determines ours. Christians intentionally engaged in *simul* sanctification can take up Barth's encouragement to see their own activity in God's own being-in-act on their behalf. Whether experiencing the highs of their *iustus* determination or the lows of their *peccator* determination, because of Christ's *simul* solidarity with the world, Christians may in turn engage with the world fully equipped with the christological grounding of each person's truth and lie, joy and agony. In other words, for Barth, "seeing through" to others' created glory is the very opposite of being blind and callous to their suffering. Contrary to Platonic conceptions, Jesus' solidarity with us translates to our own meaningful solidarity with others in happiness and in sorrow. Conversely, a church that falsely short-changes the extent of Christ's solidarity with others is a church that will not only be "incapable of weeping with them who

---

53. *CD* III/3, 526. By Barth's semi-parallelism I mean to connote nothing more than the *simul*'s inherent asymmetry. Also, Barth's final phrase in this quotation is not to be missed in reference to our earlier consideration of true humanity and angels.

54. *CD* III/3, 525.

55. *CD* IV/4, 7.

56. *CD* III/3, 459.

weep, it is also incapable at bottom of rejoicing with them who rejoice."[57] In this vein, might we go so far as to say that the best efforts of social justice are rooted in our awareness of the *simul*? Barth answers this question in the affirmative. Of all people, the Christian is most clear about the contrast between the righteousness of the Kingdom and the "as of yet unredeemed existence around him." It follows that the Christian is more keen to address the issues of the "prison or mad-house." In fact, asserts Barth, it is precisely "because the Christian hopes for the ultimate and definitive, he also hopes for the temporal and provisional."[58]

Understanding that our ambassadorship of Christ in this world, unlike that of the angels, is fraught with *simul* incongruency, how can we go about interacting with typically disenfranchised people in ways that avoid the paternalistic or patronizing approach of so much Christian ministry? How can we in the church avoid doing more harm than good in our efforts towards social justice and, to use Barth's words, "sanctification and conversion"? After the Conclusion of our study I will offer a short section, "Final Reflections," touching again on these themes.

---

57. *CD* III/1, 407; see Romans 12:15.
58. *CD* IV/3.2, 938.

Conclusion

Consummation

*"It is the same revelation which we have had,
but it is now without a veil"*[1]

WE HAVE REACHED THE CULMINATING POINT OF OUR STUDY. CHAPTER 1 assessed Barth's adaptation of Luther's *simul*, recognizing it to be more Christ-defined and thereby its scope more universal. Chapter 2 introduced the consideration of a christological *simul iustus et peccator* from which our human duality derives. Within the Chalcedonian definition we sought to establish with Barth a double duality; first that of God and human in one person (the traditional concept) and secondly, that of true human-false human in one person. Chapter 3 demonstrated the dangers of gradualism and synergism avoided by *simul* sanctification, as well as the benefits regarding Barth's Spirit-charged program for sanctification and conversion. Chapter 4 furthered our discussion of Barth's Christo-anthropological actualism, so critical for understanding Barth's universal application of the *simul* and so easily misread by theologians implementing less actualistic frameworks. Chapter 5 compared Barth to the monergist view of Luther and the synergist view of Wesley, questioning whether Barth's paradigm is a hybrid of the two poles or something altogether different. Chapter 6 entailed a thorough consideration of Barth's view of human freedom and the *simul*, especially as it relates to epistemological transformation in the Christian disciple. Chapter 7 submitted that Barth's theology of the cross, in its single subject economy, allowed him to maintain the severe and mutually exclusive determinations of the old human and new human inside of the one human being Jesus Christ. Barth's assessment of the cross makes exceedingly clear

1. *CD* II/1, 631.

the similarities and the differences between Chalcedonian Christology and what I have termed "Chalcedonian anthropology"; I sought to demonstrate that the latter duality is proven by resurrection revelation to be ultimately provisional in nature. Chapter 8 thereby offered a literally *new* perspective on the atonement, buttressed through a reading of Barth's association of Job and Jesus. Chapter 9 detailed, mostly from *CD* III, how I understood Barth's position regarding the annulment of the *simul* as well as its beginning. By investigating Barth's doctrine of creation, chapter 10 put forth the assertion that Barth's *simul* is reflective of the original antithesis between God and nothingness, under which Christ first placed himself so that we would know both his solidarity in the darkness and his victory over it. Chapter 11, from his analysis of Genesis 1 and Genesis 2, concluded Barth's Christ-defined matrix of *iustus* and *peccator* humanity to be emblematic of human birth but expressly not of human creation. It was clear that Barth's three forms of eternity hold together in distinct but unified fashion, so that even the more pronounced "distinctiveness" of the supra-temporal form cannot in any way fracture its unity with the other two. Chapter 12 acknowledged that, while humanity's anthro-dimensional existence in the supra-temporal realm includes the *peccator* dimension, on Barth's view it is "the eternal redemption"[2] of the Creator and Redeemer Jesus Christ that dictates the terms. In other words, the *peccator* dimension of humanity is the outlier; in the service of evil it can obscure and twist, but it has no root in creation, no ability to displace the good even in this life, and no ultimate future. It was the ongoing transcendence of good, *iustus*, humanity presented by Barth which allowed us to enjoin the intersection of Barth's Christo-anthropological actualism and *theosis*, considering his description of the angels as potentially his most forthright description of the human *iustus* determination. If chapter 13 endeavored to furnish us with new eyes in reading Scripture with Barth's actualism, chapter 14 hopefully further equipped us towards successfully navigating a confusing world by learning to see our environment through the lens of a christological *simul*. My introduction of a three heavens cosmology, derived from Barth, hopefully complemented Barth's understanding of time and eternity and contributed to pulling our perception of transcendence and eschatology from the future into the present.

Speaking of future, it is Barth's preference to use the word "Redemption," as in the title of his proposed Volume V, as an eschatological word synonymous with consummation. Again, this in no way means to communicate that redemption is not fully and conclusively accomplished, but it is Barth's recognition that on this side of the *eschaton*, we are still trapped

---

2. *CD* II/1, 209, cited earlier.

in the matrix of the *simul*. As Barth himself notes, redemption itself is a word "which presupposes an imprisonment."[3] "Redemption," therefore, is the consummation of the revelation of Christ's finished work (i.e., the final manifestation of the release of the captives).

Judgment Now

It is always a miracle when, in spite of utter perversion, the sinner may by the Spirit of him who raised Christ Jesus from the dead live in his or her true humanity, the *totus iustus* humanity that never recedes and always dwells above with Christ. Whereas in our slothful perversion we can only act disobediently and in ways unpleasing to God, and whereas in our righteousness we can only act obediently and in ways well-pleasing to God, we find ourselves "freed from our misery to the extent that in Him we too are new men and therefore the subjects of new acts." When it comes to our *simul* sanctification, we can know that any "new" acts of ours can only be rooted in our true humanity in Christ.[4] At the same time, because we simultaneously live in the overlap of our slothful perversion, we can never definitively categorize any of our motives or actions as purely new.[5] Again we note Barth's familiar phrase, "to the extent." Because of the two determinations at play in our lives, the product will always be mixed; our acts are good *to the extent* that they are. And until Judgment Day, the nature of that "extent" rests in the hands of the Sanctified One. How can pure and brackish water both come from the same mouth (Jas 3:11)? This is unexplainable, but it is also a fact of our contradicted existence. Words and acts will always be somewhat ambiguous in the age of the *simul*. Humility and discernment is required, as is a continual refocusing on Jesus Christ.[6] Barth not only wants us to know that God shares our *peccator* humanity, but that God also sees through our perversion to our true nature. It is on this basis that we can claim that, just as God sees through to our real selves, Christian faith "sees through the imperfections of being to its perfection."[7] It is for this reason, in spite of the existential, "*simul*" testimony of James (regarding pure and brackish water from the same mouth), that Barth can praise James in superlative terms as an unparalleled New Testament writing when it comes to

3. *Heidelberg*, 125.

4. *CD* IV/2, 490.

5. *CD* III/4, 536. Opines Barth, "even in our best activity we are perverted men in a perverted world."

6. *CD* IV/3.1, 383. See *CD* IV/1, 445–46, for Barth's indictment of a human being exalting oneself as judge.

7. *CD* III/1, 380.

presenting the gospel "so emphatically and unwaveringly" as a "divine claim" on every person. Instead of dwelling on *the face of our birth* (Gk) in the mirror, counsels Barth, James means for us to see through to our "proper face" (what we could call our *iustus* face) which can be seen in the Word; the epistle is urging us to reflect on the law of liberty, the "perfect law" of freedom, where each person's true identity is located in the Word, in Christ, as a "real hearer, and therefore a doer." It is here, insists Barth, where "we find ourselves as those who may and must do what they do in freedom . . . as those who are willing and ready, but also able, in the last resort to live our own lives."[8]

With all that has been said about Barth's logic of "to the extent" in interpreting ambiguous actions, and with his blurring of the lines between believers and unbelievers, it seems pertinent at this last juncture to speak positively concerning Barth's affirmation of real Christian growth and even progress, rightly understood. We asserted in the Introduction that on Barth's view, who we are in Christ and who we are in the Spirit are not two different things. Because we have arrived at Barth's understanding that flesh is opposed to Spirit only in its *peccator* iteration, we can also hold to the unity of Spirit and created, *iustus* flesh. This latter union constitutes our spiritual bodies—what we have alternately called our material souls—which are always present. Strictly from this ground, we now have a healthy non-Platonic grasp of Paul's adage: "For the flesh desires what is contrary to the Spirit, and the Spirit what is contrary to the flesh."[9] To wit, we could describe *simul* sanctification with Barth as "the struggle of the Spirit against the flesh and for the soul which must be saved at all costs."[10]

In the midst of the conflict, when God's word of final judgment is heard *in the present*, Christians are able to miraculously discriminate between the false and true person that each one is in one's *simul* contradiction: "How could man himself make this distinction? He is both the one and the other of these two creatures, and therefore he cannot separate himself from himself, freeing his real self from his false self, pulling himself out of the quagmire by his own forelock. But God can make this distinction and achieve this rescue, and He does so. Intervening, God sides with the former against the latter . . . summoning his good creature against the transgressor."[11]

God intervenes in this moment to validate the genuine "character" of his child; he intervenes against "the abstract I" because he *has* intervened

---

8. *CD* II/2, 588–89. See Jas 1:22–25, including Gk translation for 1:23 (NRSV note).
9. Galatians 5:17 (NIV translation).
10. *CD* III/4, 388.
11. *CD* III/4, 236.

in Christ.¹² On Barth's view, only the command from the Commander "has the significance and power of revealing transgression as something essentially alien, of making man independent and responsible in relation to it, of making him actively react towards it."¹³ God's Word pierces the Christian's "bad subjectivity"¹⁴ like a "battle-cry,"¹⁵ notes Barth, bolstering the believer's confidence in attaining "definite possibilities," empowering the believer to "secure bridgeheads within the confusion." And what is the overall result? Hopefully, says Barth, the Christian will live "a little better than hitherto." The believer might be able to "avoid at least some of his previous mistakes, renounce at least some of the rigid or dissolute practices in which he has hitherto lived, give up at least some of the follies and wickednesses which have hitherto sprung unchecked from the sources of his deep unwisdom, compensate for at least some of the harm he has done and take some intelligent counter-action."¹⁶

Growing in Discrimination and Certainty

The Spirit continually speaks truth to human beings. "Become who you are," says Barth, is shorthand for "Grow into your character"—the "form that already in the eyes of the eternal God and therefore in reality you are what you are."¹⁷ In the words of the Apostle, we are to "grow up in every way" into Christ our head (Eph 4:15); in doing so, we become ourselves.¹⁸ Jesus Christ, the rightful center of human existence, grants Christians "the gift of a discrimination which with growing certainty can select what is genuinely and necessarily our own."¹⁹ A person's character is purely a work of God's grace, states Barth, "[f]or it is one of the signs of His participation in the life of His creature. For this reason, and in gratitude for it, it is to be discovered, affirmed, willed and practised by us. For precisely the same reason, however,

---

12. *CD* III/4, 388.
13. *CD* III/4, 236.
14. *CD* III/4, 391.
15. *CD* III/4, 236.
16. *CD* III/4, 238.
17. *CD* III/4, 388.
18. See *CD* IV/2, 660: Barth asks, "How can the community be summoned to grow up into Him? How can it do this? According to v. 16 it can do it because its growth is already taking place quite apart from its own action." This obviously reflects our corollaries of Barth's actualism: actuality precedes possibility, and the exception proves the rule.
19. *CD* III/4, 389.

it cannot be willed and practised for its own sake."²⁰ Frustrations will invariably come, but the Holy Spirit provides believers "the power to wait daily for the revelation of what they already are, of what they became on the day of Golgotha."²¹ Freed from the burden of self-justification, and humbled by justification proper, the grace of Jesus Christ and him crucified "constantly restores and renews" the believer.²² On Barth's view, this refreshment by the Spirit happens especially in Christian community; "it happens within a human gathering, and therefore happens to [individuals]."²³ It is plain that *simul* sanctification is a corporate educational process which involves Christians learning together, by the Spirit, to discern the oppositional determinations at play in their lives and world (and yes, in their churches too!).

Hopefully Barth's warnings against judging each other and judging ourselves have not dismissed the importance of judgment. The gift of discrimination now given to believers is only relative to the final manifestation of "be ye separate" in the otherworldly "dimension of eternity," what we have called the second heaven. But we must ask: does this perspective of the second heaven push judgment off to the future in such a way as to render our present existence pointless? It behooves us to remember that the second heaven is just as present as the first. Even though we may employ the tactic of thinking away one dimension to grasp the distinctiveness of the other, we ultimately are stymied in our attempts to think of eternal dimensions in temporal terms. Living under the judgment of the second heaven means, with the Psalmist, lamenting that the poor get poorer, being confused that crime seems to pay, despairing that perpetrators are "getting away with murder," and yet all the while being assured by the Holy Spirit that the implicit judgment of the *simul*—that of Jesus Christ and him crucified—exists *now* and later, not just later. Barth obviously does not want us to tamp down our God-given sense of justice, but only to recognize that it derives from the cross, as illuminated fully and clearly on the Day of judgment (our "second heaven"). In fact, Barth—like the author of Ecclesiastes—envisions an atmosphere of justice that will far exceed any semblance of justice we have witnessed in this world.²⁴ Meanwhile, walking by faith, we are forced

---

20. *CD* III/4, 389–90.

21. *CD* IV/2, 330.

22. *CD* IIII/4, 239.

23. *CD* I/2, 697; see *CD* IV/1, 688. Barth is obviously keen to keep the church within God's reconciling economy of *pro nobis* before *pro me*.

24. Ecclesiastes 3:16–17 reads, "Moreover I saw under the sun that in the place of justice, wickedness was there, and in the place of righteousness, wickedness was there as well. I said in my heart, God will judge the righteous and the wicked, for he has appointed a time for every matter, and for every work." Again the second heaven is

to acknowledge that the inherent effects of human sin and disobedience which have been and will be decisively judged are often as imperceptible as the meaning and purpose of this current human existence.

Whether it is the parental structure early in life or the justice system later, both set up external consequences to show the intrinsic consequences of sin and disobedience; both are instituted by God as a means to witness to the judgment, striving to protect the integrity of human sanctity, pointing out to their charges that sin hurts others and themselves. Both of these institutions, like the church, are deeply flawed, but to the degree that they can use the *simul* to call out the wrong without categorizing a child as rotten, or to avoid defining a person by one's mistakes, they can have a positive influence under judgment of the second heaven, apprehending the implicit discrimination of the *simul*. Seeking to avoid natural theology, we can only read back into our lives and world with the eyes of faith under the authority of the true north of humanity, "Christ, who is our life." Only by the Holy Spirit can we apprehend the extent of human correlation to this reference point, all the while acknowledging the inevitable imperfection of our discernment of reality compared to how it really is.

The "real self," insists Barth, is the human "soul that lives by the Spirit of God." The clarity of the final judgment, which we all live under, presently escapes us. In the midst of "mutability . . . increase, decrease, change and novelty," Barth likens our lives to a voyage in process toward the final manifestation of our true selves which will only be seen fully and accurately in "the eternal consummation." In the Spirit, and in the midst of the world's choppy mutability, our souls are set by the North Star of Christ where we find "continuity, discipline and moulding" on the way to new shores which will always be new. "Who has not continually to discover himself afresh?," Barth questions, and "Who will ever cease to do this? In this respect too, we must consider the truth that 'it doth not yet appear what we shall be' (1 John 3:2)." In the meantime, asserts Barth pejoratively, "If a man regards his character as a final magnitude which he can survey and dispose and conducts himself accordingly—"I am made that way!"—he is again confusing it with his nature and himself, his soul with his small ego."[25]

---

cosmologically located between Barth's supra- and post-temporal eternities. Whether this otherworldly dimension or connection (*einem jenseitigen Zusammenhang*) is an extension of the supra-temporal or simply a transitional space where the *simul* still exists does not really matter, but apart from the second heaven, there is no accountability in Barth for the passing of the supra-temporal (the age of the *simul*) into the post-temporal (which is unadulterated existence), opening Barth up to the charge of triumphalism.

25. *CD* III/4, 389.

A New Creation

It is in the third heaven where the rule reigns and righteousness dictates in ways which in our experience can only be the exception.[26] For us, this third heaven is simultaneous to the second heaven, the dimension of judgment and clarity, where sin and death have a past but no future, and it is also simultaneous to the first. Even if it is from the first heaven that we receive the revelation of the second, and thereby the third, we can live now by the eternal Spirit from the third dimension, under the second, and into the first. We began by noting with Barth that the presence of God in this world is "the presence of the crucified"; the revelation of Jesus Christ's passion in this supra-temporal realm will be filled out in our lives in purposeful yet untold ways (Col 1:24), even while we recognize that his witness points us to life before the *simul* (pre-temporal) and beyond it (post-temporal). In Jesus Christ, "the same yesterday, today and forever" (Heb 13:8), Barth has given us a true christological anthropology and a theological matrix to see through to the pure form of humanity. In this light, might Barth give us permission to adjust his adage slightly, adding a parenthetical phrase: "I was and still am the old man . . . I am and will be (and always was) the new man"?[27] However Christians might grow in glory in our own *simul* sanctification, they can know that they are never becoming someone different from who they already really are. This is where we can declare with Barth, armed with the redeeming work of Jesus Christ, that Creation is true gospel: "God has created nothing to which he could only say No because of its inherent unreality. God's creation is affirmed by Him because it is real, and it is real because it is affirmed by Him. Creation is actualisation."[28]

What Barth calls "quickening" is when the "transformation that has happened to us" in Christ comes to bear in our lives by the Holy Spirit,[29] renewing us in the image of our Creator.[30] Quickening happens under the sound of the divine summons; it is our catching up to the reality of what *is*—becoming what has become.[31] Hopefully it has become increasingly clear that this

---

26. We consider 2 Peter 3:13 an apt description of the third heaven; it is where "righteousness is at home" or, alternatively described, the "home of righteousness" (NIV) we look forward to.

27. See *Humanity of God*, 59: Barth describes the gospel as "the message of the eternal love of God directed to us men as we at all time were, are, and shall be."

28. *CD* III/1, 345.

29. See *CD* IV/1, 648: Barth associates "quickening" with "enlightening" and "awakening" when speaking of the power of the Holy Spirit.

30. *CD* III/1, 204.

31. *CD* III/1, 340.

"catching up" of *simul* sanctification is abjectly opposed to a "capping off" conceptualization so prominent in synergist thought. Neither does renewing, as Athanasius taught years ago, have anything to do with re-doing.[32]

Because, on Barth's view, the *simul* exists in that otherworldly "dimension of eternity," so does the final judgment. Emerging out of our confusing world, this dimension is the realm of perfect clarity, what we have introduced as the second heaven. But what will happen when every human being, with clarity and yet still in *simul* contradiction, appears before the judgment seat of Christ (2 Cor 5:10; Rev 1:7)? Barth is not slow to describe the wrath of God's judgment as a consuming fire. There will be utmost accountability for all human complicity in evil, whether conscious or unconscious.[33] Under the "justice of His grace,"[34] the fear of our being totally exposed can only be mitigated by the context—the *identity* of the One who is judging us: "There can thus be no doubt that those who know Him will look and move forward to His judgment, fire and testing, not with hesitant but with assured, unequivocally positive and therefore joyful expectation. If they wait for His grace which judges, and which cuts with pitiless severity in this judgment, they still wait for His grace."[35]

Believers yearn for this consummation—the final freeing from contradiction.[36] But is it possible at this point, judged by the one who suffers the *simul* with us,[37] every human will be quickened before the throne of the Lamb who was slain?[38] Barth relates, "Only when the secret of God is

---

32. As mentioned in the Introduction, to "recreate humanity afresh" (Athanasius) could not mean starting over from scratch any more than Christ's incarnate death necessarily means re-incarnation. This is in line with Barth's view that only creation, not reconciliation, is *ex nihilo*.

33. *CD* IV/3.2, 921.

34. *CD* IV/3.2, 928.

35. *CD* IV/3.2, 922.

36. See *Heidelberg*, 90: "Faith, then, is an *anticipation* of our status at the last judgment . . . I look forward to it, thankful that I am on the way to it. I may already know what my sentence will be in the last judgment. In Christ it has already been spoken, even though for me the final act of judgment still lies in the future" (italics original).

37. See *CD* IV/3.2, 925: Barth speaks of Jesus Christ as the representative of all men quick, and all men dead. Might we conclude that the "quick and the dead" is the *simul* in *nuce*?

38. If the *simul* originates at the boundary between pre-temporal and supra-temporal eternity, then the *simul* ends at the boundary of supra-temporal and post-temporal eternity. On Barth's view, it is apparently in the dimension of the latter frontier where the final judgment occurs. Once the boundary of judgment is crossed into the unadulterated post-temporal, there will be no sad tears or scarring memories. In the meantime, "the Lamb slain not only stood, but still stands, between the throne of God

present as the Lamb which is the Lion can the majesty of God even over the heavenly creation be unequivocally seen"[39] While Barth would not contend that everyone will believe in that moment, he may indeed contend that no one will truly believe *until* that moment. Because of the all-pervasive distortion affecting God's beloved creatures, Barth apparently does not expect people in this realm to fully perceive their *peccator* humanity, crucified with Christ, in the context of their *iustus* humanity alive in Christ. Indeed, to know the former without the latter could only be crushing. Barth paints the scene: "So we wait and hope—in respect of our death—to be manifest with him (Jesus Christ who is raised from the dead), in the glory of judgment, and also of the grace of God. That will be the new thing: that the veil which now lies over the whole world and thus over our life (tears, death, sorrow, crying, grief) will be taken away, and God's counsel (already accomplished in Jesus Christ) will stand before our eyes, the object of our deepest shame, but also of our joyful thanks and praise."[40]

The trajectory of Barth's work would appear to suggest he imagines that all human beings, in spite of their struggles to see and believe in this earthly dimension, will make a free, exhaustively human, "Doubting Thomas" transition—from the challenge of believing as seeing to the exclamation of seeing as believing.[41] On Barth's view, sanctification's consummation does not occur for us until the veil is dropped, and the "it is finished" of creation and reconciliation converge with the "It is done" of redemption (Rev 21:6): "this transition and transformation is the unveiling and glorifying of the life which in his time man has already had in Christ."[42] Until then, *to the extent that we have ears to hear now what Barth calls "the last trump," we will be changed.*

---

and the heavenly and earthly cosmos" (CD IV/3.1, 397).

39. CD III/3, 471.

40. Busch, *Karl Barth*, 488.

41. CD II/1, 630–31, cited above. To reiterate the internal logic of the passage (John 20:29), while Jesus cites the blessing for those who do not see and yet believe, he expressly does not deny that all, like Thomas, will see. Again, as genuine participants in Christ's victory over evil, humans are meant to freely "repent and believe" from the midst of their *simul* contradiction; this is just as true in the second heaven (even with perfect clarity) as it is in the first heaven (as per Thomas).

42. CD III/2, 624. Barth attaches his comment concerning "the last trump" to 1 Cor 15:52.

Final Reflections

As anticipated in the Preface, my focus in setting forth *SIMUL* sanctification has been to articulate and defend my hypothesis about Barth's Christo-anthropological actualism and how it provides a superlative framework for reckoning with sin and evil in life of the Christian disciple. More broadly, I hope Barth's universal application of the *simul* has provided theological insight for the puzzlement of fruitful good in unbelievers and monstrous evil in believers. Correspondingly, I have only begun in the last chapters to consider concrete implications of *simul* sanctification in face of practical, everyday challenges and cultural issues humans face in what I have called the first heaven, that "fatal middle stretch between creation and consummation."[1] Another book would be in order to do justice to the *simul*'s application to "first heaven problems." However, I seek here to offer some brief reflections—not unlike Kierkegaard's "unscientific postscript"—related to Christian ministry. How can we as the church proceed to engage the world in light of a universal and fully filled out *simul iustus et peccator*?

1. "Christ's Love Compels Us": Motivation for Ministry

My view throughout our study has been that Christo-anthropological actualism intrinsically protects Barth from a mechanical, or objectifying, universalism without debunking predestination as he understands it. "The 'book' spoken of by God in Exodus 32:32," states Barth, "has always, and quite rightly, been connected with the election of grace . . . it is described as the 'book of life' in the New Testament (Phil 4:3, Rev 3:5, 17:8, 20:12, 15). One's name may not be in this book. It can be blotted out from it. And yet there are not two columns but only one." When it comes to predestination, Barth reinforces, there is not a "death-column."[2]

---

1. *CD* III/2, 304, cited earlier.
2. *CD* II/2, 16. In Exodus 32:32 Moses pleads: "please forgive them for their sin,

By putting so much weight on what Christ has done for the world, Barth's eschatologically charged vision allows him to work backwards from this finished work. Our study has endeavored to show the important benefits of such an approach for sanctification. However, by acknowledging that someone might be blotted out, is not Barth taking a huge theological risk? What if it were proven in the end, in the judgment of the second heaven, that some *are* blotted out? If it was to happen (that some were blotted out from the life column) it would be in Barth's view fundamentally irrational and unexplainable, because there is only one column. Still, knowing what we know, Barth's eschatology would only be unwarranted if 1) there was no biblical support for all being ultimately saved; and 2) if there was evidence, biblical or otherwise, that any human being, even one, is in hell. It is far from irresponsible to hope for all to be in the third (unadulterated) heaven, even Scripture does as much (e.g., 1 Tim 2:4, 2 Pet 3:9, 1 Cor 15:22). Of course in order to maintain this hope, a larger frame is required than just what we see and experience here from birth to death. As we have put forth in this book, Barth obviously believes Scripture provides such a frame.[3] He has presented us with a view of grace that takes judgment most seriously. If, on "that day," all who stand before the judgment seat in *simul* contradiction repent and believe in the Lord Jesus, Barth's proof will be in the pudding. But more than that, those who have operated with some kind of two column perspective[4]—pulling up short on giving a full and active salvation to all in

---

but if not, blot me out of the book you have written."

3. I recently saw the movie *The Shack*. While I do not think the perspective on free will complies with that presented in this book, in many ways I think the movie provides a thoughtful glimpse at what I am calling the second heaven, the sphere of judgment. It will be a time of accountability and clarity in the context of Christ's death and resurrection. In this inbetween time there is still some mystery enshrouding what lies ahead in unadulterated heaven (third heaven), but at this penultimate stage there also still exists a borrowed measure of accommodation to first heaven human forms of thought.

4. A two-column Dortian approach excludes a high percentage of humans from the beginning and locks them into one column or the other—the true column being only for the elect. The Arminian persuasion, conversely, somehow posits that a person may change from one column to the other in the existential moment, thereby changing the truth about themselves with their decision (or chalking-up this change of columns to the Holy Spirit's decision). Here I offer a personal anecdote regarding a pastor who was a part of the Non-Negotiables of Young Life Proclamation drafting committee. My proclamation approach, he wrote for the committee, "is a serious departure from the biblical evangelical message." Scripturally, he asserted, 1. "all humanity is divided into two groups . . . the good fish and the bad fish" (he also cited the wheat and the tares, the narrow and wide roads, the good tree and bad tree, and the sheep and the goats); 2. "All people begin in the group that isn't good to be in. But because of what Jesus has

Christ (and therefore to themselves)—will have missed out on opportunities afforded by the Holy Spirit empowerment of the sanctified life while on earth.

One of the most universalist-minded passages in Holy Scripture is 2 Corinthians 5:10—6:2. What is important here is that Paul's wide scope of salvation appears to have absolutely no diminishing effect on his zeal to preach the gospel. Paul starts with the gospel recognition of a final, fearful, judgment which will expose the hearts of all. Fired by Christ's love, he seeks to persuade others. Paul wants all to stand with confidence on that day (vv. 10–14). His own basis for standing confidently, in spite of the promise of fearful exposure, is centered on the death and resurrection of everyone in Christ (v. 15). From now on he considers "no one from a human point of view" (v. 16). Everyone in Christ is a new creation (v. 17). Indeed, God has "reconciled us to himself through Christ" (v. 18); "that is, in Christ God was reconciling the world to himself, not counting their trespasses against them" (v. 19). Because of this universal truth, Paul beseeches others to be who they are in Christ—reconciled to God (v. 20). Again Paul turns to the cross because it highlights the submission of Jesus Christ, Son of God, to *simul* contradiction for our sakes (v. 21). And again in 6:1 Paul urges his hearers not to refuse the grace of God which has been given to them in Christ. Do not put this off, Paul pleads quoting Isaiah, for *today* is the day of salvation (v. 2).

Paul's evangelical passion jumps off of the pages! Note in 5:14 it is not our love for Christ which compels us as gospel proclaimers, and it is not even Christ's love *for us* that compels us (as an external motivation), for it is simply "Christ's love compels us" (NIV) or "the love of Christ urges us on" (NRSV). It is because Christ is sharing his love for others with us (i.e., because he is our life, our true subject-self) that his love for others is *our*

---

done in his death and resurrection, it is possible to pass into the group that is good to be in"; and 3. "Third, those who are saved, redeemed, justified, born again, spiritually alive from the dead weren't any of these things previously. They became these when they did something." Interestingly, when it comes to modern-day Evangelicalism, and in spite of their differing two-column views, the Dortians and Arminians prove to be strange bedfellows. See my article "Young Life and the Gospel of All-Along Belonging," *The Other Journal*, 2010, where I compare these bedfellows to Barth (without getting into the subjective aspect of Barth's objective scope). Every theologian has to decide where to leave one's questions. In light of the marginalization of truth (either discriminatory in one or hypothetical in the other) in these less desirable alternatives, Barth's one-column risk seems scripturally well worth taking. With Barth we can hope that on "that day" every person will take advantage of the final and most definitive opportunity to participate as their true selves in the victory of Jesus Christ and him crucified over sin, death and the devil (Heb 2:14).

love for others; in him we are motivated to share the good news.[5] Even if we presently see through a mirror dimly, lacking the complete manifestation of this love, we will all know someday as we are fully known (1 Cor 13:12). Therefore even now, today, we fervently persevere in desiring others to know this love and belonging. It is Christ's love that prompts us to want what is best for others sooner rather than later. And yet, we can only love others in Christ to the extent that his love has impassioned us. The missionary impulse, therefore, is not hindered by too much gospel (making us complacent) but by too little "reception" of Christ's love (which as "received" can only compel us).[6]

Barth's theology maximizes the bold claim made on every human in this passage. He rebukes the idea that fear (as in the fear of others' damnation) is needed to provide urgency for gospel sharing. For Barth, when it comes to gospel proclamation, there is more urgency simply because there is more reality; the deepest reality of Christ's love (1 John 3:16).

2. Response-Oriented Evangelism

Many Christian community organizations and ministries articulate the idea that their unbelieving neighbors are created in the image of God. But can we go further? Can we do more to share Who the image is in whom we are created and re-created? In this book I have argued that the "image," to the extent it is defined apart from the Christo-anthropological perspective, is not enough. I wonder what the impact would be if we began to see our neighbors as already-participants in Jesus Christ and therefore as brothers and sisters in ongoing Trinitarian community? What if we were serious about including the participation of human response in the gift of grace, especially

---

5. This passage is not only noteworthy for its universal scope; it is also laden with Christ's primary human subjectivity, within which we relish our own secondary subjectivity: Christ's death is ours (v. 15), Christ's life is ours (vv. 15–17), Christ's act of human reconciliation to God is ours, God's appeal is ours as we act in Christ, in his agency, on his behalf, as extensions of himself in the world (vv. 19–20; see discussion of ambassadorship and angels in chapter 12). Paul concludes with a powerful testimony to participation in Christ's subjectivity, "As we work together with him, we urge you also not to accept the grace of God in vain" (6:1).

6. By now we know in our *iustus* humanity we do receive God's love perfectly, but "receive" here is by the Spirit against the hindrances of the flesh (the static interference if you will) which affects our perfect receptors. Importantly, this reception is not something we can capture or consciously quantify, a fact highlighted by the beautiful witness of those who love others with Christ's love without knowing the name of Christ. It's as if with inner ears they have heard the music, and, to the potential embarrassment of those who "know" the music and the words, herald the gospel in profound ways.

when it comes to our evangelistic efforts? Could it really work? At Reality Ministries we are practicing what I have begun to call "Response-Oriented Evangelism." As you might imagine, Response-Oriented Evangelism is a way of reclaiming and proclaiming the Response of Christ as primary to, and comprehensive of, our own response; the Torrances are fond of using uppercase and lowercase letters in this fashion (Response and response) to maintain the proper relationship. In the following section I will use their expression "the vicarious humanity of Christ" instead of the more technical term Christo-anthropological actualism.

Some evangelical approaches scramble to retro-fit the fundamental human *being* of persons, i.e., their ontological identity, only after they respond to God.[7] Instead of a reactionary approach, we proclaim from the beginning the vicarious humanity of Jesus Christ as active for all people, calling for conscious participation in Christ but also allowing for an evangelical cognizance of others' unconscious participation in Christ.[8] T. F. Torrance summarizes well the "vicarious humanity of Christ":

> He has acted in your place in the whole range of your human life and activity, including your personal decisions, and your responses to God's love, and even your acts of faith. He has believed for you, fulfilled your human response to God, even made your personal decision for you, so that he acknowledges you before God as one who has already responded to God in him, who has already believed in God through him, and whose personal decision is already implicated in Christ's self-offering

---

7. In a retro-fitting view of conversion, people after their decisions can be theologically "moved" from separation to union with Christ, unredeemed to redeemed, unreconciled to reconciled, unforgiven to forgiven, child of Satan to child of God, or even from union to communion.

8. As elaborated on in chapter 6, I want to make clear that when I say we in our *iustus* humanity are all participating unconsciously in Christ, this has nothing to do with coercion. If it feels that way, I would argue that it could only be because of our ensnarlment in Western conceptualizations of freedom and autonomy. In the offense of Christ's mediation, we might begrudge his thinking for us. To me this is akin to experiencing a stab of deep joy and being upset that in our existential consciousness we did not see it coming! Additionally, for all we know, the conscious-unconscious delineation may only be a first heaven situation, i.e., there is perhaps not a subconscious at all in that dimension where we are *only* in our right minds, the mind of Christ in him (1 Cor 2:16). In this sense, conscious and unconscious would prove to be purely provisional terms, so that what we mean by our "unconscious" *iustus* activity in this existence is only the un-accessed consciousness of our most capacious lives in the third heaven. It follows, of course, that neither our *peccator* unconsciousness or our *peccator* consciousness (both of which are slavishly coercive) have a future beyond the judgment of the second heaven.

to the Father, in all of which he has been fully and completely accepted by the Father, so that in Jesus Christ you are already accepted by him. Therefore, renounce yourself, take up your cross and follow Jesus as your Lord and Saviour.[9]

As T. F.'s brother, James Torrance, always reminds us—we should start theologically with the Christ of our experience, not our experience of Christ. When we put too much weight on the existential event, we are unwittingly diminishing our assurance because our assurance is properly based on having an ontology which is logically primary to the transformative experience! Ontology granted after the fact is no ontology at all. That's why great pains must be taken to avoid lapsing into a type of works-oriented approach where we create the truth about ourselves through our decisions. We've noted how even participation, appropriation, and other wonderful words can be subtly hijacked by our self-elevated agency.

However, we must also be wary of the opposite ditch: to deny the existential and to say unconscious participation (ontological) is all that God cares about is to make a farce of the New Testament narrative, not to mention Christ's command to preach the gospel and to make disciples. Further, to no longer live in ignorance and to *know* Jesus Christ (John 17:3) and the self-giving love of God is to *want* to share it; "Christ's love compels us!" Response-Oriented Evangelism, then, is not an attempt to emphasize the ontological as a replacement for the existential, but to put first things first (ontology before experience) and to emphasize the ontological as the explanatory basis of all existential moments of conversion or what some might call "Holy Spirit events."

Response-Oriented Evangelism highlights both God's Yes *to* us in Christ, and the Yes of Christ *for* us from the human side; this two-way mediation of Christ is the good soil where the grateful "yes" of our participation blossoms. The proclaimed presence of Christ among us produces the fruits of belief—what we could call accompanying "gospel embodiments"—which are expressed in myriad verbal and non-verbal ways. Far from minimizing human agency, moments of sanctification and conversion are witnesses to the fullness of Jesus Christ and who we really are in him (Col 2:9–10). Because we are personally implicated in all that our brother Savior Jesus Christ says and does, the gospel crucifies our individualism and renews our personhood; as we lose our self-perceived "agency," we find our true agency in Jesus Christ and the Persons of Holy Trinity.

---

9. T. F. Torrance, *The Mediation of Christ*, 94.

I believe this is our evangelical task: to pierce through the pluralism of the post-Christian world by making an evangelical claim on each person: "Jesus Christ is your life," God utterly loves you, and that's why "Jesus Christ is your death" (to destroy everything that might keep you from God). Therefore we endeavor to preach the mystery of *Jesus Christ and him crucified* as it has already been preached to every creature under heaven![10]

3. Disabilities Ministry

It should be clear that our theology gives us a new perspective on ministry alongside those with intellectual disabilities. At Reality Ministries we build our community around the fact that all human beings, regardless of belief, are in Christ at the center of the Father's love. In reality, no one is on the margins. Intentional proclamation time from Scripture is paramount, but instead of "us" unilaterally sharing Christ with "them" (as in the typical Evangelical model) we look forward in the Spirit to sharing Christ with each other as friends would share a meal. Our mission statement seeks to reflect this dynamic: "to create opportunities for teens and adults with and without developmental disabilities to experience belonging, kinship and the life-changing Reality of Christ's love."

Two years before the founding of Reality Ministries, our then Young Life staff team welcomed the opportunity to "do ministry" in community with those diagnosed with IDD (Intellectual Developmental Disabilities). At that time, while not original to our ministry calling as individuals, we recognized how well such ministry fit with our theological grounding for all ministry; we did not approach it the other way around (fitting the theology to the "on the ground" challenges). While a gospel proclamation that insists that there is "No Hercules at the Crossroads" is obviously pertinent for those with more apparent "weaknesses," it is just as critical for all of us in understanding the gospel of grace. Additionally, because it locates every person within the High Priestly mediation of Jesus Christ—the one for the many and the many in the one—Response-Oriented Evangelism heightens the anticipation that any one person with or without disabilities could lead another. Because Jesus is always mediating as High Priest for each one of us, each one of us is gifted with the derivative vocational integrity of being priests to one another in the traditional reformed sense of the term (i.e., the priesthood of all believers). This theological perspective has the effect

---

10. Colossians 3:4; 3:3; 1 Corinthians 2:2; Colossians 1:23

of cutting through patronizing or paternalistic approaches towards those with IDD.[11]

I have written on "disabilities ministry" in different places already[12] so I will add only a few thoughts here. If we are indeed born into the *simul*, as Barth's logic suggests in relation to Genesis 1 and Genesis 2, then it follows that how we are born (or even biologically conceived) is expressly *not* how we are created. In fact, because of the *simul* there is no theological permission for one to claim exhaustively, "This is how I was created." Because our contradicted earthly bodies bear only relative witness to our material spiritual bodies, the direct perspective necessary for this claim is inaccessible to us.[13] We can only say that everyone is broken and whole, imperfect and perfect, sick and well, etc., all the while knowing that we are the latter (i.e., whole, perfect, well) before the former (i.e., broken, imperfect, sick). When it comes to these couplets, we cannot leverage our own existential sequence to prove that we are in one category to the exclusion of the other or to set us apart from others. Barth did not often implement the words broken or brokenness to describe fallen humanity,[14] perhaps because he was wary of eliminating the articulation of human sin as an offense and hostility toward God. Regardless, there is a rich seedbed for community when members acknowledge that they are all broken and simultaneously whole, in Christ.

Theological precision is one thing, practical expression is another. Often people with developmental disabilities or in the IDD community will

---

11. Our theology hopefully prevents us from using the "last will be first" or the "least of these" in objectifying ways. We *really do* feel that we are being led to Christ by those whom we are "leading"—all of us with and without intellectual disabilities are giving to and receiving from each other. One of the best first-hand accounts of this kind of priestly leadership in a church situation is written by a layman who has a son with intellectual disabilities: Ewell, *Inclusion and Discipleship in the Church in View of the Developmentally Delayed*.

12. McSwain, "Sheep or Persons?"

13. As mentioned in chapter 12, even the resurrection is not a fully reliable indication of what our hidden spiritual bodies will be like. Jesus' nail wounds are not necessarily the stuff of the third heaven, but they are important to relate to his disciples and to us still existing in the first heaven and in the second heaven, when he returns to judge. Because they do not define me, I do not need my "clinical diagnoses" or memories of trauma in heaven. However, I do need to know that Jesus in solidarity and love understands me just as I am, and that as Son of God he assumed all infirmities which belong to my *simul* existence (i.e., anything which he didn't create and call good). Again I can hold to the fact that whatever earthly features do give way in the *eschaton*, it will be towards more distinctiveness, not less, in the revelation of human wholeness.

14. All human brokenness takes place within the One broken for us. See *CD* II/2, 464: "He Himself, the Shepherd, is now to be broken. He Himself is broken." See also *CD* IV/1, 225, where Barth associates "broken" with "sinful and lost humanity."

self-define (un-dimensionally) their existence with statements like, "God created me this way" or "you are perfect just the way you are." Even if (in describing myself, for instance) I would want to say more, and even if as a theologian I am keen to intercept trajectories and ward off potentially confusing conflations, on one level I celebrate that these statements are indeed 100 percent true about all of us! Regardless, knowing by the Holy Spirit that Christ in our midst has assumed our multifarious forms of brokenness and disability, while also (simultaneously) giving us his wholeness, binds us together. We can reserve judgment on what exactly wholeness "looks like" for each person in the *eschaton*.[15]

4. Distinctiveness and Kinship

One aspect of human wholeness we can anticipate in the *eschaton* is pure human distinctiveness. Returning to our hypothetical individual, we cannot predict which features of Pat's current physical body will carry over in the revelation of Pat's spiritual body, only that Pat will be distinctly Pat. With so much of the emphasis of this book concerning Jesus Christ *as humanity*, one fear is that my universal perspective will somehow threaten to obscure creaturely and cultural particularity; Willie Jennings describes this as a "theological sameness"[16] or a "leveling of all peoples"[17] which is oftentimes

---

15. In his Introduction for the book *Living Gently in a Violent World: The Prophetic Witness of Weakness* (by Stanley Hauerwas and Jean Vanier), John Swinton relates the story of his student named Angela, who was "profoundly deaf." Through an interpreter, Angela told the class of a dream in which she and Jesus met in heaven and talked with each other for a long time. In describing this joyful encounter, Angela said: "Jesus was everything I had hoped he would be," with which she followed, "*And his signing was amazing!*" Swinton comments that the main point of Angela's story is not that she was healed of her deafness in heaven (she obviously wasn't), but that "heaven was a place where the social, relational and communication barriers that restricted her life in the present no longer existed" (13). Jesus healed the deaf in his ministry (e.g., Mark 7:31–37), and even noted healing the deaf as a sign of the Kingdom (Isa 35:5; Matt 11:5; Luke 7:22). Will Angela be similarly healed in the third heaven? I am prone to automatically project this type of healing onto Angela and completely miss Swinton's point. In fact, my predisposition caused me to misread "signing" as "singing" the first time around! Swinton's next story is also poignantly relevant to our study. Dianna, a young lady with Down syndrome, shared: "I was born with a hole in my heart. When I was little it needed a patch and I was very ill; It might be because of this but I have always felt special . . . God is my best friend. God made me special because I was special to him" (13–14). For me, the past-tense nature of Dianna's last sentence evoked Jer 1:5: "Before I formed you in the womb I knew you, before you were born I set you apart."

16. Jennings, *Christian Imagination*, 144.
17. Jennings, *Christian Imagination*, 143.

rooted in Docetic Christology.[18] The question is, in holding to Jesus' particularity as a first-century Jew, do we have to marginalize his identity as the Second Adam (or the original Adam)? The same question could be posed in reverse. As with transcendence and immanence, Barth certainly did not think of these identities as contrastive. Our perspective in this book has taken us beyond the supra-temporal (our current conscious existence) to what I have called the "before-before," towards discerning the similarity between creation and the *eschaton*. We have contended that Barth's eschatological actualism is Docetic only to the extent that it is unmoored from the incarnation—from God's real presence in the world—the presence "of the crucified." This is where the Second Adam theme critically interpenetrates the suffering servant motif, providing us an epistemological gateway to the transcendent. Christ shares my plight, he shares my suffering, but only because of the cosmic range inherent in his deity can it be said that all human suffering, from the fall to now, is a sharing in the suffering of Christ.

Without capitulating to Docetic or objectifying anthropological constructs, Barth's theology maintains the utmost in human particularity, but this premier creaturely distinctiveness rightly pointed to by Jennings is hidden in the third heaven, the fullness of its reality only partly revealed in the immanent sphere. Admittedly, then, in maintaining my framework of three "heavens," there is a loosening of the grip on cultural particularity. We have held to Jesus' Jewishness in the second heaven, the realm of the full revelation of Jesus of Nazareth and him crucified; this is corroborated by Acts 1:11, "Jesus, who has been taken up from you into heaven, will come in the same way as you saw him go into heaven." But what about the third heaven? In other words, Jesus' bodily ascension guarantees that humans will be eternally embodied—for Barth there is never a soul without a body—but is Jesus a Jew in the third heaven? Is Jesus a man? If I as a white man cannot at least imagine myself and all human beings in Christ as dark-skinned Jews in the "new heaven" and "new earth,"[19] then these are questions not even worth

18. Jennings is legitimately concerned that an understanding of Christ as the Second Adam, the human in whom all humans are included, can overshadow the singular human existence of the Jew Jesus, a Palestinian man of the first century who was marginalized, oppressed, abused and ultimately killed unjustly. Such a Docetic perspective has historically led to supersessionist notions and colonialist manipulations, and to the extent that Barth's anthropology is Docetic, he would certainly fall prey along with others under the critique of Jennings. See an outstanding article on Barth and supersessionism, Brazier, "Karl Barth: Supersessionism and Israel, Yeshua and God's Election." See also Barth's strong affirmation of the Jewishness of Jesus Christ, Son of God, CD IV/1, 166–67.

19. Rev 21:1. In addition to the critical, non-Platonic, "earth" aspect of the *eschaton*, note the plural "heavens" in the Isaiah version of the phrase (Isa 65:17, 66:22).

asking.[20] They could only evidence an avoidance of the incarnation, where Jesus has become a stumbling block, and I am exposing myself theologically to be exactly one of those against whom Barth warns: those "rounding off of the picture of Jesus into a kind of ideal-picture of human existence which would necessarily degenerate into a free sketch of the man who was and is the Son of God, i.e., a sketch which is quite independent of the Israel-itish components of the New Testament."[21] However, while holding firmly to the incarnation and ascension, I can also firmly hold to the idea that Jesus Christ's Jewishness, "male"-ness, skin color, any disabilities, etc., do not necessarily carry to the third heaven, nor do any of ours. I say necessarily. They may. But they may not. If they do not, however, this could only mean that our spiritual, material bodies are *more* distinct and particular there then they could ever be here, in our birth bodies; all of the aspects which we hold

Isaiah 65:17 seems to corroborate our view of the difference between second and third heaven: "For I am about to create new heavens and a new earth; the former things shall not be remembered or come to mind."

20. In Barth's cosmic terms, as we have seen (chapter 10) creation is good but unavoidably results in a neutral negation which provides a "shelter" for nothingness and evil. Similarly, white skin has historically provided the shelter for whiteness, or racist "flesh," making white skin virtually synonymous with whiteness in its effects. In his speech "The Ballot or the Bullet" (1964), Malcolm X expresses the nature of this unavoidable existential conflation: "Now in speaking like this, it doesn't mean that we're anti-white, but it does mean we're anti-exploitation, we're anti-degradation, we're anti-oppression. And if the white man doesn't want us to be anti-him, let him stop oppressing and exploiting and degrading us." White people can most constructively own this semi-conflation if they know that whiteness cannot touch or diminish in the least their created and redeemed *iustus* identities. Polarization occurs when, walking by sight without the help of the *simul*, people paint each other with too broad of a brush. We could say that instead of painting each other with too broad a brush we should paint each of ourselves with two broad brushes (*iustus* humanity and *peccator* anti-humanity)! Please understand that I am *not* advocating for the kind of theological leveling which dumbs everything down and sees no contours in distinctiveness (*iutus*) or, for that matter, in deviance (*peccator*). The two broad brushes metaphor obviously breaks down if mistakenly taken to mean that within *iustus* humanity there is not distinctiveness and particularity, since quite the opposite is true. On the *peccator* side, as I argued in chapter 1, by calling myself a racist because of my unavoidable complicity in "whiteness," I desire not to lessen the drastic nature of that word ("racist"); yet, a *totus* indictment as a white man under the *simul* may allow me to detect and to dismantle racism more readily instead of too easily placing myself or others into a single predetermined category ("He's a racist," or "He's not a racist"). This assures our efforts are fundamentally mobilized against racism not racists (instead of directing our attention towards "racists" while systemic and other less overt symptoms of whiteness are left uninterrogated).

21. *CD* IV/1, 167. Here Barth expounds against any bifurcation between the New Testament and its "soil," the Old Testament.

dear now will be shown to be only derivative signs of the glorious particularity and distinctiveness that we will hold even more dear later, when we will recognize each other in most distinctive fashion. For the present, then, I suggest holding to the actualist scope of Barth's theology while taking a cue from Jennings and flagging any theology that seeks to diminish the integrity of cultural distinctiveness, even while refusing to idolize it.

Jennings magnificently portrays a redeemed world where vertical reconciliation and horizontal reconciliation are fully manifest. He imagines a "mutual enfolding" of peoples in their glorious particularity and distinctiveness, where "the words and ways of one people join with those of another, and another, each born anew in a community seeking to love and honor those in its midst." Critically, notes Jennings, this enfolding and unfolding of kinship is not expressed "through isolated individual bricolage" but through everyday "life together."[22] If Jennings is admittedly concerned that his vision of "Jesus-space" communion seems "idealistic,"[23] then our proposed Christo-anthropological approach of Barth's is even more counterintuitive. It asks us to think of idealistic as too weak of a word (compared to real and actual, albeit hidden). It is precisely because Barth sees human subjectivity as *beginning* in compliance with an eschatological vision like Jennings's, it cannot be manipulated in discriminatory, hegemonic ways towards alternative ends. It is a picture of what we might call an unfading *iustus* humanity in egalitarian Trinitarian community. Where manipulation of these relations does occur, it is plainly sin. It is not difficult to imagine how Barth's eschatological realism, with its heightened sense of hidden human community, also heightens the gravity of violence against others as self-violence on a personal and corporate scale.

5. "We Church!"

Barth's evangelical theology could be considered untenable by Evangelicals because it undercuts either a Dortian limited atonement or an Arminian decisionism. So too, Barth's refusal to give the sacraments anything more than a derivative, revelatory role to what Christ has already done for humanity (which for Barth means the opposite of anti-sacramental) might open him up to charges of a weak ecclesiology. To this is added the concern that Barth does seem to speak of humans more in individual terms than corporate; by now we can see this as a great strength of Barth's theology—he simply does not see any one person in theological isolation from another, and therefore

---

22. Jennings, *Christian Imagination*, 273–74.
23. Jennings, *Christian Imagination*, 288.

what is said regarding the theological anthropology of one human is equally said of the whole of humanity and vice-versa. In the same way that Barth's high view of Scripture is based on the higher authority of the living Word, his arguably high ecclesiology is based on the Body's submission to "the who" of its Head. Jesus Christ is the Head of the human race, and therefore the church. But by giving such a unifying ontological designation for every human (the body of believers being only "a provisional representation of the sanctification of all humanity and human life as it has taken place in Him"[24]), how *does* Barth envision the place of the church?[25]

Election as an "us vs. them"?

Barth rigorously maintains that Jesus of Nazareth, the first-century Jew, is the true Israelite, the true High Priest, and the true Adam; in himself Jesus Christ *is* the people of God. As Jennings reminds us, it is vital to recognize that Israel's calling as the elect people of God, in contradistinction to others, carries with it a vicarious and representative role. Israel's suffering is not *like* that of other nations (i.e., alongside of others).[26] Israel suffers as the elect people of God, and therefore carries within itself the suffering of all others who exist alongside it. Borrowing Barth's phrase about the church, the distinct election of Israel in its particularity is at the same time a "provisional representation" of all humanity as elect. It is this understanding of the particular people of Israel that helps us to grasp how the particular person of Jesus Christ can function as the elected of God and in his high priestly role represent all humanity as elect in himself as suffering servant. We do not need to take anything away from the integrity of the Old Testament historical narrative to consider the New Testament narrative of Jesus, about whom the Old Testament is written (e.g., John 5:46). However, under the sound of Jesus Christ and him crucified we can finally understand that we are all Israelites at the Red Sea, and we are all Egyptians. Just as Jacob represents all of God's elect, even Esau, so too Israel's deliverance at the Red Sea represents the deliverance of all, even Egypt.

---

24. *CD* IV/2, 620, quoted earlier.

25. Reality Ministries Inc. is not a church. Our family belongs to a local church body here in Durham (CityWell, founding pastor Cleve May), a church plant which was originally located at The Reality Center.

26. See Jennings (*Christian Imagination*, 258, 345–346) for an outstanding assessment of Israel's mediation through its three "senses" of suffering, drawn partly from T. F. Torrance's *Mediation of Christ*.

When it comes to Israel and the church, their unbreakable connection with each other is only because of their connection with every human being in Jesus. They, in their own distinct but unified way, at different times are the exception which *proves the rule* of the narrative of Jesus Christ. As itself a "provisional representation," the church simply cannot supersede Israel any more than it can supersede humanity. To do so would only result in the theological colonizing of humanity into a Christian sub-group, an "us," which can then be foisted in manipulative ways against "them." In this case, ironically those who allow themselves to think they are the elect to the exclusion of the majority are prone to act as if *they* are the majority culture. In this ecclesial notion, the majority of humans exist on the outside, as "others"; these others can join or enter in to the group, but by nature it is an insular group with privileged information. Once one joins the group, there is still an inherent pecking order because others joined first. If we are not careful, the church could forget (in conjunction with that of Israel) its vicarious role. The result is often an under-realized theology of creation in Christ. In other words, by not giving every human the Christo-anthropological truth of their lives from creation on, at the end of the day the representative role the church is meant to have—as the exception which *proves* the rule—can only devolve into a discriminatory posture where the church becomes the exception *to* the rule.

Inclusive Gathering

The "Inclusive" of Inclusive Gathering is tremendously important when it comes to our posture for church. Inclusive Gathering means that I am theologically including myself in solidarity with others in my neighborhood, regardless of whether they are including me; I am taking the perspective that we are all together in Christ. Do I really believe that because of what Christ has done for us all, there is no difference ontologically between me and my unbelieving neighbor? Do our congregants reflect Barth's comment that, "we have to think of every human being, even the oddest, most villainous or miserable, as one to whom Jesus Christ is Brother and God is Father, and we have to deal with him on this assumption."[27] We are not better than our neighbor. Have we considered how difficult it is to draw lines between "us and them" when we start with "we"—the universal "we" of the New Hu-

---

27. *Humanity of God*, 53. Barth continues, "To deny it to *him* would be for *us* to renounce having Jesus Christ as Brother and God as Father." Italics added. Later Barth adds, "The so-called 'outsiders' are really only 'insiders' who have not yet understood and apprehended themselves as such" (59).

manity? Even if we are a "tiny wee church," as the Scots might say, God has provided us the enlarging opportunity in Christ to be a "we church"! With the starting point of "we," when we gather a tangible subset of the "we" of our community, in our minds it is not gathering to the exclusion of others. In other words, we seek to gather others not so that they can belong, but *because* they belong. The subset gathered merely provides us, once again, with a "provisional representation" of the larger set (i.e., the larger community of persons), all of whom are sanctified and included in the New Humanity. There is tremendous power in this kind of "realist" community because its context and content is a God who exists in a communion of Trinitarian persons *in se*—the loving interpersonal relations in God into which every human is embedded, adopted in Christ. Knowing the concrete reality of the "in-Christ" dimension, our anticipation can only be heightened when two or three are gathered to encourage and build each other up (1 Thess 5:11).

The Great Commission: Give Them Their Baptism!

As we have discussed throughout this book, it is the same bedrock reality of Jesus Christ that gives power to our vocation as a worshipping community. To know one's union with Christ is to know one's union with others in the human race. As a microcosm of the whole, the church is meant to be a witness to the world, celebrating the distinction-in-unity of the Trinitarian Godhead, endeavoring together to follow Jesus Christ, the Head of humanity, cohering in a oneness of Spirit against the centrifugal forces which mean to scatter and divide. Again, the people boldly herald the gospel and invite others into the Body of Christ because they are certain these others already belong.

Always on guard against Docetism—the dissociation of transcendent from immanent—we must honor with utmost seriousness the way God has revealed himself to us: Jesus the Jew from Nazareth. It doesn't take a PhD to deduce that if Jesus has a Jewish body and the church is the "body of Christ," then there is the closest possible connection between the two. Even if we are not all Jews or all men in the *eschaton*, our location in the dead body of this Jewish man cannot be avoided.[28] As we turn to Barth one last time, note the double use of our by-now familiar word "determination" in Barth's elaboration on Romans 6:6 ("our old self was crucified with him that the body of

---

28. Of course our location in the crucified Christ is not meant to diminish every human's location in the risen and ascended Christ, but our emphasis here is against Docetic tendencies.

sin might be destroyed, and we might no longer be enslaved to sin") with its inter-textual connection (6:3–4) to baptism:

> In Him it was all humanity in its corruption and lostness, its earthly-historical existence under the determination of the fall, which was judged and executed and destroyed, and in that way liberated for a new determination, for its being as a new humanity. It was the body of everyman which became a corpse in Him and was buried as a corpse with Him. All men, "Jew and Greek, bond and free, male and female," as they are now representatively gathered in the community, were one in God's election (Eph 1:4), were and are one in the fulfilment of it on Golgotha, are one in the power of His resurrection, one in Jesus Christ . . . His body together in their unity and power.[29]

As mentioned in chapter 14, the sacrament of baptism is perhaps the most beautiful expression that the church possesses as a transformational testimony to the all-along belonging each person has in the body of Christ. What exactly does Jesus mean when he urges his charges with the words: "All authority in heaven and on earth has been given to me. Go therefore and make disciples of all nations, baptizing them in the name of the Father and of the Son and of the Holy Spirit, and teaching them to obey everything that I have commanded you. And remember, I am with you always, to the end of the age" (Matt 28:18–20)? Remembering that for Jesus the fundamental meaning of "baptism" is his own death,[30] it appears here that Jesus' point is that we are not walking out the great commission unless we are giving every person his or her baptism. In other words, it is by granting to everyone the familial solidarity that comes with our shared death and resurrection in Christ that the sacrament (when administered) has the authority of God's being-in-act behind it. Additionally, it appears that Jesus is calling human beings to a perfect obedience ("teach them to obey everything") which he knows is only real for us inside his own abiding subjectivity—his human solidarity with us in our true selves. Here the commands of baptism and obedience are deeply connected; in the washing away of our old selves we affirm our ongoing participation in him as (often hidden) hearers and doers of the Word. In the sacrament of baptism, then, we celebrate the incarnational grip of God's grace upon us in life and in death. No matter what "this age" throws at us, no matter the evil that we consciously and unconsciously

---

29. *CD* IV/1, 663–64.

30. Mark 10:38; Luke 12:50; Matthew 20:22. I would put Matthew 20:22 first in reference, but some translations do not include "baptism" in Jesus' words in this parallel passage, mentioning only "the cup."

endorse, there is another age, a bigger picture. He will see us through to a time when *all* that we do is walk in newness of life, emerging from the watery chaos, dripping with a new creation which has never been old.

Bibliography

Anderson, Clifford Blake. "The Problem of Psychologism in Karl Barth's Doctrine of Sanctification." *Zeitschrift für Dialektische Theologie* 18 (2002) 339–51.
Athanasius. *De Incarnatione Verbi Dei*. Translated by a religious of C.S.M.V. Crestwood: St. Vladimir's Seminary Press, 1996.
———. *On the Incarnation*, 13.7. Christian History Institute. https://christianhistoryinstitute.org/study/module/athanasius.
Balthasar, Hans Urs von. *The Theology of Karl Barth: Exposition and Interpretation*. Translated by Edward T. Oakes. San Francisco: St. Ignatius, 1992.
Barth, Karl. *Christ and Adam*. Translated by Thomas Smail. New York: Collier, 1962.
———. *Church Dogmatics*, vols. 1–4. Edited by G. W. Bromiley and T. F. Torrance. Edinburgh: T. & T. Clark, 2004.
———. *Dogmatics in Outline*. New York: Harper and Row, 1959.
———. *Die kirkliche Dogmatik*. 4 vols. Munich: Kaiser, 1932, and Zurich: TVZ, 1938–65.
———. *Learning Jesus Christ through the Heidelberg Catechism*. Translated by Shirley C. Guthrie Jr. Grand Rapids: Eerdmans, 1964.
———. *The Christian Life*. Grand Rapids: Eerdmans, 1981.
———. *The Holy Spirit and the Christian Life: The Theological Basis of Ethics*. Translated by R. Birch Hoyle. Louisville: Westminster John Knox, 1993.
———. *The Humanity of God*. Richmond, VA: John Knox, 1960.
Bass, Diane Butler. "Where Was God in Newtown?" *The Huffington Post*, December 18, 2012. https://www.huffingtonpost.com/diana-butler-bass/where-was-god-in-newtown_b_2324771.html.
Block, Mathew. "Why Lutheran Predestination Isn't Calvinist Predestination." *First Things*, December 2, 2013. https://www.firstthings.com/blogs/firstthoughts/2013/10/why-lutheran-predestination-isnt-calvinist-predestination.
Bauckham, Richard, Daniel R. Driver, Trevor A. Hart, and Nathan McDonald, eds. *The Epistle to the Hebrews and Christian Theology*. Grand Rapids: Eerdmans, 2009.
Braatan, Carl E., and Robert W. Jenson, eds. *Union with Christ: The New Finnish Interpretation of Luther*. Grand Rapids: Eerdmans, 1998.
Brazier, P. H. "Karl Barth: Supersessionism and Israel, Yeshua and God's Election—a Dialectical Balance." *The Evangelical Review of Theology and Politics* 3 (2015) A15–34.
Bromiley, Geoffrey W. *An Introduction to the Theology of Karl Barth*. Edinburgh: T. & T. Clark, 1979.

Busch, Eberhard. *Karl Barth: His Life from Letters and Autobiographical Texts*. Translated by John Bowden. Philadelphia: Fortress, 1976.

Carter, J. Kameron. *Race: A Theological Account*. Oxford: Oxford University Press, 2008.

Chadwick, J. H. *The Imitation of Christ*. Rewritten and updated by Harold Chadwick. New Jersey: Bridge-Logos, 1999.

Chiarot, Kevin. *The Unassumed Is the Unhealed: The Humanity of Christ in the Christology of T. F. Torrance*. Eugene, OR: Pickwick Publications, 2013.

Come, Arnold B. *An Introduction to Barth's "Dogmatics" for Preachers*. Philadelphia: Westminster, 1963.

Cooper, Jordan. *The Righteousness of One: An Evaluation of Early Patristic Soteriology in Light of the New Perspective on Paul*. Eugene, OR: Wipf & Stock, 2013.

Cox, Leo G. "John Wesley's View of Martin Luther." *Journal of the Evangelical Theological Society* 7 (1964) 83–90.

Dodds, Gregory D. *Exploiting Erasmus: The Erasmian Legacy and Religious Change in Early Modern England*. Toronto: University of Toronto Press, 2009.

Dorries, David. *Edward Irving's Incarnational Christology*. Fairfax, VA: Xulon, 2002.

Dever, Mark. "Nothing but the Blood." *Christianity Today*, May 1, 2006.

Erasmus, Desiderius. *On the Freedom of the Will: A Diatribe*. In *Luther and Erasmus: Free Will and Salvation*, translated and edited by E. Gordon Rupp, 35–97. London: Westminster, 1969.

Eriks, Garret J. "Luther and Erasmus: The Controversy Concerning the Bondage of the Will." *Protestant Reformed Theological Journal* 32 (1999) n.p.

Ewell, Lloyd. *Inclusion and Discipleship in the Church in View of the Developmentally Delayed: Hearing God through Red Headphones*. Grace Trinitarian, 2017. https://www.smashwords.com/books/search?query=Lloyd+Elwell.

Fackre, Gabriel. "Affirmations and Admonitions: Lutheran and Reformed." In *The Gospel and Justification in Christ: Where Does the Church Stand Today?*, edited by Wayne Stumme, 1–26. Grand Rapids: Eerdmans, 2006.

Galli, Mark. *Karl Barth: An Introduction for Evangelicals*. Grand Rapids: Eerdmans, 2017.

Ganz, Richard. "6 ways to take your thoughts captive." *Crosswalk.com*, Dec 13, 2000. https://www.crosswalk.com/faith/prayer/prayers/take-your-thoughts-captive-509888.html.

Grafton, Anthony T., Glenn W. Most, and Salvatore Settis, eds. *The Classical Tradition*. London: Harvard University Press, 2010.

Greggs, Tom. *Barth, Origen, and Universal Salvation: Restoring Particularity*. Oxford: Oxford University Press, 2009.

Gunton, Colin. "Salvation." In *Cambridge Companion to Karl Barth*, edited by John Webster, 143–58. Cambridge Companions to Religion. Cambridge: Cambridge University Press, 2000.

Hall, Christopher A. *Worshipping with the Church Fathers*. Downers Grove, IL: InterVarsity, 2009.

Hall, Thor. "An Analysis of *Simul Iustus et Peccator*." *Theology Today* 20 (1963) 174–82.

Hart, Trevor. "Humankind in Christ and Christ in Humankind: Salvation as Participation in our Substitute in the Theology of John Calvin." *Scottish Journal of Theology* 42 (1989) 67–84.

———. *Regarding Karl Barth: Essays toward a Reading of His Theology*. Carlisle, UK: Paternoster, 1999.

Higton, Mike, and John C. McDowell, eds. *Conversing with Barth*. Aldershot, UK: Ashgate, 2004.

Hoekema, Anthony. *Karl Barth's Doctrine of Sanctification*. Grand Rapids: Calvin Theological Seminary, 1965.

Hunsinger, George. "A Tale of Two Simultaneities: Justification and Sanctification in Calvin and Barth." *Zeitschrift für Dialektische Theologie* 18 (2002) 316–38.

Jennings, Willie. *The Christian Imagination: Theology and the Origins of Race*. New Haven: Yale University Press, 2010.

Jergens, William A., ed. and trans. *The Faith of the Early Fathers*. Vol. 3. Collegeville, MN: Liturgical, 1979.

Johnson, Keith L. *Karl Barth and the* Analogia Entis. Edinburgh: T. & T. Clark, 2010.

Jorgenson, Allen. "Karl Barth's Christological Treatment of Sin." *Scottish Journal of Theology* 54 (2001) 439–62.

Küng, Hans. *Justification: The Doctrine of Karl Barth and a Catholic Reflection*. Translated by Thomas Collins et al. New York: Nelson, 1964.

Lewis, C. S. *Mere Christianity*. New York: HarperCollins, 2001.

Loder, James E., and W. Jim Neidhardt. *The Knight's Move: The Relational Logic of the Spirit in Theology and Science*. Colorado Springs: Helmerich & Howard, 1992.

Luther, Martin. *Luther's Explanatory Notes on the Gospels*. Edited by E. Muller. Translated by P. Anstadt. York, PA: Anstadt, 1899.

———. *On the Bondage of the Will*. Translated by J. I. Packer and O. R. Johnson. Grand Rapids: Revel, 1996.

Maddox, Randy. *Responsible Grace: John Wesley's Practical Theology*. Nashville: Abingdon, 1994.

Malcolm X. "The Ballot or the Bullet." Speech given in Cleveland, OH, 1964. http://www.edchange.org/multicultural/speeches/malcolm_x_ballot.html.

Mann, Gary Allen. "*Simul iustus et peccator*: Luther's Paradigm of the Christian Life and Systematic Principle." PhD diss., Drew University, 1988.

Mattson, Brian G. "Double or Nothing: Martin Luther's Doctrine of Predestination." Self-published paper, 1997.

McCall, Tom. *Forsaken: The Trinity and the Cross, and Why It Matters*. Downers Grove, IL: IVP Academic, 2012.

McCormack, Bruce. "Afterword." *Zeitschrift fur Dialektische Theologie* 18 (2002) 364–78.

———. "For Us and Our Salvation: Incarnation and Atonement in the Reformed Tradition." *Greek Orthodox Theological Review* 43 (1998) 281–316.

———. "'With Loud Cries and Tears': The Humanity of the Son in the Epistle to the Hebrews." In *The Epistle to the Hebrews and Christian Theology*, edited by Richard Bauckham, et al., 37–68. Grand Rapids: Eerdmans, 2009.

McDonald, William P. "A Luther Wesley Could Appreciate? Towards Convergence on Sanctification." *Pro Ecclesia* 20 (2011) 43–63.

McGrath, Alister E. *Iustitia Dei: A History of the Christian Doctrine of Justification*. 2 vols. Cambridge: Cambridge University Press, 1986.

McLean, Stuart D. *Humanity in the Thought of Karl Barth*. Edinburgh: T. & T. Clark, 1981.

McMaken, W. Travis, and David W. Congdon, eds. *Karl Barth in Conversation*. Eugene, OR: Pickwick Publications, 2014.

McSwain, Jeff. *Movements of Grace: The Dynamic Christo-Realism of Barth, Bonhoeffer and the Torrances.* Eugene, OR: Wipf & Stock, 2010.

———. "Sheep or Persons? What Luke 15 Has to Say about Agency and Persons with Intellectual Disabilities." *Participatio: The Journal of the Thomas F. Torrance Theological Fellowship,* Supp. vol. 3 (2014) 165–81. Reprinted in *Trinity and Transformation: J. B. Torrance's Vision of Worship, Mission and Society,* edited by Todd Speidell, 175–92. Eugene, OR: Wipf & Stock, 2016.

Migliore, Daniel. *Commanding Grace: Studies in Karl Barth's Ethics.* Grand Rapids: Eerdmans, 2010.

———. "*Participatio Christi*: The Central Theme of Barth's Doctrine of Sanctification." *Zeitschrift für Dialektische Theologie* 18 (2002) 286–307.

Neder, Adam. *Participation in Christ: An Entry into Karl Barth's Church Dogmatics.* Louisville: Westminster John Knox, 2009.

Need, Stephen W. *Human Language and Knowledge in the Light of Chalcedon.* American University Studies. Series VII: Theology and Religion 187. New York: Lang, 1996.

Nimmo, Paul. *Being in Action: The Theological Shape of Barth's Ethical Vision.* London: T. & T. Clark, 2007.

Nouwen, Henri. *In the Name of Jesus.* New York: Crossroad, 1989.

Oakes, Kenneth. *Karl Barth on Theology and Philosophy.* Oxford: Oxford University Press, 2012.

Origen. *Origen: On First Principles: Being Koetschau's Text of the De Prinipiis into English, Together with an Introduction and Notes.* Edited by G. W. Butterworth. Gloucester: Smith, 1973.

Perszk, Ken, ed. *Molinism: The Contemporary Debate.* Oxford: Oxford University Press, 2011.

Peterson, Robert A., and Michael D. Williams. *Why I Am not An Arminian.* Downers Grove, IL: InterVarsity, 2004.

Price, Daniel J. *Karl Barth's Anthropology in Light of Modern Thought.* Grand Rapids: Eerdmans, 2002.

Rogers, Eugene F., Jr. "The Eclipse of the Spirit in Barth." In *Conversing with Barth,* edited by Mike Higton and John C. McDowell, 173–90. Aldershot, UK: Ashgate, 2004.

Root, Michael. "Continuing the Conversation: Deeper Agreement on Justification as Criterion and on the Christian as *simul iustus et peccator.*" In *The Gospel and Justification in Christ: Where Does the Church Stand Today?,* edited by Wayne Stumme, 42–61. Grand Rapids: Eerdmans, 2006.

Rosato, Philip. *The Spirit as Lord: The Pneumatology of Karl Barth.* Edinburgh: T. & T. Clark, 1981.

Siggelkow, Ry O. "A Response to Doerge on Barth and Hauerwas." In *Karl Barth in Conversation,* edited by Travis McMaken and David W. Congdon, 125–28. Eugene, OR: Wipf and Stock, 2014.

Sonderegger, Katherine. "Sanctification as Impartation in the Doctrine of Karl Barth." *Zeitschrift für Dialektische Theologie* 18 (2002) 308–15.

Speidell, Todd, ed. *Trinity and Transformation: J. B. Torrance's Vision of Worship, Mission and Society.* Eugene, OR: Wipf & Stock, 2016.

Spross, Daniel B. "The Doctrine of Sanctification in the Theology of Karl Barth." *Wesleyan Theological Journal* 20 (1985) 54–76.

Stumme, Wayne, ed. *The Gospel and Justification in Christ: Where Does the Church Stand Today?* Grand Rapids: Eerdmans, 2006.
Swinton, John, "Introduction," in *Living Gently in a Violent World: The Prophetic Witness of Weakness,* by Stanley Hauerwas and Jean Vanier. Downers Grove, IL: InterVarsity, 2008.
Summers, Thomas Osmond. *Systematic Theology: A Complete Body of Wesleyan Arminian Divinity,* vol. 2. Nashville: Methodist Episcopal Church South, 1888.
Tanner, Kathryn. *God and Creation in Christian Theology: Tyranny or Empowerment?* 1988. Reprint. Minneapolis: Fortress, 2004.
Thistlethwaite, Susan Brooks. *Sex, Race and God: Christian Feminism in Black and White.* 1989. Reprint, Eugene, OR: Wipf & Stock, 2009.
Torrance, T. F. *Royal Priesthood.* Scottish Journal of Theology Occasional Papers 3. Edinburgh: Oliver & Boyd, 1955.
———. *Theology in Reconstruction.* Reprint. Eugene, OR: Wipf and Stock, 1996.
Vickers, Jason E. "Wesley's Theological Emphases." In *The Cambridge Companion to John Wesley,* edited by Randy L. Maddox and Jason E. Vickers, 190–206. Cambridge Companions to Religion. Cambridge: Cambridge University Press, 2010.
Walls, Jerry L. "John Wesley's Critique of Martin Luther." *Methodist History* 20 (1981) 29–41.
Webster, John. "Introducing Barth." In *Cambridge Companion to Karl Barth,* edited by John Webster, 1–16. Cambridge Companions to Religion. Cambridge: Cambridge University Press, 2000.
———. *Barth's Moral Theology.* Grand Rapids: Eerdmans, 1998.